THE CHILD, HIS PARENTS
AND THE NURSE

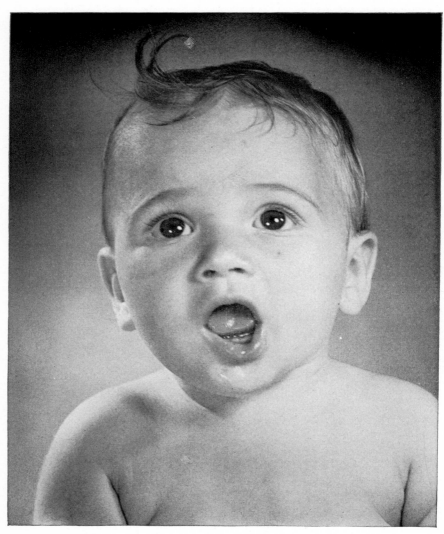

(From Louise Barker, Chicago, Ill.)

The Child, His Parents and the Nurse

FLORENCE G. BLAKE, R.N., M.A.

Associate Professor of Nursing Education,
(Nursing Care of Children)
University of Chicago

FOREWORD BY·

ADRIAN H. VANDERVEER, M.D.

Formerly Associate Professor of Pediatric Psychiatry,
University of Chicago

Philadelphia   Montreal

J . B . L I P P I N C O T T   C O M P A N Y

Distributed in Great Britain by
Pitman Medical Publishing Co., Limited
London

Library of Congress
Catalog Card Number
53-12287

PRINTED IN THE UNITED STATES OF AMERICA

To Davy, Joey, Ke Mei, Kamela,

Bobby and Carol Ann

And the other children I have known

in many lands.

Preface and Acknowledgments

In 1946, the Kellogg Foundation gave a grant to the University of Chicago to establish an advanced course in "Nursing Care of Children" for graduate nurses who wished to specialize in the field of child care. In 1949, the Illinois Department of Health and the United States Children's Bureau began yearly grants, which made it possible to continue the course and also to develop the course in accordance with the student's educational requirements. The service demands of busy hospitals did not supersede the needs of the students, and I had freedom from administrative responsibilities to concentrate on teaching in the wards of hospitals and in the various community agencies which co-operated with us.

Many people have contributed to the development of the advanced course in "Nursing Care of Children" and have made individualized nursing care a reality for those students who were specializing in the care of children. Without their support and assistance, it would have been impossible to experiment to find ways of helping students learn and apply some of the principles of nursing which are being presented in this volume. Miss Nellie X. Hawkinson, former chairman of the Department of Nursing Education at the University of Chicago, and Miss Frances Thielbar, the present chairman of the department, have supported the student's interests and given me freedom to develop the course in accordance with my philosophy of pediatric nursing. The doctors and the nurses in The Bobs Roberts and the Chicago Lying-In Hospitals have assisted in student teaching and have given us the privilege of using their clinical services in ways which have educational value for the students. Without their interest, the students would have been deprived of opportunities to learn to give individualized nursing care. I should like to express my appreciation to the following people: Dr. F. Howell Wright, Dr. Douglas N. Buchanan, Dr. Mila Pierce, Dr. Helmut P. Seckel, Dr. Albert Dorfman, Dr. Donald E. Cassels, Dr. James D. Stuart, Dr. Nathaniel S. Apter, Dr. William J. Dieckman, Dr. M. Edward Davis, Dr. H. Close Hesseltine, Miss Ann Kirchner, Miss Dorothy M. Morgan, Mrs. Laura Wielgus, Miss Ruth Gittinger, Miss Carol Jacob, Miss Beverly Davies, Miss Lois Moss, Miss Marcy Liemer, Mrs. June Dougherty, Mrs. Faith Fuerbringer, Mrs. Margaret Leeper, Mrs. Beulah Jeffery, Miss Virginia Lane, Miss Molly Quinlan, Miss Candace Heinley, Mrs. Eleanor Theissen Ewert, Miss Olive Sahar and Miss Elizabeth Craig. Miss Elizabeth

McKinley and her staff of social workers in the two hospitals mentioned above made valuable contributions to the course. Professional workers in the following schools and community agencies welcomed our students and planned conferences which increased their ability to observe the children and broadened their understanding of the services they were rendering to children and families: The University of Chicago Nursery and Laboratory Schools, Illinois Hospital School, The La Rabida Hospital for children with rheumatic fever, the Infant Welfare Society, the Visiting Nurse Association, The Dorothy Kahn Nursery School for children with cerebral palsy at the Michael Reese Hospital, the Christopher and the Spaulding Schools for handicapped children, the City of Chicago Department of Health and the University of Chicago Settlement House.

I am also deeply grateful to many people for the privileges of study which I have had during these past seven years. I have studied with outstanding teachers and have worked with children and adults under the supervision of professional workers who were trained in the understanding of behavior. The course in Psychoanalytic Child Care which is given at the Chicago Institute for Psychoanalysis and is supported by yearly grants from the Field Foundation gave me an educational experience which was unlike any I had ever had before. It deepened my understanding of children and parents and broadened my philosophy of nursing and nursing education. During the course I have come to appreciate the value of sustained relationships with children and parents and feel that no professional educational experience is complete without them. As a part of the 3-year course in Psychoanalytic Child Care I had the opportunity of conferring with Dr. Adrian H. VanderVeer. Together we discussed nursing problems and ways in which psychoanalytic concepts might be applied in the care of sick and convalescent children. I am deeply grateful to him and to Dr. Emmy Sylvester, Miss Helen Ross and Dr. Irene Josselyn who supervised my work with children.

Mrs. Barbara Merrill and Miss Harriet Ray read the manuscript and gave me valuable suggestions which assisted me in making the final revision. Miss Ethel M. Long made my first experience in pediatric supervision a challenging and satisfying experience. Mrs. Mary Kunst gave me increased understanding of children with reading difficulties. Mrs. Charles Fawkes and Mrs. Charles V. O'Kane typed the manuscript from my longhand copy, which was no easy task to accomplish. Mr. and Mrs. Walter Smalakis permitted Louise Barker to photograph 8-month-old Joseph Michael so that his picture might be used to illustrate the infant's avidness to learn about his world. Dr. Cecelia G. Katz and Dr. Edoardo Weiss taught me the meaning of understanding and encouraged me in writing this book. To all of these friends I wish to acknowledge my sincerest gratitude.

This book is the result of many people's study of human development and behavior. I am indebted to the many individuals and publishers who have permitted me to reproduce material in this volume. I have attempted to acknowledge sources of information in the list of references which appear at the end of each chapter, but it is not always easy to separate my own ideas from those I have gleaned from reading, from listening to teachers and from the stimulating students whom I have had, and to know from whence all my ideas have come. Through the years I have been doing research in libraries, hospital wards, schools and homes to discover the factors which promote healthy development and the principles of working with children and their parents. The results of my study have been compiled in this volume.

The children and the parents whom I have known have also contributed to this book. In each illustration cited the children's names have been changed, and identifying material has been altered to protect the children. If this book deepens nurses' and parents' understanding of children and parents and makes it possible for them to obtain increased pleasure in their experiences with them the purpose of the author will have been realized.

FLORENCE G. BLAKE

The University of Chicago

Foreword

Every educated person knows of the astounding progress made by medical science in the past 80 years. The germ theory of disease, aseptic operative technics and chemical research have enabled man, for the first time, to investigate normal and disturbed bodily functions on a grand scale. Discovery followed discovery; bacteriology, biochemistry, physiology and pharmacology mushroomed into sciences in their own right. Truly, we seemed to have entered the "golden age" in medicine. The total conquest of disease was felt to be imminent.

During the same period, psychiatry underwent its own revolution, largely through the work of Sigmund Freud, who exposed the origins of neurosis and thus laid the basis for a rational, etiologically oriented treatment method. His most important discoveries were: (1) That all behavior is the meaningful expression of fundamental emotional needs, (2) that behavior patterns are a resultant of interaction between basic human drives and life experiences, (3) that the most significant, character-forming interactions occur in childhood, largely within the family and (4) that unsatisfying or antisocial patterns of need-expression can be changed, either in adult life or (more easily) in *statu nascendi*.

The above psychiatric concepts were absorbed rapidly by literature and later by social work and education but they penetrated the field of medicine proper much more slowly. There were at least two reasons for this lag. In the first place, the new discoveries in psychiatry were made largely by men who did not hold academic positions and therefore exercised little influence on general medical thought. Secondly, the two lines of investigation (physiologic and psychiatric) led to divergent viewpoints about the human organism. Psychiatry, emphasizing basic drives and impulses, regarded man as a unit, whereas the deification of the test tube and the microscope inevitably led to a more compartmentalized picture of man as a collection of separate, healthy or sick, organ systems. That this latter point of view entailed some disadvantages became apparent later, as the most thorough physical studies failed to explain fully the causes or the fluctuating course of many clear-cut disease entities (such as ulcerative colitis, asthma and peptic ulcer). Moreover, more and more patients were seen whose symptoms had no discoverable physiologic basis at all. Finally, it was observed that students, trained in specialized laboratory procedures during the early part of the medical curriculum, made poor practitioners in their clinical years. They could not think of their patients as human beings—an art which the family physician never had lost. It became apparent that too much "science" was leading to a deterioration in the art of medicine and that there were too many clinical facts which physiology alone could not explain.

At this point medicine began to take psychiatry into its fold. Psychiatrists were appointed to teaching positions; they contributed their specialized knowledge to the study of medical and surgical patients; they took part in clinical conferences; psychiatric courses and contact with live patients were made a part of the first-year course in several medical schools. Contact with physicians in other specialties during World War II helped to dispel the suspicion with which the psychiatrist's activities had been regarded. His knowledge came to be appreciated as a kind of specialized common sense rather than the mumbo jumbo of a witch doctor. With the penetration of medical teaching and practice by the psychiatric point of view, doctors began to observe more closely the feelings of their patients—toward their families, toward themselves, toward their bosses, toward the hospital and toward their physicians. The importance of emotions became recognized more generally in disease, in speeding or hindering convalescence and in determining the patient's adjustment to treatment. Pediatricians especially were receptive to these ideas since they had long observed directly the effects of parent-child interaction in their practice. The profession as a whole has made great strides in psychological understanding, but more remains to be done. Many medical schools still have no pediatric psychiatrist on their staffs as yet; enuresis is generally treated by drugs, and some hospitals still routinely restrain all children under 4 years of age.

Since, at present, the nurse is the doctor's subordinate, directing her activities according to his orders, progress in nursing follows that in medicine. Therefore, it is natural and timely that the psychiatric point of view should be introduced into nursing education. Nurses need this knowledge no less than do physicians, for their contacts with hospitalized patients are bound to be more intimate and lengthy than the busy doctor's. The nurse is thus often the recipient of the patient's strongest attachment; this is particularly true with young, hospitalized children who miss their mothers acutely and seek substitutes for them. This fact gives the pediatric nurse great power over her charges—power which she can wield for their good or ill. If she understands the causes of anxiety in child and parents, she can minimize the disturbance which hospitalization and illness always entail for both. If, on the other hand, she is callous, harsh or hostile, her behavior can maximize the effect of hospitalization into a real psychic trauma.

However, it is not only in the hospital that the nurse can help children. As Miss Blake demonstrates so comprehensively, a sensitive nurse can give real psychotherapeutic support to the whole family from their first prenatal clinic visit on. The nurse is, indeed, one of those key people (along with doctors, dentists, teachers, social workers and psychologists) who is in a position to make a significant contribution to community mental health. She can do this without abandoning her profession and without stepping on the toes of more specialized psychotherapists. She merely has to enlarge her awareness and use what she sees in her patient contacts. To make the most of her opportunities, of course, the nurse, like the doctor, needs some special knowledge. She must understand the meaning of behavior in both child and parent; she must learn to appraise it objectively, rather than react to it personally; she must know something about the needs and conflicts typical for various ages, the feelings of children about illness and the disruptive effects of separation from parents; she should understand how the members of a family interact with each other; she must develop some capacity for introspection; and to permit herself to do all of the above, her own life must be reasonably satisfying.

Miss Blake's ideas will not find immediate acceptance, for the nursing profession, no less than the medical, has its resistances to change and to psychological insight. We all prefer to overlook emotional conflicts in others because seeing them stirs up those unresolved difficulties which lie within us all; it is much easier to turn away. However, the writing is on the wall and cannot long be ignored. Directors of schools of nursing should be the first to read it, for no changes in teaching can be effected without conviction at top administrative levels. Points of view filter downward more easily than upward. More physicians and hospital administrators must learn about the workings of the mind and must be willing to adapt their practices to human nature, for, without their guidance and support, the nurse cannot broaden her activities and become a co-worker rather than an assistant. The last resistance which will have to be overcome is probably the most difficult, for it is fostered by the entire pattern of nursing education as practiced today. I refer to the fact that, like the physician, the nurse is trained primarily in technics. With practice, a minimum expenditure of mental energy is required to carry them out, and their stereotyped repetition gives a sort of rigid, routinized reassurance, particularly to those of

a compulsive disposition. A rut is a comfortable place to be in because its limits are so well defined!

The kind of nursing envisioned by the author demands a different orientation—to the patient rather than to the procedure. Such
an attitude requires flexibility of character—a quality which every
human being does not possess. Its application requires effort and may
demand courage, too—courage to report significant behavior to
supervisor and doctor without assurance in advance that they will be
interested, courage to make suggestions that may be ignored or
ridiculed. Every nurse is not suited for, and many would not be
interested in, this type of work, but the viewpoint at least should
be part of her training. As this book is read and as more like it are
written—and written they will be!—I am confident that we will see
in nursing education the same evolutionary change that is happening
in medicine—from routine care toward what might be called "com-
prehensive nursing."

A. H. VANDERVEER, M.D.

Contents

1

Introduction:

The Nurse's Role in Preventive Mental Health
Programs of the Future

One of the principal functions of the family is the preservation of the art of parenthood.[4] It is as important to the preservation of society as are the production of food, the prevention of physical disease and international control in the use of atomic energy.

Essential in the art of parenthood is the capacity to establish and to maintain constructive and satisfying relationships with others. This capacity has its origin in the earliest years of a child's life and is influenced by all that happens to him from the moment of his conception.

To become prepared for parenthood the individual needs satisfying experiences with people from the moment of birth to the time that he establishes a home and begins to rear his own family. The newborn infant is completely helpless and would perish at birth were he not protected and cared for immediately. He cannot reach out toward other people, but his helplessness, dependent nature and behavior disclose that he is in great need of loving care at birth and in the years to come. Today we have ample evidence to substantiate this fact. Bowlby,[4] who studied the work of psychiatrists, psychologists and child-guidance workers in various countries of Europe and America, says:

Among the most significant developments in psychiatry during the past quarter of a century has been the steady growth of evidence that the quality of the parental care which a child receives in his earliest years is of vital importance for his future mental health. Such evidence comes first from the psycho-analytic treatment of adults and then from that of children. It has been greatly amplified during the past decade by information gathered by psychologists and psychiatrists working in child guidance and child care—two fields affording unrivalled opportunities for first-hand observation both of the developing child and of his milieu.

The earliest years of a child's life are the most critical ones for his personality development because in those years the basis for give-and-take relationships with other people is formed. Experiences

1

in the earliest years of a child's life set the patterns which will be the models upon which he patterns most of his future experiences with other people. If he finds love, protection and sympathetic understanding in his earliest years, he will grow up expecting love from others and can accept it when it comes. He also can give love without expecting any immediate return from his generosity.

Understanding early care provides the child with a background of memorable satisfactions which make it possible for him to summon feelings of trust and belief in his world whenever he meets new experiences which are trying, confusing, stressful and unfamiliar to him. Experiences of stress will come, for they are a part of the growing-up process and are a certainty in the lives of every human being. The future of the individual and the world is uncertain and unknown—no one knows what tomorrow will bring. But whatever comes we know that he will need inner strength, courage and faith to meet and to master those conflicts and problems.

To ensure optimal physical growth and personality development, the infant needs a *continuous,* intimate relationship with a warm, giving mother (or permanent mother substitute) .[4] The newborn infant starts life with a potent vital force of energy which he needs for growth and adaptation to his environment. When the infant experiences fulfillment from repeated satisfying experiences with his mother, he acquires feelings of trust and security, and his energy is freed for growth and adaptation to his environment. If the child's needs are unfulfilled, his energy is expended in anxiety and he is deprived of the vitality that he requires for physical and personality growth.

Growth brings changes which heighten the infant's capacity to perceive, discriminate and attach himself to the person who meets his physical and emotional requirements. At birth the infant is too ill-equipped to attach himself to anyone, but he can feel, smell and respond to receptiveness, emotional warmth and the physical ministrations which provide for his growth needs and relieve him of discomfort.

With growth comes increased kinesthetic, visual and auditory perception. Between the fifth and the eighth months of extrauterine life the consistently loved and cared-for baby can differentiate his mother from strangers. He can see the person who protects, loves and provides him with comfort and what he needs for growth. He attaches himself to this person, follows and imitates her and needs her as a constant companion until he is physically and psychologically ready to broaden his horizons and to develop relationships with children and adults outside his immediate family.

The young child's mother is a part of himself; she is his strength and his support, and he needs her love as much as he needs food and shelter. Without her constant support and guidance, he has insufficient energy to master his infantile impulses. Without her loving care he cannot master the rage that comes when his desires are not gratified immediately. He has no inner resources to withstand the anxiety that comes if he is separated from her. The child under 3 lives in the here and now. What is out of sight is gone; it does not exist for him. He can perceive only what is before him and what is happening to him now. "Today," "tomorrow," "later" have no meaning to the young child. His mental equipment is not sufficiently developed to anticipate the future, and he cannot maintain relationships in absentia for more than a day.

Through the infant's attachment to his mother, his personality grows. He learns to master some of his infantile impulses such as sucking, biting, soiling and a desire for immediate gratification; he gains increased mastery of his environment, and of his fear of loss of mother. He learns to relate himself to his father, his brothers and sisters, his relatives and friends, but during the first 3 years of life his mother is his primary object of interest and concern. With strangers he is shy, cautious and uncertain, and when venturing into strange territory he is apprehensive and wary until they have proved to be safe. Through his attachment, trust and confidence in his mother, and his mother's recognition of the signs which indicate her child's readiness to give up infantile ways of behaving, he also acquires the capacity to tolerate increasingly larger doses of frustration and to channel his natural aggressive impulses in ways which bring release but are within the realms of childhood social acceptability.

The child's inner resources are strengthened as he acquires the above accomplishments, and he becomes ready to separate himself from his mother for short periods of time. His "following" response becomes dulled, and he welcomes broader social experiences and new territories to conquer. As he becomes surer of himself and safer in his world, and has increased ways of meeting his own needs for gratification, he ventures into the back yard or down the street to play near other children.

When he is about 3 years of age he is ready to utilize short periods of separation from his mother. He can go to nursery or play school, for instance, if he is familiar with its environment, knows his mother will return and take him home and is familiar with the person who will provide him with protection, care and emotional satisfactions while he is separated from his mother.

In 1948, the Social Commission of the United Nations felt that a study of the needs of homeless children was indicated. This commission described homeless children as "children who are orphaned or separated from their families for other reasons and need care in foster homes, institutions or other types of group care."[4] Dr. John Bowlby of England was appointed to make the study. In 1950, he visited several countries of Europe and the United States of America to study the mental health needs of homeless children. In each country that Bowlby visited, he studied the work of specialists in the field of child care and guidance and reviewed their literature.

Bowlby's[4] report, published in 1951, contains facts and recommendations that are startling but vital for the care of dependent children, those who are emotionally disturbed and those who are ill with physical disease or conditions which require hospitalization.

Bowlby's facts and recommendations are thought-provoking and challenging but difficult to implement in our society; his recommendations for the care of sick children would be a tremendous undertaking, requiring years for accomplishment. However, progress is never achieved without recognition of the need for changes, nor without whole-hearted conviction that it would bring values that surpass those that exist in our society today.

Bowlby's facts and recommendations merit study, and for this reason they are being presented here. They may be a basis for evaluating the services which are now being provided for mothers and children and for thinking through ways in which our profession can expand its contribution to society.

Bowlby's report has stimulated the writer to contemplate the changes that would be necessary to carry out his recommendations. It has also made the writer increasingly aware of the many conditions, attitudes and problems that block our profession's opportunities to improve services to families. These are being presented for study and evaluation.

The changes that are being presented for study and experimentation represent goals which the writer has acquired through study of human development; through clinical experience with children and parents in hospitals, homes, clinics and schools for normal and handicapped children; and through observation of the needs, the aspirations and the problems of basic and graduate students of nursing. They are based upon the clinical study of specialists in the field of psychiatry, psychology, nursery school education and child development and guidance, and upon observation of the needs of children and parents in sickness and in health.

The viewpoints presented in this book are not static or infallible—they are ever-changing. They change with new insights and knowledge that come from research, study and clinical practice; they will be forever changing as long as professional people are open-minded and searching for clearer understanding of human growth and the factors which retard and promote its healthy development.

Each new insight acquired from observational study must be reviewed, tried and re-evaluated in light of the results it brings to human beings. The suggestions which follow and the factors which prevent their realization need the same treatment. Each person must study and adapt the suggestions to his own situation and experiment to discover their reliability, weaknesses and strengths.

The outstanding fact which the Bowlby report presents is that deprivation of love and security during the period that the child is dependent upon his mother for sound personality growth can damage him and cripple his capacity to form and to maintain relationships with others throughout his lifetime. Maternal deprivation occurs when the child's mother (or permanent mother substitute) is emotionally or physically incapable of providing continuity of loving care and security for her child, and when the child is separated from his mother and is unable to have her care or the care of another woman whom he has learned to trust.[4]

The extent of crippling is determined by the degree of deprivation that the child experiences, the stage of development he is in when the deprivation occurs and the circumstances to which the child is subjected during the period of separation. The longer the separation and the less substitute mothering the child is provided with, the more injurious are its effects. Vulnerability to maternal deprivation decreases to some extent after the age of 3 to 5 years. If the child has had continuity of care preceding this period, he has acquired inner resources which assist him in adapting to situations that bring limited amounts of stress. After the age of 3 to 5 years the emotionally well-adjusted child can maintain a relationship with his mother in absentia if he is well prepared for the experience, is cared for by familiar people who understand his physical and psychological requirements and is able to keep in touch with his mother through frequent visiting which permits her to give him care during the periods when they are together.

The fact that deprivation of love and the insecurity which it brings can produce disturbed relationships which interfere with the normal course of human personality development is not a supposition; it is a known fact that is substantiated by clinical evidence. Evidence comes not from one study but from many—

from direct observational studies of "the mental health and development of children in institutions, hospitals, and foster-homes," from retrospective studies "which investigate the early histories of adolescents or adults who have developed psychological illness" and from follow-up studies of "children who have suffered deprivation in their early years with a view to determining their state of mental health."[4]

Bowlby[4] cites the work of Bakwin, Goldfarb, Bender, Ribble, Spitz and Wolf, Gesell and Amatruda, Burlingame and Freud and others who did studies to determine the effects of maternal deprivation on infants and young children. Those who did direct observational studies found that deprivation of maternal love and security adversely affected intellectual, physical, social and emotional development and brought symptoms of mental and physical illness in many instances. The follow-up studies of infants who suffered complete maternal deprivation disclose the fact that many were damaged permanently with resulting affectionless psychopathic characters. They had received too little love to identify with people and become socialized through relationships with them. Others developed neurotic patterns of behavior which brought conflict, anxiety and tension and impaired their capacity for successful marriage and parenthood. Why some deprived children escape irreversible personality damage is as yet unknown.

Bakwin[2] summarized the literature from 1909 on the subject of maternal deprivation. Bowlby[4] quotes his summary, and, because it has implications for those in our profession, it is reproduced here:

> Infants under 6 months of age who have been in an institution for some time present a well-defined picture. The outstanding features are listlessness, emaciation and pallor, relative immobility, quietness, unresponsiveness to stimuli like a smile or a coo, indifferent appetite, failure to gain weight properly despite the ingestion of diets which, in the home, are entirely adequate, frequent stools, poor sleep, an appearance of unhappiness, proneness to febrile episodes, absence of sucking habits.

Spitz and Wolf[8] found that similar symptoms developed when infants between 6 to 12 months of age became separated from their mothers. They named the symptom syndrome "anaclitic depression." The deprived infants whom they studied were apprehensive, withdrawn, anorexic, sad and unresponsive to play materials and to people who approached them; they were retarded in their total development. The syndrome occurred in infants who had experienced a good relationship with their mothers during the first 6 to 9 months of their lives and then were suddenly separated from them. They had had warm relationships with their mothers, but when separation became necessary they had no substitute to meet their emotional requirements.

Spitz and Wolf[8] studied 95 children with anaclitic depression and found that nearly all those who had experienced a wholesome relationship with their mothers suffered with the foregoing symptoms. Bowlby[4] says this means that "the depressive response to separation is a normal one at this age." Bowlby's[4] comments on the prognosis of anaclitic depression are as follows:

Although recovery is rapid if the child is restored to his mother, the possibility of psychic scars which may later be reactivated cannot be disregarded, while, if the condition is permitted to continue, recovery is greatly impeded. Spitz & Wolf believe that there is a qualitative change after three months of deprivation, after which recovery is rarely, if ever, complete.

Symptoms of emotional illness and retardation of development may also occur when babies are separated from their mothers between the third and the sixth months of life.[4] Symptoms of ill health develop more slowly in this age group but are alleviated much less easily when the infant is restored to his mother.[4]

Children in the second and the third years of life respond to maternal deprivation in ways which are equally disrupting to their potentialities for growth.[4] Observers discovered that they were in acute despair and responded to their feelings of loss of love with violent expressions of anger. Their symptoms were equally severe but instead of responding positively to substitute mothers, as do younger infants, they rejected them and remained in an anxiety-ridden state for a prolonged period of time. Gradually, they showed outward signs of recuperation, but a regressive state persisted for weeks and in some instances for months. They lost their capacity for bowel and bladder control, became clinging and demanding, possessive, rivalrous and intolerant of the slightest degree of frustration.

Not all children of 1 to 3 years respond in the same way to maternal deprivation.[4] Those who have never experienced close, warm and growth-producing relationships react differently from those children who have had a continuous relationship with a warm, giving mother. The latter group react differently because maternal care has given them an object of love which has become personally important to them. When they are removed from it, they experience tremendous loss, and react with feelings of grief, anger, fear and revenge. Bowlby[4] says:

Those who have been brought up in institutions and have had no permanent mother-figure show no responses of this kind at all, the result of their affective life already having been damaged. Though the in-experienced nurse welcomes the child who regards one adult as being as good as another and criticizes the family baby who reacts violently as having been "spoilt," all the evidence suggests that the violent re-action is normal and the apathetic resignation a sign of pathological development.

Bowlby[4] describes the immediate after-effects of deprivation which were observed by Burlingame and Freud and other clinicians. He says:

Those most commonly observed are (a) a hostile reaction to the mother on her return, which sometimes takes the form of a refusal to recognize her, (b) an excessive demandingness towards the mother or substitute mother, in which intense possessiveness is combined with intolerance of frustration, acute jealousy, and violent temper tantrums, (c) a cheerful but shallow attachment to any adult within the child's orbit, and (d) an apathetic withdrawal from all emotional entangle-ments, combined with monotonous rocking of the body and sometimes head banging.

Separation of short duration creates anxiety-ridden mother-child relationships which require understanding to alleviate. Children under 3 years of age who have experienced separation of short duration show changes in their behavior. They become increasingly more clinging and resistant to having their mothers out of sight for an instant. They remain deeply attached to their mothers but in an acutely anxious way. If the child's mother understands the reason for his anxiety-ridden relationship with her, and accepts and alleviates it through consistent giving that re-establishes his trust, security and confidence in her, evidence of anxiety gradually diminishes.[4]

Prolonged separation interrupts the continuity of the mother-child relationship and jeopardizes the possibilities of re-establishing a positive relationship when the child is returned to his mother.[4] His response to his mother or the new mother substitute upon his return to her will be dependent upon the degree of suffering that he experienced and the methods that he utilized to alleviate his anxiety.

The mother's response to the behavior changes which separation anxiety and anger arouse is another factor of great import in determining the ultimate effect of separation upon the child's per-sonality development. If the child's mother is sensitive to what the child has experienced, accepts the way he manifests his anxiety and hostility toward her and is ready and able to respond in ways which will relieve his inner turmoil, the possibility of the child's re-establishing a positive emotional relationship with his mother will be increased. On the other hand, if the mother responds to her child's anxiety and distress with lack of understanding and counteraggression because she is unable to accept a child who is withdrawn or expresses his angry and revengeful feelings overtly and is fearful of future separation, then more regression and fixation at babyish stages of development will be inevitable. Under such circumstances the child not only would lose further trust in people but also he could not help but feel that the world was hostile and depriving. Emotional and social growth cannot progress under such circumstances, for personality development is dependent upon the progressive growth and expansion of the mother-child relationship.[4]

Bowlby's report presents etiologic knowledge that is a challenge to our profession. It has implications for those in the fields of maternity, pediatric and public health nursing and also for those nurses who plan and implement curricula in our schools of nursing. Students of nursing will be stimulated by the report for it implies the need for changes which would give them increased opportunity to learn to work with families and to serve society in new and challenging ways.

Dr. G. R. Hargreaves,[6] Chief of the Mental Health Section of the World Health Organization, gives the following answer to the question, "What is mental health work?"

. . . mental health work consists in *doing* as well as *talking;* it depends on action rather than "evangelism." It is directly analogous to public health work. It should consist in the attempt to remove from the human environment those factors which are harmful to health, and, on the other hand, to provide those factors which support and promote growth.

Continuity of loving maternal care is the child's birthright and society's need. It meets his greatest need for growth, happiness and social productivity and is as important to society as it is to the individual. Without satisfactory growth-producing parental relationships the individual never can realize his full potentialities and acquire the true art of parenthood. The deprived child becomes the depriving parent. Unless efforts are directed toward assisting the children and the parents of today, little hope for a healthier and more peaceful world of people can be anticipated.

There are many causes of maternal deprivation and many ways in which our profession can help to eliminate conditions that interfere with normal personality development. Parents die and leave their children orphaned, but more emotional deprivation is caused by emotional instability which brings unreadiness for parenthood, illegitimacy and broken homes.[4] Much deprivation stems from ignorance or an unawareness of the essentials for physical and psychological growth. Economic factors that make it necessary for mothers to work is another frequent cause.

Practicing the art of parenthood requires maturity. No other professional career requires as much intuitive sensitivity and warmth, insight and giving as does parenthood. Giving requires surplus energy.[1] The amount of energy available for creative parenthood is determined by the individual's physical health and psychological level of maturity.

Parents also need relationship experiences which will foster further growth of their personalities and make parenthood a more satisfying and fulfilling experience. Many of today's citizens approach parenthood unprepared and respond with feelings of perplexity and insecurity. Confusion and anxiety take energy, prevent the individual from giving wholeheartedly and create needs which require satisfaction.

The expectant mother's needs are probably more urgent than those of the expectant father, though his needs must not escape the interest and the attention of professional workers. Child-rearing during the earliest years of a child's life is largely the responsibility of the mother. Even when the primiparous mother is well prepared for the experience from creative early life experiences within her own family, she experiences some measure of anxiety because she has had no previous experience which gives her assurance that she will be adequate as a mother.

Continuity in the mother-child relationship is essential for both the child and the personality growth of the mother. Thus far continuity of care has been emphasized as being important to the child. It is equally essential for the mother. Bowlby's[4] summary of the relationship needs of mother and child is given in the paragraphs which follow:

. . . the infant and young child should experience a warm, intimate, and continuous relationship with his mother (or mother-substitute), in which both find satisfaction and enjoyment. The child needs to feel he is an object of pleasure and pride to his mother; the mother needs to feel an expansion of her own personality in the personality of her child: each needs to feel closely identified with the other. The mothering of a child is not something which can be arranged by roster; it is a live human relationship which alters the characters of both partners. The provision of a proper diet calls for more than calories and vitamins: we need to enjoy our food if it is to do us good. In the same way the provision of mothering cannot be considered in terms of hours per day but only in terms of the enjoyment of each other's company which mother and child obtain.

Such enjoyment and close identification of feeling is only possible for either party if the relationship is continuous. . . . Just as the baby needs to feel that he belongs to his mother, the mother needs to feel that she belongs to her child and it is only when she has the satisfaction of this feeling that it is easy for her to devote herself to him. The provision of constant attention day and night, seven days a week and 365 days in the year, is possible only for a woman who derives profound satisfaction from seeing her child grow from babyhood, through the many phases of childhood, to become an independent man or woman, and knows that it is her care which has made this possible.

Many expectant mothers need help to become prepared for motherhood so that they can enjoy their babies to the fullest and give them what they require. The understanding nurse can help mothers to become prepared for motherhood. She can meet their needs during the prenatal period, during labor, during the postpartum period and in the years when their children are developing. She can increase mothers' insight into the growth process, lessen their anxiety and give them strength and confidence in their own ability to care for and guide their children.

To support a mother, the nurse needs knowledge, sensitivity to what she is experiencing and a capacity to respond in ways that brings her reassurance, security and increased confidence in her own capacities. One of the purposes of the author in this book is supplementation of the nurse's knowledge of the biologic, physical and medical sciences, by increasing her understanding of personality growth and the factors which promote its healthy development.

There are other causes of maternal deprivation that have implications for those in our profession. Illness which necessitates hospitalization and separation brings more maternal deprivation than many in the medical and the nursing professions realize. Preventive work has decreased the morbidity rates; fewer children are being admitted to hospitals than there were formerly. Nonetheless, our pediatric wards continue to have a high census in most seasons of the year. In all of our pediatric wards there are some children with preventable illnesses and some who could be taken care of by their mothers in their homes if medical and nursing services were available to them there. There are also infants and young children in hospitals and convalescent homes who are experiencing unbearable stress because their mothers are not with them to make the new and frightening situation seem less dangerous.

Assisting in a preventive mental health program which aims to lessen the above causes of maternal deprivation would entail a task which seems to be near to insurmountable for our profession. At the moment public health nurses are already overburdened. They now have case loads which cannot possibly be handled successfully. Pediatric wards and maternity nurseries are inadequately staffed, and the nurses are weighted down with responsibilities that were unknown to nurses a few decades ago. Progress in the medical sciences has increased the nurse's responsibilities. There are new complicated procedures, new treatments and routines which require the nurse's attention and time. As a result she has little time to observe the children to discover what they are needing emotionally. New responsibilities have been added, but there has been little increase in staffing to balance the demands which are being made upon nursing services.

Bowlby's[4] recommendation to expand home services to mothers of sick children would prevent separation and require expansion of our nursing services. Mothers caring for their sick children at home would need a great deal of physical assistance and emotional support. Without it many would not be secure enough to keep their children at home and care for them there. Providing this service to mothers would require the acquisition of new attitudes and skills, but it would protect children's growth potentials and provide them with continuity of maternal care when they need it the most.

However, there always will be infants and young children who require care in a hospital. Many illnesses are severe and beyond the mother's capacity to nurse. To expect her to do so without the continued assistance of a professional nurse would be asking the impossible of her emotionally. Many illnesses require surgery and treatment that would be unavailable in the home. In such instances hospital care is the only solution.

Our professional task is to co-operate with others in finding ways to provide children with the kind of hospitalized care that prevents the psychological wounds (commonly referred to as traumas) which jeopardize their opportunities for personality growth. This is our problem. We can face it, study it and plan ways to prevent emotional ill health or we can rationalize the unpleasant thought from our minds by saying that a shortage of nurses blocks the realization of any new goals which we might strive to attain. There will be obstacles to surmount—not trivial ones but difficult ones that seem to be overpowering at the moment. Obstacles *are* existent. To deny them would be an indication of our escape from reality.

America's hospitals are the biggest and the best in the world; they are magnificently constructed, tastefully appointed and equipped with every piece of new apparatus which has been found valuable in the care of the sick. Yet many people say that they find them cold, rigid, impersonal and foreboding because they lose their identity as individuals and fail to get the understanding that their human needs require. This too is a reality! To deny it is to escape from what is before our eyes and meets our ears. It is a painful fact to face, but it is a reality.

If any country possesses the potentialities for change it is America! Its citizens have resources and the drive to excel and give to humanity. Many in our society delight in seeing children in beautifully decorated buildings, having been indoctrinated with the idea that the giving of buildings represents the highest form of generosity. Would that it were possible for the people in our country to get equal gratification from seeing children better cared for in their homes and in the hospital when it is a necessity! After hospitals are built and appointed, often funds are depleted, leaving insufficient resources for providing patients with professional nursing care. Nor is money available to implement programs of education which would prepare nurses to meet patients' total requirements. If change were viewed as important to society's progress, the wealthy benefactors and citizens of our country would leave no stone unturned until the new goals were accomplished. Society is unaware of its citizens' needs—and unaware of the nursing profession's needs.

It is not necessary to search the literature to substantiate the findings that Bowlby presents; evidence of the effects of maternal deprivation exists in nearly every nursery for the newborn and in every pediatric ward in the country. There are infants and children in our hospitals today whose physical needs are being met, but in another sense they are neglected because they are being subjected to tremendous stress which they are incapable of mastering without their mothers or a familiar, satisfying substitute. Mothers who have experienced the after-effects of hospitalization with their children can provide further evidence, and they will if we are ready to listen and to accept it.

Many in our society will be skeptical of the foregoing theories and will hesitate to accept the conclusion of psychologists, psychiatrists and those in the field of child research and guidance. Some in our profession and others will say: "Those theories are untrue. The infants and the young children in our wards are not hostile to their mothers or toward personnel. They are quiet, cooperative and serene." Outwardly, many young hospitalized children do appear to be serene, but if one observes further one will see that these children have not mastered their situations, for they have been too helpless to do so. They have buried their hostility and denied their fear, withdrawn from people and utilized a veneer of superficial nondiscriminating friendliness and exaggerated conformity to protect themselves from the complete loss of love which would threaten their very existence. Their behavior hides their feelings from themselves and unfortunately from many others as well. They have adapted to a stressful situation, but in ways unhealthy for their personality development.

Further description of the children referred to above will serve to demonstrate the behavior which is often misinterpreted as a constructive adjustment to hospitalization. It will also guide the observation of those individuals who are motivated to study the conditions which are existent in our hospitals today. These children respond to everyone in the same "friendly" way. They do not differentiate the visitors from the nurses or the aides. Anyone who approaches them gets a smile, be it a volunteer on her first day to the ward, or a medical student who is desirous of listening to an unknown patient's heart. If one studies the faces of these children, one will see that their smiles lack depth and their eyes are without the sparkle that comes when one views a person who is important to him personally. These children are conforming, passive and amenable to everything anyone suggests. Instead of resisting intramuscular injections and other frightening and painful treatments, they accept them without a whimper, smile after they have been given, and sometimes even add, "It doesn't hurt, I'm not afraid." They accept new routines without resistance or any sign of displeasure. They rarely, if ever, talk of their mothers or verbally anticipate visiting hours. When their mothers depart from their ward they show no outward response of anger or sadness. They accept their mother's presence with complacence and sit apathetically while they are together.

Bowlby[4] cautions his readers against being deceived by the above type of response to prolonged separation. He says that the children who respond in the above way are those who "go to pieces" when they leave the hospital or the institution. Being deceived by the above type of behavior is understandable, for most people do not know its seriousness. They do not know that it is an unnatural way for children to respond to a painful, frightening situation. Unless one has an opportunity to learn about normal behavior, one has difficulty in recognizing deviation from normalcy.

Comparison of normal children outside the hospital with those described above will show marked differences in behavior. When a normal toddler meets a stranger, he does not smile at once and conform to his directions. If the stranger approaches him with something with which he is unfamiliar, he runs to his mother for support; and when he gets it, his facial expression and behavior show a deep feeling response to her love. If he falls and runs a sliver into his knee he screams and runs to his mother for help. He is not a coward, a "cry baby" or a fighting little animal; he is responding normally.

There will be many who believe that skillful care for young children during periods of separation can provide substitute satisfactions and eliminate the hazards of separation. Clinical evidence does not support this assumption. Even when substitute mothering is provided for young children and the transition from home to institution is handled skillfully by understanding personnel, behavior changes are difficult or impossible to prevent. Bowlby[4] quotes from a monthly report written by Burlingame and Freud who directed the care of children in a residential nursery in England during World War II. Their observations were as follows:

In dealing with new cases of this kind we have attempted to work out a process of "separation in slow stages" so as to mitigate its consequences for the child. Though this has proved beneficial with children from three or four onward, we have found that *very little can be done to prevent regression where children between 1½ and 2½ are concerned.* Infants of that age can stand sudden changes and separations of a day's length without any visible effect. Whenever it is more than that they tend to lose their emotional ties, revert in their instincts and regress in their behavior. [Bowlby's italics]

The children entering the residential school referred to above were normal, healthy children. They had no disease to combat and no painful treatments to experience, but regression and behavior changes occurred even when skillful substitute mothering was provided for them.

Infants and children are not the only ones who experience distress with hospitalization. Mothers also experience it when they leave their children in the hospital, for mothers, too, need a continuous relationship with their young children, and they suffer great anxiety when they are forced to leave them in the hands of nurses and doctors with whom they have had too little experience to feel confident of their abilities. Many mothers feel that they are being forced to abandon their children when they leave them in the hospital. They are skeptical of the care that they will receive, and it is understandable why they respond in this way.

A baby or a young child needs a mother who knows and accepts him as an individual with his own needs and characteristic ways of behaving. A child never can be free from anxiety when his mother is gone and he is being confronted constantly by a myriad of strangers who do things to him that he has never experienced before. The young child cannot possibly adapt himself to such stress without injury to his developing personality.

The nurse can bathe, feed, dress, play with, medicate and treat the young child, but she cannot give him what he needs most—a continuous relationship with the person whom he has learned to love, trust and depend on. It takes time to understand a young child's individuality and to find ways that meet his needs for comfort and growth. The best-prepared nurse cannot do for a young child what his own mother can do. She does not know the baby and has no personal meaning to him. He does not desire to have a relationship with her; he needs a relationship with his mother and when he is sick his need for her is intensified. Edelston's work[5] substantiates the above concept. He studied 42 children who had experienced early maternal deprivation with hospitalization and found that the experience had precipitated, if not caused, behavior disorders which were severe enough to necessitate treatment. He says:

Coming at a time when the young child is more helpless than ever owing to his illness and feels the need for mother's care and affection most, removal from home must be a most distressing experience and will undermine his trust and confidence in his parents . . . a true understanding of the position is quite beyond the child's ego-centric outlook and he consequently feels (or even actively misinterprets) the situation as a "rejection" or a punishment. The inevitable emotional insecurity which is aroused I consider to be identical with the anxiety arising from "fear of loss of the mother" (in the psychological sense), which lies at the root of so many neurotic disorders.

Carrying out the changes which would be necessary to accommodate mothers of small children in pediatric units would bring rewards for families, students and medical and nursing personnel that far surpass those which they are experiencing now. Children's physical and psychological health would be safeguarded and strengthened to meet an unknown future. Mothers would feel they had contributed to the restoration of their children to health, and medical and nursing personnel could feel gratified from the real and worth-while contribution that they had made to the families' peace of mind and health. There would also be opportunities for nurses to increase their skill in working with parents. Such opportunities are not now available in most pediatric units. Students of nursing need this experience if they are to become prepared to fulfill their future professional roles.

Spence,[7] who has worked in English hospitals where mothers were admitted with their young children, reports his observations and indicates the value of maternal care for sick infants, mothers, nurses and medical personnel. His observations are as follows:

The most difficult and time-absorbing task in nursing is the care of the youngest children, who must be nursed, fed, and changed at frequent intervals of the night and day. If in addition there is much technical treatment the care of one seriously ill infant becomes one woman's work. If there must be off-duty periods, it will be two women's work. If we introduce the three-shift system, it will be three women's work. While these infants are in hospital their mothers are at home suspended in anxiety. It would seem logical, therefore, that a solution of the problem should be found in admitting the mothers to the hospital to nurse their own children. This is no theoretical proposal. I have worked under this arrangement in my hospitals for many years, and I count it an indispensable part of nursing in a children's unit. Nor is it a revolutionary idea. By far the greater part of sick children's nursing is already done by mothers in their homes, and the mother's nursing unit is merely an extention of this responsibility. Not all illnesses will be suited to this nursing, but the majority of all children under the age of 3 derive benefit from it. The mother lives in the same room with her child. She needs little or no off-duty time, because the sleep requirements of a mother fall near to zero when her own child is acutely ill. She feeds the child; she tends the child; she keeps it in its most comfortable posture, whether on its pillow or on her knee. The sister and nurse are at hand to help and to administer technical treatment to the child.

The advantages of the system are fourfold. It is an advantage to the child. It is an advantage to the mother, for to have undergone this experience and to have felt that she has been responsible for her own child's recovery establishes a relationship with her child and confidence in herself which bodes well for the future. It is an advantage to the nurses, who learn much by contact with the best of these women, not only about the handling of a child but about life itself. It is an advantage to the other children in the ward, for whose care more nursing is liberated. In teaching hospitals it is of further advantage to the students, who gain a practical experience of the form of nursing they will depend on in their practices and learn to recognize the anxieties and courage which bind the mothers to their children during illness: a lesson which fosters the courtesy on which the practice of medicine depends.

Many hospital personnel will resist Bowlby's foregoing recommendation for changes in methods of caring for babies and young children in hospitals, and there are reasons why they will. Many in our profession have not had the opportunity to study children. They do not recognize the behavior characteristics that spell distress and threaten the child's mental health. There are others who have observed the damaging effects of maternal deprivation but have not reacted strongly enough to mobilize their creative efforts to find ways to alleviate them. Others have reacted to their observations and attempted to stimulate the interest of their associates in the nursing and the medical professions. Some changes have come through concerted effort; other suggestions have met with resistance that has not been overcome. Bowlby[4] suggests that reluctance to accept the findings of research workers and the opinions of those trained in the understanding of human behavior may possibly come because acceptance "would involve far-reaching changes in conceptions of human nature and in methods of caring for young children."

Making changes which would meet the needs of young children and mothers would require drastic reorganization in many institutions. In some it would mean rebuilding; in others it would necessitate the rearrangement of furniture and the cutting down of available beds for young children. Such reorganization would involve money and the formulation of new administrative policies.

There are other changes, however, which would be more difficult to realize. They would require temporary personal sacrifice on the part of those providing care for sick children in hospitals. Only with a change in thinking and the acquisition of new attitudes and skills would such reorganization be possible. Hospitals would need to use more flexible methods of care which mothers help to formulate and execute. Mothers would require teaching, encouragement and support. Understanding and a capacity to work with all kinds of mothers, including those who are frightened, ambivalent or overprotective, would be necessary to meet their requirements.

Effecting changes which would prevent mental ill health and bring increased services to families would require unity of purpose, emotional preparedness and concerted action on the part of all hospital personnel. Daring to change requires conviction, courage and confidence in one's ability to master the problems in interpersonal relationships that it brings. In 1953, emotional preparedness and unity of purpose and philosophy are far from a reality. But it is something within the realms of possibility—not this year or the next, perhaps, but in the decades to come.

Many in our profession will resist Bowlby's recommendations because they sense their inability to cope with the problems which would be an inevitable part of change. It is understandable why they feel this way. Their professional training has not prepared them for the close interpersonal relationships which changes in the care of children would bring. They have not learned how to work with parents; they do not know the satisfactions which could be derived from it, for no one ever has assisted them in discovering them.

Women enter the field of nursing motivated to work with people, but many are graduated from schools of nursing disillusioned, frustrated and resistant to changes which would keep mothers and young children together. The causes are undoubtedly multiple. Many cannot be eliminated, but others could be rectified if financial assistance and wholehearted interest were a reality. What brings the change in attitude, the disillusionment and the frustration? What makes graduate nurses resistant to mothers in the pediatric and the orthopedic wards and to babies in their mothers' room in the maternity hospital? Is this resistance within the student when she enters the school of nursing? If it is not existent on admission to the school, how does she acquire it and how can we prevent it from developing within her? If it is existent when she enters the school, how could we help her to change her attitudes so she could develop the skills necessary to work with parents?

Observation of student nurses at the time they enter schools of nursing shows that the majority are idealistic, enthusiastic, creative, thoughtful and receptive. They enter the school of nursing motivated to work with people. They are fired with a desire to serve humanity. They want to be close to people, understand them and be generous in their giving. Within them there is a need to be with people and a need to be giving to them. If this were not true, many would seek preparation in a field which would isolate them from warm relationships with others. However, many young students do not know how to establish relationships with patients. They are ill at ease and uncomfortable with them unless they have something specific to do for them.

There are many factors which create the feelings of uneasiness commonly experienced by the young student when she begins her clinical practice in the clinics and the wards. Students are sent to the ward to do, and usually the doing is directed down to the minutest detail. They have practiced and repracticed on Mrs. Chase, the nursing arts laboratory manikin; they have mastered the art of giving a bath and making perfect corners of a bed. They have learned the accepted arrangement of equipment for the evening care procedure. They know where the talcum powder can, the bottle of alcohol and the bath basin should be placed, and they know the accepted method of covering the patient before they fanfold the upper bedclothing to the foot of the bed.

Although the student avidly awaits the day when she can go to the ward and see patients, she often returns from her experience unable to describe the behavior and the emotional needs of the patient whom she has bathed. She does not go to the ward with her interest centered on the study of patients but on technics and the steps which are required to complete them in a way which brings supervisory acceptance. She has learned little about people and she does not know patients want understanding and interest in them as persons infinitely more than interest in their beds and their surrounding environment. Most patients do not care how the equipment is placed or how meticulously their bedclothing is folded to the foot of the bed. Their interest is centered on themselves, and they want both physical and emotional comfort. Sick people are regressed people in need of dependent satisfactions and personal interest. They long for motherly interest and the kind of care which is based on their own individual needs. They need someone to talk to who will listen and recognize their need to be considered as persons—not as patients with interesting diseases but as human individuals different from all other persons in the ward.

Student nurses need freedom to understand their patients and to relate to them in a way which meets their needs. They are equally in need of the knowledge which observation of their patients would bring, for it is necessary for their personal and professional growth. Some of our students of nursing never have freedom to center their interest on patients as a means of learning to understand them. From experience they have learned that their security depends upon pleasing the instructor, the supervisor or the doctor. This takes energy, for teacher or doctor acceptance too often requires concentration on making sure that the procedure or the routine is carried out *exactly* as it has been taught. Under such circumstances the students have little energy left for patients and they feel it! They are preoccupied, scared and intent on acquiring the supervisor's and the doctor's acceptance. In the process they are often frustrated, for they get neither their acceptance nor the gratification that comes from learning to understand their patients. In addition, their growth becomes stifled because they have had too little freedom to develop the creative powers within them.

By the time many students reach the maternity service, they have lost a great deal of their interest in people, for they have had too little help and too little time to develop their capacities to study and work with them as persons. Many have become engrossed in pathology, symptoms, drugs and treatment. They have had little opportunity to discover that people are interesting, understandable and a source of knowledge and pleasure. They do not know that the science of human behavior can bring richer and more satisfying professional relationships, for they have not had the opportunity to study it in the classroom or in the wards. Maternity nursing is often looked upon as a tedious experience. It is not unusual to hear students say: "Maternity is not exciting. There is no pathology to study, and the care is routine, monotonous and a bore!" Why do the students feel this way? Why are they not challenged by maternity nursing? Why do they leave the laboring mother alone and remain insensitive to the mothers' need to have their babies with them and to learn about their needs and care?

Many nurses react in the above way because they have lost interest in human needs through experiences which have brought frustration rather than gratifying human relationships. Their need for understanding patients and learning to work with them has been thwarted; it has not been kept alive and allowed to grow. Frustration brings anxiety and the need to defend oneself against it. Interest in pathology, exciting procedures and new and complicated treatments gives them a substitute interest and lessens the anxiety within them. But, unfortunately, it brings neither personal satisfaction nor the individual nursing care which people require.

Many students come to the pediatric service equally unprepared to work with children. Many students are more ill at ease with children than they are with adults. They do not know what normal children are like and they have had few opportunities to know them. Yet immediately upon arrival in the pediatric ward they are expected to take care of sick children. They cannot give them total care when they have not been oriented to their basic requirements or to a method of study which helps them to discover the meaning of their behavior.

The unprepared student often finds her pediatric nursing experience unsatisfying. Because she is unprepared to understand children, she again concentrates on procedures and gets along fairly well with babies and critically ill children. With convalescent and ambulatory children, however, she is often at a total loss to know how to handle herself or the children. It is not unusual to hear comments like the following ones: "I was told to take a basket of toys to the ward and play with the children. I took the basket of toys but I didn't have the remotest notion of what to do with them. The ward was full of children calling, 'Play nurse, come here,' but I didn't know how to approach them or what to do with them. It was the most miserable week of my training, and I never wanted to face children again. Pediatrics is the last specialty I would ever choose."

The unprepared student often leaves the pediatric service with attitudes which thwart her personal growth and potentialities to be of service to children and parents. Instead of finding the care of children enjoyable and stimulating, many students of nursing find it painful, and not infrequently humiliating as well for they discover that they are inadequate and uncertain in their feminine roles. Perhaps the foregoing comments will recall the reader's early experiences in a pediatric ward. Perhaps she may remember her feelings of inadequacy when a child had a temper tantrum as she approached him with a dose of medicine. Maybe she will remember a child's saying, "I hate you—go away," and the thoughts that came as she groped for a way to handle her feelings so she could continue to work with the child. She may also remember some periods that she spent on evening duty with a ward of boys who were infinitely more interested in playing pranks on her than in going to sleep. The memory of private room sections where mothers and children roomed together may arouse strong feelings in the nurse who was placed there without any understanding of what mothers or children require. Many nurses who had the latter experience left the service feeling that mothers were a hindrance and should be excluded from hospital wards. It is understandable why they feel this way. They were miserably uncomfortable because they did not know what to do or say. They had no children to take care of, and substitute satisfactions were impossible because they did not know how to approach mothers, gain their co-operation and assist them in caring for their children. How could they assist them when they had not yet learned how to work with children themselves?

Students of nursing need a background of knowledge in biologic, physical, medical and nursing sciences because the principles underlying the physical care of sick patients are based upon them. Patients would not be safely nursed without this knowledge. They also need knowledge of the medical sciences, for understanding of the etiology, the symptomatology and the treatment of disease is essential in the care of sick patients and necessary if one is to function effectively in preventive health programs. Courses in nutrition and the nursing arts are equally important, for the application of the knowledge gained from these sciences gives the student the physical skills which are necessary to restore her patients to physical health.

Students of nursing recognize their need for knowledge in the above sciences but they need education and experiences which increase their capacities to apply it in ways that bring satisfaction to others and to themselves. The student's interest in learning to work with people must be utilized, strengthened and kept alive. It is important for the student. It is also important to society. One's professional training should bring satisfactions and personal growth. Unless it does, neither self-realization nor full social productivity can be realized.

Changes in nursing school curriculum are indicated for several reasons. Students are seeking a different kind of professional education than they are getting in many of our schools today. To keep their interest in people alive, new kinds of educational experiences are imperative. To expand nurses' capacities to work with people, they need increased insight into human needs, as well as skill in working with people.

If we want to prepare nurses to understand their patients and function in units where mothers and young children are accommodated together, education and training will need to begin when the students enter the school of nursing. To prepare students to understand the nursing care requirements of mothers and children, education and supervised experience must *precede* the students' clinical practice in maternity and pediatric nursing. Students must come to these services with a knowledge of family life and its importance to the growing individual and to his parents and with an interest which motivates them to want to acquire ways of contributing to it. They will also need to come prepared and motivated to study patients as a means of determining their total nursing needs. For this, students of nursing need orientation which increases their understanding of human growth, the dynamics of personality development and the forces, the strivings and the fears that motivate human behavior.

In addition to the above orientation, students of nursing need experiences which assist them in acquiring the art of observation. They should have opportunities to observe human behavior *before* they go into the wards to care for the sick in order that they may understand what they see. Observational opportunities are available in every hospital and community in the country. All of the following are found in some communities, and many are available in small towns: there are prenatal, well-baby and pediatric clinics, pediatricians' and obstetricians' offices, nurseries for the newborn, nursery, primary and secondary schools, play schools, playgrounds, Church schools, recreational clubs and homes where families reside.

Observation and participational experiences would provide the students with opportunities to observe behavior characteristics of children at different age levels, to study parent-child, teacher-child, nurse-patient and doctor-patient relationships, and to study environments that are planned to meet children's needs. Participation experience in a nursery or play school of normal children would enrich the student's knowledge and provide her with opportunities to study her reactions in her relationships with the children.

Students of nursing require more than supervision in the carrying out of procedures and routines. They need help that assists them in developing those qualities most essential for the art of nursing. Theory and observational experiences provide knowledge, stimulate the formulation of new attitudes and motivate the students to increase their powers of observation and to acquire new skills. However, to make knowledge functional, students need opportunities and help to apply it and to observe its effects in their relationships with others. For this the student nurse needs supervised clinical practice which helps her to evaluate her relationships with patients in clinics and wards and to develop her own philosophy and skills in working with people. Each student will utilize knowledge and experience in her own way. She needs freedom and encouragement to rely on her own feelings and opportunities to work out a professional and life philosophy that is her very own.

The student nurse is in a process of growth and needs further emotional preparedness if she is to become ready to function creatively in a professional role. She, too, has emotional and social needs and must receive before she can give. From the time she enters the school of nursing and throughout her professional training period, she needs emotional warmth, acceptance, understanding, guidance, recognition and interest in her as a person. The student nurse requires surplus energy for giving the same as any other human being does. An emotionally deprived nurse cannot supply the emotional nourishment that a sick child or adult requires. Nursing makes many demands upon the nurse; unless those demands are balanced with satisfactions, either the patient or the nurse herself is going to be deprived of basic requirements for health.

The student nurse can develop skill in working with people only if she has help—she needs supervision that meets her human needs. The above concepts merely serve to summarize the student nurse's emotional needs. This subject deserves further study, for the product a school graduates is influenced by the relationships she experiences as well as by the curriculum content.

Another method of assisting student and graduate nurses in gaining increased understanding of parents and children is the utilization of the psychiatrist and the social worker in maternity and pediatric wards. The nursing profession is already utilizing the help of those specialists on its faculties. They are giving lectures and seminars, but there is further assistance from them that students of nursing are seeking and need. All social agencies have psychiatric consultants who function in an advisory capacity to their staffs. Is it inconceivable to think of psychiatric and social worker consultants for nurses in the maternity and the pediatric wards?

Changes in nursing education will require increased financial assistance if the profession is going to expand its services to the individuals in our society. *They can come in no other way, for the kind of learning and practice essential to improve nursing practice cannot come when service demands of a busy hospital supersede the educational and the emotional needs of the students.* This condition exists in the great majority of our schools of nursing today. It takes time to learn to study patients, to learn to meet their physical and emotional needs and to evaluate one's relationships with others. It also requires the help of additional faculty members who are prepared to help students work out their relationship problems with people in ways that bring increased satisfaction to themselves and to those they are preparing to nurse, support and guide.

Students preparing for practice in other professions have long periods *preceding* clinical practice which require giving and also the assuming of responsibilities. When they meet responsibility, they are ready to assume it because they have received that which helps them become ready to assume it. Is it not equally important for those young women who are preparing to enter the nursing profession? Why are the student nurse's opportunities for emotional and educational growth jeopardized? Why is she expected to carry responsibility for the care of patients *before* she has had opportunities to learn what is entailed in nursing them? Why is she expected to meet the needs of patients, doctors and hospital administrators before her own needs have been met? Is it not unreasonable and unsound educationally? The student nurse does require clinical practice and an adequate amount of it; but we want her to develop into a person who is capable of professional work; like other students she needs a period of learning that is free from service demand pressures.

When the student nurse is graduated, not only is she confronted with the care of patients but also she is expected to know how to supervise practical nurses, auxiliary workers and student nurses who are functioning under her direction. Many of the practical nurses and auxiliary workers are wives and mothers who have had opportunities to learn about family life. They have less technical skill and scientific knowledge than the graduate nurse but they have had other educational opportunities not available to student nurses. Could such a coincidence account for some of the problems in interpersonal relationships existing in our hospitals today? It is another subject which merits study.

Any change in hospital service is doomed to failure without the entire staff's wholehearted acceptance and readiness to participate. To become prepared to effect changes in hospitals, in-service preparation for graduate nurses and auxiliary workers is indicated.

During this period when we are studying our professional services to mothers and children and are planning ways in which we eventually might realize "rooming-in" in maternity and pediatric wards and home services for sick children, many things can be done to improve the quality of care given to children in hospitals and to prepare students of nursing for their future roles in society.

Bender[3] studied 6,000 emotionally disturbed children and made recommendations for the care of dependent children. Her recommendations point up a goal which children need to have realized in our hospital wards and convalescent homes today. She says:

. . . we must feel challenged to provide a different kind of early care for dependent children. Foster care should begin in the earliest months, but it cannot protect the child unless he has *continuous* experience in the *same* home with a warm loving foster mother. Practically speaking, this will be NO easy program to achieve. In the meantime, some modification in institutional practice would seem desirable. Perhaps it would help if attendants were chosen with some eye to warmth of personality, and if assignments of work were made which allowed a continuous relation between the baby and the adult to whose care he is assigned.

One of the most urgent changes that seems to be indicated is the instituting of the case method of patient assignment, which ensures greater continuity of care for the children and increases the student or graduate nurse's opportunities for learning. The hospitalized child is in great need of a continuing relationship which will provide those essentials that a warm, understanding and sensitive mother provides. Case method of assignment never can provide the consistent care that can be given by mothers but it does lessen the contacts to which children are subjected and offers something that more nearly resembles the kind of supportive, warm care to which they have been accustomed before.

Both nurses and children need continuity in their relationship together. Nurses need it to learn about children and to grow through understanding of them. As the nurse works with a child her interest in him as a unique individual becomes heightened. They begin to respond to one another, and a relationship develops which involves the feelings of both the nurse and the child. The nurse's maternal feelings become motivated, and she can give more of herself emotionally, which is what the child needs to regain his health and to continue to grow. It is also what the nurse needs, for as she gives to the child and assists him in regaining his health and mastering his situation in the hospital, her personality has opportunities for growth as well.

Feeling relationships rarely occur when assignments are made to duties rather than to children, for the care of children is done according to ward scheduling rather than in response to their individual needs. Frequent change in patient assignment is also depriving. Neither child nor nurse can become familiar with one another and involved in a relationship which provides satisfactions and growth for them both.

Individual care requires flexibility in hospital routine and flexibility and warmth in the personalities who are providing it. It is of paramount importance for the infant and the young child who is as yet unable to adapt himself to fixed regimens without suffering and emotional shock. The illness and the treatment required are traumatizing in themselves. In many instances this cannot be prevented, but if, in addition, the child must experience inconsistency, coldness and rigidity in care, his welfare becomes increasingly more precarious.

The functional method of assignment commonly practiced in pediatric wards centers the nurse's interest on routines, technics and procedures and fails to provide children with any semblance of maternal care. The child needs to feel that he belongs to some one person who cares, and this need is as important for the child in the ward as for the one in the home. When a functional method of assignment is used, the child is subjected to a variety of human attitudes and feelings and to great diversity in manual skills. He has no one person to depend upon, and he can never feel safe, for he has no consistent experiences which help him to anticipate support, care and fulfillment from those in his environment.

Basic to the art of child care is the capacity to provide the child with the kind of relationship that makes it possible for him to grow through mastery of whatever situation he is in. Establishing and maintaining a constructive, satisfying relationship with a child requires knowledge of children's developmental needs, study to discover his individual requirements, understanding of oneself and intuitive capacity and skill in supplying him with what he needs to master his current life situation, be it illness and hospitalization, life in a new school environment, or a conflicting situation which is a normal part of growth. If the child's problem is the kind that requires mastery of a hospital experience and recuperation from illness, the nurse needs knowledge of his illness and the medical and physical care required. She also needs understanding of his basic human needs.

The remaining chapters of this book have been written to deepen readers' understanding of children and parents and to increase their enjoyment of them as persons. The material in this book is divided into age periods for the purpose of clarity and organization. It does not mean, however, that each phase of development is a clearly demarcated period in the life of the child. Each phase of development continues into the next period and becomes fused with it.

REFERENCES

1. Alexander, Franz: Emotional maturity, Ment. Health Bull. **26**:1, 1948.
2. Bakwin, Harry: Emotional deprivation of infants, J. Pediat. **35**:512, 1949.
3. Bender, Lauretta: There is no substitute for family life, Child Study **23**:74, 1946.
4. Bowlby, John: Maternal Care and Mental Health, Geneva, World Health Organization: Monograph Series No. 2, 1951.
5. Edelston, H.: Separation Anxiety in Young Children: A Study of Hospital Cases, Genetic Psychology Monograph **28**:3, 1943.
6. Hargreaves, G. R.: The development of mental health work, World Ment. Health **5**:2, 1953.
7. Spence, J. C.: The care of children in hospital, Brit. M. J. **1**:125, 1947.
8. Spitz, A., and Wolf, K. M.: Anaclitic Depression; an Inquiry into the Genesis of Psychiatric Conditions in Early Childhood II, p. 313 in The Psychoanalytic Study of the Child, vol. 2, New York, Internat. Univ. Press, 1947.

2

The Prenatal Period and Its Influence
on the Mother-Child Relationship

THE CHILD'S PHYSICAL HERITAGE

From the moment of conception, a child's heredity is established. As the male sperm cell with its 24 chromosomes enters the nucleus of the female egg cell, contributing chromosomes from the latter are released.[13] The united 48 chromosomes, half contributed from the mother and half from the father, comprise the *child's physical heritage.*

In each chromosome there are countless genes which are the real determinants of the individual's heredity. It is the genes which determine the color of the child's eyes, hair and skin, his bodily proportions, his activity type, his sex and his potentialities for intellectual, physical and emotional growth. The genes will also determine the individual's response to his environment during the earliest periods of his extra-uterine life.

INFLUENCE OF THE MOTHER'S PHYSICAL AND EMOTIONAL HEALTH ON THE FETUS

Influence of Maternal Physical Health on the Mother and the Developing Fetus

The physical health of the mother at the time of conception and during the prenatal period will affect the growth of the organ-

29

ism which has begun its life as a minute cell within her body. Her physical health determines the kind of internal environment she will provide for the developing fetus. Absence of disease in the mother ensures fetal development in accordance with its inherited potentialities. The mother's physical health during pregnancy affects her feelings of well-being. The fewer physical ills and discomforts she experiences, the more ensured are her happiness and her relationship to her child.

Studies have demonstrated the effect of adequate nutrition on the health of both mother and child. In one study of 216 pregnant women, Burke, Beal, Kirkwood and Stuart[2] found that every stillborn, all prematures but one, every functionally immature infant, most of the infants with congenital defects and every infant but one who died during the first days of life were born to women who had had inadequate diets during pregnancy.

Ebbs, Tisdall and Scott[6] of Toronto studied the influence of prenatal diet on 300 mothers and their children. One group of 100 women was given additional foods to supplement their diets and to guarantee an excellent nutritional intake. Another group of 100 women was given instructions pertaining to their dietary needs during pregnancy. A third group of 100 women served as controls. This latter group was neither instructed nor given food with which to supplement their diets. During the maternity cycle, the women's health was appraised by obstetricians who were uninformed of the dietary status of their patients. At birth the babies were given physical health ratings. The women on the supplemented diets were healthier during pregnancy and recuperated more effectively in the postpartum period. Their babies were healthier at birth and had fewer illnesses during the neonatal period. Three per cent of the babies born to mothers on unsupplemented diets died during the early weeks of life. There was no mortality in the group of babies born to mothers on supplemented diets. The incidence of prematurity, stillbirths and abortions was higher in the group of mothers who had ingested poor diets during pregnancy.

Other studies have disclosed similar findings which indicate the nutritional needs of the expectant mothers. Adequate intake alone will not ensure optimal physical health for the mother during the maternity cycle, nor will it ensure the birth of a normal full-term infant. However, its influence on maternal health and in producing normal fetal development is well established and should receive adequate emphasis in the care of prenatal patients.

The physically and mentally perfect infant meets with fewer hazards and adapts to extra-uterine existence with greater ease. Adaptation to extra-uterine life is a difficult process for the newborn infant. *To assist the fetus in becoming ready for living as an independent organism it needs adequate nutrients and a peaceful, parasitic existence* in utero. The normally developed infant is received more readily and accepted more easily. Abnormalities are a threat to the child's physical and psychological growth.* Many times they are more of a threat to emotional than to physical growth. Many children with congenital abnormalities survive but fail to grow emotionally because they are deprived of the emotional acceptance they require for wholesome personality growth.

INFLUENCE OF ENVIRONMENT ON THE HEALTH OF THE CHILD

Although a child's inherited constitution produces his uniqueness and affects the manner in which he will adapt himself to society, environmental factors, particularly those involved in the interpersonal relationships within the family, are believed to play the greatest role in the development of personality.

To ensure optimal growth, the newborn infant needs a mother who is prepared to receive him with unconditional acceptance, warmth and freedom to use her intuitive powers of motherliness. The relationship a newborn infant experiences with its mother is the first and most meaningful experience of its life. It influences the kind of adjustment the child will be able to make to extra-uterine existence during the newborn period and throughout his lifetime. It influences his feelings about the world and all his future relationships with people.

Environmental factors begin to have their influence on the child from the moment of his conception. The emotional atmosphere into which he is received is dependent upon the character structure of the partners who conceived him. The motivations which prompted the individual's conception and the feelings in the minds and the hearts of the parents who conceived him will provide the soil from whence the child's personality must grow. Everything that has happened to the woman prior to the birth of her child affects her receptivity and her capacity to give to her dependent, helpless babe. Her early experiences within her family and her community, the emotional support she receives from her husband and the kind of help she has from professional workers during pregnancy—all influence her feelings concerning herself,

---

* Further development of this topic appears in Chapter 3.

her pregnancy and the responsibilities and privileges entailed in motherhood.

Influence of the Mother's Emotional Health

A pregnant woman's emotional health is as important to the child as her physical health. Her mental health determines how she is able to utilize health instruction. A pregnant woman who is fearful or frustrated may not be able to assimilate an adequate diet. This may be so even when intellectually she accepts the theory that adequate nutrition is an essential part of her care during pregnancy. The pregnant woman who responds to inner anxiety with bouts of overeating will have difficulty in complying with the instructions devised to prevent her from gaining excess weight during pregnancy.

The pregnant woman's mental health also influences her physical state and therefore influences the development of her unborn child. Escalona[7] writes of Sontag's studies of the effect of anxiety and emotional tension in producing unfavorable prenatal conditions for the unborn child. Sontag believes the mother's emotional state can affect the functioning of her autonomic nervous system and produce increased activity in the fetus. He believes fetal hyperactivity has an effect upon the infant's capacity to make a comfortable adaptation to extra-uterine existence during the early months of its life. Deutsch[5] feels there is insufficient evidence to prove maternal tension does influence the fetus, but she believes there is much evidence to support Sontag's theory. Deutsch[5] states there is evidence to prove that pre-existing unconscious anxiety affects the physiologic phenomena of pregnancy. Therefore, she believes it is not illogical to assume it can affect so integral a part of the mother's body as the fetus.

Pregnancy brings changes into a woman's life. It upsets established equilibrium; it is a potential threat and therefore can be a precipitating factor in the production of anxiety and tension.[5] To many women marriage brings security, a satisfaction of dependent longings and a solution to disturbing conflicts.[5] As Deutsch[5] has suggested, the "we" that comes with marriage gives many women ego-strength and produces harmony within their personalities. In instances in which marriage has an overabundance of this meaning for a woman, pregnancy may bring insecurity and varying degrees of emotional disequilibrium.[5]

How a woman accepts her pregnancy is determined by the personal meaning it has for her. Throughout her lifetime the woman has been confronted with experiences in interpersonal relationships which have made her ready or unready for motherhood. These experiences have produced a capacity for giving or a need to deprive. Each pregnant woman is an individual with feelings and attitudes toward her pregnancy which are personal and meaningful to her. *The expectant mother's attitudes, feelings and fears in relation to her pregnancy need consideration* if she is to be assisted in making a good adjustment to this new venture which is a fulfillment of her deepest and most powerful wish. Whenever and wherever the nurse meets her, the pregnant woman as a person must be her primary focus of interest. To consider only the woman's physical health and needs without considering her response to pregnancy is to neglect a phase of nursing which has great import for the individual.

DEVELOPMENT OF THE WISH FOR A CHILD

The wish for a child has its origin in the early years of the child's life. The wish comes before the child has become aware of sex differences or aware that mothers and fathers have an intimate relationship with each other. The little girl finds interest in play with dolls. In her second year she is observed mothering her dolls. She assumes a mother role and makes her dolls her babies. She bathes, dresses, feeds and puts "her babies" to bed. The dolls become the recipients of her care. In play she is no longer a baby; she is a mother. Without any direction or prompting, the young child reverses her role in her play with dolls.[9] Through this play she is beginning to solve her conflict between independence and dependence.[9] This kind of play is observable in the period when the child is attempting to gain a degree of independence from her mother and when she begins to assert her rights in expressing herself. She wants and needs her mother's love and care, but she also wants to control, dominate and be permitted to carry out her own desires. In this period she often wishes she could make her mother into a baby whom she could discipline, love and control.[9] Children frequently express this wish to their mothers or their nurses in their play. It is not unusual for the little girl to say, "Come, let's play house. You pretend you are the baby. I'll be the mother."

The little girl's early experiences with her mother, and the knowledge she acquires concerning the feminine role, influence her play and produce patterned behavior and attitudes toward her dolls. In the third year girls discover they are feminine like their mothers and that women have babies. Their interest in doll play increases. Observation discloses their intense absorption in dramatizing the mother's activities. This is play; it is also preparation for their future feminine role. The relationship the small child has with her mother is reflected in her play with dolls. She gives to her dolls what she feels she has received or what she wishes she might obtain from her mother. She accepts, rejects or shows ambivalence to her dolls depending upon the attitudes and needs that have been created within her.

The patterned behavior the child acquires through her relationships with her mother will eventually express itself in the relationship she will have with her own children. These attitudes and forms of behavior will be influenced by the way she meets and solves other conflicts that occur in the process of her personality development. However, it is her earliest experiences that will color the kind of solution she will be able to make to all subsequent problems with which she is confronted.

In the late preschool period the girl observes sexual differences and her feelings about herself become influenced by the attitudes of the people in the world about her. Between 3 and 4 years of age the little girl's experience widens and she begins to develop relationships with boys. She observes their anatomic differences and expresses her feelings about them in behavior and words. From observation of girls' behavior and verbal communications it is evident the discovery of anatomic differences influences their feelings about themselves and their femininity.* Universally girls envy boys; our culture is responsible for it. Our civilization is oriented more to men than to women. It is not unusual for parents to prefer boys to be their first-born child. Our civilization boasts material possessions that can be displayed and admired. When the little girl observes the boy's penis, it represents to her a possession that can be shown off. Many little girls say they feel boys have more than they and show their feelings of inadequacy and anger in their behavior. If the little girl has learned that girls have an organ in their bodies where babies can grow, she wishes she could have a baby for she feels a need to prove that she is as good as a boy.

Growth and the experiences of childhood bring wishes and fantasies which must be repressed until the individual is ready for motherhood. Between 3 and 5 years of age girls have fantasies about having babies. These fantasies come as a result of the girl's attachment to her father, and her desire for the kind of love relationship with him she observes to be existent between her parents. In the course of normal development the fantasies become repressed because the wish cannot be fulfilled in reality. During

---

* Further development of this topic appears in Chapter 6.

the school age period, the girl's interest becomes centered on learning about the world and in making satisfying adaptations to new group and school experiences. Her wish for a child is not conscious in this period of development.

When pubertal changes come, the girl's wish for a child is revived. In adolescence the wish is threatening and even dangerous, due to reality limitations and social standards. Because reality limitations exist, the drive or wish becomes sublimated into constructive activities where she can play the role of a substitute mother. At this period she is interested in children and child care. She seeks care of neighborhood children for it gives her some of the gratification for which she longs. It is at this period that preparation for marriage and child care should be given, although experiences within her family have been preparing her for them from the moment of her birth. In adolescence a girl's interest and receptiveness are at a peak. She is motivated to learn and is an apt pupil at this time because instruction fulfills a need which has deep meaning for her. During the first year or two after marriage, the wish for a child is not usually the woman's most prominent wish. Energy is being utilized in making physical and emotional adjustments to her partner and to the many new experiences involved in married life. When the adjustment period is over and a satisfying relationship is established, energy becomes available for the realization of her dreams for a child.

NEED OF THE EXPECTANT MOTHER FOR UNDERSTANDING CARE—ITS INFLUENCE ON FUTURE FAMILY INTERPERSONAL RELATIONSHIPS

Child welfare involves more than the child; it involves those within his home and his community. Pediatric, maternity, orthopedic and public health nurses have relationships with parents and the children they have produced. Pediatric nurses are not directly concerned with prenatal care or the instruction of expectant fathers. Pediatric nursing, however, is concerned with child welfare. The pediatric nurse meets parents and children in the well-baby clinic, in the hospital ward, in the school and in their homes. To understand the child, the nurse needs to know those closest to him. His parents make up his environment. It is his interpersonal relationships with those closest to him that make him what he is. To care successfully for the child wherever he is the nurse needs to consider the child's parents and keep him in touch with them. In the well-baby clinic and in the home the nurse deals with mothers more than with their children. Her success in helping them in the clinic, the ward or the home depends on her ability to understand and to accept them as individuals and as parents.

INFLUENCE OF PRENATAL CARE ON THE PREVENTION OF BEHAVIOR DISTURBANCES

Good prenatal care motivates and prepares parents to utilize the assistance available to them not only during the maternity cycle but during the formative years of the child's life as well. When a woman becomes pregnant, she longs for and is in need of someone to talk to and to guide her. In the prenatal period she has a real need for supportive care. In many instances she also needs specific instruction which will help her feel prepared for her future responsibilities. Good prenatal care can do much to prevent behavior disturbances in the child. It is for this reason that those interested in the field of child care and family life view the prenatal period as a period of vital importance. When expectant parents' needs for acceptance, understanding and enlightenment are met, they become receptive and motivated to seek and to utilize the help of professional workers in the guidance of their children.

KNOWLEDGE, ATTITUDES AND SKILLS—REQUIREMENTS FOR HELPING EXPECTANT PARENTS

Success in helping expectant parents depends upon the worker's knowledge, attitudes and skills. The nurse needs knowledge to help her to understand what the individual may be experiencing as she ventures into a new experience which is making new and difficult demands upon her. She needs knowledge to understand the common problems, the usual worries, conflicting feelings and fears, and to appreciate from whence they come. Such knowledge helps the individual to be nonjudicial, understanding and accepting. The professional worker needs attitudes which make it possible for her to accept the individual regardless of the kinds of fears, feelings or behavior she expresses. She needs skill in creating an atmosphere which makes it possible for the woman to disclose the feelings, thoughts and fears which are bringing her discomfort and making pregnancy unsatisfying to her. The capacity to develop a constructive relationship with the individual stems from a true interest in people, a genuine desire to understand them and a real capacity to accept them as they are. This requires a goodly degree of self-understanding. Examining one's own feelings, prejudices, attitudes toward the attitudes of others, and the expectant parents' reaction to her, aids the nurse in developing her skills in working with people.[17]

The expectant mother needs a nurse who has skill in listening, the capacity to relieve conscious fears and the ability to help her without being authoritative or directing. Unless a nurse can listen she will not discover the expectant mother's feelings, attitudes and fears or meet the needs that exist within her. A nondirecting interested nurse assists the expectant mother in developing her own potentialities, and relieves the anxiety and frustration which prevent her from solving her own problems. Women have intuitive feelings and an abundance of good common sense. If they are encouraged to use them in planning their own schedule of care and in planning for the future needs of their infants they will acquire increased confidence in their own abilities.

EMOTIONAL CHANGES OF PREGNANCY

The pregnant woman needs understanding of her emotional responses to the changes which are occurring within her body. Pregnancy brings emotional as well as physical changes within the individual. Benedek[1] says that hormonal and metabolic changes bring increase in vital energy, new feelings, a revival of old fears and conflicts and a tendency toward introspection. The emotional changes revive the woman's early childhood thoughts about pregnancy and bring to the fore the early emotional reactions she had concerning those impressions. Anxiety which was formerly mastered becomes reactivated; it brings tension and emotional and physical discomfort.[5] New emotional needs are created and they strive for gratification.[1] The pregnant woman's interest becomes centered on herself, her body, her feelings and her unborn child. She becomes withdrawn, contemplative, anxious. She becomes less sensitive to the needs of her husband and other children. This is not because she loves them less, but because physical and emotional changes heighten her self-interest. She daydreams about her baby, his sex and the possibilities of his future achievements. Yet the fetus is not a real object to the woman in the first trimester of pregnancy; it is but a part of her body which is controllable, and capable of being molded into the kind of a child she is desirous of having.

Daydreaming brings regression. Dependency longings which formerly were handled with ease become revived and seek satisfaction. Unsatisfied dependent receptive needs bring frustration, anger and tension. When there is frustration more regression occurs, and dependency needs become further intensified. Unfulfilled needs prevent the development of motherliness, a quality of importance to both mother and child.[1]

Many pregnant women, especially primiparae, experience anxiety which brings regression and utilizes energy they need for normal adaptive behavior. When an abundance of energy is being expended in anxiety, the woman is less able to master her feelings and to control her behavior. She becomes irritable about trivial matters, more demanding and more difficult to satisfy. She becomes less able to tolerate frustrations that formerly she could handle with comparative ease. These characteristics within herself make the woman uncomfortable and unhappy. Many women feel guilty for having these feelings. When they express them they condemn themselves. Others condemn the pregnancy; some condemn their husbands. In this way feelings and the expression of them can influence interpersonal relationships within the family.

PREGNANCY-CREATED FEARS REQUIRING ALLEVIATION

The pregnant woman needs freedom from anxiety, frustration and deprivation so that happiness and psychological growth can be achieved. A pregnancy fraught with psychological suffering cannot help but influence the mother's attitudes and feelings toward her unborn child. Therefore it can influence the kind of relationship she will be able to establish with her infant in the crucial newborn period. When the mother sees her child as the cause of her discomfort, feelings of resentment tend to occur.

Fear of abortion, of producing a stillborn or deformed child, is common in pregnant women and stems from experiences which are a part of growth. These fears reflect the inferiority feelings they experienced in preschool years when they compared themselves unfavorably with boys. Another source of fear of abortion and stillbirth lies in the feelings the girl may have had in connection with masturbation.[5] Some little girls feel they have injured their genitals and therefore are unable to produce a child.

Many women unconsciously expect a deformed child as punishment for hostile wishes and feelings they had concerning their mothers in the period when they were competing with them for the love of their fathers. "Is he normal?" is the first question the mother usually asks when the delivery is completed. Observation during the postpartum period shows further evidence of the existence of their fear. One inspection of the newborn infant does not suffice to satisfy the mother's need to prove to herself that she has given birth to a perfect infant. She continues to explore and to inspect her child's body. She needs this opportunity and it is one which should not be denied her. Only as she examines her infant each time the fear is revived will her fears be dispelled.

The physical and emotional changes that come with pregnancy create anxiety in some pregnant women. They are often sensitive, self-depreciative and concerned lest their misshapen body bring the disapproval of their husbands. Some women are disturbed because their feelings toward their mates change with pregnancy. In some women the sexual drive becomes intensified; in others it becomes modified and sometimes even nonexistent. The possibility of change in the relationship to their husbands after the infant's arrival becomes a threat to some. They fear their love for their child will detract from the love they feel for their husbands. Others are insecure concerning their capacity to meet their husband's expectations of them as mothers. Many have doubts concerning their ability to love and to guide their children. These doubts reflect ambivalent feelings which are common to pregnant women. Senn[12] studied expectant mothers in a prenatal clinic. He found they were more apprehensive about their ability to fulfill the mother role than they were about their capacity to survive delivery and to produce a living child. Our middle-class culture sets high standards for motherhood. It is little wonder the expectant mother grows introspective and attempts to evaluate her readiness and her capacity to fulfill the mother role.

The expectant mother who experiences conflicting feelings needs to know they are universal for they influence her feelings about herself and the child. Many women are overjoyed when they learn they are pregnant. They feel good physically, anticipate motherhood and revel in becoming prepared for it. They are proud of the pregnancy and reflect it in all they say and do. Their pregnancy is proof to themselves and the world that they are adequate in performing their greatest function in life. The majority of women, however, experience conflicting feelings.[17] They experience joy and fulfillment, yet they feel resentful, miserable and afraid. They want the pregnancy, yet there are feelings within them which often prevent them from accepting it with complete joyfulness. Many of the negative feelings are suppressed; they are too unacceptable to be tolerated. Yet they are common to a vast number of pregnant women. This fact, however, they do not know. Many of the suppressed feelings are acted out in direct and indirect ways. They become expressed in their relationships to their doctors, to nurses and to members of their family.

It is not the place of the nurse to stimulate the expression of the above feelings but if a woman actually verbalizes them the nurse can be of tremendous service if she can accept and clarify them. To stimulate the expression of unconscious feelings is dangerous for it precipitates anxiety, which nurses are unprepared to help the woman handle. However, many of these feelings are conscious and are expressed with extreme guilt, which can be alleviated with acceptance and a knowledge of their universality. When the woman discovers her feelings are natural, common and acceptable, she need have no guilt concerning them. When guilt is removed, she will not need to hide the feelings from herself by overprotective care of her child.

Helping the expectant mother discover the unreality of her fears through support and the acquisition of knowledge and skills which increases her understanding and self-confidence alleviates anxiety and feelings of inadequacy. Nurses have neither the background of knowledge nor the skill required to go to the basis of her fears, but they can give the pregnant woman an opportunity to express her conscious feelings and anxieties. In the majority of instances expression of fear brings relief of tension when accepted without derision, criticism or mirth.[16] In the process of listening, reassuring and relieving anxiety, the nurse becomes a supporting person from whom the woman can take strength and gain some measure of satisfaction of her dependent longings. In this way the nurse can lessen frustration, making it possible for the woman to use her energy more constructively in preparing herself for labor and to welcome her child with a greater degree of motherliness.

It is important that nurses recognize a patient's need for specialized service. When a woman's problems indicate her need for expert help, the function of available agencies should be interpreted to her. In many instances it may be the nurse's responsibility to help the patient to feel a need for and to accept the help of a social worker or psychiatrist.

Assisting the expectant father in gaining insight into the responsibilities entailed in his role is another way in which nurses can function to help expectant mothers have a more comfortable and enjoyable pregnancy. The expectant father needs to have the natural emotional changes that come with pregnancy interpreted to him. The expectant mother needs his support, understanding and acceptance; she needs to have her husband appreciate and fulfill her need for increased attention and satisfaction of her intensified passive, dependent tendencies. He needs to be able to give in to her whims and her occasional impulsiveness and to accept the fact that her interest has been temporarily withdrawn from him and become centered on herself and their child that is to be. *This* is the expectant father's role! He needs to know there is a relationship between his affectionate and understanding care of his wife and the kind of responses she will show in her relationship to their child when it is born.

The expectant mother needs specific guidance during the prenatal period to alleviate her apprehension concerning her ability to give care to her child. Anticipatory guidance can reduce the fear existent in many primiparae. The nurse can teach expectant mothers the principles of child care and can assist them in gaining skill in handling a small infant. When expectant mothers have gained security and confidence, they can handle the problems of the postpartum period with greater equanimity. Freedom from anxiety will free their energies for giving to and loving their newborn infants. A prepared mother will give her infant security and comfort more abundantly than the mother who is anxious, uncertain and overwhelmed. An anxious mother cannot make a secure child; anxiety is communicated, and its effect upon the newborn infant is apparent to the skilled observer.

To prevent anxiety the nurse needs to know the expectant mother's philosophy, plans and attitudes pertaining to infant care before she attempts to give her any anticipatory guidance. If the mother is encouraged to discuss her ideas concerning infant care, the nurse can discover the areas in which she is well prepared. It will give the nurse an opportunity to commend her and to increase her self-assurance. She can discover how she feels about breast feeding and can encourage her if she shows no adverse feelings concerning it. When negative feelings pertaining to breast feeding are encountered, it is important that the woman is not made to feel anxious or guilty about her attitude. Instead, the woman must be understood and not judged. There are many reasons why women do not want to breast feed their babies. Many are not emotionally ready for motherhood and the giving which it entails, although biologically they are capable of producing a child. There are many who are repulsed at the idea of nursing a child. They feel it is exhibitionistic, primitive, confining and disfiguring. Many fear lest their milk will not be good enough for their babies. There are those who feel it is not a socially approved method of feeding an infant. Although they have a wish to breast feed their baby, they are fearful lest they be criticized.

A mother must want to breast feed her baby if it is to be a satisfactory experience for her and her child. If she has negative feelings toward the process but breast feeds because she feels it is expected of her, the infant will get mother's milk but not the mothering which is his source of comfort and security. Indoctrinating women with the concept that breast feeding is the only method of choice for feeding a newborn infant is an unwise procedure for it brings feelings of uneasiness to many women. Many times, for physical, economic or psychological reasons, a mother is unable to breast feed her baby. If she has been made to feel that the bottle deprives the baby of essential mothering, feelings of guilt, inadequacy, inferiority and despair often arise.

The expectant mothers who want to breast feed their babies or are undecided which method of feeding to use need encouragement, and oftentimes sanction, from their doctors and nurses. Interpreting the emotional values inherent in the breast feeding experience helps many expectant mothers to follow their inner feelings. When an expectant mother expresses indecision, she is probably seeking information which will help her think through her problem concerning feeding. The nurse can provide explanations but they should be given in such a way that the mother is motivated to make her own decision.

There is little doubt that breast feeding meets the baby's emotional and physical needs more completely. When a mother gives her breast to her child, she is giving of herself emotionally as well as physically. The breast is a gift of love to the infant; it is the very essence of mothering when it is given by a woman who desires to do so. It provides the closeness to his mother which gives the child a feeling of pleasure and security as well as food that is appropriate for his needs. Many authorities believe that breast feeding immunizes the child against anxiety. A baby can be satisfied more quickly when breast feeding is available. He does not have to wait for the bottle to be warmed, and until a satisfactory nipple is obtained. The milk flow is better regulated from the breast, and the infant can suck until he is satiated. The quantity is not controlled from without but is controlled by the infant's own inner need for food, sucking and emotional warmth.

Breast feeding is also of value to the mother; it is conducive to the development of a wholesome mother-child relationship. It not only meets the infant's need for pleasure and closeness; it also meets the mother's need for a continued symbiotic relationship with her child.[1] Breast feeding should bring pleasure to both mother and child. It is the mutual satisfaction they give to one another that forms the basis of a constructive, happy experience together.[1]

The expectant mother will profit most from anticipatory guidance which teaches the principles of child care and prepares her to observe her infant. As expectant parents talk about their plans for the care of their infant, the nurse can discover wherein they need a specific kind of help. When she has this information, she can supply the instruction they require. Expectant mothers usually want to know how to feed, handle, bathe and dress an infant. They need to know about essential equipment and clothing, but most they need to know that their infants will be *unique individuals needful of care which is adapted to their own specific and characteristic needs.* They must be helped to know their child will require *study* to determine his unique emotional and physical requirements. Only as needs are known and interpreted can they be met in a way which fulfills the infant's total requirements. There is no single principle as important in the entire realm of child care. In the prenatal period the *principles* of child care should be taught. Prescribed authoritarian dictums do not increase the women's confidence or prepare them to meet their infants' needs. There is no universal formula for guidance which is appliable to all infants. Interpreting the emotional concomitants of physical care increases the expectant mother's understanding and prepares her to observe and to meet her baby's needs in her own way.

In teaching expectant parents emphasis should be placed on the infant's need for individualized care. Expectant mothers need readiness to apply the basic knowledge in the care of their individual child. They also need readiness to use their own intuitive powers in experimenting to find ways of bringing physical and emotional satisfaction to their infants and to themselves. They need freedom to think, to plan and to do what their inner feelings guide them in doing; they need guidance which aims to increase their independence and feelings of self-confidence.

NEED OF THE EXPECTANT FATHER
FOR PREPARATION FOR HIS ROLE

ANXIETY, A COMMON EXPERIENCE OF THE EXPECTANT FATHER

Pregnancy makes demands on expectant fathers and creates anxiety in many of them. Maternity is a family affair. The pregnancy is theirs and it has an effect upon the expectant father as well as upon his wife. Both individuals have a tremendous emotional investment in it. The expectant father is meeting a new situation which makes financial, emotional and social demands upon him.

The man's emotional attitudes toward fatherhood and its responsibilities, his acceptance or lack of acceptance of it, have its roots in early childhood and have evolved from the interpersonal relationships within his family. Pregnancy can be a threat to the expectant father as well as to his wife. His needs may be threatened by his wife's pregnancy. He may feel rivalrous with the child to be, or even abandoned.

NEED OF THE EXPECTANT FATHER FOR FREEDOM FROM ANXIETY IN PREPARATION FOR FULFILLMENT OF HIS ROLE

The expectant father needs to understand the psychological changes occurring in his wife not only because she needs his support, love and acceptance, but also because his anxiety will be relieved when he learns it is the somatic changes which cause some of his wife's interest to be withdrawn from him and to become centered on herself and her child. He needs to know it is only temporary and not the result of changes in her feelings toward him. His feelings will affect his state of comfort and influence the kind of support he will be able to give his wife throughout the maternity cycle. They will also determine the kind of relationship he is able to establish with his child when it is born. The more united the expectant parents are in their feelings and philosophy, the more ensured is the family relationship.

The expectant father's preparedness to meet his wife's needs during labor and the postpartum period relieves his anxiety and fulfills his need to be adequate in his important supportive role. *He needs to feel a part of the experience.* He needs to be included when all plans are being made for the care of his wife and their baby. He needs understanding of labor, and how he can participate during it. It will help him to feel needed and vitally involved in the birth of his child. Many expectant fathers are not aware of the responsibilities they will have in the postpartum period. If, in the prenatal period, they are helped to anticipate and to accept the responsibilities they will meet in the neonatal period, they will be more ready to meet them cheerfully. A readiness to assist with household chores is not the only task of importance—of equal importance is the expectant father's readiness to provide the encouragement and support which are a part of the foundation upon which the mother-child relationship is built.

NEED OF EXPECTANT PARENTS FOR PREPARATION FOR LABOR

ALLEVIATION OF FEAR BY PREPARATION

Both expectant parents have fears pertaining to the labor experience that is to come. The expectant mother fears lest she not survive the delivery of the infant. She may also fear that pregnancy and delivery will leave her with a body that is irreparably changed or damaged, for in some there is a deep fear of bodily injury. The expectant father is usually apprehensive; he is concerned for his wife's safety and sometimes threatened with possible loss. He wants to understand labor and wants help in knowing how to support his wife during the event.

The way in which labor is approached and experienced will have an effect upon the family unit. It will influence the parents' feeling toward each other and toward the child that is to come. It will also influence the way the parents will come to the postpartum period—with feelings of fulfillment and joy and a readiness to establish a warm relationship with the newcomer, or feeling bitter, resentful and unreceptive to the child who is dependent upon a continued close relationship with its mother. When the experience is fraught with anxiety, frustration, anger and an undue amount of pain, they will have less energy available for meeting their respective roles during the neonatal period. The mother needs an emotional and physical reserve available to regain her strength and prepregnancy state of emotional maturity. Energy is necessary for the development of motherliness. Her husband needs energy available to carry out his supportive role—a role which has its impact on the early mother-child relationship.

Preparation for labor should be provided early in the pregnancy so that fears may be dispelled and replaced by positive emotional values and feelings that bring confidence, security and a readiness to participate in the experience without dread or fear. It is not easy to dispel the fears existent in expectant parents; it takes more than a description of the signs and symptoms which indicate the onset of labor and an explanation of its mechanisms.

The conception of labor which expectant parents bring into the pregnancy was acquired early in their lives. Throughout their lives they have been exposed to the feelings of others concerning it; they have taken in more than information; they have absorbed the emotional attitudes and responses of those they have heard discussing it. Many of these individuals as children received no answers to the questions which perplexed and confused them. When explanations fail to come, children are forced to invent their own. These fantasies, the product of their own imagination, remain with them; they become the source of their superstitious beliefs, unrealistic fears and emotional reactions. Many have been exposed to abnormality and difficult pregnancies and deliveries, and have generalized that it is characteristic of all births.

Many women are unbelievably ignorant in regard to their own anatomy and the way their bodies function. Many cannot accept pregnancy and labor as a natural feminine function for which their bodies are biologically well prepared. It is the anxiety and the tension the above thoughts and feelings produce that make it difficult for them to keep in control of themselves in the birth-rooms, and interferes with the functioning of their physiologic mechanisms. The nurse knows the signs which indicate normal progress. She knows that labor is safe, but many women have had no experiences which make it possible for them emotionally to accept this concept. A capacity to feel with the frightened individual is a quality of great import. Without this ability, the nurse will be of little support to her patients.

ASSISTING MOTHERS IN ACCOMPLISHING NATURAL CHILDBIRTH BY PREPARATION AND SUPPORT

Study of women in labor has shown that prenatal preparation alleviates anxiety and makes it possible for many women to participate in the delivery of their babies. Read,[11] Goodrich,[8] Thom,[14] Vollmer[15] and many others have worked with expectant mothers during the prenatal period, preparing them for labor and to participate in the delivery of their babies. Studying the relationship between prenatal attitudes and the behavior of women during labor, they found that preparation influenced the progress of labor, its duration and the degree of discomfort the individual experienced. They found that the majority of women were able to participate in the process of natural childbirth if they were prepared for labor psychologically and physically, had exercised to increase the elasticity of their abdominal and perineal muscles and had mastered the art of relaxation.

Some women were unable to profit from preparation because of early life experiences. Their inability to utilize instruction and to be influenced by the psychological approach of that preparation was due not to ignorance—it was due to deeply buried anxiety which could not be reached by those untrained in the technics of psychoanalytic therapy.

Those who have worked with mothers who experienced natural childbirth have concluded that preparation for and support during labor were the factors of greatest importance in ensuring success. During the prenatal period, the expectant parents' needs were met through constructive doctor-patient and nurse-patient relationships. The women's confidence in professional workers was increased. They were ready to place their trust in those who were caring for them during labor. In the birthrooms they met with the same understanding help they had received during the prenatal period, and the expectant fathers were permitted to support their wives up until the time their babies were ready to be born.

EMOTIONAL CARE DURING LABOR

EMOTIONAL CARE DURING LABOR TO MEET THE FAMILY NEEDS

To help expectant parents gain trust and confidence, an atmosphere of human kindness and understanding needs to pervade the birthrooms. For many women it is their first experience in the hospital. They must adjust themselves to a new environment as well as to the feelings inside them. Many women enter the birthrooms ready to trust and place their confidence in the nurses and doctors. Others need satisfying experiences with them before they become assured they are in safe hands.

Understanding care and kindness has far-reaching effects for each member of the family. It not only gives the expectant parents what they need at a critical period of their lives, it also contributes to and has influence upon the infant's physical and psychological health. When expectant parents receive understanding care in the birthrooms, they become prepared to utilize the help of nurses in later situations for through experience they have discovered them to be helpful people.

Expectant parents need nurses in the birthrooms who are prepared to function in emotionally supporting ways. The attitudes and feelings of the nurses in the birthrooms are reflected in all they say and do to their patients and those closest to them. Nurses need understanding of the meaning of emotional care. This requires sensitivity to and an ability to interpret the emotional needs existent within both individuals and a capacity to meet them. If the nurse has within herself a desire to understand the expectant parents, and provide them with the knowledge, encouragement and support they individually require, she will reflect these wishes in all she does and says.

The woman in labor needs someone with her, for loneliness is threatening when one feels endangered emotionally or physically. The woman in labor longs for her mother, though her relationship with her may be such that her mother could not meet her needs were it possible for her to be in attendance. The nurse represents the mother or elder sister figure to the woman in labor. The laboring woman will welcome her nurse's personal interest, support, giving and understanding of her need for emotional acceptance. She will delight in having nourishments served to her during the long period of waiting. She will appreciate having someone to talk to who is interested in her as a person. It will help her to feel she is a person with personal identity rather than a patient in a strange, impersonal setting. Little signs of thoughtfulness like finding magazines for her to read, or interpreting what she will meet in the delivery rooms will do much to help her to feel accepted and the important person she really is.

During labor, the expectant father has a need to feel welcome, important and helpful in the birthrooms. The truly skillful nurse meets his needs because she is sensitive to and aware of its importance to both individuals.

From the time the expectant parents enter the hospital, they need support and information which will keep them informed about the progress of labor and the meaning involved in each new development. The laboring mother needs preparation for each new procedure and an interpretation of its need for her. She needs her apprehension accepted when she is subjected to procedures unfamiliar to her. Many women have unconscious feelings and childish fantasies which prevent them from accepting routines in a fearless way. In many women, there is a fear of death which is difficult to control and to tolerate.[16] Many are fearful lest they lose control and do things which will make them ashamed of themselves. Without support many do lose control but it is not without feelings of remorse and sometimes even of despair.

When the laboring mother has had prenatal preparation for labor and is desirous of experiencing natural childbirth, she needs constant support to maintain faith and confidence in herself. She will need her faith in the technic of relaxation strengthened so she can practice it successfully during her labor. She will also require reminders which help her to feel the need for abdominal breathing during the first stage of labor. At the end of the first stage of labor when she grows fatigued and questions incessantly about her progress, she needs a nurse who is patient, tolerant and ready to give the explanations and support she needs to know how to help herself. It is in this period the woman needs the greatest amount of reassurance and a feeling that those attending her have confidence in her ability to participate in the delivery of her child. When contractions grow stronger and produce stimulation which forces the woman to bear down upon her rectum, there is often fear lest she eliminate stool and urine involuntarily.[10] To prevent fear and tension which will only inhibit uterine contractions and bring an increased amount of pain, the woman in labor needs help in understanding that this is inevitable and acceptable.

In the second stage of labor, when the woman is struggling to maintain her strength and her faith in her own powers, she needs a nurse who is convinced of the value of natural childbirth for the mother, her husband and the child which is nearly ready to come. A nurse's belief in the woman's capacity to experience natural childbirth communicates itself to the woman who is desirous of actively participating in the entire process of bearing her child. If a nurse is genuinely sympathetic to the woman's desire to help in delivering her own offspring, she will support her in ways a nurse who is without this conviction can never do. Supporting is not done with words alone; it is done through acts and the communication of feelings which give the woman strength successfully to achieve her goal. Unless a woman has confidence in the nurse, she will be without the support she requires. She may achieve her goal independently but to do so alone is a feat few women are able to accomplish.

When a woman aspires to participate fully in the delivery of her child and then discovers she cannot master the anxiety which is aggravating her discomfort, she needs help in accepting the situation even though she requires sedation or anesthesia. There are women who are unable to achieve their goal for physical or psychological reasons. Some will need help in accepting sedation or anesthesia; others ask for it and then later feel they have been inadequate and a failure. To prevent feelings of remorse and self-condemnation in the postpartum period, the frightened woman who cannot complete the participation process needs reassurance that she is not a failure at the time sedation or anesthesia is required.

FULFILLMENT FROM NATURAL CHILDBIRTH

Until recently, the young women of our country have not considered the possibilities of natural childbirth. Delivery was performed according to the dictates of those in the medical and nursing professions. Though women may have wanted to express themselves and assert their rights in producing their child in their own way, they were inhibited by a multitude of personal and cultural factors. Many did not know it was possible. It was only when Read's method of helping women achieve natural childbirth became tried and accepted that widespread interest became centered in it.

Today the picture has changed. More and more women are demanding natural childbirth. From reading and from listening to the personal experiences of friends, women have become interested in natural childbirth and are seeking help in accomplishing it.

Observational experience has demonstrated that natural childbirth is possible; it has also demonstrated that it gives many women an emotional experience that should not be denied them. The majority of women who participate in the delivery of their babies experience feelings of ecstasy and fulfillment. Observing the behavior of these mothers as their babies are born and placed within their arms gives proof of the value and meaning which it has for them. They receive their infants with their minds, heart and bodies. Birth does not separate them from their babies; they are reunited immediately. A new kind of emotional bond becomes established between the mother and her child and it begins the close emotional relationship which is so necessary for them both. With natural childbirth the mother feels love for her child at once and it brings reassurance to her. Birth has not destroyed the gratification she experienced when the fetus was a part of her and with this emotional response her security is increased. She has been assured of love for her child. This feeling of reassurance brings relaxation and freedom for rest which the recuperation process requires.

Observational experience has also demonstrated that natural childbirth has values to the child and his father. Unaffected by drugs or anesthesia, the child was alert and already participating in its own adjustment; he was receiving his first taste of the outer world from the receptive arms and heart of his mother, the person who would be most important to his survival and his capacity to receive and to give human love. The reunion of husband and wife was a moment of mutual happiness. He met a woman who had experienced fulfillment through his love for her. She had produced a child which she could present to him. Together they were ready to share their love and life with a newcomer.

QUESTIONS TO GUIDE OBSERVATION

1. How do you imagine a woman might feel coming into a prenatal clinic for the first time?

2. Why are pediatric nurses concerned with the prenatal period?

3. Recall experiences that you have had in a prenatal clinic. What did you learn about the women you saw in the clinic? What did they talk about? What seemed to concern them most? Did you feel that you had sufficient time to give them an opportunity to talk to you? When you did have time, did you find the experience satisfying or uncomfortable? Why do you think you may have felt the way you did?

4. Observe two women in a prenatal clinic being interviewed by a graduate nurse. Describe what you saw and record the conversation of the interviews as you remember them. How did the nurse approach the women? What were the women's responses to her? Did the women feel comfortable enough to talk freely to the nurse?

What specifically do you think helped them to feel comfortable? How do you think the women felt about their pregnancy?

5. Observe a class for expectant mothers. Describe what you saw. Did the expectant mothers seem to be interested? How did they show it? How did the instructor get the mother's interest? Did the instructor present the material in a way that was understandable to her group? Did it stimulate questions, comments and a desire for further understanding? Do you think the content of the class was appropriate for expectant mothers? Give the reasons for your answer.

6. If a woman told you that she was pregnant and asked you where she should go to get prenatal care, what would you do?

7. What do you think the content of a series of classes for expectant mothers should be? For expectant fathers? Do you think that there should be classes for expectant parents or do you think that an individual series for mothers and fathers is preferable?

8. Of what value are classes for expectant parents?

9. How can experience in labor affect the mother-child relationship?

10. Describe an expectant mother you cared for in labor. What did she do, say and feel that increased your understanding of her? What did her behavior tell you she was needing? How did you meet her needs? What changes in behavior did you observe in the different stages of labor? What were her immediate responses at the completion of the laboring process?

11. Observe a woman experiencing natural childbirth. Describe what you saw, heard and felt. What was your response to it?

12. Recall your birthroom experience. What were your feelings concerning the experience? Describe some of the women's responses to labor, to you and to the doctors. Describe some observations that you made of expectant fathers during their wives' labor experiences.

REFERENCES

1. Benedek, Therese: The psychosomatic implications of the primary unit, mother-child, Am. J. Orthopsychiat. 19:642, 1949.
2. Burke, B. S., Beal, Virginia, Kirkwood, S. B., and Stuart, H. C.: Nutrition studies during pregnancy, Am. J. Obstet. Gynec. 46:38, 1943.
3. Burke, B. S., and Stuart, H. C.: Nutritional requirements during pregnancy and lactation, J. A. M. A. 137:198, 1948.
4. Davis, M. E., and Sheckler, C. E.: De Lee's Obstetrics for Nurses, Philadelphia, Saunders, 1951.
5. Deutsch, Helen: An introduction to the discussion of the psychological problems of pregnancy, p. 11 in Problems of Early Infancy, New York, Josiah Macy Jr. Foundation, 1948.

6. Ebbs, J. H., Tisdall, F. F., and Scott, W. A.: Influence of prenatal diet on mother and child, J. Nutrition **22:**515, 1941.
7. Escalona, Sibylle: Summary abstract of three articles by Dr. L. W. Sontag and associates, p. 18 in Problems of Early Infancy, New York, Josiah Macy Jr. Foundation, 1948.
8. Goodrich, F. W.: Emotions in pregnancy and labor as related to natural childbirth, p. 35 in Problems of Early Infancy, New York, Josiah Macy Jr. Foundation, 1948.
9. Jacobson, Edith: Development of the wish for a child in boys, p. 139 in The Psychoanalytic Study of the Child, vol. 5, New York, Internat. Univ. Press, 1950.
10. Kartchner, F. D.: A study of the emotional reactions during labor, Am. J. Obst. Gynec. **60:**19, 1950.
11. Read, G. D.: Childbirth Without Fear, New York, Harper, 1944.
12. Senn, M. J. E.: Anticipatory guidance of the pregnant woman and her husband for their roles as parents, p. 11 in Problems of Early Infancy, New York, Josiah Macy Jr. Foundation, 1947.
13. Scheinfeld, Amram: You and Heredity, Philadelphia, Lippincott, 1950.
14. Thom, Herbert: Training for Childbirth, New York, McGraw-Hill, 1950.
15. Vollmer, A. M.: Clinical experiences and observations on the use of relaxation methods in obstetrical practice, p. 50 in Problems of Early Infancy, New York, Josiah Macy Jr. Foundation, 1948.
16. Zabriskie, Louise, and Eastman, N.: Nurses Handbook of Obstetrics, Philadelphia, Lippincott, 1952.
17. Zimmerman, Kent: The public health nurse and the emotions of pregnancy, Pub. Health Nursing **39:**63, 1947.

3

Nursing Care During the Adjustment Period (Birth to 3 Months):

Its Influence on the Child's Feelings About the World

The meaning which birth has to the child and to his parents needs consideration, for it provides the background of knowledge necessary for the understanding of their emotional and physical requirements during the adjustment period. When the physical and psychological significance of an experience is understood and accepted, attitudes toward nursing are broadened and there is increased capacity for service to patients. There is also increased opportunity for the nurse to gain gratification from her work. Understanding the general meaning which birth has for parents and the child increases one's capacity to observe and to interpret the specific meaning that it has for a specific individual. It also increases one's capacity to meet the needs which have arisen within that individual as a response to it.

THE NEWBORN INFANT'S BEHAVIOR AND ITS MEANING
THE MEANING OF BIRTH TO THE INFANT

During intra-uterine life the fetus experienced a peaceful, comfortable, parasitic existence. He was warm, protected and secure because the closeness (or what is called the symbiotic relationship)

53

with his mother provided all the essentials necessary to meet his physical and his emotional requirements. The intra-uterine environment presumably was relatively free from disturbing stimuli; it brought him no frustration, pain or fear; it provided all the essentials necessary to reach that state of physical development necessary for adaptation to life outside the uterus.

Biologically, the normal full-term infant is ready for extrauterine existence and for participation in his own adaptation. He has developed from a minute cell into an organism capable of meeting the next step in the developmental process; he has achieved the capacity to meet the physical frustrations that will provide the stimulus for further maturation and growth. He is capable of meeting the physical frustrations that come when he has feelings of suffocation and pangs of hunger. He has the physiologic mechanism that makes it possible for him to breathe by himself, to search for food and to suck, swallow, digest and excrete its byproducts. He has the physiologic mechanism which enables him to signal his needs to those who attend him. He enters the world with certain perceptive abilities and a capacity to respond to persons and things within his environment. He has the capacity to develop emotional feelings and attitudes toward all he experiences. Within him at birth are the potentialities for physical, mental and psychosocial development.

The newborn infant is ready to be received as a human individual and ready to become acquainted with the outer world. He is also ready to adjust to a different kind of physical environment. No longer does he require continuous contact with his mother's protective womb. *But this new individual is helpless, dependent and needful of the kind of nurturing that will make it possible for him to adapt to the outer world with a minimum amount of discomfort and a maximum amount of pleasure.* The fulfillment of this need is of utmost importance to his physical well-being and to his personality development.

Although the infant is biologically prepared for birth, the experience is anxiety-provoking and threatening because it separates him from his mother, the source of all his physical and emotional security. At birth the infant experiences frustration and intense anxiety; he reacts to it physically and as though it had affected him emotionally. It is difficult to believe that the first cry is for solely physiologic reasons. Observations of older infants seem to justify the assumption that emotional feeling is already present in the first cry. From our knowledge of observed trauma in later separation between mother and child, it seems logical and sensible to assume that this first separation from the mother has deep and emotional significance. Many authors believe the birth experience is the prototype of all later anxiety.

The Infant's Cry as a Defense Mechanism

The infant's first cry seems to serve two purposes—it forces air into his lungs and initiates the breathing process, and it indicates his urgent need for help in what he must feel to be a strange and unpredictable environment. Infants are born with a capacity to feel, and with protective mechanisms to use whenever they are biologically or emotionally threatened. Their cry is the only way they can express the feelings of discomfort, that may come from hunger, loneliness, fatigue, functional insufficiency or disease. The way they feel is demonstrable in their behavior, which has meaning and significance—it is a response to physical and psychological needs. It needs interpretation, for the way needs are met is dependent upon the adult's understanding of them. The infant's helplessness makes him totally dependent upon those within his environment.

PHYSICAL NEEDS DURING THE ADJUSTMENT PERIOD

The Newborn's Organism—Unstable and Unorganized

The newborn infant is different from the adult in more ways than in size and proportion—he is different physiologically, chemically, anatomically and emotionally, and he requires care based on his infantile nature and needs. Adaptation to extra-uterine life makes demands upon his total organism. Although he is ready to be born, he has many immaturities as far as his bio-chemical make-up is concerned. He is unstable, unorganized and variable; his equilibrium is delicately balanced and easily upset. *He needs stability and an environment which takes his immature characteristics into consideration.* Slight changes in diet and environment can produce changes in the salt and water content of his blood and tissues and in the metabolic, respiratory and heart rate. They can produce fluctuations in temperature and changes in the functioning of the gastro-intestinal tract.

The newborn infant's first need is for oxygen. From the moment of birth, when the cord is cut, he must oxygenate his own blood and tissues. Nature has provided the newborn with cells which function at a low level during the first minutes of his life. They take little oxygen, which makes it possible for him to withstand a 10- to 15-minute period of apnea. Failure to breathe by the end of that period brings damage to the organism, especially to the brain cells of his body. With the first insufflation, the aperture in the septum of his heart closes and his heart begins to pump blood in a different course, which is now independent of his mother's circulation. The blood now goes to the lungs for oxygenation; its change in pressure closes the ductus venosus, the ductus arteriosus and the foramen ovale. Complete closure is not instantaneous—it requires several days to establish postnatal circulation. During this period duskiness of the face and the extremities frequently is observed. Peripheral circulation is slowest to become established. Until it is established, deep cyanosis of the hands and feet is not unusual.

In respiration more is involved than the expansion of the lungs, inhaling and exhaling; there must be gaseous exchange, an oxygenation of all tissues, elimination of carbon dioxide and an uptake of water. What initiates the respiratory process at birth is as yet unknown. The respiratory center in the medulla of the brain is sensitive to changes in blood oxygen content or tension. Whether the respiratory activity of the newborn is a response to low oxygen tension or to changes in the acid-base (pH) balance produced by the carbon dioxide in the blood is unknown. The "Multiple Factor Theory" is probably the best explanation, for at birth there are a multiplicity of factors impinging on the organism to intiate the respiratory process.

The newborn infant needs protection to ensure full expansion of his lungs. The lungs of the newborn infant are adhesive, and pressure is required to inflate them. The initial insufflation requires from 15 to 30 cubic centimeters of water pressure. Later, when adhesiveness is nonexistent, insufflation requires only 8 cubic centimeters of water pressure. Full expansion of the lungs does not occur before the end of 2 or 3 days. Abdominal binders, if used, should be applied lightly, to prevent pressure on the diaphragm which would interfere with full expansion of the lungs. Pressure on the diaphragm also brings discomfort to the infant. Turning the infant from side to side and preventing gastric distention favors lung expansion and prevents respiratory distress.

Observation to prevent obstruction in the respiratory tract is of extreme importance for the infant's comfort and safety. Respiration for the newborn is automatic and comfortable if there is no obstruction in the respiratory tract. Mucous obstruction brings respiratory distress and feelings of suffocation, and may even produce death. When an infant's respiratory passages become filled with mucus, he is unable to signal his need for help. Ordinarily mucus will drain from the respiratory passages if the infant is kept on his side with his head lowered, but in some instances aspiration of the mucus may be necessary. An aspiration bulb always should be kept in readiness for use whenever distress from mucus is observable. Large amounts can interfere seriously with an infant's capacity to get his need for oxygen supplied. An insufficiency of oxygen produces cyanosis, distress and sometimes sternal retraction if the oxygen hunger is excessive. The sternal retraction comes as the infant attempts to meet his oxygen want by using his intercostal muscles to elevate his ribs to increase the size of the intrathoracic cavity.

When there is no obstruction and the infant's oxygen supply is meeting his needs, respiration occurs as a result of diaphragmatic activity. The infant's chest with its straight and elevated ribs has a barrel-shaped appearance. Breathing is abdominal, and irregular in depth and rhythm. Sometimes the respiratory movements are scarcely visible or audible. Downward movement of the diaphragm increases negative pressure within the lungs and causes air to flow into them; its upward movement decreases negative pressure and forces air from them. Later in infancy the thoracic muscles function in the respiratory process, and their use changes the shape of the chest.

During fetal life, the red blood cell count is approximately one million higher, and each cell contains more hemoglobin. To meet the oxygen requirement of the fetus, red blood cells are produced by the blood islands in the liver and the spleen as well as in the bone marrow. Taking oxygen from the maternal stream is a more difficult process than taking it from inhaled air. Therefore, fetal hemoglobin is different in quantity and amount. Prior to birth, the blood islands in the liver and the spleen begin to obliterate, and the function of hematopoiesis is taken over almost entirely by the bone marrow.

At birth, blood changes occur because the newborn does not need as many red blood cells as did the fetus. The newborn receives more oxygen through his lungs than he received via his mother's placenta during fetal life. The blood changes are physiologic ones to which the newborn must make an adjustment. Destruction of red blood cells and hemoglobin begins at birth. As red blood cells and hemoglobin are destroyed bilirubin is produced and absorbed into the blood stream.

The above blood changes produce icterus neonatorum, the characteristic jaundice which appears on the second or third day of extra-uterine life. The newborn's liver is immature. It cannot remove bilirubin from the blood stream rapidly enough to prevent discoloration of the skin and other body tissues. Because the jaundice is physiologic, it requires no treatment or special nursing care. Some infants are more jaundiced than others, the degree of jaundice being determined largely by the infant's liver function. Gradually liver functioning becomes more adequate. Bilirubin is absorbed and excreted more readily and the jaundice disappears during the second week of the infant's extra-uterine life.

During the first week of extra-uterine life, there may be a tendency toward bleeding. The liver needs vitamin K to produce prothrombin, the blood constituent which influences coagulation time. At birth the infant's intestine is sterile, and bacterial flora are necessary for vitamin K production. On the eighth day of extra-uterine life, the prothrombin level increases and the bleeding tendency diminishes. Vitamin K given to the mother prior to delivery is a means of providing the infant's body with an amount sufficient to prevent bleeding in the period when the infant is otherwise unprotected.

There are functional endocrine disorders which occur in the period of adjustment to extra-uterine life. In utero, the adrenal glands functioned more actively than is required after birth. As a result there is diminution in the size of the gland during the first weeks after birth. Why there is need for enlarged adrenal glands during fetal life and at the time of birth is yet unknown. There has been speculation concerning two possible theories, one of which is that the stress of pregnancy upon the mother requires increased adrenal activity, and the changes within her endocrine system bring changes in that of the fetus. Another theory suggests that it is a physiologic phenomenon which occurs to assist the infant in handling the stress and the strain involved in the birth and the adaptive process. This theory also fits in with the hypothesis that birth constitutes an emotional trauma to the child, since we know that states of intense emotion increase the flow of epinephrine.

There are other functional endocrine phenomena observable in the newborn infant. It is not unusual to observe stimulation of the infant's breast tissue due to the presence of maternal lactating hormone. Stimulation to the point of the production of colostrum is not an unusual occurrence. Likewise, in approximately 5 per cent of female infants, the estrogenic hormone in the infant's circulating blood produces a blood-tinged vaginal discharge from the sloughing of the adult type of mucosa which developed in response to the mother's hormones within the infant's body. The adult type of mucosa remains a part of the infant's genital tract only so long as there is estrogenic substance in the blood stream.

Metabolic changes occur during the period of adaptation to extra-uterine life. The newborn baby loses 10 per cent of his body weight in the first days of extra-uterine life. It is unwise to prevent fluid loss with forced feedings of water or glucose during the first 24 hours after birth. Rest is a greater need in this adjustment period. Much of the weight loss is due to loss of tissue fluid which is not needed after birth. During fetal life a large quantity of tissue fluid is required to carry on the metabolic processes. Birth weight is usually regained by the tenth day of life but the increase in weight is tissue, not water.

At birth the infant's heat-regulating apparatus is immature and unready to function in controlling his body temperature. The heat-regulating mechanism in his brain does not have to function prior to birth for his mother's body keeps him at a constant optimal temperature. The newborn's physical characteristics require a stable environmental temperature of between 70° and 75° Fahrenheit to keep him comfortable and to keep his body processes functioning to capacity. His heating plant is small in comparison with his large radiating skin surface, from which heat loss is great. He can neither shiver nor perspire to regulate his internal temperature. Until his nervous system has matured and gained sufficient practice in controlling his body temperature, he must be clothed in accordance with his specific requirements.

The newborn infant needs observation and protection from infection; his immature biophysiologic organism requires that it be so. In utero he was well protected from pathogenic organisms. At birth he becomes exposed to organisms to which he has little or no resistance. Although his body fluids do contain some immune bodies from his mother's circulation, they do not provide him with sufficient protection from disease. Any infection, even of a minor nature, produces physiochemical changes that threaten the life of the child.

The newborn has many characteristics which make him particularly vulnerable to infection. His lungs are not fully expanded, and his hematopoietic system is undergoing change. His skin and the mucous membranes of his respiratory tract are fragile and excellent areas for bacterial growth. His gastro-intestinal tract is unstable and sensitive, and the hydrochloric acid content of his gastric juice is not high enough to destroy ingested organisms. Minor infection produces vomiting and diarrhea which can bring serious alterations in the electrolyte balance.

Individual aseptic technic and careful observation are essential in the care of the newborn. He needs care which is meticulous, safe and gentle. Personnel must be free from infection and cognizant of the infant's need for a protected, controlled environment. They must examine the baby for any signs of abnormality and be alert to any signs indicating the onset of any kind of skin, respiratory or gastro-intestinal infection. Changes in behavior, especially in relation to the feeding situation, should be noted carefully. Observing the color, frequency and consistency of the stools, and the condition and the color of his skin, is an essential protective measure. It is the early signs and symptoms that must be discovered, for early treatment prevents the hazards which disease brings.

Disease has an impact on the child and on his parents. Disease not only brings hazards of a physical nature which require treatment that is painful, frustrating and anxiety-provoking, but also it brings separation from his mother at a time when closeness to her is essential to him emotionally. Disease also brings discomfort to the parents. It separates the mother from her child at a time when she has a great need for him. Disease brings fear and feelings of helplessness which interfere with the development of the natural mother-child relationship.

The newborn infant needs undisturbed rest to regain his strength after the strenuous activity of being born. He must have sufficient energy to make the adaptation to extra-uterine life with ease and full utilization of his own adaptive capacity. The newborn shows his need for rest by sleeping and by his unfavorable reaction to anything that disturbs him. In utero he was required to adapt himself neither to bright lights, loud noises, pangs of hunger and feelings of overdistention, nor to sudden movements which brought fear with loss of equilibrium.

Only through the prompt satisfaction of his needs for food, love and comfort will the infant have the undisturbed rest his nature requires. Relaxation and a state of equilibrium (security) are achieved when the infant gets what he needs to relieve him of discomfort. He will need "bubbling" after his feeding to prevent discomfort and interference with his rest. All infants swallow air as they are nursing. To prevent distention and pain, the infant should be held upright against the mother's chest and gently patted on the back until he has expelled the air from his stomach. Some infants require "bubbling" at intervals during the feeding. It requires observation to determine technics of care which an individual baby requires to keep him physically comfortable.

EMOTIONAL NEEDS DURING THE ADJUSTMENT PERIOD

Individual Differences

The newborn infant is born with self-regulatory capacity which should be respected in providing care for him. *He needs a schedule of care based upon the knowledge acquired through observation of him as a unique individual.* His behavior is the clue to his needs; and prompt satisfaction of his individual instinctual drives is the true essence of mothering.

Each baby is a unique being. There are no two of them who are exactly alike; they differ physically, mentally and emotionally. One visit in a newborn nursery will prove this point to the sensitive observer. As one gains familiarity with babies in a newborn nursery, their individual personality differences become increasingly more striking. Each infant has his own innate drives which vary in intensity, rhythm, mode of expression and the way in which they become satisfied. There are newborn infants who respond rapidly to any stimuli from within or from the outer world. There are others who show less sensitivity to these stimuli. Some are vigorous in their response to inner needs and in making them known; others are complacent, calm and inactive. One infant, for example, will calmly sleep through his bath and the weighing procedure. Another will show signs of acute discomfort when his clothing is removed and he is placed upon a scale which requires adjustment to new feelings and a change in body position. Some infants require the gentlest of handling to prevent tension reactions while they are becoming acclimated to the realities of extra-uterine life. Others seem to adapt themselves to extra-uterine life with ease. Some infants require a great deal of physical contact to maintain their equilibrium; others require less and display stress reactions when they are handled frequently. Each infant has his own characteristic way of behaving. His physical body and characteristic way of responding to pleasure and pain comprise the personality of the newborn.

The way in which the child's individual differences are accepted and met influences his physical health and personality development. The mature giving mother studies her child. She discovers the nature of his needs and determines their rhythm and intensity; then she experiments to meet them in a way which brings him the maximum amount of pleasure. Warm and skilled nurses do the same thing. They provide nursing care as the infant shows a need for it. They bathe those babies who are awake and in need of comfort and solace. They take the hungry babies to their mothers and provide rest for those who are in need of it. Their interest is concentrated upon the babies rather than upon the mechanized steps involved in routinized, rigid nursery procedure.

The Newborn's Personality—Unformed

To become ready for the socialization process, the infant requires a long period of complete dependency, for his personality is unformed and unstructured. The infant's nature makes him a demanding, dependent, uncontrolled individual. *In this period of development, he requires unconditional acceptance, complete permissiveness and unrestricted love.* His need for this kind of nurturing is in proportion to his degree of helplessness.[19]

Within the newborn infant are the potentialities for physical and psychological maturation. These potentialities will unfold and develop in accordance with their own genetic pattern if they are protected, nurtured, stimulated and guided as they are ready for guidance. Gradually, in the months and years to come, the child will show his readiness to acquire new physical capacities and a greater degree of ability to meet the demands of his world. During early life, however, he is physically and emotionally unready to adapt himself in other ways than have been cited already.

The newborn infant wants what he wants when he wants it; he functions on what is called the "pleasure principle." He has no mental, physical or emotional equipment to do otherwise. He has neither the capacity to meet his own desires nor the power to reject those experiences for which he has no readiness. He is completely governed by his inner drives, or that part of his personality which is called the id. These inner drives strive to gain immediate gratification, irrespective of the needs of others within his environment. The infant has no interest except to gratify his cravings which are urgent, powerful and uncontrolled. He has no other interest because he has not had enough experience with his mother to find himself or to discover there is another person whose love he is desirous of having. He is uncontrolled because his nervous system and personality are not sufficiently developed either to give him control of his body mechanism or to help him gain mastery of his behavior. He can only feel; his response to pleasure and pain is immediate and automatic.

Fulfillment of the infant's biologic and emotional needs helps him to master anxiety and influences his feelings about himself. The young infant has no physical or psychological capacity to withstand the frustration that develops when food and love do not come; he has no inner resources to use in the mastery of anxiety. Frustration brings anger and anxiety; it brings tension which overwhelms and threatens his homeostatic balance. He must master the anxiety to obtain equilibrium. He does so when he makes a connection between his own signal of need and the coming of food and love. When his signal of need is fulfilled, it comes as a response to his own activity. This gives the infant some control over his helplessness, for it brings someone to his aid. Prompt fulfillment must surely influence his feelings about himself. It seems entirely reasonable to assume that the very foundation of self-confidence is laid in this period. Prompt fulfillment does ensure the infant's safety. It is reasonable to assume that when his needs are met, he will eventually come to feel the world is friendly, warm and giving.

Benedek[5] refers to French's hypothesis that hope is the habit which is built on feelings of confidence in the person who cares for him. Prompt satisfaction of inner drives during the period of greatest insecurity, helplessness and dependency lays the foundation for feelings of optimism, a quality that is invaluable to the child later in life when he is meeting its inevitable frustrations. Likewise, deprivation in early life creates feelings of pessimism, futility and hopelessness.

The young infant needs what he wants when he wants it for it gives him the security he needs for growth. It is the one and only time in his life he can make demands and still be loved. In this period no demands should be made upon him. Each period of life must be lived to its fullest. There is nothing which more adequately prepares the child for the next step in development than to experience fulfillment of the needs which are developmentally characteristic of the period he is living in at the moment. Experiencing fulfillment in this period of development provides the emotional security his nature requires. One of the greatest needs of the child is to have a sense of security, the foundation for which is laid in early infancy by the loving care he is given. Fulfillment gives the infant a feeling of belongingness, a feeling which is the right and the need of every child.

The sooner an infant establishes the connection between need and an expectation of satisfaction, the more likely he is to acquire feelings of trust and security. It is exceedingly important that the infant's first experiences be positive ones, for each experience deepens the infant's slowly developing concept of those within his environment. Positive experiences tend to eliminate unnecessary tension and to facilitate ease of satisfaction each time the need arises. However, negative, frustrating experiences seem to invest the need with anxiety which makes it difficult for the baby to become satisfied. Gratification thus increases the experience of satisfaction, whereas frustration makes the child so demanding that it becomes increasingly more difficult for the adult to meet his needs in a way that brings him pleasure.

A "spoiled" child is one who does not know what he wants. He was never satisfied in infancy, and because it happened before he was able to understand he is in a perpetual state of fear lest his needs remain unsatisfied. Meeting the infant's needs does not "spoil" a child—it is lack of confidence that gratification will come that makes an infant or a child overwhelmingly demanding, perpetually dissatisfied, unhappy and fearful.

The young infant needs freedom from the anxiety which frustration produces so that he may have the gratification necessary to gain positive feelings toward himself and those within his environment. The care an infant is given should make it easy for the infant to love his mother. His nature requires that he receive love before he is able to give it. He will learn to love in proportion to what he has received; he will learn to meet society's demands because of his desire to please and to maintain the affection of the person he has come to love. It is the love he feels for his mother, his first object of love, which will make it possible for him to accept the frustrations which are a part of the socialization process. When a love relationship is established, the child will get a reward for modifying and giving up the instinctual pleasure he experienced as a young infant. The love relationship develops when he discovers that the source of his pleasures comes not from himself but from someone apart from himself—his mother.

Fulfillment of needs serves many purposes. It serves a self-preservation function, for it provides the energy he requires for adaptation and growth. It brings pleasure and therefore has social and emotional significance. It influences his receiving tendencies and his capacity for object relationships because fulfillment helps him to sense the love of another and to turn to others for the satisfaction of his needs. It also makes functioning according to the "reality principle" a possibility. When he has had sufficient gratification of his inner drives and has developed a close affectionate attachment to his mother he will be able to accept limited amounts of discomfort because he knows that if he waits he will achieve greater pleasure in the future.

To reach maturity one must learn to function in accordance with the "reality principle." The basis for achieving this capacity is in infancy. It is the love the infant receives as his receptive-dependent needs are gratified which makes it possible for him to modify and to redirect his drives into socially accepted, productive and self-fulfilling channels.

Birth separates the infant from his mother physically, but he continues to need a close symbiotic relationship with her. He is not ready for complete interruption of the closeness he experienced before birth. In many infants the need for closeness to the mother is observable soon after birth. One observes signals of distress which seem to be relieved only when the infants are held close, cuddled and soothed. When their need for closeness is met promptly it is not long before better equilibrium is established. The need for closeness becomes less frequent and intense and can be satisfied as love is provided with the feeding process.

Newborn infants vary in their need for food and their capacity to obtain it. Some demonstrate a desire for food soon after birth; others seem uninterested in the breast or the bottle until the second or third day. Many infants need help in learning to eat. The best method of helping an infant is to provide him with food as soon as he shows a need for it, and to accept the fact that it will take him time to learn to suck from the bottle or the breast. Often mothers expect instantaneous success in feeding their babies. If they know learning is required, they will remain poised and let the infant experiment until he learns to hold the nipple in his mouth and to suck effectively.

When a normal full-term baby is hungry, he cries, nuzzles, sucks his fists and searches for food, for his rooting, sucking and swallowing reflexes are well developed. If his cheek is placed against his mother's breast, the smell of the milk and his need for food will motivate him to root for the nipple.[3] Holding the infant's cheeks to force his mouth onto the nipple impedes his progress toward the source of satisfaction. Instead of rooting toward the nipple, he turns toward the nurse's hand. He does not find food and he becomes angry. He fights and becomes difficult to pacify.

Meeting the infant's hunger and love needs promptly within the first few weeks after birth is of special importance. Experiences combining food, sucking and having contact with his mother are the infant's chief and most important sources of satisfaction.[11] When food comes in response to the infant's signal of hunger, he experiences pleasure and relief from discomfort. Repetition of this kind of experience accustoms the infant to the pleasure which sucking and food bring. He becomes positively conditioned to the feeding process and to the person who provides it. When once conditioned, he will be more apt to accept food whenever it is offered.[11] Through experience he discovers that sucking and taking in food bring him feelings of comfort and freedom from pain and fear. When pleasure is experienced in the first functions in life, there is greater likelihood that subsequent body functioning will also bring satisfaction.

When food and love do not come, and there is no outlet for his tension, the infant shows symptoms of what has been described as a "traumatic state." His reaction to internal tension (anxiety) affects his entire body. He behaves as though he were afraid he had been abandoned. He screams, waves his extremities, grows tense and excited. His pulse and respiration rates increase, his face and his body grow red and pressure within the skull is evidenced by a tense fontanel. When an adult is threatened he, too, experiences anxiety which brings symptoms similar to those described above. He does not scream and wave his extremities but he often feels like doing so.

"Traumatic states" are damaging to the infant. Not only do they bring reddened, scratched faces and excoriated knees and toes, but also they utilize needed energy, bring on exhaustion and traumatize the psyche. Trauma early in life is most injurious, for it cuts through and affects every developmental potential. Should a similar unit of trauma be inflicted upon a school-age child, less damage would result because it would affect only one segment, and not the total personality.

In the first months of extra-uterine life the infant is not well organized, and his pattern of need for food may vary from day to day or from week to week. Some babies become stabilized rapidly and establish a consistent rhythm of need for food; others require more time to adjust to conditions of extra-uterine existence. It takes longer for the latter group of infants to establish a regular pattern of need for food.

To ensure physical and mental health the infant needs to regulate the time for eating and the amount of food and sucking he desires at a time. Refusing the infant food and love when he needs them, or compelling him to eat when he feels no hunger, encourages negative responses to food and deprives him of the opportunity to gain needed gratification from those within his environment. It disturbs the rhythm of his instinctual drives and forces him to experience pain when he should be experiencing nothing but pleasure.

The way the infant's need for food is met sets his life pattern of instinctual gratification; it influences his physical adaptation to extra-uterine life and lays the foundation upon which his personality must develop. The infant needs to take in feelings of love as he takes in food. Infants associate the feeding process with the attitudes of the mother or the nurse as she gives food to them. The infant's emotional needs are satisfied when love is a part of the care which comes as a response to his biologic needs. His need for emotional warmth from a giving mother is as urgent as his need for food; he is lost without it. When love and food are given concomitantly, the infant becomes satiated, relaxed and ready for sleep.

In each phase of personality development there are developmental tasks and conflicts which must be mastered. Unless those of this early period are successfully mastered and resolved, progress to and adjustment in succeeding phases is uncertain. The tasks of the next phase of personality growth will be more difficult to master when there has been no resolution of early conflicts and poor solutions made to the problems of the earlier period. It is repetition of inappropriate and unsatisfying experiences which brings distortion and imbalance within the personality structure.

When the infant's biologic needs are met with love, his potentialities for future growth are protected and stimulated in accordance with his needs. Preventing the traumatization which comes from unmastered anxiety provides the infant with the vital energy (or libido, as it is often called) he needs for physical or psychological growth. From a succession of gratifying life experiences, the young infant learns to trust and to depend upon others within his environment. In this way the development of his ego begins. Ego growth is rooted in the satisfaction of his needs and the development of trust in those about him.

Pattern of Instinctual Gratification

Need	Signal	Satisfaction	Physical Response	Emotional Response
Relief from hunger and closeness to his mother	Nuzzling Rooting Restlessness	Food and satiety Pleasure (love)	Relief from pain Relaxation Sleep	Confidence and trust in mother Self-esteem Faith, hope Safety (the world is friendly and loving) Freedom from fear (security) Equilibrium (peace of mind)

The diagram on the preceding page shows the desirable pattern of instinctual gratification and the emotional attitudes derived when maternal care meets the specific needs of a newly born child.

FAMILY-CENTERED MATERNITY CARE AND ITS INFLUENCE ON FAMILY INTERPERSONAL RELATIONSHIPS

Need for Changes in Maternity Care

Family members need each other in the postpartum period. Changes in our society which brought hospitals and their mechanized care did not alter the emotional needs of those within the family; they have served merely to inhibit woman's natural instinctive tendencies to mother her child when he needs her closeness most, and to prevent the father from meeting his needs and carrying out his important supportive role.

Maternity units with segregated nurseries developed a half century ago to reduce maternal and infant mortality rates, but the system has separated the family and has failed to meet its needs. When the maternity units were built, it became customary to receive maternity care in institutions and home delivery became almost extinct in urban areas. The new maternity care did accomplish its aim and mortality rates were reduced markedly, but routinization in the care of babies and mothers was the outcome. Rigid 4-hour feeding schedules were inaugurated, and individual patterns of behavior were ignored to meet the needs of the nursery regimen and of the medical and the nursing staffs. Mothers were denied the privilege of learning to know and to care for their babies, and fathers were considered a hindrance in the maternity unit.

Many mothers followed the hospital pattern of infant care upon return home from the hospital because they had had no authoritarian support or guidance to do otherwise. Rigid instructions for infant care were given to mothers, who were expected to carry them out. Many mothers were too insecure to rely upon their own intuitive feelings. Authority directed them and they followed, for they were too inexperienced and afraid to do otherwise.

Psychoanalytic study revealed the importance of early infant experience to emotional health and brought new understanding of emotional growth and the dynamics which distort and retard normal development. It stimulated widespread interest which led to the development of the Mental Hygiene Movement. Professional groups became interested in prevention and treatment of personality disorders. Child guidance centers developed, and parents sought their help. Workers in the guidance clinics studied the children and their background of experience within the family as a basis for therapy. They found that early experiences had brought discomfort and trauma to both child and parent.[22] The indoctrination to which mothers had been subjected had brought conflict and tension. It prevented mothers from utilizing their intuitive feelings to meet their infants' needs, thus bringing feelings of inadequacy and guilt. The babies were subjected to deprivation, and problems in interpersonal relationships developed. There is no question but what numerous influences impinged upon children and affected their normal development. However, the early feeding situation assumes prime importance, because it is the child's first exposure to interpersonal relationships.

The knowledge which has come from the fields of psychoanalysis and child development is influencing the thinking and the feeling of the entire population, especially of the younger generation. It is also bringing changes within the medical and the nursing professions, and influencing the kind of care being provided for both parents and children. The emotions have come to be recognized as extremely important for physical as well as for mental health. Today professional groups are attempting to develop the kind of service for society which will bring optimal physical and mental health. Medical groups interested in family life have studied their needs in relation to maternity care and have advocated changes in obstetric practices. They have concluded that Gesell's suggestion of "rooming in" is an appropriate plan for meeting the needs of all family members. "Rooming in" makes it possible for mother and baby to be together and recognizes that the father has emotional needs which require fulfillment at this time.

"Rooming in" has not been accepted generally by the medical or the nursing professions, although it has been tried and proved to be of inestimable value in bringing unity within the family. However, the public has developed increased interest in child care and sees the benefits which might be derived from a new type of maternity service. Expectant mothers are indicating their desire to have their babies room with them, and many are unsatisfied when hospital regimens will not accommodate them.

MEANING OF BIRTH TO THE MOTHER

How the mother responds emotionally to physical separation from her child will be determined by her personality structure and the meaning which the pregnancy had to her personally.[5] The symbiotic relationship gave the mother a feeling of unity and oneness with her child. Physical separation brings the mother new problems of adjustment which she must face and surmount. These changes bring a need for reorganization within her personality.[5]

Most mothers long for a continuation of the symbiotic relationship with their babies. It is natural for them to want their babies with them for the presence of their infants fulfills one of their deepest needs. Separation brings feelings of emotional emptiness, anger and anxiety, and contributes to the development of "postpartum blues." These emotional reactions utilize vital energy which should be available for regaining strength and adaptation to the experiences which are a natural part of the postpartum period.

The hormonal changes of pregnancy continue to exert their influence on the mother's psyche during the postpartum period. She needs to love and to be loved. In this period she is preoccupied with herself and her child and the care she knows he needs and longs to be able to give him. If these natural feelings are not inhibited, and she is permitted to express and utilize them, she will continue to center her interest on her child during the weeks to come. A century ago, when women delivered their babies at home, they often confined themselves to their rooms for several weeks after delivery. They breast fed their babies and continued to have close warm experiences with them. This was the natural thing to do, for mother and baby needed each other.

Emotional Needs of Mothers

The mother needs a continuation of the symbiotic relationship with her child. "Rooming in" meets this need; it prevents feelings of emotional emptiness, for when the mother feels a need to be close to her child she is able to satisfy it. It also prevents anxiety, for the infant is there to prove to her that she has produced a normal, living child. If the interim between delivery and contact with the baby is prolonged, anxiety mounts and every conceivable malady is suspected. Every nurse has heard the questions and comments that reflect the new mother's anxiety. When the baby is at the mother's side, she has no need to worry lest his needs are not being met. His presence gives her the peace of mind she requires. She can love and caress him, admire and talk about him.

If the above needs are those which mothers long to have satisfied, is it any wonder they show feelings of resentment and rivalry toward the nurses who take their babies from them? Is it any wonder mothers think nurses are insensitive when they whisk their babies from them without considering their need for one another? Is it not understandable why they think nursery routine is more important than they? Why do mothers and fathers, too, congregate at the windows of the nursery and spend long periods gazing at their babies? Have we paused long enough to wonder how they must feel as they watch others doing for their babies what they are longing to do? Does our skepticism of "rooming in" stem from truly objective study of its potential value to families, or are there other reasons why we are reluctant to give up the care of babies to their mothers? These are questions that need honest and objective study.

In the period after delivery all mothers have a need for their husband's attentiveness, support and interest in the baby. If in the prenatal period he has been helped to become aware of the emotional reactions that are common to women in the postpartum period, he will be more ready to give his wife the understanding she craves and requires. Her husband's pride in her encourages the development of maternal feelings. When the baby is beside her, and she has opportunities to observe her husband's response to their child, she experiences unbounded pleasure and pride in their achievement. Shared experiences of this kind bring families closer together.

In the period after delivery all mothers have a need to feel dependent and to find gratification for that need. *A mother needs freedom from frustration and anxiety so she may experience pleasure in her new role.* Although early ambulation is desirable from a physical standpoint, mothers should not be forced into self-care before they are ready for it. Pregnancy and the strain of labor have produced a regressive state.[5] The needs arising from it must be met with understanding and acceptance.

The degree of regression varies among women in the postpartum period. Some grow from the regressive state rapidly and are eager to begin assuming responsibility for themselves and for their infants. However, there are others who need a longer period of dependency before they can assume their new role and the responsibilities entailed in it. Others reject dependency care because they have a need to hide its existence from themselves. If a mother is unduly fatigued and in need of dependent care, too much responsibility in the care of either herself or her infant prolongs regression and makes it impossible for her to be giving to her baby. Meeting physical and emotional needs does not increase dependency; instead, it gratifies the woman and frees energy which will enable her to cater to her infant's needs.

A constructive nurse-mother relationship is necessary to meet emotional needs. Each mother needs observation so that her specific needs may be recognized and met in accordance with her level of maturity. Unless a good mother-nurse relationship exists, most mothers find it impossible to disclose their feelings and express themselves sufficiently to make their needs known.

Most mothers have a great need to talk about labor, their babies, their own care and all the problems which concern them. When mothers begin caring for themselves, they need to know the care their bodies require and why special care is essential. They will have innumerable questions about breast and perineal care and each question merits respect and an answer which increases the mother's understanding of her own care.

Many mothers have problems they need to talk over with a supportive person. Many mothers have had unhappy experiences during pregnancy and labor, and need to give vent to their feelings concerning them. There are mothers who were not able to face the fact that having a baby entailed responsibility as well as pleasure. The arrival of the child forces them to face reality quickly, and some mothers become overwhelmed with the problems that confront them. Many are totally unprepared to provide maternal care for their babies.

Relieving fear which prevents mothers from enjoying their babies is one of the most important essentials in the nursing care of the postpartum patient. Talking brings mothers relief from tension and helps them to master their feelings, gain perspective and acquire readiness to cope with their problems. It also brings gratification, for an accepting, sympathetic listener enhances their feelings of self-esteem and satisfies their dependent longings. When mothers express fears pertaining to the care of their infants, the nurse can help them to see they are understandable, and that she is ready to help them gain skill and confidence. From such experiences the nurse will also gain gratification. She brings comfort to her patients and obtains the information she needs to prepare them to meet their responsibilities successfully.

It takes time for maternal feelings to develop. Maternal feelings do not come to every woman with the birth of her child. In many women the natural instinct needs encouragement and time if it is to unfold, develop and bring satisfaction into the mother-child relationship. The production of prolactin influences the development of maternal feelings. Prolactin is not produced in the first days after delivery. Until it is, a lag in the development of positive emotional responses to the infant is the rule rather than the exception.[5]

When the mother has experienced intense discomfort during labor and has required deep sedation and anesthesia there is more apt to be a lag in the development of emotional feelings of motherliness. The majority of these women awaken uncomfortable, fearful and unaware of what has happened to them. They have heard no birth cry and have had no opportunity to hold the child who was once an integral part of them. They have experienced no positive emotional response which has reassured them of oneness with their child. They often feel no love—only a deep sense of loss and emptiness which disturbs them and threatens their peace of mind.

Many mothers who have been asleep during delivery react to their babies as though they were changelings and feel remorseful, guilty, inadequate and afraid as a result. It is difficult for these mothers to feel that their babies belong to them. They become disturbed and attempts to suppress such feelings are inevitable for they are painful and disquieting. Emotional experiences of this nature bring insecurity to the mother-child relationship.

The way in which a mother will respond to a situation of this kind depends upon her personality structure and the kind of help she is given early in the postpartum period. Benedek[5] has found that some women react to an experience of this kind with depressive symptoms which produce withdrawal from the child. Others, she has observed, become rejecting and see the child as the one responsible for the unacceptable feelings within them. Still others, because of their character traits, find it necessary to repress the feelings and handle them by providing overprotective and overindulgent care for their infants.

Mothers who feel estranged from their child or who show a lag in the development of motherliness need help in handling their feelings constructively. If nurses can understand and accept a mother's inability to feel warmth and a close affectionate bond with her child, they can lessen her anxiety and help her face her feelings without self-condemnation and guilt. Then the mother will have no need to repress her feelings. Understanding comments such as the following help the mother to know that her feelings are not unique and despicable, but the result of circumstances which have inhibited a more positive response to her child: "It must be difficult for you to realize it is your own baby when you were asleep throughout the delivery. So many mothers feel that way at first. It takes several days, sometimes even longer, to become acquainted with your baby and feel love for him."

MOTHERS' NEED FOR HELP IN BECOMING FAMILIAR WITH THEIR BABIES AND THEIR CARE

All mothers need time and help to develop a positive relationship with their babies and to become emotionally prepared to give care to them. The nurse's first task is to help mother and child find pleasure in being together. The mother needs help in finding ways to bring gratification to her child. As she becomes proficient in this she will develop affection for her child and feelings of confidence in her own ability.

Assisting the mother and the baby in establishing a feeding regimen in which each derives satisfaction from the other is a nursing skill of great import. The mother who wishes to breast feed her baby will need preparation for the experience and help to find a position that will be comfortable for both the infant and herself. The mother will need to know that the infant's first grasp of the nipple may bring discomfort, and that it is important that the baby get the entire nipple and part of the areola into his mouth to prevent nipple soreness and to stimulate the flow of milk. When an infant is hungry he accepts the breast more readily. His avidness in going to breast and the pleasure he finds in the activity bring a positive response from the prepared mother and encourage her to continue breast feeding.

The above response is often referred to as the "contentment response." When the baby is hungry and feeding, both mother and child have pleasure; there is mutual satisfaction. The mother satisfies her child's need for food and love, and the infant lessens the tension within his mother's breast and evokes a feeling of motherliness within her. From this mutually enjoyed experience, a bond of love becomes established which creates the warmth and security necessary for physical and emotional growth.

The mother who wishes to bottle feed her baby also needs help if it is to be a successful experience. Newly born infants have an abundance of mucus in their respiratory tracts which often causes gagging and "spitting up" during the feeding. Regurgitation with bubbling during the first weeks of life is not uncommon. Sometimes infants regurgitate milk through their nostrils, and unless mothers know these common characteristics they become concerned lest their babies are abnormal. The mother will need her nurse with her at feeding times until the baby has learned to suck and to "bubble," and until she has achieved a feeling of confidence in her ability to meet her baby's needs independently. The primiparous mother will need help in knowing when her baby is satiated. If she is not given this help she is apt to concentrate her interest on getting the bottle emptied rather than on the degree of comfort existent in her baby.

When there is routinization in postpartum care, the above kind of supportive nursing care is difficult to provide. Babies are taken to their mothers at scheduled hours, regardless of the infant's or the mother's needs at the time. If the baby is unready for food, or exhausted from a prolonged period of crying, it is impossible for mother and baby to find comfort in one another. When the baby refuses the breast, the mother grows anxious instead of experiencing the pleasure she needs for growth of her maternal instinct. Repeated experiences of this kind deprive the mother of the experiences she needs for growth. Many mothers feel guilty when their babies will not eat and discontinue breast feeding because they think their milk or breasts are not acceptable to the baby.

Aldrich[1] and his group at the Rochester Child Health Project found that many infants showed a need for food more frequently than every 4 hours during the earliest months of extra-uterine life. Yet in most maternity units the rigid 4-hour schedule is still in existence. They also found that crying in the newborn nursery could be reduced by 50 per cent when additional staff were added to the nursery and taught to pick up the babies and to attend to their individual needs. In many newborn nurseries, nurses are not allowed to pick up babies to soothe and to comfort them. There are no chairs provided in many nurseries, and the nurse who intuitively responds to the infant's needs rather than to the need for nursery efficiency is often frowned upon, criticized and labeled a nonconformist.

In the "rooming in" units nursing care can be more individualized. There are no rigid schedules and routines. Instead there are mothers, fathers and babies learning to live together with comfort and satisfaction. The mother and baby are cared for as a unit. They are part of a family, and the nurse concentrates her efforts on helping its members gain increased understanding of one another. If the nurse is observant and interested in people, she also has many opportunities to learn about family life.

If mother and baby are rooming together, the mother will have many opportunities to become prepared for the time when she will want to meet reality situations with supervision. A mother will show signs which indicate her readiness to care for her baby. Until she does, it indicates she needs the nurse to assume the responsibility for her. As she observes the nurse caring for her child she will gain familiarity with him and reassurance concerning his needs. She will also be stimulated to want to try her hand at giving him care. If, in caring for the baby, the nurse bases what she does on the needs of the child and interprets the reasons for her care, the mother will be helped to see the need to do likewise. There are endless opportunities to teach mothers what they want and need to know.

Mothers who are unfamiliar with newborn infants need to know the details concerning their normal characteristics. The earlier they are able to accept their infant's physical characteristics as normal phenomena, the less anxiety they will experience. Many mothers cannot verbally express their wonderment and fears as they view their infant's physical characteristics. For this reason it is important that the nurse anticipate the mother's need for information, and give her help in understanding that which is normal. Many of the physical and emotional characteristics presented previously can be interpreted to mothers. There are others which bring concern unless they are understood; these will be discussed subsequently.

The newborn infant's head appears large in proportion to the remainder of his body. Often the head is elongated or asymmetrical because of the molding that occurs during the process of birth. The extremities are short and held in a characteristic flexed position. The hands with their short fingers are clenched, and the grasp reflexes are strong. The feet have short toes and a pad of fat over the arches gives them their flat appearance.

Pressure on the veins of the scalp produce edema, commonly referred to as caput succedaneum. The soft spots, or fontanels, permit brain growth and require no special protection. The face is broad, the eyes widely separated, the nose small and broad and the jaw receding. Sucking develops the muscles of the jaw, and the receding chin is usually only a temporary characteristic.

Hiccoughs are frequent in the young baby. The liver is large and when his stomach is full pressure against his diaphragm irritates it. Usually the hiccoughs disappear as soon as the stomach empties itself. Occasionally a milk curd becomes regurgitated into the esophagus, and this may stimulate the nerve supply of the diaphragm. A drink of water usually removes the curd and stops the hiccoughs.

Tiny reddened areas produced as capillaries are ruptured during birth are often observable on the eyelids, the forehead and the base of the neck. These areas are called telangiectases. Comedones are commonly seen on the tip of the nose. These areas are pinpoint white papules which remain until the sebaceous glands begin to function.

Strabismus remains characteristic until the nerves to the muscles of the eyes are sufficiently matured to make focusing possible. The 1 per cent silver nitrate solution instilled into the conjunctival sac of each eye at birth to prevent ophthalmia neonatorum often produces irritation. It is not uncommon to observe a discharge in babies' eyes in the first day or two after birth. Often the discharge is profuse, and with it there may be swelling of the eyelids. Hemorrhagic spots on the conjunctiva are the result of trauma; they disappear early in the child's life.

Sleeping postures and behavior are individual and show considerable variation. The infant's head usually is turned to the side and held in a position characteristic for him. The infant needs a firm mattress and back support when he is turned on his side. Changes in position prevent body asymmetry and give the infant comfort. During sleep many babies startle easily and show quivering movements of the jaw and the extremities.

Changes in the skin become observable during the first weeks of life. During intra-uterine life the skin was covered with a cheesylike substance called vernix caseosa, a protective covering during the period the skin is bathed in amniotic fluid. When the vernix is removed with warmed oil, the skin usually appears smooth, delicate and red. Sometimes desquamation and dryness of the skin appear as a response to changes in the extra-uterine environment. Downy hair, called lanugo, is often seen on the back, the face and the legs. It usually disappears during the first weeks of extra-uterine life. In the first days after birth the skin may show a response to ingested protein—a rash called toxic erythema which may be diffuse or localized. The areas are red and raised and they disappear as rapidly as they come. New babies' buttocks become reddened and excoriated if they are not kept clean. Special care to prevent excoriated buttocks is of extreme importance. They bring the infant discomfort and disturb the mother's peace of mind.

The cut cord protrudes from the infant's abdomen, and is tied with a cord or closed with a Hesseltine clamp. If a clamp is used, the cord usually drops off by the end of the first week. Gradually the stump dries and separates itself, leaving the umbilicus dry and healed. No special care is required unless there is irritation or discharge, then the area requires cleansing with alcohol. Until the umbilicus is completely healed, tub baths are contraindicated. Until tub baths can be given, cleansing the skin with oil or water-dampened cotton is all that is required.

Circumcision is often advised for the phimosis commonly observed in newborn infants. When phimosis exists, it is difficult and sometimes impossible to retract the foreskin of the penis for cleansing purposes unless adhesions between the glans and the foreskin are freed. If circumcision is advised, it is usually done on the eighth day of life when the prothrombin level has increased.

When a baby is circumcised, he needs special care during the procedure and after it is completed. The infant needs conforting during the procedure. Stroking his head as he is permitted to suck upon a sugar tip helps to lessen the discomfort he feels as he is restrained and operated upon. When surgery is completed he needs immediate comforting in the arms of his mother, not only to relieve the infant's discomfort but also to relieve the mother's tension and reassure her that her baby is not suffering. Many mothers are anxious when they know their infants are being circumcised. Comforting the infant takes time but might it not eliminate the need for restraining his legs to prevent him from kicking off the circumcision dressing? Observation for signs of bleeding should be made during the ensuing hours. This the mother could be taught to do and in the process she would feel needed and important to her baby. After 24 hours, the circular dressing can be removed from the infant's penis and replaced by a square of gauze lubricated with petrolatum.

Mothers' Need for Supervised Experience in the Care of Their Babies

Gradually, as the mother becomes familiar with her infant, with his patterns of behavior and with the care he requires, her anxiety will decrease and she will be ready to respond to and to gratify more of his needs. At this time she needs a supporting nurse to encourage her to respond to her inner feelings and to help her become accomplished and self-assured. The mother will need the help of a nurse who can put her at ease and convey feelings of confidence to her so she can be free from anxiety, enjoy the experience and function to capacity. To do this successfully, the nurse needs genuine faith in mothers' ability to mother their infants. The inexperienced mother needs a helper, not a critical, punctilious person who gives her feelings of inadequacy rather than the feeling that she is being accepted as a person who has every potentiality of becoming a good mother.

Supervision in this instance is more than teaching a mother the steps of a mechanical procedure; it is guidance to help the mother achieve fulfillment in her mother role. To accomplish this purpose the nurse needs to be able to relinquish the care of the baby to its mother and to permit her to have the experience she needs to develop security, confidence and pleasure. The nurse also requires freedom from a need to direct so the mother will have opportunity to use her own initiative and power in the solution of her problems.

The more the nurse can help the mother find answers to her own questions as she begins to function more independently the more occasions she will find to reassure her and approve of her judgment and intuitive capacity to mother her child. This kind of supervision will give the mother professional sanction and emotional strength. She will be ready to meet her problems at home. The incidence of maternal panic reactions to a new situation of responsibility will be lessened both because she has become assured of her capacity and because she has gained sufficient familiarity with her infant to feel secure.[7] The infant will be more assured of security, for he will have a mother who understands his individuality and is able to respond to his needs in a way which brings him total satisfaction.

FAMILIES' NEED FOR HELP IN PLANNING FOR THEIR INFANTS' HEALTH SUPERVISION

Before the family leaves the hospital, they will need to know that community facilities function to provide health supervision and guidance in the care of their child. Some mothers may need the help of the visiting nurse before it is time to take the baby to the doctor for health supervision. When a mother's need for help is recognized, the nurse can interpret the functions of the visiting nurse and give her assistance in knowing how to obtain her services.

New parents need to know that monthly visits to a pediatrician or well-baby clinic are advisable and that immunization for whooping cough, tetanus, diphtheria and smallpox should be begun by the infant's sixth week of life. If the family wishes to bring their child back to the well-baby clinic in the medical center where the baby was born, it is advisable to secure an appointment for the mother while she is still in the hospital. If the parents prefer to take their baby to a city child health conference, they will probably need assistance in locating the one nearest their home.

FATHERS' EMOTIONAL NEEDS

The father needs recognition as an important part of the family unit. "Rooming in" helps to fulfill this need and to make obstetric care a family affair. In the "rooming in" units the father is welcome not only because his wife needs him but also because he, too, needs opportunities to make an adjustment to the changes that have occurred within his family. In many instances he is as dependent upon his wife's emotional support and interest as she is upon his. The arrival of a new child makes additional demands upon him, and unless his needs are met he may become frustrated and resentful, and seek to meet his dependency needs in nonconstructive ways. Saul[18] and others have found that alcoholism, psychosomatic illnesses and other neurotic disorders may appear or become reactivated at the time an infant is born.

Observation of the husband with his wife and baby can give the nurse clues concerning his attitudes, interests and needs. Men who are insecure concerning their masculinity feel threatened if they are expected to give an infant care; others find gratification as they care for a child. If the father shows a desire to hold and care for his child, he will welcome permission to do so. Participating in the care of his child helps many fathers to accept and become identified with him. If he can gain satisfaction from the infant, he will feel less threatened and more capable of showing pride in his wife's demonstrations of motherliness. Through shared experiences of this kind, family relationships become strengthened, and the possibilities for happy home life are increased.

"ROOMING IN" AND THE TRADITIONAL MATERNITY UNIT

"Rooming in" has been presented as an ideal plan for meeting the needs of those parents who are ready for and want the experience of being together. The needs of the family unit have also been presented. "Rooming in" has also been viewed as a plan of care which could bring nurses increased professional satisfaction and knowledge of family life and personality development.

"Rooming in" is not only a physical arrangement which accommodates mothers and babies in the same room; it is a plan of care based upon the needs of those persons who come to the maternity hospital for care. Those who wrote the pamphlet "Family Centered Maternity and Infant Care"[22] describe the meaning of "rooming in" in the following sentences:

. . . rooming-in is not to be viewed merely as a specific plan for space arrangement or as a particular kind of equipment or organization, but rather as an integrated, interdepartmental program of professional assistance which is aimed to help parents achieve happy family unity and warm parent-child relationships.

Nurses can make a contribution to the realization of the above objective. Many of the family's needs could be met in our traditional maternity units if their routines and regulations were studied with a genuine desire to find ways of providing family-centered maternity and infant care.

The ideas which follow are presented as possible changes for bringing increased services to families, and for providing nurses with the experiences they need to develop increased skill in the kind of interpersonal relationships necessary for professional success. They are presented for study and for evaluation. If incorporated in our traditional units, increased service to families and broader educational experience for nurses would be provided. They would give nurses the kind of experience they need to help mothers know how to establish a self-regulatory regimen of infant care, for they would have learned how to observe, interpret and meet emotional needs as well as physical ones. Learning the routines and procedures in a newborn nursery and maternity ward does not prepare nurses to function in mental hygiene programs, nor does it prepare them for their own future maternal roles.

1. Assign nurses to the care of mother-father-child units. Increase the nurse's interest in observing individual personality characteristics and the interpersonal relationships of each family unit as a basis for a nursing care plan which extends throughout their period of hospitalization.

2. Increase the nurse's interest in the above by teaching that care of individuals requires more than a knowledge of procedures and the principles underlying them; it requires recognition of needs and skill in fulfilling them.

3. Provide the kind of supervision that increases the nurse's capacity to perceive, feel and become more skillful in responding to the needs existent in their patients.

4. If a family assignment plan is not feasible, assign nurses in the nursery to the babies they will care for throughout their period of hospitalization. Do the same in the mother's unit and encourage co-operative planning between the two nurses who are giving care to the family unit.

5. Permit flexibility in routines to make it possible to meet the needs of the family. Encourage nurses in the use of their intuitive capacities, and permit them to bring mother and baby together when they are in need of each other. Encourage nurses to recognize the father's need to view his baby and to talk about the new experience he is having.

6. Encourage the nurse to establish a relationship with the parents by interpreting her role and plan of nursing care for them. Help the nurse see the need to help the parents feel she is sin-

cerely interested in providing the kind of care that will assist them in becoming prepared to meet their infant's needs at home.

7. Provide classes for mothers in the maternity unit. Use the discussion method of teaching to provide mothers with an opportunity to make their needs known.

8. Utilize each contact to increase the mother's understanding of her child and the care he requires. Help her to gain the security and the confidence she requires by giving her opportunities to feed, diaper and handle her baby when she shows a readiness to do so.

9. Provide opportunities for mothers to bathe and to dress their babies in the unit before they leave the hospital. Supervision by the nurse who has come to know and understand the mother will bring the most desirable results.

10. Interpret community resources to parents who indicate their need for supportive guidance after discharge from the hospital.

ROLE OF THE NURSE IN THE HOME

It is not only the infant who must make adjustments in living during the first months of his life; his parents have many adjustments to make as well. The arrival of a baby brings changes into the husband-wife relationship. Now they must share each other with their baby. They must also share their baby with each other. They have new roles to fulfill. No longer are they only husband and wife; they are father and mother as well. They sense the expectation of their mate in their new parental roles. They also sense the expectations of the society in which they live. Now a new support is required of each other. They must understand and emotionally support each other as parents of their child as well as support each other in their husband-wife relationship. The way these interpersonal family adjustments will be made will depend upon the maturity of the couple and upon their capacity to accept and to understand one another.

The period when the parents begin to assume complete responsibility for the care of their infant at home is a crucial time for each member of the new family. The care of the young child is the mother's role. She knows it, feels it and senses the implications of her responsibility. If the period of hospitalization was an unusually short one, the mother's responsibilities will loom larger to her because she will not have recuperated sufficiently to feel ready to meet them. If she has had no help in the hospital in becoming prepared for the care of her baby, the public health nurse's task will be a greater one. It will not be one that can be accomplished in one or several brief home visits.

Nurses working with mothers in the community will need to take additional factors into account. The mother is at home facing new problems of adjustment as well as new problems of responsibility. In the hospital the mother may not have grasped the reality of the situation she was going to meet. But now, in her home, she must face it, react to it and handle it in whatever way she can.

During pregnancy, as stated previously, the expectant mother attempts to evaluate her capacities to be a mother. She also visualizes in fantasy what it will be like to be a mother. Until she experiences it in reality, however, she knows neither her own abilities nor the amount of self-sacrifice which will be required of her as a mother. Nor does she know whether or not it will bring her the satisfactions her personality needs require.

Mothers react to their new responsibilities in different ways. Many women find that being a mother brings fulfillment and satisfaction of one of their deepest desires. Their infants' care and dependence upon them is gratifying and fulfilling; it is the answer to something they have waited and longed for. However, other mothers may not be able to experience that degree of gratification and fulfillment. Instead of fulfillment, they may feel fatigued, overburdened and resentful. Sacrifice of their own personal wishes to meet their infant's needs 24 hours a day may bring frustration, disappointment in themselves and discouragement. They may discover that being a mother changes their pattern of living from one which brought pleasure to one which seems heavily weighted with demands, restrictions and limited opportunity for freedom and self-expression.

The above feelings are understandable when there is insight into the experiences with which the new mother must cope. Some mothers have had professional careers or work outside their homes prior to the delivery of their babies. Through their work they may have met their needs for achievement, recognition and stimulating give-and-take relationships. These women may discover that motherhood has brought conflicts they have never experienced before.

Cultural factors have an effect upon the mother's feelings and attitudes and therefore upon the kind of adjustment she will make to motherhood and its responsibilities. The mother has absorbed her culture's concept of motherhood. Within her are the standards, goals and ideals she has assimilated from life within her family and society. She may accept the standards of her culture and experience great frustration in her attempts to achieve them. Or she may reject them and formulate new ones in keeping with her evaluation of her own needs and capabilities. Regardless of what she thinks about her culture's standards, social pressure will force her to feel she should strive to attain them.

Middle-class concepts of motherhood are idealistic and in many ways incompatible with human nature. They tend to increase mothers' feelings of inadequacy and bring anxiety rather than pleasure. They tend to expect mothers to suppress their feelings and concomitant reactions, be completely infallible and self-sacrificing and capable of applying every suggestion and principle of child care that textbooks present.[15] It is natural for mothers, and fathers, too, to have some negative feelings toward their child and the responsibilities he requires. Parents cannot always be loving, free from hostility and resentfulness. Parents have feelings, needs, conflicts and fears which express themselves in their behavior whether they will it or not.[15] They prevent parents from following the textbooks' suggestions and from achieving what they consciously desire of themselves for their children.[15] Levy and Munroe say:[15]

> The effects of calling attention to the dangers to children of parental emotions and of giving parents carefully indexed guide-books for handling their feelings seem to have been this: it has made parents think they must compete with St. Anthony or St. Anne as guides of children's lives and has succeeded in leaving them feeling defeated and frustrated when their own standards of behavior fall below heavenly example.*

An understanding of human nature is important for the nurse who is attempting to help women make an adjustment to their new maternal roles. If the nurse's ideals of motherhood are those which expect a degree of perfection which is incompatible with human nature, she will have difficulty in permitting mothers to express their feelings, ideals and frustrations. Mothers sense the nurse's expectations for she discloses them in her relationships with them. An accepting nurse conveys her feelings in her approach and helps the mother feel comfortable and more accepting of herself. An unaccepting, perfectionistic nurse makes the mother feel defensive and uncomfortable.

The nurse with realistic concepts of motherhood will be more effective in helping mothers recognize and accept their feelings and modify their ideals to a level which they can achieve with less conflict, anxiety or guilt. With such help mothers will be able to experience more pleasure in the care of their babies. They will also be able to feel a sense of achievement which was impossible while they were struggling to reach unattainable goals.

---

* Reprinted from *The Happy Family,* by John Levy and Ruth Munroe, by permission of the publisher, Alfred A. Knopf, Inc. Copyright 1938 by Ruth Munroe Levy.

Nurses who are sensitive to the many adjustments which family members must make in the process of becoming parents will approach them with sympathetic understanding. They will appreciate the struggle they are having as they attempt to harmonize their inner needs with those of each member of their family, and with the expectations of the culture in which they live. The nurse who goes into a home with a background of understanding will anticipate that tensions and conflicts will be existent there. She will give the mother an opportunity to talk about the concerns and perplexities she has experienced since coming home with her new baby. She will attempt to establish a positive relationship with the mother by meeting her needs of the moment. If she has known and helped this mother during the prenatal period, a constructive relationship will already be established. Then her task is to maintain it. This is usually accomplished best if the nurse continues to focus her interest on the mother and all that is of concern to her. If she centers her interest and attention on the baby, the mother may feel neglected and be unable to seek the assistance she needs for herself.

Telling a mother to recognize and to accept her feelings is of little value. A mother needs to feel the nurse's acceptance of natural feelings through her response to the conflicts and the stresses she knows are characteristic during the period the family is becoming adjusted to a new way of life. The situation which follows indicates the application of this principle.

The J. family had their first baby after a year of marriage. Mr. J. was a student working his way through college. Mrs. J. worked as a librarian until she was 8 months pregnant. Neither parent anticipated the changes the arrival of the baby would bring. Mrs. J. knew something of infant care but was totally unprepared for the irregularity in need for food which is characteristic of newborns during their first weeks of life.

When the nurse visited the J. home 6 days after the mother's return home from the hospital, she found a tired, distraught woman and a crying baby. Immediately Mrs. J. said things were going nicely but added she had been up 4 times during the night with a crying baby. She talked of the pleasures of motherhood but as she did the lines in her face deepened and she fussed constantly with the belt of her dress.

After listening to the mother tell about her experiences during the past days the nurse said, "It must be terrible getting up so often during the night. I'd feel like sending the baby back to the hospital after one night like that. Getting up that often would exasperate the most patient mother." Mrs. J. looked at the nurse and said, "Do you *really* think so? That's the way I felt, but I didn't dare let on to my husband I felt that way. When I got up the fourth time I wondered why I had ever married. I longed to go back to the library and have the peace and quiet that existed there."

The nurse said, "Screaming grates on everyone's nerves. Until a mother has time to understand her baby and find ways of keeping him comfortable, her responsibilities seem more weighty than she can bear." After these words Mrs. J. burst into tears and said, "No one ever told me what it would be like. I never realized a baby would require so much. I haven't time for any of the things I used to enjoy. Do you think I can ever become a mother?"

This visit was the first of many visits. In each visit Mrs. J. unburdened herself and discovered her feelings were no different from those experienced by other mothers in similar circumstances. She was lonely in the first weeks after the baby arrived and welcomed the nurse's visits. Gradually she learned that she, too, needed relaxation, and was able to leave the baby with a neighbor while she went off for short periods of recreation. Her fear of being an inadequate mother was not based on reality but she had set standards for herself that no mother could attain without a degree of self-sacrifice incompatible with comfort. Mrs. J. was an excellent mother. There were things she could not tolerate comfortably but that is true of every mother. There is no perfect mother, and gradually Mrs. J. faced this fact and stopped striving for something no human being could ever attain.

Encouraging the mother to talk about her daily routine has been found to be a more effective method of helping mothers than direct questioning.[9] Direct questioning is apt to put mothers on the defensive. It is not a method of approach that encourages mothers to express themselves freely. If mothers are encouraged to talk about their daily routines, the nurse is more apt to discover the problems the mother is facing. They may be in relation to the baby or to her feelings concerning her adequacy as a mother. On the other hand, they may be in relation to her feelings of loneliness as she finds herself isolated from activities which formerly brought her pleasure. If there are other children in the family, she may be finding problems in helping them to become adjusted to the new baby. There may be conflicts with relatives, or problems in relation to the family income. If the mother feels free to talk, she will disclose her way of caring for the baby and adjusting to the problems of being a mother.

Mothers need to talk about their daily routines and the trials and tribulations which are a part of it. It must be so for that is what mothers talk about when given the opportunity. So often their problems seem insurmountable and unique to them alone. They do not realize that other mothers also doubt their own judgment or find adjustment difficult in the very ways they are experiencing. Sharing their problems with another often brings emotional release. Often mothers gain new perspective in the process of talking. They return to their work with renewed energy or discover their tasks and problems are less difficult than they had thought them to be.

Observation, and listening with a genuine desire to understand, will give the nurse clues to help her to know wherein the mother feels a need for support, reassurance or direct assistance in the solving of a specific problem in relation to either herself or other members of her family. In talking of her daily routine, the mother may question or show an unusual amount of concern in relation to one or more aspects of her child's care. Her questions or concern often serve to point up the area or areas in which she feels most anxious in her relationship to her infant.

Mothers question or express concern for a multitude of reasons. In some instances they may want specific information or concrete suggestions as to what to do. In other instances they may be seeking help in gaining understanding of their child's behavior. They may be in need of the nurse's evaluation of them as a mother or reassurance that their methods of care are appropriate for their child. Many times there are no direct questions but from the mother's behavior one cannot help but sense feelings of anxiety which she is unable to communicate in words.

What the mother gains from the nurse's visit will depend upon the relationship she has with her. Fries[9] says, "It is essential that all the relationships of professional workers to parents be as satisfactory as the desired parent-child relationship, in order to enable the carrying out of a constructive program." From such a relationship the mother gains strength through her identification with a supporting, understanding and helpful person. She becomes more able to meet her infant's needs, and experiences greater joy in being a mother to her child. When the mother enjoys her baby and is comfortable in her relationship with him, personal growth for both is more ensured. Realization of this goal for the mother should be the nurse's objective, for it is through satisfying experiences with his mother that the child's feelings about the world are influenced.

ROLE OF THE NURSE IN THE CARE OF NEWBORN INFANTS WHO DEVIATE FROM NORMALITY

In maternity units there will be mothers and babies who cannot be together because illness, prematurity or the presence of a physical deformity necessitates that the babies be isolated in special nurseries where facilities for their physical care are readily available. Many of these babies will require care in incubators or oxygen beds. Some will remain in isolated units in the maternity wards; others will be transferred to pediatric wards within the same building or to children's hospitals where specialized care is available. When the baby must be transferred from the maternity unit, the distance between mother and child becomes greater both physically and psychologically.

Physical Handicaps and the Physical and Psychological Health of the Child

When an infant has been born prematurely or malformed or becomes ill, additional care will be necessary to meet his particular physical requirements. When an infant deviates from normality, his physical condition and requirements are appraised by the physician. In some instances the infant may need a special kind of environment to keep his tissues oxygenated, and to supply additional warmth, humidity and protection from infection. He may require special technics in feeding or holding, and treatments which are unnecessary for the normally developed and physically healthy child.

The presence of a physical handicap threatens both the physical and the emotional health of the child. The way it threatens his physical health is plainly observable; the way it affects his emotional health, however, is often much less appreciated. Prematurity, illness and some physical handicaps bring frustration at a period when an infant has no resources within himself to master the feelings it precipitates. Deviation from normal not only brings prolonged and continued separation from his mother at a period when he most needs closeness but in addition it often brings physical pain, fewer periods of undisturbed rest, confining restraints of one kind or another and curtailment of much craved and needed sucking activity.

In providing care which is needed to meet the infant's particular physical requirements, the nurse must not lose sight of his emotional requirements, which are the same as those cited as being necessary for the normal child. Equally as much as the normal child, he needs trust, freedom from anxiety and the feeling that the world is a friendly place. He is a human being first and foremost. Instead of thinking of him as one afflicted with a particular disorder, the nurse must see him as a person who is being affected by his immaturity, handicap or illness.

In giving care to an infant the nurse needs to ask herself the following questions: "How does this baby's physical condition affect him? What emotional satisfactions should he be receiving? How does nursing care which is necessary to meet his physical requirements frustrate his emotional longings? Are there ways I could provide substitute satisfactions and lessen the frustration the infant is experiencing? How can I plan his care so he can get the maximum amount of undisturbed rest? How can I work with the infant's parents so they may become prepared and confident of their ability to give their child care when he is ready to leave the hospital? How do I feel about this child and his parents?"

Starting life with a physical handicap cannot in most instances be prevented, but emotional deprivation and the handicaps it brings to the individual can be augmented to a great degree. The infant not only needs individualized care in the hospital but also he needs parents who can receive him with unconditional acceptance, hopefulness, freedom from fear and confidence in their ability to provide him with the care his unique emotional nature and bodily status requires. Unless hospital personnel recognize their responsibility to both the child and his parents, life for each member of the newly formed family may become heavily weighted with fears, trials, sadness and suffering.

The birth of an infant who is different from that accepted by society as normal affects every member of the family; it does not affect only the child who is born handicapped. Killilea's[13] story of Karen clearly exemplifies this fact. Karen was born prematurely and was also affected by cerebral palsy. Her physical handicap had an impact upon every member of her family. From the moment of her birth it affected her parents, her relatives and her older sister, and later her younger brother. When plans were made for Karen, the needs of the other members of the family had to be considered.

THE BABY WHO DEVIATES FROM NORMALITY AS A THREAT TO HIS PARENTS' EGO

Giving birth to an infant who deviates from the parents' concept of perfection or normality is a threat to their egos. The more the infant deviates from normality, the more powerful the impact of the experience upon them seems to be. The mother has separation from her baby to cope with and together the parents have the problem of meeting a reality situation which is frightening, frustrating and painful and in many instances also near to overwhelming.

Being an adequate parent is difficult even when one's baby is completely normal. Today's world is uncertain, complex, trying and chaotic in many ways. Parents face many problems and responsibilities in raising children today. To expect the parents of a handicapped child to meet their problems stoically and independently is to expect the impossible.

Too frequently nurses expect these mothers to be stoics, unfeeling and totally capable of meeting their problems and responsibilities unaided. They have difficulty appreciating what an experience of this kind can mean to parents and are therefore unable to help them feel there are persons who understand something of what they are experiencing.

The parents of a handicapped child cannot be casual and objective, for they experience pressures unknown to those with normal children. To fail to recognize the peculiar pressures that touch the parents of a handicapped child is to ignore those factors of deepest concern to them. It is not easy for parents to see that there are more severe handicapping abnormalities than the one with which their own baby has been born. Nor is it simple for them to understand that surgery can correct the defect or that specialized care can provide what the infant needs to reach a state of normality. Parents cannot be objective and relaxed and see their child as a person first and foremost when they feel disappointed, angry, guilty and frightened because they are being forced to meet and to handle a situation for which they have had no previous preparation.

Reminiscing about one's earliest experiences in a pediatric ward should help the nurse gain insight into the feelings human beings experience when they must meet situations for which they are unprepared. Perhaps the nurse can recall the feelings stirred up within her when she was assigned to give care to a baby with an abnormality necessitating specific nursing care she was totally unfamiliar with. Certainly she felt fearful and inadequate. And in many instances she may have experienced feelings of anger as well. The following thoughts must have run through the minds of many students: "Why must I take care of this baby? Why was he not assigned to someone else? What have I done to deserve this assignment? No one has ever taught me how to care for a baby with this kind of abnormality. How do they expect me to do it?" The unprepared nurse's concern is with the abnormality—not with the child as a person.

The nurse's concern cannot be with the child as a person when she is anxious and preoccupied with feelings of fear, anger, resentment and perhaps even revulsion toward the baby. Yet the baby is not hers. She has not created it, and her emotional investment is minimal in comparison with that which parents invest in the child which they have conceived. The nurse has only the problems of the moment to meet; the parents have those of a lifetime before them. They not only have their own feelings with which to cope; they know the feelings, prejudices and attitudes which many in our society have toward the imperfect child and adult.

Is it any wonder that parents' thoughts and concerns center around their own feelings, their child's defect and what it means to them personally? Is it any wonder they cannot immediately see their child as a person and the meaning the defect or handicap might have for him personally? It is their personal problems and anxieties which prevent them from seeing the hopeful side and believing that their child can lead a normal, happy and useful life even though he has begun life with a physical handicap.[16] It is their doubt of themselves and their society that makes it difficult for them to face the responsibilities before them. If the child has been born with a physical handicap they sense he will have greater and more prolonged dependency needs. They know that his education and training will need to be specialized and that there will be burdens hard to bear. Is it not understandable why parents cannot immediately mobilize their energies to accept the child and meet the demands before them?

Before parents can establish a wholesome relationship with their child, they have to work through their own personal problems which the birth of an immature or imperfect infant has precipitated. Until they get relief from their anxieties and feel confident of their ability to raise their child, they will not have sufficient energy to give to him.

The most important factor in any child's development is a constructive wholesome relationship with his parents in the formative years of his life. In writing of a handicapped child's need for parental acceptance, Norris[16] says:

We believe that this is even more true in the case of a handicapped child since his capacity to master his environment is so very dependent upon the inner security which comes from having an unquestioned place in his own family and which is a reflection of the parents' acceptance and confidence in him.

Emotional Responses to the Birth of a Child Who Deviates from Normality

Facing one's problems and responsibilities and working them through to a point where one obtains relief from his anxieties takes time and supportive understanding. While parents are working through their problems they need understanding from those in the hospital and the community. They also need strength, hope and specific guidance which helps them to gain confidence in their own abilities to provide their baby with the care he needs both physically and psychologically. The earlier this help is given, the less suffering both parent and child will experience and the more ensured will be their relationship together.

The mother needs help in meeting reality while she is in the maternity unit. The first thing she wants to know is the condition of her infant at birth. If she does not learn its state of health immediately, she imagines every conceivable malady and often her imaginings are worse than reality. Periods of wondering, doubting and fearing seem interminable and unbearable. They utilize energy the mother will need when she learns the truth. Eventually she must know, and the sooner she is helped to meet reality the better. She cannot begin to make an adjustment until she knows to what she must adjust. Many mothers say the truth was easier to bear than the period of time they experienced evasion and what they interpreted as unconcern on the part of hospital personnel.

It is the doctor who tells the parents the condition of their baby at birth and gives the parents understanding of the etiologic factors of the physical deformity or immaturity, the methods of treatment and the prognosis for future development. He will help the parents accept reality and guide them in finding solutions to their problems and in making plans for the kind of treatment and care the infant will require. If he sees the family is in need of additional help, he will obtain the assistance of a social worker or a psychiatrist or refer the family to an available community social agency.

The nurses caring for the mother and the baby need to be ready to work with the doctor, social worker or psychiatrist. She needs to know the doctor's and the social worker's approach to the family and the plans they have formulated to assist them with their problems. Together they need to plan ways in which they can function as a unified team in the service of the family. After the doctor has talked with the parents about their baby, the nurse needs to be ready to observe the mother's reaction to the news she has received. The mother's reaction and behavior will provide the information all those working with the family need to help her through a very trying period of her life.

The way a mother will respond to news concerning the physical condition of her baby will depend upon her personality structure and the meaning which the birth of a handicapped child has to her personally. Not all mothers will react with similar feelings or express them in the same ways. Besides responding with fear many women react to the birth of an imperfect or premature infant with feelings of self-depreciation. It is a blow to their pride; a narcissistic injury. The baby has been a part of their bodies and they react as though it were they who were injured or imperfect. Some parents respond with feelings of guilt. They question their dietary intake, hereditary background, thoughts and activities and think something they have done or thought must have caused this to happen to them. Killilea[13] said, in writing of the feelings she and her husband had when they discovered their daughter had cerebral palsy, "And doubt presented even more agonizing questions. Privately each considered the other's family—was it hereditary? Or worse—somehow is it my fault? Of what am I guilty?"*

If the pregnancy was unwanted, parents may feel they are being punished and deserving of such a calamity. Some feel ashamed and inadequate. They want to hide the news from their family and friends for they expect the impact of social stigma to be directed at them and their child. And often it is.

Many people in our society react to a handicapped child and his parents as though they were dangerous, "bad," frightening and a blight on the face of the earth. Many people do not know the true etiologic factors which produce physical handicaps. Nor does the public at large know that handicapped children are usually mentally normal, feeling little people. Many in our society are suspicious, fearful and filled with superstitious beliefs. They are cruel to the handicapped child and to those who produce him; not always because they are sadistic and hostile people but because they are filled with "prejudice which has its roots in ignorance—an unawareness of the facts."[13] Killilea[13] said the world at large regarded their family with humiliating pity or suspicious scorn. That is what the parents of a handicapped child fear and it is a fear which has basis in reality and one which would be threatening to any family.

Anger is another reaction parents of a handicapped child may experience. They feel angry that Providence has ordained them to be the parents of a deformed child. They respond with feelings of great pity for themselves, wish to be rid of the responsibility confronting them and wonder why it has happened to them. For 9 months they have anticipated the arrival of a perfect child. In fantasy they have visualized it and throughout the waiting period they have anticipated the pride they would feel in displaying their child, and in parenthood. Instead of a healthy, big, beautiful baby, they may instead have a fragile, miniature infant, or one with a harelip or some other anomaly. The imperfect child frustrates the parents' wish for a perfect child. Sometimes the anger that frustration brings becomes directed at the child. When it is there is apt to be tension, guilt and overprotectiveness for it is a feeling which most mothers cannot tolerate in themselves.

Then there are those parents who feel grief-stricken for the child and see the abnormality as a threat to his happiness, adjust-

---

* Reprinted with the permission of the publishers from *Karen* by Marie Killilea. Copyright, 1952, by Marie Lyons Killilea. Published by Prentice-Hall, Inc., New York.

ment to life and state of well-being. Many mothers become depressed when they learn they have given birth to an imperfect baby; others lose control of themselves and overtly express their feelings of frustration, anger and fear.

There are mothers who want to be alone with their sorrow and they withdraw and keep their feelings and thoughts within them, but the majority of mothers want someone with whom they can talk and share their burdens. Anxiety increases their dependency longings and they need strength and support from others. Feelings of guilt are often the first to be uttered. It takes time for a mother to assimilate and to accept emotionally the explanation she had from her doctor. She may talk about her feelings to the nurse as well as to the doctor and when she does it is important that she feels she is being understood. Responding to expressions of guilt with statements like the following ones usually make a mother feel misunderstood: "Forget it—that's no way to feel" or "That is foolishness. Didn't the doctor tell you that the medical profession had never discovered the parents to be responsible for this kind of condition?" If a mother expresses feelings of guilt she feels that way whether or not it is foolish or inappropriate. A mother will feel infinitely more understood if someone helps her to know that is the way many mothers feel and it is natural to respond with the above kind of reaction. If a mother is permitted to express what she really feels and finds that her feelings are understood, she will be able to understand more readily the explanations given to relieve her anxiety and guilt.

The most effective way of helping parents of a premature or handicapped infant gain relief from feelings of guilt is to accept them and their baby. Lemkau[14] makes the following statement which is pertinent to this point:

. . . a premature birth is abnormal. People frequently feel that what is abnormal is wrong, is evidence of sin. They tend to feel guilty about the unusual situation. Physicians and nurses are frequently trained to suspect syphilis in any unusual obstetrical event. In spite of educational efforts to the contrary, they may also harbor a feeling that there is some guilt or inadequacy involved on the part of the mother and may let her, deliberately or unconsciously, know that they feel so. Quite aside from the medical facts which appear to make them untenable scientifically, such attitudes are generally agreed to be harmful to patients and to stand in the way of setting up helpful relationships with them.*

The mother who feels depressed and grief-stricken for herself needs sympathy, acceptance and comforting. If she wants to talk

---

* By permission from *Mental Hygiene in Public Health*, by Paul V. Lemkau. Copyright 1949. McGraw-Hill Book Company, Inc.

about the experience she should be encouraged to do so. Having a baby that deviates from normality is a shock to most mothers. And most people need to talk about experiences which have activated strong feelings within them. Through talking to someone who understands, parents can gain perspective. Gradually they begin to put the fact of the child's physical make-up in its proper place. They face the fact of the handicap, come to recognize that the child is a person who needs their acceptance and mobilize their energies in getting ready to give their infant love and care.

Telling the mother not to cry, to forget about the handicap or to think of how fortunate she really is because there are many things that could be worse, serves only to make her feel misunderstood. Such attitudes merely serve to force her to repress her feelings and inadvertently tell her that it is unacceptable or "bad" to have feelings of grief and even worse to express them.

It is natural for a mother to react with negative feelings upon giving birth to a baby with an abnormality. Every woman wants a perfect baby. It takes emotional maturity and superb ego strength to accept an imperfect infant.

Many parents' background of experience has not helped them to develop the security and inner resources necessary to handle the feelings which come when they are threatened with the reality of an imperfect child. These parents need acceptance and understanding. There is a reason why they cannot accept reality and responsibility or they would not respond with behavior which discloses the threatening feelings they are experiencing. They need to know that all parents in similar circumstances respond with disappointment, tears, frustration and sometimes even with anger or outright rejection.

Many people in our society are raised with the feeling that direct emotional expression is undesirable. Our culture says, "You must act grown-up and have no anger or fear. Crying is babyish—a sign of immaturity." As a result it is difficult for many professional people to understand a mother who cries or who expresses her anger or fear. But many mothers and some fathers, too, need to cry. And many of them have feelings of fear, shame and hostility which need to be expressed.

Repressing one's feelings brings anxiety, guilt and feelings of inadequacy which become expressed in nonconstructive ways; facing one's feelings is the first step toward giving them up. It is much easier to accept one's feelings if they are accepted by another. When parents of a handicapped child can face their feelings and learn to handle them they do not have to utilize their energy in defending themselves against them. Instead they have energy for giving and freedom to use their creativeness in their relationship with their child. As long as there are repressed feelings and anxieties there will be barriers which come between them and their child and prevent the establishment of a wholesome relationship with him. Instead of acceptance, there will be ambivalence, over-protection or denial leading to unhappiness for all members of the family.

There are further ways the nurse can function to help parents surmount their problems and become ready to receive and care for their infants. If the baby is a premature infant and in an isolated nursery in the maternity unit, the mother can be taken to see her baby if she expresses a desire for it and if there are windows through which she can see. Unless the infant is too fragile or ill, the mother needs to know it is possible for her to see her baby. Some anxiety is allayed when the mother sees that her baby is perfect though small. Often a mother's fantasies are not in keeping with reality. If she has fantasied the baby imperfect, observation will help to convince her that her fears are unfounded.

The following example serves to clarify the above point:

Mrs. J. had delivered a premature infant. The morning following delivery, she was anxious and withdrawn. She seemed preoccupied and restless and could not seem to get herself comfortable. The nurse established a relationship with her and said, "It must be very uncomfortable not having your baby with you. Each time you see the other mothers having their babies, you must wish you could have yours too." Mrs. J. burst into tears and said, "I just know I will never have him. I miss him so. If only I could see him!" Then the nurse said, "I saw your baby this afternoon through the window of the premature station. He is small and delicate but perfect in every way. I could move your bed down there and you could see him too." "Is he *really* all right?" Mrs. J. said fearfully.

After Mrs. J. had seen her baby, the tears began to come and she said, "I was *sure* he was a monster. I just couldn't believe the doctors when they told me he was normal though small and doing well." She talked on and on, about the delivery, her fear lest the baby was imperfect, and her disappointment in not carrying the baby to term. As she talked she became more relaxed, her tears lessened and it seemed as though some of her tension was relieved. Soon after the experience, she became more comfortable and fell asleep.

When a mother's baby is premature or ill, she cannot cuddle, feel, feed and nurture him. Earlier in this chapter, the importance of a continued symbiotic mother-child relationship was cited. The maternal instinct expands and matures as the mother gives of herself to the child. It is more difficult for a mother-child relationship to develop when others are ministering to her baby. Many mothers feel resentment toward those who are more skilled and able to give their babies care. Feelings of inadequacy often develop because they feel others are more capable than they.

When a mother is separated from her baby at the time of birth, she will need help to develop feelings of motherliness toward her child. If she expresses concern, she needs to know that it is because she has been deprived of the opportunity to develop it in the usual kind of way. It will be reassuring to her to know that maternal feelings do not come with delivery but with closeness and through opportunities to meet her infant's needs. If the mother is interested in maintaining her breast milk supply and the baby will be able to go to breast in a limited period of time, she should be encouraged to do so. This is important not only for the baby but for the mother as well, for in maintaining her milk supply she gains increased confidence that she will have something of herself to give her baby when he becomes ready for it.

Nurses in premature stations and in pediatric wards have many opportunities to help parents adapt themselves to separation from their infants. Leaving the maternity hospital without a baby is a difficult task for parents. They have anticipated homegoing with a baby and a feeling of emptiness is often experienced. Permitting the parents to visit the unit whenever they feel it is necessary, and sharing with them the changes in development which are occurring in the infant, will do much to keep the family in touch with their child. Questions will undoubtedly be numerous and often telephone calls may be out of proportion to the seriousness of the situation but parental behavior discloses needs which require sympathetic understanding.[14]

As the nurse in the premature station or the pediatric ward learns the way the infant expresses his individual instinctual drives and seeks to satisfy them, the parents will profit from having this knowledge shared with them. It will help them to know their baby's individuality to a greater degree and to recognize his need for a self-regulated plan of care at home. Care in an incubator or in a busy hospital ward is not the kind of atmosphere conducive to the best kind of personality growth.[14] In the home the care can be individualized to a greater degree, and the importance of it for the premature or the handicapped baby who has started life under adverse circumstances cannot be minimized.

When the prematurely born infant has been moved to a less protected environment or when an ill infant's condition has improved, the mother needs opportunities to develop a closer relationship with her baby. Killilea[13] expresses what she and her husband felt when they touched their daughter for the first time. She said:

When the transfer was completed Dr. John turned to Jimmy and me and smiled and left us beside our baby. We both worked hard that we should not weep and then, O wondrous act! we touched her. . . .

We looked at each other and knew that we were thinking the same thing. With the surreptitiousness of two thieves escaping with an original Rembrandt we gently loosened the blankets on the side and with quick glances toward the door peered beneath. . . .

Our visits were doubly rich now since we had the communion of touch.

Preventing overprotectiveness is important to safeguard the child's emotional growth. It can be prevented by building up the mother's feelings of adequacy, by relieving anxiety and guilt and by helping her to know that her baby has reached a state of normalcy through specialized premature care, or with surgical or medical treatment. If the mother can be with her child and give him care while he is in the hospital, she will be aided in developing maternal feelings and helped to recognize the unreality of her fears. She will need supervision that increases her confidence and helps her to see her infant requires not oversolicitude but the kind of emotional warmth on which a normal baby thrives.

Accepting overprotectiveness is equally important for it is often the way a mother needs to solve her problems concerning her premature or abnormally developed child. People adjust to crises in their own way, and their way must be respected. When a mother is threatened she experiences intense anxiety. She must mobilize the ego defenses she has at her disposal to save herself from anxiety and possible disorganization. That is what every person does in a crisis. If he did not summon his defenses to his rescue he would break emotionally. Fortunate is the person who has defenses and inner resources to use in times of stress which bring great frustration. Some people do not have them; they become emotionally disturbed not because they are not willing to take responsibility but because their life experiences have not fully prepared them to make adjustments to situations demanding a great deal of tolerance to disappointment and frustration.

Instead of accepting and understanding the deep purpose overprotection has for a mother, many nurses are critical of her oversolicitude and fail to help mother or child. When a nurse is critical of a mother's overprotectiveness, the latter becomes more hostile and tense and deepens her defenses against her feelings and anxiety. She feels misunderstood and a good relationship with the nurse becomes an impossibility. Instead of helping the mother, the nurse blocks every avenue of communication with her. A mother cannot be receptive to a nurse when she feels misunderstood. Often, in her desire to help the child, the nurse does not recognize the problems and the needs of the mother; unless they are recognized and taken into account, efforts to help will be of little avail. In fact, the nurse's efforts may increase the child's problems because his mother's anxiety has been increased rather than lessened. The situation and explanations which follow exemplify some of the foregoing concepts:

Baby S. was born with a harelip and a cleft palate. When his mother awakened from anesthesia in the birthroom, she asked to see her child. When he was not shown to her immediately, she sat up and attempted to see her baby. At that time she was told that her baby had a harelip. She demanded to see her baby at once and her wish was granted. Her first response was a scream. Then came expressions of frustration, disappointment and fear. "It's not my baby. Take it away," she screamed. Mrs. S. needed help and her doctor, priest and social worker provided it while she was in the maternity unit.

To the social worker Mrs. S. expressed her disappointment in the following way: "I wanted a perfect baby. I can't tell my family about this. I wanted a baby so much and now I have one with a hole in his face. That's all I can see, is that hole." In another interview the mother expressed pity for herself and showed signs of depression. She cried a great deal, longed for her baby but, simultaneously, had visions of an infant disfigured in the way previously described.

Before Mrs. S. left the maternity hospital she was decidedly less anxious. When her social worker commended her upon the adjustment she was making, she indicated the way she was handling her anxiety. She said, "I *had* to pull myself togther. I had no alternative. I realized I just couldn't go on feeling sorry for myself. The baby needs me now and I want to go all the way for him. I'll do everything possible to make it up to him." Mrs. S. had to pull herself together because as she said she *had* no alternative. The degree of anxiety she was experiencing was her signal. She had to defend herself against anxiety to save herself from disorganization.

Pity for herself had become replaced with pity for and an overprotective attitude toward her son. Although Mrs. S's. social worker knew that her pity and overprotectiveness were a defense covering negative feelings and in all probability would lead to overprotection, she knew it was the only way she could solve her problem at the present time and she respected the adjustment she had made.

When Baby S. was 9 days old he was transferred to the pediatric unit for surgery. On the twelfth day of his life a repair of the harelip was done. On the day of operation the father visited. He said his wife was not able to come but he hoped she would find it possible to come before long. He said, "Whenever we speak of the baby my wife bursts into tears. She's wanted a baby to take care of and she's feeling lonely and depressed. She cannot seem to see him except as she saw him on that first day of his birth." Mr. S. was encouraged when he observed the remarkable surgery which had been performed and said he knew his wife would be overjoyed when she heard the news.

The following day Mr. S. brought his wife with him to visit the baby. He had prepared her for what she would see and was ready to provide the support he anticipated she would require.

When Baby S.'s mother saw him she lost control of herself and wept bitterly. "Poor, poor little boy. He is suffering so much," the mother said. She clutched at the nurse and looked to her for physical contact and some words of sympathy. "What is it that hurts the most?" the nurse asked. To these words the mother responded with affect which disclosed the deep pain she was feeling. "It's just that I wanted a perfect child so much," she said. "Of course you did," the nurse said. "Every mother wants a perfect child. All mothers who have babies with harelips feel that way. It *is* a great disappointment and it is natural for you to feel this way."

Cautiously Mrs. S. stroked the baby's head as she bent closer to him, and over and over again she repeated, "Poor little fellow. My poor dear little boy. How much pain you have to stand." The infant was not suffering—he was sound asleep and looked as peaceful as any normal infant looks when he is resting. What made the mother think he was suffering greatly? There was nothing in the reality situation which indicated pain or even the mildest degree of discomfort. But she was in acute pain and could not yet feel that the baby was not a part of herself. In addition she *needed* to feel pity for her child!

Baby S. was his parents' first child. Both parents had wanted this baby and the pregnancy had been comfortable and satisfying. Because Mrs. S. had been separated from her baby since birth, the staff thought she might need and desire an opportunity to become familiar with her son and the individual care he required. This opportunity was presented to her and she expressed interest in wanting to be with him.

There were mornings Mrs. S. came to the ward and mornings she could not. No effort was made to hurry her into taking responsibility in the care of her child for it was apparent that she was not yet ready for it. Seeing her child was obviously a painful experience for her. At first she could only tolerate short periods with her son and in those periods it seemed that she saw only his lip and felt only the anguish she was experiencing within her. This too, was natural and understandable. She had had no opportunity to develop maternal feelings and what she saw at the time of his birth brought pain instead of pleasure. Besides only a few days had elapsed and she had had insufficient time to recuperate from her labor and the emotional trauma she had experienced.

When Mrs. S. was with her son she asked innumerable questions about the lip repair. She noticed the swelling, the asymmetry of his lip and was greatly concerned when she noticed milk welling up into his nostrils. She held and cuddled him and gradually over a period of several days, she began to show evidence that comforting brought her pleasure.

The nurse caring for the baby had conferred with the doctor and social case worker. She learned of the mother's response to the baby at the time of his birth and discovered ways she could work with the mother to help her begin to see the baby as he really was—not as an uncomfortable, malformed child but as a comfortable, human being with a lip that had been made whole.

To give Mrs. S. an opportunity to talk if she wished to, the nurse said, "It must have been hard for you when you left the hospital without your baby." "It was hard," Mrs. S. said tearfully. "It was the hardest moment of my life. I had a bundle there. I put it in my arms and made believe it was a baby. I've missed him so. For so long we wanted a baby to take care of." She talked of her labor, the feelings she had when she learned her baby had a harelip and the struggle she was having to rid her mind of his deformed face. "I keep seeing that hole in his face. Is there something the mother does that causes it? I tried to do everything right. I ate good food and never exceeded the diet my doctor recommended," she said.

Mrs. S. needed to talk about the experience she had had. She continued to carry a picture of a deformed child in her mind and it was one of the barriers which kept her from developing a relationship with her son. For days Mrs. S. continued to talk about the infant's lip, and the suffering he was experiencing. Gradually, with the nurse's help, the mother began to see her baby as he really was. She began to recognize his freedom from discomfort, the beauty of his eyes and body, and the behavior characteristics which made him unique and a person to be loved.

Throughout this period, Mrs. S. was receiving the help of her priest. She expressed her faith and said it gave her strength to face the family and the problems she was encountering in herself. She wanted to be accepting and do only those things which were for her child's best welfare. She was using every power she knew as she struggled to find a solution to what is probably one of the biggest problems she will ever have in her lifetime.

A month later Mrs. S. brought her son into the hospital clinic. She was carrying her baby and his face was fully exposed for all to see. The nurse met her in the hospital corridor and after her greeting, she looked at the baby and said, "What a lovely baby. How beautifully he has grown with your care!" Mrs. S. looked at her son admiringly and said, "And to think I once thought I could never look at him. There was a time when I thought I could never take him home. He has a scar on his lip and an opening in his mouth yet to be repaired but we love him just the same."

Baby S.'s mother was beginning to face reality. Her son had an imperfect lip and a cleft palate yet to be repaired which his mother neither denied nor tried to hide. Undoubtedly, she wished he had a perfectly formed body for that is the wish of every parent but her wish did not seem to be blinding her to the fact that he had within him the potentialities for growing into a happily adjusted child. Undoubtedly, too, she still had many problems yet unsolved but she had taken the first steps in making an adjustment to life as it was.

In the years to come the baby's parents will need further support and guidance from their case worker for there are yet many problems for them to surmount. More surgery will be required and in all probability speech therapy and special dental care will become necessary. In addition, the baby will need the health supervision of a pediatrician.

Fortunately for this family all medical resources will be available to them for they have a pediatrician who will supervise the child's emotional and physical health, utilizing all the resources of the medical center he is in.

There will be many families in similar circumstances who will not be so fortunate as the S. family. They may not know their community's facilities or they may be residing in a community where there are limited agencies to serve families who are in need of special services. In these instances the family physician and the community nurse need to work together in giving the family the help they require. Each state has a department through which care can be provided for the care of the handicapped child. The community nurse needs to be familiar with the services of her state and work with the physician in interpreting their function and in planning ways in which state services may be obtained.

QUESTIONS TO GUIDE OBSERVATION

1. How important do you feel the adjustment period is to personality development?

2. Do you feel the time spent in helping mothers to become familiar with their babies in a maternity ward is time well spent? Why have you answered this question as you have?

3. Why should a pediatric nurse be concerned with the care an infant and his parents receive in a maternity unit?

4. When you were a student in a maternity ward, what feelings pertaining to the nursery routines did mothers disclose to you? How did they feel about having their babies in the nursery? If they showed apprehension concerning their ability to give their child care, how did they show it?

5. When you were a student in a maternity unit, what observations did you make which showed fathers' reactions to the arrival of a new child in their family? Do you feel they should be considered in a maternity unit? Why? What did you observe when they were not considered?

6. Talk with a mother of a newborn infant who is hospitalized in a pediatric ward, and write a report of the conference including the following points: How did you approach her? Did you feel she welcomed an opportunity to talk to a nurse who knew her baby? What made you think she did (did not)? What did she tell you about her prenatal period, and her experiences in labor? How do you think she feels about her baby's illness or abnormality? Do you think she is having sufficient opportunity to develop a relationship with her baby? Did she show any resentment because visiting hours were limited, or because she was not permitted to do things for her

baby? How might she show this though she is unable to express it verbally? What do you think she could be permitted to do for her baby in the pediatric ward? What value would she and the baby receive from it?

7. Observe an ill newborn baby in the pediatric ward. What needs is he having frustrated by his illness? How could you meet his needs more adequately? What changes in nursing care would be required? If the infant's mother is in the maternity ward, and a visit to her is not contraindicated for any reason, give her an opportunity to talk about the experience she is having and record your observations.

8. How do you think a mother might feel producing an abnormal infant? What different responses might mothers have? If a mother in the maternity unit delivered a baby with a cleft palate or another congenital anomaly, and you were assigned to her care, what would you do?

9. Observe in a well-baby conference. Did you hear mothers talking about their problems after leaving the maternity unit? What did you hear which gave you insight into the problems a new mother has at home? How will you use this insight?

10. If you were a public health nurse and had a new mother, father and baby in your district, what would be your plans in working with the family?

REFERENCES

1. Aldrich, C. A.: Neonatal crying, Hospitals 20:68, 1946.
2. ———: Babies Are Human Beings, New York, Macmillan, 1946.
3. ———: Ancient processes in a scientific age, Am. J. Dis. Child. 64:714, 1942.
4. Bakwin, Harry: Psychological implications of early child care, Am. J. Nursing 51:7, 1951.
5. Benedek, Therese: The psychosomatic implications of the primary unit: mother-child, Am. J. Orthopsychiat. 19:642, 1949.
6. Corbin, Hazel: Changing maternity service in a changing world, Pub. Health Nursing 42:427, 1950.
7. Escalona, Sibylle: The psychological situation of mother and child upon return from the hospital, p. 30 in Problems of Infancy and Childhood, New York, Josiah Macy Jr. Foundation, 1949.
8. Fries, M. E.: The psychosomatic relationship between mother and infant, Psychosom. Med. 6:159, 1944.
9. ———: The child's ego development and the training of adults in his environment, p. 85 in The Psychoanalytic Study of the Child, vol. 2, New York, Internat. Univ. Press, 1947.
10. Hickok, V. F.: Changing maternity and newborn care in hospital, Pub. Health Nursing 42:435, 1950.
11. Jackson, Edith: Should mother and baby room together?, Am. J. Nursing 46:17, 1946.

12. Jackson, Edith: The initiation of a rooming-in project at the Grace-New Haven community hospital, p. 45 in Problems of Early Infancy, New York, Josiah Macy Jr. Foundation, 1947.
13. Killilea, Marie: Karen, New York, Prentice-Hall, 1952.
14. Lemkau, P. V.: Mental Hygiene in Public Health, New York, McGraw-Hill, 1949.
15. Levy, John, and Munroe, Ruth: The Happy Family, New York, Knopf, 1943.
16. Norris, Miriam: Social factors influencing the development of the pre-school blind child, p. 13, in The Pre-school Blind Child Project (pamphlet) , New York, American Foundation for the Blind, 1952.
17. Ribble, Margaret: The Right of Infants, New York, Columbia, 1943.
18. Saul, Leon: Emotional Maturity, Philadelphia, Lippincott, 1947.
19. Spitz, Rene: Steps to maturity: what it means to grow up, Child Study 28:3, Winter, 1950-1951.
20. Trainham, Genevieve, and Montgomery, J. C.: Self demand feeding for babies, Am. J. Nursing 46:767, 1946.
21. Problems of Early Infancy, Transactions of First Conference, New York, Josiah Macy Jr. Foundation, 1947.
22. Family Centered Maternity and Infant Care, Supplement 1 to Problems of Infancy and Childhood Transactions, Fourth Conference, New York, Josiah Macy Jr. Foundation, 1950.

4

Development and Care During the Rapid
Growth Period (3 Months to 1 Year)

PRINCIPLES OF INTRODUCING NEW FOODS INTO THE INFANT'S DIET

SUCKING, AN INSTINCTUAL NEED

LEARNING THROUGH SENSORY AND MOTOR EXPERIENCES

WEANING—THE INFANT'S FIRST CRUCIAL STEP IN ADAPTATION TO
REALITY

ABRUPT WEANING, AN INJURY TO PERSONALITY DEVELOPMENT

The first months of life are trying ones for the newly born infant and his mother. The infant must become adjusted to the
physical changes which birth necessitates and acclimated to life
outside the uterus. The adjustments he must make are drastic ones.
He is testing out his own powers of adaptation and the friendliness
and reliability of those within his environment. If it is his mother's
first experience in mothering she is equally uncertain of her powers.
She, too, is testing out her capacities. Constantly she is evaluating
her competence and comparing herself with others and the standards
she has set for herself.

During the first months of life the infant can give little in return
for all he receives; he is demanding, impatient and irregular in his
need for food, sleep and closeness to his mother. His mother cannot organize her day and be assured her aspirations and plans can
be achieved. At times the baby may demand food every 2 hours;
at other times he may sleep for from 5 to 8 hours. Sometimes he
may take several ounces of formula or nurse at the breast for a prolonged period of time. At other times he may need only a few sips
of milk to satisfy his requirements. Sometimes his need is for milk;
at other times he may only be seeking relief from tension which
comes as he sucks and feels the warmth of his mother's arms about
him.

The infant's irregularity of need for food and emotional warmth
in the adjustment period is a response to instability of his bio-

105

physiologic mechanism; it is also probable that it arises from feelings of uncertainty. The newly born infant is meeting a totally new and perplexing experience. Feelings of uncertainty are a natural part of any new experience. It takes *time* for many adults to discover a new situation is safe, friendly and responsive to their needs. Until they do become comfortable in a new situation their energy is not totally available for productive activity, be it work, study or the development of interpersonal relationships with others. If this is true of adults, is it any wonder an infant's behavior is inconsistent during the adjustment period? It takes *time* for him to become assured of safety and fulfillment also, and time spent in helping him to feel this security is time well spent.

About the third month of extra-uterine life, a change in behavior becomes observable if the infant has had his biologic needs gratified by a secure, giving mother. His behavior becomes more predictable and organized. He adapts more easily and remains comfortable for longer periods of time. He is a little less impatient, a trifle more tolerant of discomfort and seemingly more sure of his safety. He is beginning to discover that gratification comes when he needs it. He begins to see and focus on the person who gives him pleasure. This is a biologic and psychologic coincidence. He begins to respond to pleasurable feelings, sights and sounds with smiles as well as with random muscular movements.

The first smiles which come some time between 6 weeks to 2 months evidence increase in neurologic development; they also evidence the infant's capacity to respond to human love and care. Although the baby is indiscriminating at this period and smiles at any human face that brings him comfort, his smiles give. They give his mother pleasure—a glorious reward for all she has given to keep him free from anxiety and comfortable as he adjusted to the new world he is in. To many mothers the first smiles bring reassurance that they are loved, increased pride and a heightened feeling of accomplishment and satisfaction. They feel loved, appreciated and wanted. It gives them security, and reassures many concerning their capacity to mother their babies. As a result they have more love to give.

Between 6 weeks and 4 to 5 months of age, the infant's auditory and visual discrimination becomes heightened. Between the fifth and the eighth month of life, his powers of discrimination progress and he develops the capacity to differentiate his mother from others. He knows who takes care of him, provides protection and gives him pleasure. He attaches himself to this important person, follows, imitates and expects complete fulfillment from her. If he obtains the satisfaction his nature requires and anxiety is kept at a minimum, his relationship with his mother expands, and by the end of this period it becomes one of deep meaning for the child.

During the first year of life physical and psychologic growth is marked and rapid. Through satisfying experiences with his mother, *the infant needs to gain trust and security in his world, adapt himself to new methods of eating, acquire increased mastery of his body and environment and become prepared for weaning which is his first crucial step in adaptation to reality.*

PRINCIPLES OF INTRODUCING NEW FOODS INTO THE INFANT'S DIET

By 3 months of age a pattern of need for food, love and sleep has usually become established and the infant is ready for a new kind of feeding experience. When the baby's needs become more predictable the mother can plan a schedule of care with the assurance that drastic changes will not usually become necessary. However, flexibility will continue to be needed by the infant for several months. As he grows, needs will change, but there will not be the irregularity characteristic of his behavior earlier. About the third month of life the infant becomes ready for new foods and capable of adjusting himself to a new method of feeding.

The way new foods are introduced into the infant's diet is important to him physically and psychologically. The feeding experience should continue to bring the infant gratification if he is to develop a feeling of love for and trust in his mother. The *feeling* the infant has toward his food is as important as the food itself. To ensure the continuation of a wholesome mother-child relationship *the infant needs a mother who understands and accepts the learning which is required when new foods and new methods of feeding are introduced into his daily regimen.*

DEVELOPMENT OF READINESS FOR SOLID FOOD BY THE INFANT

A need for solid food comes when the infant's biophysiologic mechanism requires an increase in calories and nutritional essentials that cannot be supplied by milk. Some doctors recommend that solid foods be introduced into the infant's diet during the early weeks of the infant's extra-uterine life. Others recommend that they be withheld until a baby shows increased physiologic readiness for them.

It is an interesting phenomenon that readiness to ingest solid food coincides with the infant's need for an increase in nutritional essentials. At 3 months of age, when his nutritional requirements increase, neuromuscular and jaw development has made him ready to ingest solid food. In the newborn the jaw is receding and small in comparison to the size of the tongue. When solid food is placed on the neonate's tongue, reflex action pushes his tongue forward and he is unable to get the food into the back of his throat, from whence it can be swallowed. By 3 months of age a change has occurred. The infant's jaw has increased in size and his tongue no longer completely fills his mouth. When a *small* amount of solid food is placed well onto the back of his tongue with a coffee spoon, he is able to swallow it with comparative ease.

Respecting the developmental process makes learning a more natural and comfortable experience for the baby and prevents discouragement in the mother. Some big, strong babies are able to take solid food before 3 months of age, but the majority of average-sized babies seem to do better if their mothers wait until they have developed biophysiologic readiness for them.

The introduction of new foods into the infant's diet brings a characteristic emotional response. The food not only tastes differently, it *feels* unlike anything he has been accustomed to before. It is not unusual for the infant to react to the feeling of the spoon and new food with anger. Nor is it unusual for a hungry baby to scream in response to the frustration he feels when food does not come as rapidly as it did from the breast or the bottle. A hungry baby wants what has given him relief from discomfort before and he wants it immediately! Waiting frustrates him and he responds with anger. It is the natural way for a baby to react. He has not the capacity to handle his feelings in any other way.

A characteristic motor response is also often observable. When an infant receives a new food instead of the accustomed bottle or breast and he is angered by it, he will usually do one of three things. He will spit it out, choke on it or refuse to open his mouth. Spitting out and refusal is a natural part of the learning experience. It requires time for a baby to learn to accept new foods which are given in a way which is unfamiliar to him. Taking solid foods requires changes in the functioning of the muscles of his jaw, tongue, throat and gastro-intestinal tract.

THE INFANT'S NEED OF HELP IN LEARNING TO ACCEPT NEW FOODS

The mother or nurse needs to be prepared for what she will experience when she begins to help a baby learn to eat solid foods. If the mother anticipates the above reactions and she knows turning the baby to the side will prevent aspiration she will be more secure and able to accept natural behavior with complacency and poise.

In all new experiences the infant needs the help of a patient, serene and confident mother who gets pleasure from feeding him. The prepared mother helps the child tolerate the frustration he feels. She aids him in accepting a change in his feeding regimen with a minimum of discomfort. She knows she can help the baby enjoy the experience, and he will after he has had repeated pleasureable experiences which prove to him that good things come even though they come more slowly than he has been accustomed to having them come before.

The prepared accepting mother is more successful. Her freedom from anxiety lessens the infant's tension and provides him with the energy he needs to master a new learning experience. This will not only bring the infant pleasure, it will also bring satisfaction to his mother. When the infant's mother or nurse finds success in helping him adapt himself to a new learning experience, feelings of love and pride arise. Mutually enjoyed experiences strengthen their relationship and bring them closer to one another emotionally. It is this kind of experience that prevents feeding problems and personality distortions from arising.

Experimentation is necessary to discover a method of feeding satisfying to the individual infant. Many babies accept new foods best when they are most hungry; others, however, cannot tolerate the frustration that comes when the bottle or breast is withheld. The latter infants accept solid food willingly only after they have obtained relief from discomfort with a portion of their milk feeding.

When an infant has his first experiences with solid food in a hospital, he needs the same kind of understanding help in becoming adjusted to a new feeding regimen. Many times hospitalized infants are resistant to change. Often it is because they have been ill. Their energy is depleted and they cling to that which has given them comfort before. However, in other instances, it is because the infant's needs are not respected. He is awakened for a feeding and has no desire for food and certainly no interest in adjusting himself to new foods or a method of feeding which requires effort on his part.

Unless the infant's pattern of need for food is respected, meal time will bring him discomfort and the nurse will invariably be frustrated in her attempts to help him accept new foods. Both infant and nurse will be deprived of valuable learning experiences. Instead of a pleasurable experience together, it will be a duty to perform for the nurse and a painful feeding for the infant. Their relationship will not be strengthened—in fact, it probably never will develop, which is depriving to the nurse as well as to the baby.

The infant needs solid foods introduced into his diet gradually. Usually cereals and puréed fruits are the first solids introduced. When the infant has learned to accept one kind, the other is introduced. Then other foods are added in the following order: vegetables, soups, meats, egg yolks, puddings, whole eggs. Cereals and fruits usually are given with the morning and the evening feedings. Vegetables, soups, egg, meats and puddings usually become a part of the midday meal. In this way the infant is helped gradually to become accustomed to the meal customs characteristic of our society.

To prevent resistance to a new feeding regimen new foods should be added to the infant's diet as he develops willingness to accept variety and new textures and tastes. Babies differ in their readiness to ingest new foods. Some accept almost any new taste or texture; others are hesitant and require a longer period to develop readiness to take them or to develop a taste for foods to which they have not yet become accustomed. Forcing and hurry slow the learning process. They may even block it completely if the child is subjected to repeated experiences which bring pain instead of pleasure. Forcing and hurry create tension and negative feelings toward food and the person who gives it. The baby grows more resistant as pressure is put upon him and the mother's tension mounts as frustration increases. It does not take many painful unhappy experiences to make mealtime a battle of wills instead of a comforting and successful experience.

The Infant's Need of Opportunities to Become Accustomed to Variety in His Diet

In the period from the third to the eighth month of life the infant's appetite is at its peak and he needs opportunities to learn to eat a wide variety of fruits, vegetables, cereals and meats. During this period physical growth is rapid and his need for food is great. He accepts new foods more readily then than he will later when his appetite temporarily declines as physical growths slows down.

It is natural for infants to show dislike of some foods. There are always substitutes of equal value. Later the food can be offered again. Eventually, he probably will learn to like it but if he does not he needs the privilege of selecting those foods for which he has appetite.

After the first year of life, it becomes increasingly more difficult to introduce new foods in the infant's diet because he becomes more discriminating in his taste. Babies who have not become accustomed to a variety of foods earlier often show reluctance to accept foods at this time.

Babies who are hospitalized over long periods of time during the first year of their lives also need opportunity to become accustomed to variety in their diets. If thought is not given to planning the infant's menu, he may miss opportunities for which he has a readiness to profit.

The Infant's Needs Determine His Feeding Schedule

During the first 6 to 9 months of life, the infant's pattern of food need will vary. Refusal of a feeding of solid food need not concern a mother unless there is other behavior which suggests ill health. Refusal of solid food is characteristic behavior when the infant's pattern of need for food is changing. Growth brings changes. Gradually the interval between feedings lengthens. He consumes more at a feeding and therefore remains satiated for a longer period of time.

Babies whose individual patterns of need for food are observed and respected place themselves on a 4-meal-a-day schedule about the fourth or fifth month of life. Those who have been permitted to regulate their own dietary needs place themselves on a 4-and then a 3-meal-a-day schedule earlier than do those infants who have been fed according to a prescribed schedule.

Helping Mothers Understand Their Infants' Needs in the Feeding Process

Many mothers need help in knowing how to introduce new foods and the foods essential for normal growth. Given the principles of introducing solid foods, most mothers are able to apply them to the needs of their babies with ease. They are able to follow their infants' cues of readiness, experiment and permit them to take whatever quantity they desire. Unless a mother expresses a need for more help, it is wiser to refrain from suggesting a schedule for introducing new foods. Prescribed schedules frequently produce tension in mothers. Many feel compelled to follow them. When the schedule fails to meet the infant's needs (which is more often the rule than the exception) feeding difficulties arise.

Some inexperienced mothers need additional help. Some mothers may need help in recognizing their infants' signs of readiness for solid food; some may require encouragement before they are able to trust their intuitive capacities. There will be others who will seek specific instructions about timing and amounts to introduce. The mother who seeks detailed and specific directions is usually an insecure mother who has insufficient trust in her own judgment. She needs support and specific guidance temporarily, and she should receive the help she is seeking. However, the nurse must be sensitive to the mother's potentialities for assuming increasing amounts of responsibility. A mother who seeks specific directions is a mother who needs encouragement and increased respect for her own judgment. This the nurse can provide. She can give it as she lends a supporting hand to the mother who is meeting an experience for which she feels lack of preparation.

SUCKING, AN INSTINCTUAL NEED

PURPOSE OF THE INFANT'S SUCKING

The infant needs a mother who understands his drive to obtain gratification from sucking and who permits him to have all the sucking experience he requires. Sucking gives a baby comfort and relief from the oral and the bodily tension characteristic of this phase of psychological development. His mouth is the zone which gives him his greatest pleasure. It is the reason this phase of growth is commonly referred to as the oral phase of personality development.

The infant wants and needs to suck to obtain his milk; his psychological and physical needs are not satisfied without it. When the infant is fed from a nipple which has too large holes in it, the infant gets milk but little or no sucking is required to obtain it. Sucking not only relieves tension and gives the baby pleasure, it also provides him with important learning experiences. A baby needs to work to get his milk for it gives him an opportunity to master a small frustration. When he works and masters his frustration he gets pleasure which motivates him to want to grow and to master increasingly more difficult ones. The baby who never works to get his milk never gets the pleasure that comes from mastery and he is less prepared for taking solid foods than is the baby who has already surmounted one difficult task. Sucking also contributes to jaw development, a factor of physiologic importance.

One of the first ways an infant learns is through oral experience; he takes in not only milk but also the feelings his mother or nurse has as she feeds him. The changes that come as the infant is cuddled and gently stroked as loving words are added to the feeding experience are clearly observable. The infant squirms, waves his arms and, if he is over 2 months of age, he smiles as he feels his mother's love. Eventually, he chuckles, even at the expense of losing his grip on his beloved nipple! When the feelings of the mother or nurse are negative instead of positive, a different response is elicited from the infant. He grows tense, sometimes even rigid.

His sucking activity wanes or is completely inhibited, and his facial expression denotes fearfulness. Some babies scream as they feel hostility and anxiety in the mother or nurse; others withdraw and lose interest in sucking activity.

When an infant is fed from a gadget fastened to his crib or carriage, he gets food but nothing else. He is deprived of one of the most important experiences of his life. He cannot associate love with food and his capacities for relationship experiences may become impaired.

Early in life many babies discover the relief of tension and comfort which comes as their fingers come in contact with their mouths. At first when oral tension or hunger is experienced the baby roots to find something to get into his mouth. Sometimes he uses the sides of his crib to suck upon but eventually random movements bring his hand in contact with his mouth. He sucks; he finds a new way of obtaining pleasure. He repeats it again and again and soon a characteristic pattern of behavior becomes established. He uses it to relieve tension that exists when he has no need for food. Through his own activity he has met one of his own needs. He has discovered a way of obtaining relief from tension and pleasure independently.

DISCARD OF SUCKING WHEN CAPACITY FOR OTHER GRATIFICATION DEVELOPS

The infant will continue to suck his fingers until his need for sucking is satisfied and he has discovered other tensional outlets which bring him pleasure. When the infant's neuromuscular development has increased, and he is given opportunities to use his hands in playful activities, he will have less need to suck his fingers because life is full of other pleasures.

Through sucking the infant gets more than relief of tension; he learns the properties of some of the things in his world. He will continue to learn via his mouth long after his need for sucking has lessened. He will investigate his toys and other objects with which he comes in contact not only with his hands but also with his mouth as well. In the process he will learn something of their properties. He will discover what things are eatable and what are not. He will learn how things *feel*. He will begin to distinguish between softness and hardness, roughness and smoothness. He will learn what feelings and taste bring pleasure and those which do not.

Because the infant's mouth is his natural avenue of investigation, small objects that can be swallowed and sharp objects that pierce should be kept out of his reach. This is a protective measure to ensure safety; it is also a measure to prevent frustration that the infant is unready to tolerate.

Snatching objects from the baby with admonitions such as "No, no" or "Naughty baby" are experiences from which the baby should be protected. He cannot understand them. Nor has he the capacity to suppress his natural desire to investigate things with his mouth.

The above statement does not mean the mother must never say "No, no" to her child. It is not the words "No, no" which are detrimental. It is the feeling tone which motivates the use of the words which is important. If their use was motivated by anger, the child will feel the hostility behind the words. However, if the mother is motivated to use the words because she feels protective and sees her child's need to learn to distinguish between appropriate and inappropriate activities, the child will sense her protective feelings and be able to tolerate the frustration if he has reached the level of development which makes this possible.

If the child has not reached the level of frustration tolerance necessary to withstand his mother's "No, no's," other methods of guidance are indicated. Substituting a safe object for a dangerous or unacceptable one is a method of preventing undue discomfort. Sometimes removal from the frustration is the wisest solution. If the infant is outdoors on the grass, for instance, and he picks up a pebble and places it in his mouth, his mother should remove it, of course, and kindly and firmly say "No, no." If the infant is ready to endure this frustration, he will adjust himself to it. However, if he is unready to learn that there are things which cannot be safely mouthed, he will show it in his behavior. Then there is no alternative but to comfort him and to move him from the situation to one which is nonfrustrating.

Growth and inner and outer circumstances influence the child's need for sucking. Sucking becomes less intense when the baby begins to vocalize and to use his mouth for exploring purposes. It may, however, be needed again when he is teething and when he is being weaned from the bottle or breast. In times of stress or at times when he is experiencing undue anxiety, he may resort to finger sucking for solace or relief from tension.

A baby needs help in finding substitute outlets which bring him pleasure. He can obtain them through play and through his mother's positive responsiveness to his new accomplishments. If he is not helped to obtain substitute gratifications, he will cling to sucking to meet his emotional needs and become retarded in his development.

Babies who are ill and must experience the grief and anxiety that come from separation from their mothers often revert to sucking. It is a way of obtaining quick relief, and they *need* it. However, in convalescence many infants continue to spend much of their waking hours sucking. They do it because they are uncomfortable from loneliness and have no experiences which bring stimulation and pleasure. Stephie, age 1 year, exemplifies children's use of sucking to alleviate anxiety.

Stephie had Cooley's anemia. She required hospitalization for study and blood transfusions. She was grief-stricken after she was separated from her mother and withdrew from the nurses. She became apathetic, and sucked on her fingers constantly. Play materials were on her bed, but she never used them. Instead, she rolled into a ball in the corner of the crib, lay quietly and sucked on her fingers. When a nurse approached her, she grunted disapproval and withdrew farther into the corner of her bed. When the nurse put out her arms to her, she withdrew. She wanted and needed her mother, and a strange nurse was no substitute. Instead, she gave the nurse her two dolls.

Food was offered, but Stephie pushed it away. She pointed to the bottle of milk and it was given to her. She evidenced a desire to hold it herself and ardently disapproved of the nurse's touching it. The nurse continued to sit beside her throughout the self-feeding activity.

When Stephie finished her bottle she grunted and pointed to the thermometer tray, which sat upon the table. The thermometer and bottles were removed. Then the tray and the metal pieces which held the bottle were given to Stephie. She fingered it, removed the metal ring and pointed to the box of tissues. One by one Stephie removed the pieces of tissue. She tore them up, put them back into the box, and repeated the play many times.

Then Stephie pointed to the bath basin within her table. In it was a clean washcloth. This she used to chew upon as she continued her play. She put things into the basin, took them out and then began handing one thing at a time to the nurse. Then Stephie would indicate her desire to have them back, and as the interplay continued, Stephie's facial expression began to change. She beamed, began to smile and became more daring in the things she did. She would drop a piece of tissue to the floor, eye the nurse and chuckle when she discovered the nurse would playfully return it. She came closer to the nurse and when a spoonful of cereal and applesauce was presented, Stephie took it willingly and eagerly. It was the first solid food Stephie had had since coming into the hospital 3 days before.

Through this interpersonal experience which provided stimulation and an opportunity to test out the nurse's attitudes and feelings, Stephie gained some trust and pleasure. She did not need to withdraw and use her thumb for comfort. Other opportunities for pleasure were offered, and when Stephie found they brought pleasure, she was able to utilize them. Through this experience Stephie discovered that those in her new world were friendly and giving. And her nurse became aware of Stephie as a person! Both had satisfaction from the other, and a bond of mutual friendliness was established. No longer was Stephie a patient who withdrew from contacts and spent her time sucking her thumb. She was a responsive person with a great capacity for fun and growth.

Replacement of the Sucking Impulse by the Impulse to Bite and Chew

Between the fifth and seventh months of life, the child's behavior begins to change. He feels safer in his environment and has more energy available for new pursuits. In addition, physical growth slows down and provides the infant with increased energy for development in other areas. He becomes more aggressive and seeks more active experiences which provide him with opportunities to develop his body and his perceptual abilities.

The vital source of energy within the child, or *libido* as it is often called, stimulates the constructive aggressiveness necessary for learning, for overcoming obstacles and for developing initiative and the creativeness within him. When the child's vital energy is directed constructively he adapts and gradually becomes a socialized, happy, constructive individual. When this vital energy cannot be expressed in constructive channels because his needs are not understood and his efforts to learn are thwarted, it becomes blocked or repressed, bringing retardation in emotional development, distortions in personality or psychosomatic illness.

When the infant's lower and upper incisors begin to erupt between the sixth and the eighth months of life, his sucking impulses lessen and become replaced by impulses to bite and to deal with things more aggressively.[6] At first a baby's only method of getting food is by sucking. The puréed cereals, fruits and vegetables are manipulated in his mouth just as he manipulated the nipple to obtain his liquid food. However, his behavior changes when his teeth begin to erupt. His gums become uncomfortable and he bites more than he did before and chews to obtain comfort. He bites on the nipple, the spoon and his toys. If he is deprived of these pleasures he becomes irate and tearful and loses opportunities to learn to bite and chew.

The infant needs his biting impulses understood and help in finding socially accepted outlets for his urge to bite, chew and deal with things more aggressively. His aggression is not destructive; it is constructive and necessary for his development. The infant needs to learn that biting on the breast is not appropriate not only because it hurts his mother but because it is important that he discover one does not have to bite on the breast to obtain pleasure. If his mother presses gently on his jaw he will be frustrated but he will have learned it is an unacceptable way to get pleasure. If he is given other things to chew upon he will have the help he needs to find socially accepted outlets for his urges.

The Infant's Development of Readiness for Dietary Changes

When the baby begins to chew he has reached a new phase of development and shows he has acquired the physical readiness and interest necessary to experiment with a new learning experience. Helping the baby learn to chew foods is easy if his interest in learning is utilized at the time it becomes observable. This principle is true in all areas of learning. The adult's task is to recognize the signs that show his interest and a desire to experiment with something new and give him leeway to develop his own powers in his own characteristic way.

When the baby begins to chew he will welcome a teething ring and hard foods to chew upon. Chopped foods, a bone to chew upon, zwieback, a stalk of celery and toast are foods that will help the baby develop skill in chewing. When chopped foods are first introduced, he will most likely chew it a few seconds as he cogitates about it, and then spit it out. Gradually, however, he will get the idea that they are eatable, tasty and to be swallowed. By the time he has cut his lower and upper incisors, he should be able to eat table foods that are cut up into small pieces.

The infant will enjoy new table foods most if he is allowed to use his hands and to participate in his own feeding. Placing bits of a new food on the tray of his high chair encourages him to investigate and to taste them independently. In the process, however, he will first want to discover their properties. He will feel and smear them and glory in the activity if his mother has no negative feelings concerning his natural exploratory inclinations. At this time the use of an ice-tea spoon for feeding vegetables, cereals and fruits is a great advantage to both mother and baby. The mother has a spoon with a handle long enough to control and the infant can hold the lower part of the shaft and help direct the bowl of the spoon to his mouth.

The infant's interest in manipulating the spoon and exploration of his food is evidence of growth. If it is encouraged with genuine pride in his growing desire for new experiences, he will know his activity is acceptable and he will want to repeat the act. Permitting the infant to have a part in the experience should enrich the mother-child relationship. The infant will feel pride in his growing capacity to co-ordinate and to master a situation, and the mother will gain a sense of pride in her youngster's growing independence.

In this period of development the infant should become emotionally and physically prepared for self-feeding. If he is permitted to explore and to do the parts he is capable of doing, his co-ordination will increase and he will become motivated to want to gain complete mastery of himself in the feeding situation. With guidance, he will acquire this capacity in the period of life which is to come.

LEARNING THROUGH SENSORY AND MOTOR EXPERIENCES

Physical growth of the body is continuous and individual and proceeds in an orderly fashion. Each child possesses his own unique potentialities for physical growth and his own characteristic way of responding to both pleasurable and problematic situations. Some infants grow rapidly; others develop at a slower pace. Most infants will creep before they walk but there will be a few who skip the crawling and creeping stages completely. Although there is orderly progression which takes the child from one stage into the next, there will be wide variations in the way children grow and the time when they will acquire new skills. Both heredity and environment influence growth and determine the tempo at which it shall progress.

PROMOTING GROWTH AND PERSONALITY DEVELOPMENT BY CARE AND GUIDANCE

All Aspects of Growth Are Interrelated. The child grows as a whole. All aspects of his development are interrelated, each part being dependent upon the other. As physical growth progresses the infant becomes ready for new experiences which give him opportunity to practice his developing capacities. As he acquires skills, his confidence and pride expand and his personality development becomes influenced.

Learning is more than the acquisition of motor and intellectual skill; it is a social experience involving feelings and one in which both the infant and his teacher (mother or father) participate. The impetus to learn through self-directed activity comes as a consequence to physical maturation. However, progress in learning will be determined largely by the emotional interaction which takes place between the two persons involved in each new situation. As the infant develops increased sensory and motor power and begins to experiment with a new skill, he becomes aware of his mother's response to it. At first her response is only felt. Gradually, however, as maturation takes place, he becomes increasingly more capable of perceiving her response from her gestures, words and tones of voice.

Because the infant's emotional relationship with his mother is one of the strongest motivators of growth in this period, her attitudes and feelings concerning the developmental process are of extreme importance to him. *The infant needs a mother who provides optimal physical health, has respect for the developmental process and interest in his need to explore and provides the tools he requires for development.*

Good Health Is Essential for Growth. Protecting the child from disease and malnutrition with immunizations, adequate nutrition and good physical hygiene will assist him in utilizing his inherent potentialities for growth. When an infant is ill and his energy is being used to combat disease and fatigue, the tempo of his growth is retarded until physical health and emotional equilibrium are restored. A malnourished child is listless and uninterested in developing his skills; he has not the vitality he needs for physical or personality growth.

However, the infant needs more than adequate nutrition, good physical hygiene and immunization to learn to use his mind and body functionally; he also needs continuity in his relationship to his mother, emotional warmth and acceptance. Babies thrive only when physical hygiene is accompanied by those ingredients essential for mental health.

The Newborn Infant Has No Voluntary Control of His Body. At birth the infant has no voluntary control of any part of his body. He cannot lift his head from his crib or move one arm without moving the other. When he is uncomfortable not only does he scream, but also his total musculature is set into action. If he is hungry he moves toward the side of his crib in search of food, but if the cribside is very far away he is unable to get to it. When he is on his abdomen he can turn his head to the side but if he becomes uncomfortable in that position he can do little but cry.

Growth Brings New Abilities and Changes in Behavior Which Require the Fulfillment of Newly Developed Needs. Gradually the baby acquires control of his head. By 1 month of age the infant can lift his head from the bed and from his mother's shoulder when she holds him against her in an upright position. By 3 months of age he can control his head and move it with purpose.

By 3 to 4 months of age the infant's requirements begin to change; he needs the interest of his mother expressed in additional ways. Earlier he was satisfied if his biologic needs were met with physical love and acceptance. Now he wants more than that; he wants and needs stimuli which give him a new kind of pleasure. Age-adequate stimuli promote maximum physical, mental, social and emotional development. *The infant will reach out for the experiences he is ready for, which will stimulate his growth. He will also reject those experiences he is unable to utilize comfortably.*

By 3 to 4 months of age the infant has acquired some degree of eye muscle control and his interest in objects increases as he moves his head in an effort to get the visual stimulation he desires. At birth his eyes moved independently and he could not focus on an object held before him. At about 3 months of age, however, he can focus, follow an object and move his eyes together unless he is attempting to visualize something very close to him.

Nervous system development which makes eye muscle control possible indicates the infant's readiness for short periods of sensory stimulation. At this time he will enjoy and profit from short periods of propping which permit him to view the world from a new angle. One needs to protect the baby from fatigue to prevent the experience from becoming painful instead of pleasurable. When he begins to wiggle to get himself down from the propped position, the infant is telling us he has had enough and is needful of a change in activity. It is his way of showing rejection of an experience which he cannot utilize comfortably.

Between the third and the sixth months of life motor development increases rapidly. Gradually, the infant discovers he can move himself up in his crib by pushing his heels against it. Kicking exercises his legs and arms and helps him to acquire better co-ordination. By the fifth month of life when he is on his back he can flex his knees, push on his feet, arch his back and raise it from the bed. After his bath when clothing does not impede movement he will enjoy and profit from periods of unrestricted activity.

Between the fourth and the sixth months of life the infant discovers he can use his hands and feet. First, he finds he can bring his hands together and when he does he views them in ways he has not been able to do before. He finds they are good playthings and he spends much time examining and manipulating them. Soon he will begin to show increasing capacity to handle a rattle and to enjoy dangling, noise-creating toys suspended across his crib. At a later time he will discover his toes and like his fingers they will become objects with which to play.

There are other accomplishments the infant acquires between the fourth and the sixth months of life. When he is on his abdomen he can raise his head and shoulders and reach out toward objects and draw them to him. Behavior at bath time begins to change. He can splash with both his feet and his hands and can manipulate objects within the water. At this time he not only grasps objects, he also releases them from his hands even though his toys drop from the tub or onto the floor and out of sight. He does it over and over again and will continue to do so for months to come.

The infant is not being obstinate when he drops things from his bathtub, high chair or crib; he is merely practicing a newly acquired skill. Teaching him to drop them into a can or box will help to solve the mother's problem but to expect consistent compliance with her suggestions is expecting control he has not yet acquired. Scolding inhibits his development and fails to understand his need for this kind of activity. Tying toys to his cribside or high chair does not solve the problem for as yet he has not acquired the capacity to retrieve them.

Between the fourth and the sixth months of life the infant acquires the capacity to roll himself from one side to the other and he needs protection to prevent falls while he is learning. He struggles to get himself rolled over. With exercise he accomplishes the feat but often he lands on the other side with a thud. This does not inhibit his progress, however. He continues to practice because activity is pleasurable, and because there is impetus from within to master his body. Very soon he can accomplish rolling over with ease. It is hazardous to leave the infant lying on anything which does not protect him from rolling to the floor. Because one cannot anticipate when new skills will be acquired, it is wise to scrutinize the child's environment and eliminate those things that might bring physical injury and fear-provoking experiences.

As the baby gains increased perceptual and motor power, he will need tools to develop them. The infant's behavior will communicate his readiness for new sensory and motor experience. If toys are kept within his sight and reach, he will reach out for them when he is ready to use them to his advantage.

The infant is not discriminating in his choice of play materials; *his only requirement is equipment, space and freedom to learn.* He not only wants freedom; he needs it. His play equipment does not have to be the expensive commercially made variety. Commercially made rattles, balls and water toys are useful to the baby, but he can learn from equipment readily available in the hospital or the home. Pieces of cloth of different textures and cellophane bags of paper can provide both touch and manipulatory experiences. Various-sized pill boxes with bottle tops inside and covered with cellophane tape make wonderful objects with which to play. Strings of spools or colored napkin rings can be examined, pounded and thrown. Empty bread crumb cans or adhesive roll cartons can be rolled, banged and eventually used as cylinder blocks. Cottage cheese containers and empty boxes can be grasped, moved and used as receptacles for smaller objects. Measuring spoons, aluminum pans and covers provide many opportunities for profitable play experiences.

Development of perceptual, motor and intellectual powers influences the development of the ego or that part of the personality which makes adaptation to reality a possibility. The ego is the "I" of the personality, the part which adapts to the needs of the infantile urges (id) and the demands of the outer world. It is the part of the personality which helps the child to tolerate increasingly larger doses of frustration and to master the anxiety that comes as his desires come in conflict with the desires of others in his outer world. Eventually, with future experiences with his parents, the child's conscience will become an internalized part of his personality structure. When this personality growth has occurred, his ego will be the mediator between his id, his conscience and outer reality.[8]

As the child acquires new skills, his feelings about himself expand; his ego becomes strengthened. He becomes proud of his achievements and more confident of his own ability. He gains mastery of his body, learns the properties of things within his reach and acquires inner resources as he finds ways of obtaining gratification through his own bodily activity.

By the sixth to the ninth month of life the infant's neuromuscular development makes it possible for him to enjoy many new activities. Previous exercise has strengthened his body. As a result, he is able to propel himself by wiggling and by pushing against an upraised knee. He can pull himself forward if he has a bed pad or rug to pull upon. And he can sit up and hold his upper torso erect. He loves to exercise this power and he is reluctant to lie down unless he is tired or busily engaged in the examination of an object which is intriguing to him.

Soon after birth the infant is responsive to sounds, but at birth he does not react to noise for his eardrums are surrounded by embryonic epithelial tissue. There is also absence of air in the auditory canals. However, in a day or two, the infant begins to respond to sharp, loud noises. If the adult's hands are clapped loudly, the normal newborn infant will respond with extension of all four extremities. This response to loud, sudden noises is called the "Moro" reflex. It disappears about the third month of life when myelination of the nerve sheaths become more completely developed.

Gradually it becomes apparent that the baby enjoys sounds and distinguishes between those which are pleasurable and those which distress him. By 3 months of age the crying of many infants ceases when they hear their mothers' voice or other melodious sounds near them. They enjoy the sensory stimulation which comes from music, or from the sounds which come when a bell or metal disk is struck.

In this period the child uses his hands with increased skill and glories in exploring objects of any variety. He picks them up with his whole hand. He fingers them, pounds and rolls them, and as he does so he listens to the noise he is creating.

When the infant begins to manipulate toys and discovers that he can create sounds through his own activity, his feelings about himself are influenced and gradually he begins to discover himself as a person. His response to his own activity shows the feelings which come as he makes his new discovery. He shows delight and a tremendous sense of power! Through repetition of experiences which help him to discover that his own activity brings changes in things and people, he eventually discovers himself as a person. The noise he makes is not always melodious to adult ears, but to him it is glorious because it is he who has the power to produce it.

As growth brings increased activity, the infant needs space to move in and new objects to explore. He shows feelings of dissatisfaction when he is confined in his crib, baby tender and high chair. His curiosity is avid, and his need to exercise comes in response to powerful inner drives. One who studies the infant's behavior cannot doubt this characteristic for he sees what happens when he spies a new object, goes to it and works to satisfy his curiosity and to master it. Bob's behavior illustrates this point.

Bob was 13 months old when he was presented with a new toilet chair. First he looked at it, felt it and mouthed its back. Then he handled the front piece and discovered it was movable. He lifted it up, swung it over the back and returned it to its original position. After he did this four times he turned the chair on its side and examined the under surfaces. Then he put it into a standing position and put one foot through the hole in the seat. He wasn't satisfied with this so he put his other foot in. Then he met a problem. He needed help to get out.

Meeting a problem did not thwart Bob. He continued to find out more about the chair. Again he tipped it over but this time he discovered he was cornered between the wall, his crib and the chair. He looked at the observer, then at the chair. He tried to crawl over it but the chair tipped and he withdrew. He tried to get under the bed but that did not work. Then he thought of moving the chair over toward the wall. He came out of the corner, put the chair upright and turned his interest to something else. He had mastered the chair and was ready to find something else to conquer.

When the baby begins to pull away from his mother and to reach out for new experiences, she is faced with a new problem. Many mothers and nurses find it difficult to relinquish the pleasure that comes from holding, cuddling and controlling a baby. Some mothers experience an acute sense of rejection when their babies prefer sitting in their high chairs or on the floor to play. There comes a time when the baby pushes his mother's hands from the bottle, preferring to feed himself. If his cues are noticed and accepted there will also be times when he prefers his food while he is sitting in his high chair. There will also come a time when he resists his mother's desire to rock him to sleep. Instead, he will show indications of preferring a short period of unrestricted activity on his bed or a few moments to cuddle a soft toy before he falls asleep. When he begins to show resistance to accustomed pleasures it does not mean he is ready to give them up consistently, however. When he is especially tired or in need of some extra cuddling, he will again resume his old patterns of behavior.

In the hospital, changes in behavior come when the infant's illness subsides and he becomes familiar with the new person who is giving him care. As he becomes more comfortable in his environment he will show signs that indicate his readiness to experiment with some new activities. He needs opportunities to learn and to get pleasure from learning. However, the hospitalized infant, needs more than toys suspended across his crib. He needs the emotional interplay that comes when his nurse sees him as a human being who is needful of stimulation, encouragement and experiences appropriate for his level of development and his degree of illness.

When growth brings new needs, the infant requires a mother or a nurse who is ready to modify her patterns of behavior to meet his needs for growth. If his mother or nurse has accustomed herself to a meticulously neat home or hospital unit, and a schedule which does not include guidance of an exploring child, changes in the infant's behavior will bring other problems which require an adjustment being made to them. It is not easy for mothers or nurses to change, especially if it deprives them of satisfactions to which they have grown accustomed.

The mother's responsiveness to her infant's accomplishments nurtures growth in all areas of development. When the infant discovers new ways of obtaining gratification his need for physical closeness gradually diminishes and becomes replaced by a need for encouragement and maternal responsiveness to his new activity and play. *The infant needs a mother who finds satisfaction in his accomplishments.* Her pleasure in his growth not only stimulates him and encourages him to strive to accomplish increasingly more difficult tasks, but also communicates her acceptance of him as a person. Psychologically, it gives him permission to grow and to develop those qualities which he will need to achieve eventual self-realization. In such an atmosphere of acceptance, life will continue to bring experiences which are enjoyed by both mother and child. In this way his social and emotional growth are nurtured.

When a child's drive to master himself and his environment is thwarted, he becomes frustrated, angry and disappointed and has to make an adjustment to it. How he responds to his frustration will depend upon the strength of his impulses (constitutional make-up), the manner in which his mother responds to his natural aggressiveness, and the way in which the child perceives her behavior.

There are some babies who fight to gain gratification of their drive for motor activity even at the expense of threatening their relationships with their mothers. Babies who have inherited strong constitutions often resist the frustration which inhibition of their natural tendencies brings. If an infant's aggressiveness is unacceptable because his growth deprives his mother of her gratification, their relationship becomes threatened. The infant is then forced into conflict between his need for activity and his need for acceptance. Motor development may advance because his nature demands it, but growth in other areas may become retarded in the process. Unless his mother gains insight into his needs to the degree that she can see things from his point of view and acquiesce to his needs, disturbances in relationship become inevitable.

There are other infants who withdraw and regress when they sense their mothers do not accept their developing constructive aggressiveness. When their desire to learn is thwarted, they are confronted with a painful, frustrating experience. Instead of fighting to obtain gratification, they regress and cling to the dependence and security that has brought them satisfaction before. Thumb-sucking, dependency and passivity are often prolonged for this reason.

Another example of regression is one commonly observed when an infant's readiness to participate in his own feeding is thwarted. When he reaches for the bottle or spoon and his hands are held at his sides, or he is given the feeling that his behavior is unacceptable, he withdraws and loses his urge to practice a skill he is ready for and interested in learning. Instead of fighting to retain the spoon or refusing to eat, he regresses and becomes acquiescent to his mother's needs which she communicates in her relationship with him. He lets his mother feed him either because he has too little strength to fight a powerful person or because he is unable to tolerate the anxiety he feels when his mother is dissatisfied with his activity.

Through acquiescing to his mother's demands, the infant described above maintains his security with his mother, but he resents her lack of interest in his needs and pays a high price for what he receives. Instead of growing, he regresses, for acceptance is his most essential requirement. A year later when his mother recognizes that his skills do not compare favorably with those of other children, she attempts to force him to develop them. By that time a pattern of behavior has become established. The mother has failed to utilize her infant's interest and cues of readiness for learning, and he has retained immature ways of obtaining gratification and feelings of resentment toward the person who thwarted him earlier. When his mother attempts to turn over the feeding process to him, he refuses to practice that which he would have enjoyed earlier, and often it is with a resistance that is indomitable.

Forcing a baby to inhibit his need for motor and sensory growth in order to obtain acceptance and the love his emotional nature requires limits his opportunities for personality growth. It rejects his inherent nature and limits him in acquiring the inner resources he will need to adapt to reality situations in the future. If early in life he has had too little help in acquiring the ego strength he needs in order to deal with reality situations, his problems will be multiplied because he will be expected to endure frustrations for which he is inadequately prepared. Weaning is an example of a reality situation he will be expected to meet. The way in which preparedness influences the infant's adaptation to the weaning process will be discussed in the next section of this chapter.

Between the eighth and the tenth months of life, most babies learn to creep, crawl and pick up small objects with their thumbs and forefingers. When a baby has developed the capacity to creep and crawl, he can get places and investigate everything he has been eyeing and taking in visually for the past few months. About the tenth month of life he picks up objects with what Gesell[5] calls the "pincer" grasp. Every small object he sees stimulates him to practice his newly acquired skill. It is in this stage of development that it is especially important to keep small objects out of his reach.

Next the infant learns to pull himself up into a standing position, but getting down requires another skill he must learn. When he first pulls himself up into a standing position in his play pen, he will summon his mother or nurse to help him down for he is in a precarious new position and he knows it—he is thrilled with his accomplishment but a trifle wary about what he should do next. If his mother flexes his knees and puts him down or shows him how to get his hands onto the horizontal bar of his play pen and slide down, he will soon learn to do the task independently.

Whenever a child succeeds in accomplishing a new feat, he seems to be under compulsion to repeat it over and over again. It is as though he felt he had to practice until he had reached a stage of perfection. And this is exactly what he must do! His practice has purpose—it gives him exercise and the confidence that comes from mastery and prepares him for tackling a new task.

Learning to walk is the infant's next task, and when he has perfected this skill he will be off searching for new territories to conquer. Some babies begin learning to walk as early as the tenth month of life. Others are constitutionally different and do not develop the control necessary to keep them upright until the fifteenth month of life. Often during the process of learning to walk the infant reverts to creeping for exercise and to get himself places more quickly and safely. It is not long, however, before he gives up creeping entirely; he does so when he feels safer and a need for it becomes nonexistent. When that time comes he uses his energy in acquiring variations in upright location.

Freedom to exercise his new skills brings confidence, strengthens his body and brings changes in his posture. When a baby begins to walk, he is awkward and unsure of himself. He separates his feet and wobbles from side to side to maintain his balance. His abdomen protrudes beyond his chest, and lordosis is characteristic. The exercise he gets as he learns to walk, run and climb develops the muscles which will straighten his back and hold his chest high and his chin and abdomen in. It is exercise which will make it possible for him to walk with his feet pointed straight ahead and together. Good posture develops by the fifth year of life if normal activities have been permitted.

HELPING MOTHERS MEET THEIR INFANTS' NEEDS FOR NEW SENSORY AND MOTOR EXPERIENCES

Helping mothers recognize their infants' developing needs is done most effectively as anticipatory guidance. When signs of readiness are anticipated for mothers most of them are able to provide the experiences their infants require.

However, there will be some mothers who miss their infants' cues because their own needs blind them to the needs of their babies. When a mother blocks her child's opportunities for growth because of her own needs she is unaware that she is doing it. She is also unaware of the needs within herself she is seeking to satisfy. This is not something for which the mother should be punished by criticism. Had her early needs been met she would know intuitively what her infant required.

Instead of admonition the mother who frustrates her infant's opportunities for growth needs the kind of assistance that will bring satisfaction to her as well as to her child. With help many of these mothers can gain insight into their infants' needs. They can also be helped to find ways of obtaining substitute satisfactions for themselves. If the nurse can help the mother develop technics of guidance which bring her feelings of success, she will contribute to the happiness of both mother and child. When a mother finds that her thoughtfulness and effort have stimulated her infant's growth, she will feel rewarded. It will help her to relinquish her infant's dependence upon her, and tolerate the interruptions and increased responsibility which an exploring infant's activity requires. Giving the mother opportunities to talk about her infant's accomplishments gives her gratification and helps her to appreciate the role she plays in her child's growth toward self-mastery.

Another way of helping a mother find substitute satisfaction is through guidance which assists her in developing her latent powers of observation. Many mothers do not know how to observe because they have never been motivated to learn. As a result they have never discovered the pleasure that can be derived from it. Without powers of observation, infant care can become monotonous and frustrating. With the ability to observe, infant care provides opportunities for constant learning and the pleasure that comes when babies' needs are fulfilled.

Care based on observation of the infant's needs not only brings him pleasure and provides what he needs for growth but also gives his mother the satisfaction that comes from knowing a piece of work is well done. When the mother has observed and interpreted her child's behavior and has responded to the need he disclosed in that behavior, she senses she has contributed to his fulfillment. It is this realization which brings feelings of accomplishment and pride in her capabilities.

When a baby gets what he needs to achieve his goal, be it relief from hunger or opportunity to practice a new skill, he communicates his feelings of gratitude and gives his mother pleasure. He feels understood and loved! He conveys these feelings not in words but in his behavior. He responds to the person who has provided fulfillment. It is the positive responses which give the mother her pleasure. Helping the mother learn how to get this kind of responsiveness is one of the objectives of health supervision. It is also the objective of the supervisor who is guiding her students toward increased enjoyment in working with children.

WEANING—THE INFANT'S FIRST CRUCIAL STEP IN ADAPTATION TO REALITY

Necessity of Gratification and Frustration for Growth

Spitz[9] says the infant requires age-adequate stimulation through gratification and through frustration for personality growth. Up until the sixth or the seventh month of life our concern is in the infant's gratification, for he needs a period of complete fulfillment to become ready to meet the crucial frustrations necessary for personality growth. When frustrations are introduced at the time the infant is ready for them he profits from them and reaches a stage of greater independence which brings him new pleasures as a substitute for the old. Spitz[9] says:

> In the course of the life of the infant and the growing child the time for imposing necessary frustrations is when the child has reached the level of physical development, nervous and muscular, to carry out the demand; and when he has reached the level of psychological development which is needed to understand the demand or the prohibition, to adapt to it, to deal with it, and to turn it into an advantage in his further development. When that stage has arrived the demand should be made.

To continue to give the child whatever he wants when he wants it beyond the time he shows readiness to master the frustration or demand is as damaging as neglect.[9] This is true because it fails to take into account the child's need and desire to grow increasingly more independent. The mature mother or nurse will expect neither too much nor too little of a child; she will neither demand the impossible nor retard his progress toward independence.

It is the *time* and the *way* demands are made upon the child and the way he is helped to master the anxiety which comes with frustration that is important for emotional health. To know when to introduce age-adequate frustrations or demands is a difficult problem. Children's drives differ in their intensity and tolerance for frustration shows wide variation.

The child's behavior at the time a frustration is introduced is a more reliable index of his readiness to adapt to reality than is his chronologic age. Textbooks can give the approximate time when children develop bodily and mental skills. They cannot, however, give a formula which will be the answer to an individual child's capacity to meet specific frustrations involved in the socialization process. A child's readiness for frustration is not only the result of physical maturation; it is also determined by his previous emotional experiences with his mother.

The child's behavior will provide the clues the mother or nurse needs to socialize a child in a way which brings satisfaction to him and to society. The child will show us the way if we learn to observe and to interpret his behavior. He will show signs of physical and psychological readiness and signs which indicate his feelings concerning the demand being made upon him.

The infant needs help in becoming ready to endure frustrations. He also needs understanding of the feelings that arise as his desires are thwarted. Then he can relinquish old patterns of behavior and gain pleasure in the acquisition of the new.

READINESS FOR WEANING AS PROTECTION OF THE INFANT'S MENTAL HEALTH

Finding Pleasure in Motor and Sensory Activity Helps the Infant Tolerate Frustration. Through exercise and play the infant finds he can get pleasure from his own activity; it prepares him to give up that which has given him pleasure earlier. If his cues have been utilized and he has had opportunities to explore he will begin to separate himself physically from his mother about the sixth or the seventh month of life. At approximately the same time he will begin to show interest in learning to participate in the feeding process. He will push his mother's hands from the bottle and show his inclination to hold it himself. A little later he will reach toward the cup, clasp it in his hands and draw it to his mouth. He may spill the contents in the process but his interest in self-activity needs recognition and encouragement. At the breast he will show his readiness to be weaned when he shortens his nursing time and strives to have more activity than the position in his mother's arms permit.[10]

Acquiring Positive Feelings Toward the Spoon and the Cup Helps the Infant Become Prepared for the Weaning Process. Like the early spoon feedings, experiences with the cup should also bring pleasure. The infant can be helped to enjoy drinking from a cup just as he learned to enjoy the use of the spoon. When the infant's need for sucking has lessened and he has acquired positive feelings with the use of the cup, he will begin to show signs that indicate his readiness to discard the bottle or to lessen his time at the breast. If breast feeding must be discontinued before the sixth month of life the infant will need to be weaned to the bottle rather than to the cup.

Between the fourth and the sixth months of life most infants are ready to learn to take sips of milk from a cup. If the baby is being breast fed, sips of pasteurized milk can be offered to test his interest in learning. Learning to drink from a cup is a slow process. The infant learns best if small amounts are given and his efforts are rewarded with words or gestures which communicate his mother's pride in his accomplishment.

Acquiring the Capacity to Feel Love from His Mother's Smiles, Words and Gestures Prepares the Infant for the Weaning Process. If the infant's early feeding experiences have combined food, physical closeness to his mother, smiles and loving words not only will he have learned to anticipate fulfillment of his needs but also he will recognize her as an object apart from himself and be able to take in feelings of love and acceptance in ways other than through close physical contact. He will be able to sense love in his mother's words, smiles and gestures because they have been repeatedly associated with the most pleasurable part of his early experience. He will *know* and feel that love comes from behavior as well as from the bottle or breast. The acquisition of this capacity will further assist him in adapting to weaning.

AN UNDERSTANDING METHOD OF WEANING AS PROTECTION OF THE CHILD'S MENTAL HEALTH

When the infant has acquired the above accomplishments he has the inner resources he needs to begin the socialization process which will bring both frustration and rewards. He has the ego strength necessary to withstand short periods of frustration. He does not have to have his food at once. He can wait a few minutes while it is being prepared if he is placed where he can see and hear his mother as he plays with his toys.

He is also ready to begin the weaning process which is a stimulus to growth. Weaning is one of the first crucial steps an infant must take in learning to adapt to reality. If it is done gradually at the infant's own rate of speed, he will accept and profit from it. In many instances he may even welcome it because he finds enjoyment in a new activity. It will bring some measure of frustration because weaning necessitates giving up something which is a familiar pleasure but it will also bring enjoyment. Successful weaning gives the infant increased mastery of himself. It is this and the mother's pleasure in his accomplishment which will provide the substitute satisfactions that make the frustration possible.

The baby needs to be weaned in accordance with his capacity to tolerate frustration. When the infant takes a goodly quantity of milk from the cup and enjoys the experience, the bottle or the breast can be eliminated at that particular feeding. When his intake from the cup is small and he expresses resentment at the use of the cup, his feelings merit respect and his former method of feeding should be resumed. Behavior of this kind is observed most often in the evening when the baby is tired and has insufficient energy to adapt in his accustomed way. Fatigue brings regression. When the baby is fatigued he needs the solace which comes from the bottle or the breast.

If the infant's cues are followed, weaning becomes a gradual process and one that stimulates healthy personality development. It is not something which is done according to a prescribed schedule; it is an experience which is planned in accordance with the infant's capacity to meet a new way of doing things. It is not a depriving, heartless process but an experience in helping the baby find satisfaction in the growing-up process.

It is the child's feelings of love for his mother and his identification with her which motivate him to want to do those things he sees his mother doing. When he is ready to experiment with a new method of drinking, his interest should be utilized for it is then that new accomplishments are acquired most easily. When the above method of weaning is utilized, most babies use the cup exclusively by the end of the first year of life. Some babies continue to need a bottle in the evening beyond that time but the majority will give it up willingly if they are given a substitute pleasure at the time of sleep.

Maintaining poise and affectionate understanding during weaning prevents the infant from experiencing anxiety with the withdrawal of the breast or the bottle. During weaning the infant's intake of milk often becomes lessened. This will be temporary if the mother accepts it as a natural occurrence and inhibits her inclination to force the infant to take something he does not desire. Additional play experiences with the mother in this period will help him know that he is still loved even though the breast or the bottle has been withdrawn. Weaning comes at a time when he is awake for longer periods of time and ready for more active periods of play and social stimulation.

The satisfactory completion of weaning marks the decline of the dominance of the oral phase of personality development which is characterized by complete dependency, utter uncontrolledness and the need for maximum oral gratification and physical closeness to the mother.

ABRUPT WEANING, AN INJURY TO PERSONALITY DEVELOPMENT

STUNTING OF PERSONALITY GROWTH BY INSUFFICIENT GRATIFICATION

Weaning can be a traumatic experience which retards future emotional growth. If done abruptly before the infant's needs for sucking and impulses toward the breast are satisfied, it brings feelings of loss of love and anger, for food and love have come to have synonymous meaning to him.[6] When an infant does not receive optimal gratification during the oral phase of personality development, he continues to have unsatisfied dependent longings. These longings affect the adjustment he makes to all subsequent phases of psychosocial development. Instead of feeling loved, he goes through life feeling unsatisfied and reacts as if he felt he had not received all he had coming to him. His wants are insatiable for he attempts to compensate for quality by demanding a quantity which is completely unattainable in reality. Within him there is a pervading feeling of discontent which destroys his ability to be satisfied with what he gets and leaves him perpetually tense and anxious. When this occurs, the individual is said to be fixated at the oral level of personality development.

The individual who has been deprived during this period of his life may solve his problem in one or several ways. He may deny his dependent longings and become a "go-getter," an executive or one who directs the activity of others. He will undoubtedly be successful but within his unconscious is a feeling of resentment and longing because he did not get enough of what he needed. His conflict eventually may become expressed in psychosomatic or mental illness, or he may go through life feeling dissatisfied with all his accomplishments. There are others who erect no defenses against their dependent longings. They are the ones who are always taking yet never getting enough to satisfy them. They take from society instead of contributing to it not because they want to be greedy, self-centered and demanding but because they have not received enough to gain the ego strength necessary to seek satisfaction through their own activity and to adapt to the realities of adult life and learn to function on the "reality principle." They cannot wait for gratification and give up their own desires; they continue to function on the "pleasure principle" throughout their lives.

NURSING CARE IN PROTECTING THE INFANT FROM TRAUMA

When a child is ill he needs protection from frustration which he is unable to tolerate. When an infant is ill he has little energy to use in making an adjustment to a new kind of feeding experience. If he is a breast-fed infant he needs his mother with him to prevent the anxiety that comes when breast feedings are discontinued abruptly. If the mother cannot be with her infant and hospitalization demands abrupt weaning from the breast, substitute consistent mothering is imperative. This is necessary for the above reasons and to assist the infant in accepting a new food and a new method of feeding.

When an infant has an illness which necessitates the elimination of oral feedings, he will need a great deal of motherly care to prevent overwhelming anxiety. A pacifier, unless contraindicated medically, often brings a degree of comfort if it is used in addition to other comfort-giving nursing care. An infant will swallow air as he sucks upon a pacifier but he will get infinitely less air into his gastrointestinal tract than he would if he spent long periods in screaming.

If illness strikes when the baby is in the process of being weaned to the cup, he may temporarily show his need for sucking by turning away from the cup or pushing it from the nurse's hands. This indicates the baby's unreadiness to resume his former pattern of behavior.

Convalescence brings a change of needs which require satisfaction. If his needs for play and social stimulation are satisfied, his readiness for weaning will again manifest itself. If his needs for play and social stimulation are not met, he will cling to the bottle and not progress to the stage he was in prior to the acute phase of his illness. When the baby has recuperated from the acute phase of his illness, the nurse can test his capacity to accept the cup from her. If progress is made, it shows that the baby is ready to continue weaning. If the above principles are utilized in handling weaning, the baby will profit from the experience. Unless the infant can have a continuing warm relationship with a nurse, little accomplishment can be expected. The situation which follows describes an infant's response to the maternal deprivation that came when illness necessitated abrupt weaning and separation from his mother. It also describes the specific nursing care which relieved his distress.

Prior to his illness, Jerry was an active, healthy, 5-month-old youngster who got relief from tension through his sucking activity, through gross motor play and through bodily contact with his mother. Jerry's illness came on suddenly. He was happily playing when all of a sudden he seemed stricken with acute abdominal pain. He shrieked, pulled his legs up on to his abdomen and turned pale. Nothing would pacify him, which was unusual behavior for Jerry. Previously, a little cuddling or rocking would relieve his distress, and in a short time he would again be ready to resume his play or go off to sleep. His mother tried to breast feed him, but he turned from an experience which formerly he had welcomed with eagerness. Before long he began to vomit and in the course of the next few hours he passed blood and mucus from his intestinal tract.

Fortunately, Jerry's mother recognized the seriousness of his condition and brought him into the hospital, where a diagnosis of intussusception was made. A part of Jerry's intestine had telescoped itself into the portion of intestine immediately below it cutting off circulation and bringing acute pain, vomiting, small stools of blood and mucus, and eventually symptoms of prostration or shock.

Jerry was taken to surgery soon after admission to the hospital. The intussusception was reduced with manipulation, and Jerry was returned to the ward in excellent physical condition. Both arms were restrained at his sides to prevent him from removing the catheter which was inserted into his stomach and connected at the other end to a Wangensteen suction apparatus. His left leg was also immobilized to a board to keep the intravenous needle secure in his ankle vein. Over his abdomen was a dressing which protected his surgical wound.

It was not long before Jerry began to show signs of acute emotional distress. Sedatives did not quiet him, nor did they bring a state of relaxation which Jerry was seeking through the only channels available to him. One leg was free of restraint and it was in constant motion. He screamed incessantly. His body was rigid, and his fontanel tense.

Jerry's illness necessitated abrupt weaning from the breast and a hospital experience which brought not only the pain of separation from his mother but also restrictions that prevented him from obtaining any relief from tension through his own activity. Jerry was suffering from an acute state of anxiety. He could not have fluids by mouth, nor could he be freed from immobilization without jeopardizing the position of the catheter or the intravenous needle securely fastened in his vein. Besides, he needed the oxygen that flowed into the tent enclosing the upper part of his body.

In an attempt to give Jerry relief from his tension, a pacifier was placed against his lips. The avidity with which he sought the pacifier and utilized it to obtain relief and relaxation was sufficient evidence to prove it was an effective temporary substitute for the breast he so desired and needed. He sucked vigorously, and as he did relaxation came. The tension lessened. The nurse could see it subsiding and she could feel it in his legs, arm and body. Jerry went to sleep, but his sucking continued.

The next day the catheter was removed, and an oxygen tent was no longer necessary. Periodically, when Jerry showed a need for physical closeness, the restraints were loosened and Jerry was held in his nurse's arms. His leg was still immobilized for intravenous fluid therapy, but care in lifting and handling Jerry prevented the needle from becoming dislodged from its position in the vein. The following day oral feedings were resumed, and in another 24 hours Jerry was ready for milk feedings. His mother came at intervals to feed him, and it was not long before Jerry began to smile and to resume his former patterns of playful activities.

QUESTIONS TO GUIDE OBSERVATION

1. What are the factors that help a new baby to become better organized?

2. If a mother indicated her need of help in knowing how to accustom her baby to new foods, what would you do and say?

3. Of what importance are the mother's feelings in the feeding situation?

4. How can thumb-sucking in the preschool period be prevented?

5. Describe an infant under 1 year of age who is your patient.

What are his needs? How does he communicate them to you? How did you feel about him when you were first assigned to him? After 2 weeks? What new things have you learned about him that help you provide more individualized care for him?

6. What makes babies bite? How would you feel if a year-old child bit you? What would you do?

7. Observe a baby of 10 to 12 months of age. How does he respond to different sensory stimuli? Of what value to you is a knowledge of sensory perception and the way in which it develops?

8. Observe a baby of 1 year of age and describe his motor development. Is he functioning according to the norms of development? If not, why isn't he? How has his physical condition influenced his motor development? How does his mother respond to his need for motor activity? What is the infant's reaction to his mother's response?

9. Observe infants of 1 month, 6 months and 1 year of age. Indicate some of the differences you observed in their motor activity. Observe 2 or 3 infants of approximately the same age and indicate the differences in their behavior. Describe their personalities, showing how they differ from one another. Have you any clues as to the factors which make them different from one another? If so, what are they?

10. What are some of the characteristics of infants in this phase of personality growth? What difficulties, if any, have you had in your relationship with infants in this period of development?

11. How can the nurse establish and maintain a positive relationship with an infant in this period of development?

12. If a mother in a well-baby conference anticipated weaning her baby in the near future and asked you for help in learning how to do it, how would you help her?

13. How does weaning affect personality development?

14. Observe a newly admitted baby who had been breast fed prior to his illness. What behavior characteristics did you observe? How did he respond to separation from his mother? How may this illness affect his personality development? What nursing care is required to prevent personality injury?

15. How does one know when a baby is ready to adapt himself to frustration? What are the signs indicating that a baby is ready to begin the weaning process?

REFERENCES

1. Aldrich, C. A.: Babies Are Human Beings, New York, Macmillan, 1946.
2. Burlingham, Dorothy, and Freud, Anna: Infants Without Families, New York, Willard, 1934.
3. English, O. S., and Pearson, G. H.: The Psychosexual development of the child, Chapter 2, p. 18, in Common Neurosis of Children and Adults, New York, Norton, 1937.
4. Fries, Margaret: The child's ego development and the training of adults in his environment, p. 85 in The Psychoanalytic Study of the Child, vol. 2, New York, Internat. Univ. Press, 1947.
5. Gesell, Arnold, and others: Forty weeks old, p. 116 in The Infant and Child in the Culture of Today, New York, Harpers, 1943.
6. Isaacs, Susan: The Nursery Years, New York, Vanguard, 1929.
7. Lemkau, Paul: Mental Hygiene in Public Health, New York, McGraw-Hill, 1949.
8. Saul, Leon: Bases of Human Behavior, Philadelphia, Lippincott, 1951.
9. Spitz, Rene: Steps to maturity: what it means to grow up, Child Study 28:3, 1950-1951.
10. Spock, Benjamin: Weaning from bottle to cup, p. 182, and Weaning from the breast, p. 45, in Common Sense Book of Babies and Child Care, New York, Duell, Sloan & Pearce, 1945.

5

Development and Care During the Training Period (1 to 3 Years)

NEED OF INFANTS FOR HELP IN LEARNING TO SHARE THEIR OBJECT
    OF LOVE

ACQUIRING BOWEL CONTROL

ACQUIRING BLADDER CONTROL

RIGID PERFECTIONISTIC TRAINING A HINDRANCE TO THE CHILD IN MAKING
    A HEALTHY SOLUTION TO HIS PROBLEM

ILLNESS AND SEPARATION FROM THE MOTHER AND RESULTING
    REGRESSION

LANGUAGE GROWTH

DISCIPLINE AS UNDERSTANDING GUIDANCE

In this phase of personality development the child is ready to gain increased mastery of himself and his environment. It is a safer and much less threatening period because the child is a little less helpless and has the capacity to meet more of his own needs for gratification. *In this phase of development the child needs to gain increased mastery of his fear of separation and to learn to share his object of love. He needs to learn some of the customs and standards of his society, to grow increasingly more able to communicate with speech and to find ways of expressing his new-found individuality and powers in ways that will enhance his growth potentials.*

The child can accomplish the above tasks if he has received optimal gratification in the preceding months of life and is guided by adults who understand his feelings concerning the problems and anxieties he is expected to master now. It is not easy for the child to give up the pleasures of the earlier period and to learn to meet some of the standards of his society. However, he can and will if he is ready and desirous of learning and finds life in this period enjoyable and nonthreatening to his peace of mind. If he has had his early needs fulfilled but finds in this period more frustration than he can master, his energy will be used to handle anxiety. As a result he will have insufficient energy available for personality growth. If the problems of the period bring more pain than joy, regression to a stage which formerly brought satisfaction is apt to be the outcome.

NEED OF INFANTS FOR HELP IN LEARNING TO SHARE THEIR OBJECT OF LOVE

By the end of the first year of life, the child's relationship with his mother has grown deeper and become personally more meaningful to him. He recognizes that it is his mother who provides protection, love and pleasurable experiences and that he could not survive without her.

The change in the intensity of the child's relationship with his mother and the recognition of his own dependence upon her makes him long for her constant attention and interest, and fearful whenever she is out of his sight. The game of "Peek-a-Boo" which the baby plays is more than an enjoyable game; it is a way of mastering his fear of separation from his mother. In bringing his mother back through his own power, he gains some degree of mastery of his separation anxiety. Later "Hide and Seek" serves a similar purpose. He discovers through playing that his mother will search to find him and he discovers he has the power to bring her back through his own activity.

For the first year of life the child feels he is the center of the universe and is unaware that there are others who are also important to his mother. However, he gradually becomes increasingly sensitive to the fact that there are others whom his mother loves. If the infant has older brothers or sisters (or siblings, as they are often called), he becomes resentful and rivalrous with them. He wishes they were nonexistent so he might be the recipient of all his mother's love.[6] However, he discovers that his mother expects him to like them and to share her love with them. These feelings bring conflict and fear. *The infant needs help to accept his older siblings and to learn that he is still loved even though he is the possessor and expresser of hostile feelings toward others in his family.*

Many mothers need this phase of development interpreted to them so they can be ready to help their babies share them with their other children. When a mother has insight into the problem with which the child is struggling, she will provide the understanding he requires. She will be able to accept her child's increased demandingness and expressions of hostility to her and to his older siblings. When a mother is helped to recognize the genesis of her child's anxiety and demandingness, she will be more able to show him she has enough love for all members of her family. It is not through words but through fulfillment of his needs that the infant discovers this. When the youngster becomes assured that his need for love and care will be fulfilled, his fear of loss of love will subside and his equilibrium will become re-established. Demanding and clinging behavior will lessen and the child's energy will be freed to begin tackling his next task.

The change in the intensity of the child's relationship with his mother, coupled with his awareness of his great need for her, serves a purpose for the child's development; it is the basis upon which the child becomes an increasingly more socialized individual. The child senses that his mother expects him to like his siblings. He learns to do so because of this expectation and because he wants her approval and needs to retain her love.[6]

If hospitalization is necessary during this phase of the child's development and hospital policy requires that he be separated from his mother, one can imagine the grief he will experience and understand how it will increase his difficulties in mastering his fear of loss of love and the other tasks of the period. The young child cannot understand why separation is necessary. Nor can he understand that his mother wants to be with him but is excluded by hospital policy. But he can feel, and frightening and angry feelings are devastating, both physically and psychologically.

Daily periods when the mother and the child can be together in the hospital will precipitate the expression of strong feelings but they are better ventilated than buried within the child. They will also help to ease his fear of abandonment. Expression of strong feelings should be anticipated for the mother and interpreted as a means of helping the child rid himself of the feelings separation has brought. Unless the mother understands the reasons for his violent reactions to her coming and leave-taking, and is able to handle her feelings which may be aroused by his impetuous and clinging behavior, she may decide to stay away to keep herself comfortable.

Opportunities to observe the developmental characteristics described above are available in pediatric wards. When a young child has had an opportunity to form an attachment to a nurse whom he has come to feel is his own, he manifests similar behavior which shows his need and wish to have his nurse as a constant companion and all to himself. Observation of Patty with her nurse serves to exemplify the behavior described above.

Patty, aged 15 months, was having a difficult time adapting herself to the deprivation her mother's illness brought. Her mother was hospitalized for tuberculosis, and Patty was admitted for observation.

Her daddy visited daily but that did not mitigate the grief she was experiencing for her mother, nor did it lessen her fear. Patty could not eat or play and grew more wan and anxious as each day passed.

A nurse was assigned to give Patty care each morning. Her objective was to establish and maintain a relationship with her which would provide opportunities for her to express her grief, anger and anxiety and to find pleasure. Each morning she bathed and fed Patty. Prior to hospitalization Patty had learned to feed herself but separation brought regression and she demanded to be fed. The nurse fulfilled her designated requirements and spent time holding and soothing her. Whenever Patty said, "Mamma, where Mamma?" and began to cry, she was permitted freedom to ventilate her feelings to obtain relief from her tension and grief.

During the first 2 weeks the nurse cared for her, Patty's anxiety was acute and she needed constant reassurance that she would have her needs fulfilled. She required holding and could not nap unless she was rocked before she was placed upon her bed. In the second week Patty began to enjoy mealtimes and could play by herself for short periods of time. Patty's nurse was also giving care to another child. When she left Patty to care for her other patient, she told her where she was going and when she would return. When she returned she would say something like the following: "Patty, I did come back. I'll always come back when I tell you I will." Patty could not understand all the words but she seemed to catch the nurse's sympathetic feeling and through repeated experiences she learned she was not alone with her grief.

Little by little Patty showed evidence that she was beginning to trust her nurse. At first she cried when her nurse left her. Gradually, however, her crying lessened and became replaced with a facial expression which disclosed remnants of uneasiness she had not yet mastered. She had experienced one separation and it could happen again. Patty's relationship with her nurse was not a relaxed one; it was anxiety-ridden because of what she had experienced before.

One day 10-year-old Jim who was ambulatory appeared in Patty's doorway. Patty grew agitated and began to chatter at the nurse they were sharing to get her undivided attention. Patty's nurse met her need for reassurance by saying, "Yes, Patty, I'm going to stay here. I love you both and I can take care of both of you." Then she continued to give Jim the help he was seeking. Soon Patty pulled at her nurse's gown, pointed to the chair and with gestures which could not be mistaken indicated her wish to have her sit down beside her. With her other hand, Patty communicated her desire for undivided attention by waving Jim from the doorway. "Bye, bye," she said, with affect which suggested the intensity of her feeling. Jim showed his understanding of Patty's words, gestures and feelings and said, "I guess she doesn't want me here. She acts as if she feels it was her turn to have you to herself. I'll go to the playroom until she is ready to let you go."

Infants in the hospital will show more anxiety, demandingness and clinging behavior than do babies at home. They have already experienced one separation and that makes them fearful lest it be repeated.

ACQUIRING BOWEL CONTROL

The Infant's Derivation of Pleasure from His Excretory Function and Products

During the first year (and throughout all of life) the infant derives pleasure from his body and its functioning. Although oral activity brought the greatest pleasure, the infant was also experiencing pleasurable sensations in other parts of his body, particularly from his skin and the organs involved in the digestive and the excretory processes. *The infant needs a mother who accepts all parts of him and also permits him to experience maximum gratification from wetting and soiling.* Only after he has experienced maximum pleasure will he relinquish it and want to do those things he sees others doing.

The young infant excretes urine and feces whenever his bladder or rectum is stimulated by pressure. He has no capacity to inhibit release of his sphincter muscles. He eliminates anywhere and at any time. It makes no difference to him whether he is on the scales completely nude or in his crib with a diaper in place to protect those about him from becoming soiled. Elimination of stools and urine releases physiologic tension and brings pleasureable sensations. The infant's primary interest is his comfort.

Toward the end of the first year of life the infant begins to demonstrate his fascination with the products of his body which are as yet undifferentiated from himself. Later he learns to differentiate feces from himself and he comes to value it as a creation of his own making. He sees nothing shameful about his feces. Instead, he finds there is pleasure in feeling, smelling and manipulating it. He shows no disgust even with its flavor. It is difficult for the baby to understand that he is accepted if his mother shows dislike of what he produces. It is also difficult for him to comprehend why soiling, messiness and interest in his creation are unacceptable to her. *The infant needs a mother who is not disgusted by his interest in the products of his excretory tract and can redirect his exploratory activities into acceptable channels without creating feelings of shame.*

The Child's Incorporation of Maternal Feelings

Before the end of the first year, the infant is keenly aware of his mother's feelings and constantly is being influenced by them. He has become adept at interpreting them from her facial expression, her tone of voice and her behavior. If she is pleased with his accomplishments, he feels it even though she utters no words. If the infant's mother accepts her child's pleasure in soiling and his interest in his productions, he will acquire the same feelings as she. This phenomenon is called *internalization*. It simply means the taking in of feelings and attitudes and making them a part of oneself.

The infant has to learn that urine and feces are waste, invaluable and inappropriate as play materials, but he can do so without feeling they are disgusting or bad. If the infant acquires feelings of shame and disgust in connection with the excretory organs, it is highly probable that he will come to associate them with his genital organs. Such feelings increase his problems in the periods to come.

LEARNING SOCIAL CUSTOMS THROUGH THE MOTHER'S INTERPRETATION OF THEM

Our society's toileting customs are different from those observed in some foreign lands. Our society imposes restrictions upon its members which individuals must learn to accept. There is a designated place and a time for elimination.

In some parts of the world children are not required to adapt themselves to such standards or customs—they never experience the "training" period. In some societies children wear no pants and there are no toilets to use for elimination. In others, children are dressed in pants that are open to facilitate elimination. Children in the latter society eliminate whenever the urge comes. If they are outside, they squat over the ground to relieve themselves. They need no help in removing their clothing or in getting onto a toilet. With neuromuscular development the interval between evacuations becomes lengthened. These children mature physically but they are not required to learn that there is a time and a place to eliminate.

The child's mother is his teacher and the interpreter of our society's expectations and standards. Learning to use the toilet is an important social affair involving both mother and child. The mother begins to make demands on her child by showing him her custom. The child begins to develop the capacity to give in return for what he has received. When he finds he gets more pleasure from giving and being "grown-up," he is willing to relinquish his primitive impulses to soil indiscriminately for he has discovered something more satisfying.

Toilet Training Influences the Child's Personality Development.
During the period the child is acquiring mastery of his body functions, maternal attitudes and feelings are of prime importance for
they become reflected in the mother's method of guidance. The
way a child is toilet trained influences his give-and-take relationships throughout his lifetime, for in the process of training he will
develop patterns of behavior that will become a part of his personality structure. The standards, attitudes and feelings he acquires
eventually will become incorporated into the part of his personality
called the superego. In the process of learning to control bodily
functions, the child's psychic structure is becoming formed. The
child's mind does not develop as a separate entity—mind and body
are a part of a whole, and the development and functioning of one
part affect the other.

Toilet Training Brings Conflict Which Requires Understanding. Training in the control of excretory functions involves infinitely more than the acquisition of socialized toilet habits; it
involves the child's feelings about his mother (authority), his body
and his capacities, and determines how he will express his emotions.
*To guide a child so that he experiences the minimum amount of
frustration, anger and fear his mother needs to feel with him and
to see the meaning of the experience from his point of view.*

Acquiring habits of cleanliness is not an easy process for the
child. He senses his mother is asking something of him which is
difficult to achieve. Even when readiness is acquired, he will feel
some degree of frustration, conflict and fear. In the training experience the child must cope with two opposing needs. He wants
and needs to be secure in his mother's love, for that relieves him of
anxiety concerning possible punishment or disapproval. At the
same time he wants freedom from the discomfort that comes whenever instinctual needs remain unsatisfied. He wants bodily comfort
but at the same time he wants self-mastery and the praise of his
mother.

During this period the child has varied feelings which he cannot communicate verbally to his mother or nurse; he can only show
them in his response to what is happening to him. However, his
mother can interpret his communications. If she has insight into
her child's feelings he will feel understood, be ready to make sacrifices for her and be able to gain mastery of himself without acquiring distortions in his personality. This is the healthy solution for

the child to make to his problem and the one he needs assistance in making.

Readiness Is Essential for Learning. *An infant needs physiologic and psychological readiness to participate in the training experience.* When a child has acquired the capacity to creep and walk, he grows increasingly more interested in everything that everyone does. He observes, imitates and glories in each of his new accomplishments. Success spurs him on. Within him there is an urge to do what others do, a need to please his mother and a potent drive to master himself.

Physiologic readiness to begin mastering bowel control comes about the time the infant acquires the capacity to stand and walk.[14] At this time voluntary rectal sphincter control becomes more reliable and he can retain feces in his rectum for a longer period of time. By this time most infants have also established a regular daytime pattern of defecation and show through their facial expression and the production of grunting sounds that they have made a connection between their need to expel feces and the activity entailed in the process. The above are the *physiologic* signs that indicate readiness to co-operate.

Psychological readiness to begin mastering bowel control comes simultaneously with the above accomplishment. After weaning, Josselyn[14] has observed that oral gratification becomes partially displaced to the anal area and prepares the child for the "training" process. This psychological change centers the child's interest in excretory functions and products and shows his *psychological* readiness to profit from a new learning experience. His interest is his cue which demonstrates his readiness to co-operate and to master his primitive impulses.

Waiting for readiness ensures not only healthy physiologic functioning but also success which brings feelings of adequacy and self-esteem and protects his mental health. However, signs of readiness do not mean that the child is able to co-operate consistently. This takes time. In the process of learning there will be times when the child is not able to wait until he reaches the toilet. Such times are inevitable and nothing to be discouraged about. If his mother understands that "accidents" are a natural part of the training experience the child will not grow discouraged and dissatisfied with himself.[12]

The infant needs his autonomy respected for it helps him to achieve self-mastery with a greater degree of comfort. If he is placed on the potty chair when he shows he has a need to defecate, he will soon co-operate if his mother shows pride and praises him for successful performance and refrains from showing disapproval at times when he is unable to function. When he is first placed on the potty chair he may whimper or show resistance to the new experience in other ways. These are natural reactions to a change in activity. In a few seconds he will have given vent to his feelings and be ready to participate. If his feelings concerning interruption of an already established way of doing things are accepted with poise, he will feel understood. A need to demonstrate resistance will then be unnecessary.

When a mother shows recognition of her child's ability to co-operate, she rewards him with her approval. He gives and gets something in return. Alexander[1] says:

> In some such manner the excrement becomes associated with the concept of possession. This explains its close relation to money, which is one of the best-established facts uncovered by psychoanalysis. Every excremental act is evaluated by the child as a kind of donation to the adults, an attitude often reinforced by the mother's great interest in the child's excrement. (The German expression for the bowel movement of the child, "Bescherung," means gift.)

The situation which follows demonstrates 4-year-old Jim's acquisition of this concept.

> Jim was playing with a toy monkey and assuming the role of the organ grinder he had been observing with keen interest. Jimmy made his monkey dance and then said, "I'm the organ grinder man. The monkey wants some money." The nurse playing with Jimmy took scraps of paper and handed them to the monkey. As she did so she said, "Here's some money for you." Jim took the money, placed it at the monkey's anal area and returned it to the nurse. In the process he said, "He puts it here. Now he is giving it to you." The nurse accepted it with pleasure. To Jim it was gift giving and the nurse received it in the spirit in which it was given.
>
> A few minutes later Jim danced the monkey across the room. At this point the stitching at the monkey's anal area broke. The beans with which the monkey was stuffed rolled out upon the floor. Jim looked amazed and anxious. The nurse said, "The monkey likes you. He is giving you something." Jim's quick response to this remark was, "No, he is giving *you* something. Do you want it? Close your eyes." The nurse closed her eyes. Jimmy picked up every bean, placed them under his buttocks and said, "Now open your eyes." Jim withdrew the beans from under his buttocks and gave them to the nurse.

At the time of the above play, Jim was in conflict and expressing it with constipation. He would hold his feces for days, but when holding back took more power than he possessed, bits of stool would come out and become strewn upon the floor. When the monkey's stitching broke and the beans rolled out, Jim may well have been reminded of his own dilemma.

Preventing hard stools and the pain associated with their elimination is of special importance during infancy and during the time the child is being accustomed to the use of the toilet. If evacuation brings him pain on the toilet he will acquire unpleasant associations with it. He will come to dread it and to refuse its use instead of enjoying it. The introduction of prune juice and additional fruits and vegetables into his diet may be all that is necessary to soften his stools and to make evacuation comfortable. In other instances, the advice of a doctor may be required.

ACQUIRING BLADDER CONTROL

THE INFANT'S DEVELOPMENT OF READINESS TO BEGIN USING THE TOILET FOR URINATION

The child needs readiness to learn to use the toilet for urination just as he needed it to master bowel control. This readiness develops later than readiness to adapt to its use for defecation. If frustration and anxiety have been kept to a minimum during the period his mother was helping him learn that there is a specific place for defecation, and if he has acquired only pleasant associations with the toilet and his mother, learning to master bladder functioning will be an easier process.

Later development of readiness to acquire bladder control is due partly to neuromuscular development and partly to the fact that urination is a more frequent occurrence. During the first year of life, a baby voids from 20 to 24 times in a 24-hour period. Gradually, his bladder develops the capacity to hold urine for a longer period of time. Then he develops sensitivity to the feeling of a full bladder and connects it with the idea that the toilet is also used for urinating and that his mother needs to know he is ready for assistance in learning. Making these connections is dependent upon both physiologic and psychological development. Until the child's brain can receive the message and respond to it with appropriate behavior, his mother can "catch" his urine if she is a keen observer and a methodical worker but the training is hers and not the child's.

Spock[21] says there is little value in attempting to help the child master bladder control unless he has developed the capacity to retain urine for a 2-hour period. This seems to be the most logical criterion for estimating a child's readiness for an occasional experience on the toilet for urinating. The capacity to retain urine for a 2-hour period is acquired usually about the fifteenth to the eighteenth month of life. Even then it is usually not a consistent pattern. At first the child may be able to hold urine for a 2-hour period only once a day. Some days he may not be able to retain it that long at all, and it may be months before it becomes regular enough to help him remain dry throughout an entire day. When it becomes a fairly consistent pattern, the use of training panties helps the child to feel more grown-up and lessens the restriction in movement that applying diapers entails. In this period he needs to be kept dry so that he becomes accustomed to the feeling of dryness and learns to enjoy it.

Helping Mothers to Gain Insight into the Facts of Development

When a mother is helped to gain understanding of the developmental process, she will base her expectations upon her child's capacities and interests rather than upon her own desire for achievement. She will know her child is not ready for an immediate regimen of frequent toileting throughout the day just because he has achieved a little more capacity to co-operate. She will make training a gradual process and expect co-operation only when she knows his bladder is about ready to empty itself.

Mothers need to know that a child goes through many stages before he is able verbally to communicate his need to go to the toilet. First, he will develop consciousness of his wetness and indicate the occurrence of urination to his mother. *This is a sign of increased maturation; it is progress in learning, and the child needs to receive recognition for each new accomplishment.* Anticipating this phase of development to mothers will prevent them from misinterpreting it. Unless mothers know that recognition of urination and wetness comes *before* recognition of his need to urinate, they might scold their children when they are in need of praise. Reporting of accidents is usual around the eighteenth month of life. The child probably will be 21 to 30 months of age before he is sufficiently aware of his needs to call for help or to get himself to the toilet before he has to urinate.

A child needs help in learning words that communicate his need for the toilet. If the same words are used each time he goes to the toilet, he will associate them with functioning and eventually will learn to use them appropriately. Giving him the correct words for the function and the products of excretion saves unlearning, for they are comprehended and learned as readily as the babyish substitutes so frequently used.

Developing reliability for toileting is accomplished largely by the child himself. If he has attained readiness, and his interest in becoming more group-up is utilized, he will take toileting in his stride, master his problem with a minimum of discomfort and be proud of his accomplishment. Complete independence and self-mastery rarely are acquired before the third birthday.

When accidents occur in times of stress or in moments of absorption in play, the child needs reassurance and understanding. An accident often hurts his pride and makes him fearful. For the moment he has lost his bodily control and his self-mastery is threatened. Putting him back into diapers or threatening to do so is depreciating. It brings loss of self-esteem and feelings of resentment. Such feelings do not prevent recurrences—they increase them by giving the child an additional problem to handle. The situation which follows exemplifies Jane's feelings about diapers and her own accomplishment.

Jane was 3 years old when she came into the hospital for eye surgery. The day after surgery, she was nauseated and vomited profusely. Because her nurse did not wish to leave Jane, she called to an attendant and asked her to bring her a diaper. She wanted it to put under Jane's head after she had washed her face and changed her bed. The minute the nurse asked for a diaper, Jane shrieked, "No, not a diaper! I'm a big girl now. Only babies wear diapers."

MAKING THE PROCESS OF LEARNING EASIER BY CLOTHING AND TOILET FACILITIES

Self-help clothing aids the child in developing independence. Pants the child can slip down or open with a zipper give him an opportunity to use his developing skill and to gain satisfaction from independent activity.

The potty chair has many advantages over the adult toilet. Its use is less fear-provoking and the toddler can eventually use it independently, which is an advantage from his point of view. In hospitals low toilets with small seats would be advantageous. If the large toilet is used for children, a small toilet seat should be placed over it and preparation to prevent fear of flushing should be given. Fear of flushing can be prevented by explanation which creates interest in listening for the noise, and by permitting the child to manipulate the device independently.

Steps which assist the child in getting on the toilet independently are invaluable in helping him enjoy the experience. The boy can use the steps and stand for urination. The desire to stand for urination is acquired naturally—when the boy observes big boys stand to urinate, he wants to do likewise.

ACQUIRING NIGHTTIME CONTROL

Nighttime control comes with development of the nervous system and is rarely acquired until the child has achieved complete independence in toileting during the daytime. When the child's nervous system has matured sufficiently to make retaining urine for 8 to 10 hours a physiologic possibility, his bed will remain dry. This, of course, presupposes that earlier experiences have been conducive to the maintenance of good parent-child relationships.

Before physiologic readiness to hold urine during sleep has been achieved, the child's bed can be kept dry but no real self-mastery is required, and often it brings discomfort and resentment as well. Many children resent being awakened from their sleep to be taken to the toilet and respond with anger or resistance. Some children stay awake after they have been toileted. In such instances awakening the child hardly seems justified. Nor does it seem legitimate to withhold fluids from a child in the late afternoon and evening to keep his bed dry. The child's immaturity needs acceptance; it should not be punished with deprivation. Some mothers take their youngsters to the toilet for urination without awakening them. This does keep the bed dry but it does not in any way help a child gain control of bladder functioning. He voids in his sleep and no learning takes place.

When a child is wetting his bed at 4 to 5 years of age, it indicates he is troubled and needs help. Occasionally, physical abnormalities or disease cause enuresis. However, in most instances enuresis is a symptom of conflict and confusion arising from disturbances in family interpersonal relationships. Many children with enuresis need psychological treatment. Often it is the nurse who must help mothers recognize the fact that their children are troubled and not ornery, lazy or mean. The nurse can interpret the functions of the child guidance clinic and help mothers feel a need for seeking guidance which will increase their understanding of their children.

Mothers who have children with problems often harbor feelings of self-doubt and inadequacy. In referring a mother to a child guidance clinic, the nurse needs to be prepared to relieve the anxiety that often stems from feelings of inadequacy, fear of psychiatric treatment or fear of the public's criticism of those who require the help of psychiatrically trained individuals.

RIGID PERFECTIONISTIC TRAINING A HINDRANCE TO THE CHILD IN MAKING A HEALTHY SOLUTION TO HIS PROBLEM

INFLUENCE OF CONSTITUTIONAL AND ENVIRONMENTAL FACTORS ON THE CHILD'S RESPONSE TO COERCIVE TOILET TRAINING

Early rigid training that fails to take the child's needs into account brings confusion, anger, frustration and anxiety. Josselyn[14] has graphically described the feelings that come when a child is confronted by a situation he neither understands nor is ready to utilize for his growth. She says:

> If the child could express his conscious and unconscious feelings at this time he might quite possibly say, "I am confused and angry and anxious. I don't understand. I have a gift which I am capable of giving to you or withholding. I like it, I am proud of it. I like its smell and its texture. It is fun to smear with it. It is something that I can enjoy myself. But you, Mother, seem to want it very badly. You want me to give it to you. At times I do not wish to give it, even though my failure means you will not love me, and that frightens me. At other times, in order to be sure that you love me, I will give it to you. But then you indicate it is bad, and throw it away. Sometimes I would rather be powerful than loved; at other times I would rather be loved than powerful. Sometimes I want only revenge for what you have done to me. At other times I just want to stay a baby."*

If a child fails to receive the understanding guidance he requires, he has to solve his problem in any way he can to bring himself comfort. When a child does not receive understanding guidance, he resents his mother's attempt to inflict her will on him, and expresses his feelings concerning it. His mother's response to his resistance, his constitutional make-up and his former experiences with her will determine how he will solve his problem. He may express his feelings and conflict with rigid compliance, constipation, indiscriminate soiling, smearing or hiding his excreta where he thinks no one will find it. He does not consciously plan the solution to his problem for he does not have the mental capacity to do so, but he does feel, observe and interpret his mother's communications to him and through this he discovers wherein his security lies.

EARLY TRAINING AND THE FEARFUL CHILD

When a mother shows disapproval or dissatisfaction with her child's achievement and attempts to force him to comply too early with punishment or threats of deprivation of love, the child becomes frightened. Fearfulness does not stay confined to one area of functioning—it spreads from the problem of achieving bowel and bladder control to other areas in which achievement is expected of him.

Some children become so fear-ridden through the toilet-training experience that they dread doing anything lest they offend their mothers and be punished by deprivation of love. They are afraid to play and can do so only when they are certain it will meet with adult approval. To retain love these children take over their mothers' attitudes, but at great expense to themselves, for

---

* Reprinted by permission of the author and the Family Service Association of America.

they become deprived of many play experiences they need in this phase of personality development. Fear of the mother (authority) remains in the child's unconscious. Thoughout his life he will be burdened with constant anxiety lest he do things that will bring the disapproval of those who are important to him.[23]

EARLY RIGID TRAINING AND RESULTING COMPULSIVENESS AND DOCILITY

There are mothers who overemphasize toilet training before their infants have had enough gratification and matured sufficiently to master their primitive impulses. These mothers do not institute early rigid training because they are thoughtless and unfeeling; they do so because their early training forced them to make unhealthy solutions to their own problems. They received little understanding from their own mothers in the training period and as a result cannot permit their babies to have the pleasure they were denied.

These mothers center their interest on toilet training and cleanliness and bring discomfort to their babies. They take them from their absorbing play, place them on the toilet and expect them to function according to prescribed schedules which they formulate. In doing so they lose sight of the importance of experiences that provide opportunities for mutual enjoyment. Because their babies have not yet acquired interest in the training experience, they are unable to participate and enjoy it. Often the babies are given toys to play with while they are kept sitting on the toilet, but they are no substitute for instinctual pleasure and they know it.

These mothers are compelled to meet their own needs for cleanliness and regularity irrespective of their infants' developmental requirements. In their eagerness they make it difficult or even impossible for their children to relinquish their interest in obtaining pleasure from excretory functioning and messing so it can become directed toward the genitals in the next phase of personality development.[4] Their concentration on cleanliness heightens interest in excretory functioning instead of lessening it; it retards progress through this phase of development. The infants sense the importance excretory functioning and cleanliness have for their mothers. Their mothers' avidity for cleanliness makes them feel that their acceptance and security are dependent on the adoption of their attitudes. And they are right—their security does depend upon their capacity to meet their mothers' needs.

When a child has obtained optimal gratification from soiling, he is able to find satisfaction for his instinctual urge to mess and smear in play with appropriate materials. In the training period the child delights in water and mud play. It serves a purpose. In play with mud, water, clay and paint, the child finds a constructive outlet for his primitive impulses. When he is permitted these activities he does not resent restrictions placed upon his desire to play and smear with feces. He uses the substitute materials and finds pleasure in play that is socially acceptable. This is called *sublimation.* It is a constructive ego mechanism of defense and a healthy way to gratify one's impulses.

However, the situation is different if the child is forced to give up soiling before he has obtained optimal gratification and readiness to master his impulses. In these instances sublimation is impossible.[3] Instead the child must control his wish to soil indiscriminately with the use of two less healthy defenses—repression and reaction formation. Through their use he makes an adjustment to his problem, but it is a poor substitute for self-mastery.

When a child is toilet trained before he is ready and interested in learning, he experiences rage and acute anxiety from which he must find relief. His impulses to soil and smear become intensified with anger and clamor for satisfaction but if he permits himself to satisfy them he becomes threatened with loss of love. Under such circumstances the child is in a predicament, and a painful one; he is experiencing conflict and anxiety. His mother forbids soiling and expects obedience, and his security depends upon his capacity to keep his feelings and urges under control. He has no recourse but to banish from his mind that which is desired, forbidden and considered "bad," and to erect defenses that will keep him safe in his mother's love. The wishes to express the anger he feels toward his mother for subjecting him to coercive training and to soil indiscriminately will vanish from consciousness; they will become *repressed.* In their place will be a conscious wish and compulsive need for *cleanliness,* order and "goodness." This defense which his ego erects against his infantile impulses is called a *reaction formation.*[7] The child then finds the odor and the sight of excrement disgusting.

Repressed memories, wishes and feelings are not gone; they remain deeply buried within the child's unconscious and influence the way in which his personality will become formed. Freud[8] described to her students the twofold characteristics of the child's early experiences in the following manner:

We have seen that the importance of any event is by no means a guarantee of its permanence in our memory; indeed, on the contrary, it is just the most significant impressions that regularly escape our recollection. At the same time experience shows that this forgotten part of the inner world has the curious characteristic of retaining its dynamic force when it disappears from memory. It exercises a decisive influence on the child's life, shapes his relations to the people around him and reveals itself in his daily conduct. This twofold characteristic of the experiences of childhood, so contrary to all your expectations, its disappearance into the void while retaining all its power to influence, has given you a good idea of the conception of the *unconscious* in psychoanalysis.

The conscious disgust toward soiling and excreta which the child acquires spreads just as fearfulness does. Gradually it spreads to distaste for all messiness and disorder of any nature. Instead of being a spontaneous, creative child, he becomes a docile, obedient, overly conscientious, meticulous individual who cannot tolerate any signs of imperfection in himself or others. His natural characteristics were never accepted and therefore he cannot tolerate them in himself or others.

The reaction formation serves a purpose, but, instead of a sublimated outlet for a natural urge, there is repression of a potent wish with no healthy and constructive means of expression. Instead of acquiring mastery of his impulses he is free from anxiety only when he does things at a certain time and in a particular stereotyped way. He is not master of himself for he cannot control impulses and feelings which are hidden deeply within his unconscious. He is governed by rules and compulsive rituals he is powerless to alter. To do so would be too threatening for he would discover anger and impulses he had never mastered.

Compulsive behavior frees the individual from anxiety but blocks his opportunities for growth, creativeness and self-realization. As he cleans and meticulously puts things in order, he gains some measure of satisfaction of his urge to mess. However, it is a far less constructive way for it never brings complete satisfaction. He never gets through cleaning and is usually dissatisfied with the results he obtains. He is rigid and inflexible for he dares not deviate from his established patterns of behavior.

Orderliness and cleanliness are desirable qualities and every child needs them, but the child who acquires these traits without fear of mother or his own hostility, or without guilt, will develop into a freer, more flexible person than the one who develops them because he was threatened with loss of love and punishment.

Projection is a mechanism of defense which many individuals utilize with repression to keep their unmastered urges and feelings hidden from themselves.[19] To hide their urges and feelings, the individual may project them onto others and accuse them of possessing the very urges and feelings he unconsciously wishes to express.[19]

Bob's behavior exemplifies the character traits that can come with repression. His hospital record disclosed the fact that toilet training was completed at 14 months of age and there was no problem behavior which brought his mother concern. He never overtly expressed his anger but bouts of diarrhea were bringing loss of weight and apathy which his mother felt needed medical therapy.

Bob was nearly 6 years old when he developed colitis and needed treatment in the hospital. He was a meticulous lad who seemed perpetually uncomfortable, anxious and docile. At the table Bob was fastidious. Whenever a bit of food dropped from his fork to the table, he looked anxious and cleaned it up immediately. He used a fork to eat his cake and frowned with dismay when he observed other children using their fingers as pushers and to eat. His bath was an important ritual and he never needed reminding to wash his hands before meals.

When his mother came to visit, he was as undemonstrative with her as with the children. They talked together but it seemed as though he was holding back positive feelings as well as negative ones. He bade her good-bye in a childlike formal way without the expression of feeling one sees in a comfortably adjusted child.

In the playroom Bob was as unspontaneous as he was in the ward. He concentrated on cars, soldiers and trucks and lined them up, rearranged them and returned them to their proper containers. He was quiet and invariably stoop shouldered as he strolled about the playroom observing the activities the other children were enjoying.

One day when Bob and 3-year-old Joan were sitting at the table together, the nurse placed finger-painting materials before them. Joan got into the paint at once and gloried in the feel of the material, showing evidence that she welcomed an opportunity to satisfy the urge which is a natural characteristic of every human being.

Bob's reaction to the materials was totally different. The minute Joan put her hands into the paint, Bob put his hands behind his back and tightly clenched them together. His facial expression changed and he showed evidence of increased anxiety as he shouted: "She's a bad girl to do that. Why did you give it to her? You're a bad nurse. Her mother won't like it if she does that."

Bob continued to watch Joan and once he looked as though he was tempted to try it. He unclenched his hands, put them onto the table, and his fingers neared the paint. Then quickly he put his hands behind his back and said, "Take it away. I don't want to do it. It's no fun."

Bob projected his own feelings onto Joan. He also generalized that all mothers would react as his mother had responded to his desires. Bob's behavior showed he was tempted to do what Joan was doing. Were this not true, why would he have needed to clasp his hands behind his back each time something compelled him to reach out toward an activity that all uninhibited preschool children enjoy?

EARLY RIGID TRAINING AND RESULTING CONSTIPATION

A child may withhold feces as a means of expressing his conflict and confusion associated with the training process for one or several reasons. He may do so because he has received so little he has no desire to give. Instead of wanting to give, he may wish to keep his possessions for himself. He becomes obstinate, unyielding and a hoarder, giving little in return for what he gets.[23] Other children may withhold feces because they have come to feel that the products of elimination are injurious. If through observation of his mother's response to his investigation of feces the child has been made to feel that it is "bad," he may fear his inability to control his own impulses and withhold to protect himself from anxiety. He may come to hate his feces for it has brought anxiety and because hating his feces is less threatening than hating his mother who brought him the discomfort.

Other children may withhold because they have been made to feel defecating is a dangerous thing to do. If a mother responds to her child's defecating with a rejecting attitude that implies she has been hurt by her child's failure to respond to her wishes to stay clean, he may interpret the activity as dangerous. He becomes anxious and defends himself against it by withholding his feces.

Constipation serves a purpose; it protects the child from anxiety. His mother's attitude makes him feel that cleanliness is her prime objective. Withholding not only keeps the child free from anxiety, it also brings pleasurable sensations in the lower intestine as well. It also brings his mother concern and punishes her for inhibiting his natural desires. From this and his power over her, he obtains pleasure which he becomes reluctant to relinquish.

Fear of evacuation may make a child resistant to the use of the toilet. Soiling with obstinate constipation occurs fairly commonly. When the physiologic need to defecate becomes too great to withstand, it overpowers the child's defenses against his fear of soiling and he eliminates bits of stool in his panties.

EARLY RIGID TRAINING AND RESULTING SOILING

Some children respond to unreasonable social demands with rebelliousness and nonconformity rather than with docility and strict obedience.[23] They show their resentment by refusing to comply and go on soiling even though they are punished physically or by disapproval. Often these children have had an insufficiency of love and express their feelings of deprivation by unwillingness to conform. They have received little and therefore have no desire to make sacrifices for anyone. They are unable to express their resentment in words, but they have the power to show their feelings in the continuation of indiscriminate soiling.[23] It is a way of getting back at mother for imposing painful restrictions.

Eventually, the child accepts his mother's standards, but a pattern of behavior has been established through the training experience, and feelings pertaining to it remain within the unconscious part of his mind and continue to exert their influence on his behavior throughout his liftime. [23] His unconscious feelings will influence the kind of response he will make when he is angered at persons or situations. Weiss and English[23] have found that some adults express the thoughts and feelings which cannot be expressed in words or actions through some organ or organ system. Instead of expressing the hostility to the person who precipitated it or finding a satisfactory solution to their problem, they utilize the pattern they acquired in childhood and express their aggressiveness in bouts of diarrhea or urinary frequency.[23] Weiss and English[23] refer to this phenomenon as the "language of the organs," and say:

The organ which "speaks" is most likely to be the organ whose function was in the ascendancy when environmental conditions were bad and produced pain (anxiety) in the mind. But constitutional predisposition, identification with a parent, or other factors, may also determine the "choice of organ."

ILLNESS AND SEPARATION FROM THE MOTHER AND RESULTING REGRESSION

INFLUENCE OF ABSENCE OF THE MOTHER ON THE CHILD'S CAPACITY TO FUNCTION

Until the child has thoroughly mastered his impulses to soil and has incorporated his mother's standards into his conscience, successful achievement in toileting is dependent upon his reward (mother's pride and acceptance). The child's most potent motivation in adaptation to the toilet training experience is his desire to please his mother and to become more grown-up. In doing so he gives but he also gets. When training is first begun, the child can function on the toilet only if his mother is with him. It will be months before he will be able to function in her absence. In the interim changes in environmental circumstances usually precipitate relapses.

A young child has little incentive to conform, or ability to control his drives when his mother is absent or unable to provide him with substitute satisfactions. If circumstances separate the young child from his mother, he may temporarily lose his capacity to control himself for the source of his satisfaction is gone. This can happen if the child is hospitalized, or if he becomes disillusioned and disappointed by his mother's interest in a new house or a new baby, or if she is taken away because of illness. However, if he has achieved personal inner satisfaction and felt pride in his achievement, his desire to control himself will become revived again if the source of his gratification is returned to him within a short time.

ILLNESS AND RESULTING REGRESSION

Illness and separation from the mother are powerful factors that interfere with the child's ability to control his excretory functioning. Illness deprives the child of energy and prevents normal adaptation if the illness is severe. If hospitalization is required and there is abrupt separation from his mother, fear and anger become aroused, making regression and loss of sphincter control inevitable. The cause is understandable. He not only loses the object of his satisfaction, but also he has hostile retaliatory impulses toward his mother for subjecting him to discomfort. In addition, he must cope with fear of abandonment in a strange, threatening situation. The child becomes flooded with emotion and tension, making self-control completely impossible in many instances.

There is more involved in changing diapers and offering bedpans than keeping the child clean and observing the way his gastro-intestinal and genito-urinary tracts respond to bodily infection or injury. Of equal importance is the nurse's observation of the child's response to the psychological experience he is having and her skill in helping him recover without injury to his personality. For this reason it is important for nurses to know what stage of development the child was in prior to illness and what attitudes and methods of training the child had experienced within his home. If the child had experienced severity in training at home, a corrective experience during convalescence might be valuable for him. To learn that all women are not alike might help him to modify his feelings toward those in authority. To experience the reverse, understanding at home and coerciveness and rigidity within the hospital will also leave its imprint on the mind of the child.

If a child enters the hospital before he has reached a stage of readiness for learning society's customs, he will not be ready for it during the period of hospitalization unless a prolonged period of convalescence becomes a necessity. In these instances the baby needs to have what pleasure he can get from excretory activity.

The nurse reflects her attitudes toward soiling and excreta as she gives care to babies. It is important that the nurse be aware of her feelings toward the child in this aspect of his behavior as well as in all others. Nurses who are critical and resentful need not necessarily injure their patients. If they understand their own feelings and gain control over their expression their patients will profit from it. The child needs a nurse who understands her young patients' need for instinctual pleasure and their feelings concerning the functioning and products of their bodies.

The child who enters the hospital with excretory control already established prior to his illness or need for surgery needs understanding guidance. In the mother's presence young children need to be introduced to the use of the bedpan and the urinal for many require their mother's approval before they can use hospital equipment. Knowledge of the child's physical and verbal signs of need will prepare the nurse for meeting his toilet needs.

Unless the child is provided with continuing nursing care and has an opportunity to form an attachment to a nurse, he will probably be unable to make his toilet needs known. If the nurse becomes "his nurse" through continued association and through successful alleviation of his discomfort from illness, separation and fear, he will regain equilibrium and have energy available to master his illness and hospital experience and re-establish his former pattern of independence during the period of convalescence.

When a child experiences anxiety due to separation from his mother and is ill, he needs a nurse who can help him accept the accidents bound to occur. Losing control of excretory functioning threatens many children. If a child shows concern when he loses control, he will need assurance that it is understandable and he will be given help to regain his power when he becomes well. If the nurse provides assurance, he will begin to respond to her understanding and kindness and be able to tell her of his needs. Comments like the following convey understanding feelings and assure the child that he will be helped to regain his former power when he recuperates: "Johnny, it is all right that you got wet. When you are sick and away from your mother that happens. It happens to all children when they are sick, lonely, cross and scared. If you want to use the toilet, you tell me. I'll help you when you are ready." The child's words for toilet and the excretory processes need to be used by those who care for him for they indicate the terminology to which he is accustomed.

There are little children who need help in gaining mastery of bowel and bladder functioning while they are in the hospital or the convalescent home, for there are many who remain for long periods of time. Learning experiences need to be provided for them. If they are not helped to master their impulses when readiness develops they will acquire patterns of behavior which are socially unaccept-able and difficult to change. The re-educational methods that will be necessary to undo the unacceptable behavior patterns will entail infinitely more frustration for these children than would be required if learning to adapt to reality had been begun when readiness was first recognized.[20]

If the nurses are convinced of the value of understanding guid-ance in the formation of personality structure, they will find ways to provide children with the kind of consistent nursing care they require to become socialized and happy individuals. Without a sustained good nurse-child relationship, hospitalized children will be deprived of opportunities for growth. They will either remain uncontrolled or become docile, obedient creatures who control them-selves not because they are self-directing and desirous of meeting the realities of our civilized way of life, but because they are afraid to do otherwise.

Many young hospitalized children use soiling to retaliate against the hostility they feel inflicted upon them from their parents who have placed them in the hospital or from hospital personnel who have somehow failed to provide them with the emotional satisfac-tions they require. They wet and soil their beds, urinate on the floor, or call for the bedpan and then refuse its use when it is forth-coming. The child may have soiled as a method of retaliation at home and discovered its effectiveness as a weapon or a means of parental control or he may have acquired this behavior in the hos-pital. During the acute phase of his illness or during the time he was reacting to strangeness and separation, he may have had an acci-dent. Instead of getting reassurance, he may have experienced dis-approval and rejection which angered and disappointed him. At the same time he probably perceived that his accident angered the nurse and made him the center of attention. Through such an experience a child not only acquires feelings which create a need to retaliate but also finds a weapon he can use to punish his nurse.

It is the easy way out to call the child who soils a problem and to respond to his behavior with scolding, rejection or disgust. These responses will not lessen soiling; they intensify the feelings which produced the behavior we view as unacceptable. It is infinitely more difficult to find the cause of his soiling and rectify the situation which creates a need to retaliate with soiling. But difficult as it is, the cause must be found for the child is dependent upon us for guidance. It is a part of nursing and without help the child's psycho-logical welfare is threatened. The cause of the behavior is in the child's environment. The behavior is merely a symptom of the emotional turmoil the child is experiencing. Only as we discover and meet his emotional needs will he be able to discard this method of solving his predicament and find a more constructive way to adjust to his problem.

LANGUAGE GROWTH
Development of Vocalization into the Capacity to Communicate with Others

Prerequisites for Speech Development. In the period from 1 to 3 years of age the child acquires increased capacity to understand others and to express his wishes, ideas and feelings in words. The mastery of speech strengthens his ego; it increases his capacity to think, reason, grasp reality and meet his own needs.

The child develops the capacity to speak in his own way and at his own rate of speed. Many infants speak their first words at 1 year of age; others remain nonverbal until they are from 18 months to 2 years of age. The child's speech development depends on both hereditary and environmental factors. The ability to hear and to retain what he hears is the first prerequisite. It also depends upon his desire to understand and to talk and upon the help he is given in mastering speech.

The infant needs a rich emotional relationship with his mother to acquire speech naturally and easily. Babies raised in orphanages, institutions and homes where there has been emotional deprivation show a marked lag in language development. Spitz[20] observed babies in an orphanage who were reared without their mothers from birth to the fourth year of life. He found ". . . that 95 percent of them had never learned to speak."

Stages of Speech Development. From birth the infant uses his organs of speech to express his feelings and to communicate his needs to others. During the first weeks of life, it is difficult to detect variations in his crying; however, before long, the mother learns to recognize the cries that communicate feelings of hunger, fatigue, loneliness and fear. From birth it is also evident that the baby derives pleasure from love which is communicated to him by words and song.

Through early feeding experiences the infant discovers the pleasure that comes from oral activity. At first sucking is his most pleasurable mouth activity. Gradually, however, he obtains another oral pleasure. Through repeated mouth play, he experiments in controlling the flow of air over his vocal cords and succeeds in producing a variety of sounds. Creating them brings pleasurable feelings and he is motivated to repeat them over and over again.

From the third month of life on, the infant grows increasingly more capable of varying the sounds he makes. By the fourth month of life he can produce the vowels and a few consonants and he uses them in all shades of intonation to express his feelings of contentment and pain. About the sixth month of life the infant's vocalization develops into the "babble" stage of speech development. He combines vowels and consonants and utters such sounds as "bah, mah, da." He vocalizes as he plays and never seems to become tired of his repetitive monologue.

When the baby vocalizes to express the pleasure he feels from his mother's care, he discovers he has an appreciative listener. Mothers welcome this tangible evidence of responsiveness and reward it with an increased display of emotional warmth. This gives the baby a new way to gain pleasure. Usually the mother "talks back" to her baby. When his vocalization brings a positive response from his listener, he seems to get the idea that he, too, can communicate. When the mother "talks back" she usually imitates the sounds her infant has expressed. As the child hears the sounds he has become accustomed to, the pleasurable feelings he experienced through his own vocalization become revived. He not only enjoys his own vocalization, he also enjoys that which is produced by another. From interpersonal experiences of this kind the desire to communicate verbally with others has its origin.

The infant's interest in developing speech is evidenced by his growing awareness of his mother's oral activity. He centers his interest on her mouth, imitating the movements and struggling to produce identical sounds. It becomes a part of their play together. Through it the infant gets love, has a model to imitate and practice and is further motivated to learn. Before a year is over he has acquired the ability to make every sound necessary for speaking.

With brain development, the infant begins to associate his mother's words with things, gestures and activities. Long before he can co-ordinate sufficiently to articulate, he has understanding of simple words and statements. If, for instance, the words "Go bye-bye" have been associated with preparations for outdoor excursions which were greatly enjoyed, the healthy 9- to 11-month-old infant will respond to repetition of the words with behavior which indicates his understanding of his mother's verbal communication.

After a period of practice and accumulating word symbols through association, the infant begins to speak. His first words usually are received with parental acclaim. Their pride in his accomplishment delights him and the quest for vocabulary begins. His ability to imitate is instinctive and from approximately the twelfth month onward his vocabulary begins to increase. At intervals there may be a lag in language growth. When an infant is concentrating on developing facility in locomotion, he may temporarily abandon his interest in acquiring speech. When locomotor skill is acquired, he usually begins to concentrate on learning to talk.

Between 2 and 3 years of age the child's vocabulary increases rapidly. He imitates or "parrots" the words of others and through this activity he learns the names of things, places, people and activities. In this period questions like "What?" and "Why that?" are used to acquire vocabulary and reassurance and to discover ways of doing things. At this stage he is under compulsion to exercise his verbal powers. He talks constantly and as much to himself as to others. His constant query, "What's this?" often seems to satisfy a need to verify his own knowledge, obtain reassurance or demonstrate that he has learned and knows just as adults know. When the adult suspects the child knows the answer to his own question and responds with, "What is it? You tell me," he very often gets both the name of the object and a response which shows profound satisfaction in his accomplishment.

Guidance Promotes Language Growth. Although a child has a seemingly good vocabulary, his limitations in understanding need to be accepted. The child learns best if few and short sentences containing words within his comprehension are used to communicate with him. Accompanying the words with the act itself helps the child gain understanding of words and to know what is expected of him.

The child needs help in developing his vocabulary and in gaining facility in the use of it. If the child can use words to communicate his wishes and needs to others and to gain increased understanding of their verbal communications with him, his opportunities for social participation will be increased. Acquiring facility in the use of language heightens his feelings of self-adequacy and independence. The more he can understand what he sees and hears going on around him, the less anxiety and confusion he will experience.

The child needs adults who will talk to and listen to him. The significance of meeting this need during the first year of the infant's life has been cited. It is equally important in the years that follow. Talking to and listening to a child gives him gratification and a feeling of belongingness and helps him gain understanding of what is required of him. It also helps him gain understanding of the people in his environment.

Listening to the child and helping him to expand his capacity to communicate with and to gain understanding of others is an important part of nursing care. Observation of behavior and the words and feelings that accompany it are a prerequisite for understanding him. The child also needs to understand his nurse. She can give him this understanding by interpreting to him all that she does and by consistently meeting his needs in her relationship with him. Meeting the above needs requires case method of assignment. It takes time and repeated experiences to understand the speech and behavior of the young child. The child also needs time to learn to interpret his nurse's communications to him.

The child not only has limitations in understanding, he also has limitations in his ability to express himself. Benedek[2] says:

Speech, phylogenetically the most recent acquirement, is abandoned quickly if the child is under the influence of affects. Not only in distress does the child cry rather than tell about his situation, but other emotions are also expressed by gesture rather than by words. The child jumps around with joy but does not say, "I am glad," or he hides his face or himself altogether if embarrassed. Children in early years actually communicate by speech only when they are calm and their attention is directed.

Benedek's statement describes the child's nature and indicates his need for acceptance in times of stress. The child uses gestures to express feelings because he has not matured sufficiently to express them in words. Even when he has acquired a large vocabulary and can express himself ably in situations which do not arouse strong feelings, he cannot function to capacity in times of stress. Hospital experiences are frustrating and threatening. It is easy to accept the exuberance that comes when a child is flooded with feelings of joy. *He needs equal acceptance when he uses crying and gestures to express his anger or fear.*

To expect a child in this period and the next to express anger, grief or fear in words or to refrain from crying or moving when he is angry, grief-stricken or afraid is to expect behavior that is inappropriate to his nature. Crying is a signal of distress. With it he is communicating his feelings. It is the only language he can use in situations that require more control than he has acquired.

In painful and frightening situations the child needs simple preparation, acceptance of his need to express his feelings in preverbal language and support which helps him to know he is not being attacked but understood. Admonitions to "Hold still" or "Stop crying" are detrimental. They merely increase his anger and fear, make him feel guilty and unloved and lessen his ability to handle himself in a painful and fear-provoking situation. Such admonitions do not communicate understanding; they are often hostile and make the child feel more threatened and tense than he did before.

DISCIPLINE AS UNDERSTANDING GUIDANCE

Necessity for Discipline to Help the Child Gain Increased Mastery of Himself Within His Social Environment

The Objectives of Discipline. The child's conflict between his need to retain his mother's love and protection and his need to express his infantile impulses was discussed in relation to acquiring bowel and bladder control. In all subsequent socializing experiences the child again feels conflict and anxiety. The kind of discipline he receives in later socializing experiences influences his personality growth as it influenced it in all preceding situations where frustration and adaptation to reality were involved.

When the child develops increased capacity in the use of his body and mind, he meets new experiences, some of which are gratifying and others frustrating. His horizons broaden and he is confronted with exciting and stimulating new interests and opportunities to learn and to practice his developing skills. However, simultaneously be becomes confronted with restrictions and demands that he has never experienced before. They thwart his wishes and bring new problems in interpersonal relationships. In this period the child also develops potentialities for increased independence. He discovers and asserts himself but it is not without some measure of conflict and fear.

The goal of discipline is *self*-control and not merely obedience to outer forces. Discipline is education; it is a method of helping the child acquire increased self-control and feelings of self-adequacy; it is guidance which assists the child in finding socially accepted ways to express his feelings, wishes and drives.

The child learns most effectively and feels better about society's rules and regulations if he is helped to gain increased powers of self-control with understanding guidance. Discipline does not have to be painful and punishing to be effective. Many adults feel discipline is a failure if it has not made the child feel miserable, afraid and repentant but study of children has not shown this to be true.

The child needs guidance which helps him to become socialized with the least possible sacrifice of his personal freedom, spontaneity and individuality. Discipline should help the child develop increased capacity for self-direction. It should increase his self-confidence and his respect for himself and his own capacities. As he becomes successful in mastering himself within his environment, he becomes more secure, freer from anxiety and better equipped to enjoy his interpersonal relationships with both children and adults.

Becoming a productive, self-reliant, self-directing, co-operative person requires both growth and intelligent guidance. Those who guide the child need to accept the fact that he is asocial according to adult standards. They also need acceptance of the fact that it takes *time* (from birth through adolescence) and *wisdom* to help the child learn to find ways of adapting that are satisfying both to himself and to those within his group and in his society. *The child needs controls from within.* Unless controls come from within, self-direction, self-realization and optimal social productiveness are an impossibility.

Consideration of the child's feelings serves to provide him with the emotional freedom he requires to reach full emotional maturity; it does not limit his potentialities for future accomplishments. *As the child develops new powers he needs thoughtful guidance to gain ego strength, to accept the limits of his environment and to help him recognize and accept his feelings and handle them increasingly more constructively.* One needs to be free of hate, resentment and crippling fears to realize one's greatest potentialities. If a child is "good," socialized and conforming only because he is afraid to be "bad" or to call his soul his own, he will be no pleasure to himself for he will be eternally frustrated. He may eventually contribute enormously to society but in the process he may miss the fulfillment that comes from total self-realization and genuine social productivity.

To adapt to group living successfully the child needs parents who have a good constructive relationship with him. What really helps the child to develop a socialized way of behaving is the *feeling* he has toward those who are guiding him. The foundation of that feeling lies not in the moment, but in the important preceding periods when the mother-child and father-child relationships had their origin.

Limits Are Necessary for Security and Growth. Children are born asocial; they are not born with a sense of right and wrong and a knowledge of those things and activities which are dangerous. Nor are they born with inner controls that inhibit asocial, impulsive behavior. They acquire this knowledge and find socially acceptable ways of channeling their asocial tendencies through constructive experiences with the adults in their environment.

Disciplinary restraints will frustrate the child and make him angry momentarily, but *he needs and wants them* to learn, to protect him from destroying property, hurting himself and others and bringing undue discomfort to the adults within his environment. Hurting others makes a child feel guilty and fearful lest the person retaliate in like manner. And oftentimes he does, if a child persists in inflicting discomfort upon another. It is kinder to redirect or to inhibit a child's aggressive or exploratory impulses *before* our anger is aroused. If we are free of anger we can think more clearly and redirect in a way that will be accepted more readily and that will be less frightening to the child.

A young child needs to feel strength in his parents and to know they are in control, for their strength and wisdom aid him in developing a strong ego. The child wants to gain mastery of himself but first he needs to know what is expected of him. It reassures him to know that there is someone who cares for and loves him enough to protect him from doing those things he ought not to do.[13] He needs to know his parents are there to help him become more socialized. He needs to feel their faith and confidence in his ability and to desire to grow increasingly more able to control his asocial impulses and become a more self-reliant little person.

Without protective limits set for him, a child's personality cannot grow. He will be fearful for he can never be sure of the response he will evoke in his parents. Permitting the child to have complete and unrestricted freedom fails to prepare him gradually for life in our society. Eventually, the child will desire social experiences with children and adults outside his home. Unless he is prepared for co-operative living within his family he will be deprived of the satisfactions that come from social experiences with others.

Without protective limits the child will become either an unrestrained, impulse-ridden, unhappy, perplexed child or one who is inhibited because he is afraid to be otherwise. The impulse-ridden child is one who has been deprived of the help he needed to meet restrictions. Instead of becoming a more controlled and self-reliant child, he has become increasingly less tolerant of restrictions and responds with anger to smaller and smaller doses of frustration. The inhibited child becomes so because he has been given no help in finding safe, acceptable behavior. He fears loss of love and protects himself by doing only those things he sees his elder siblings or parents doing.[15] In the process he becomes deprived of experiences, gratification and emotional freedom. In the following statement, Josselyn[15] shows the child's need for a balance between freedom and controls:

Wise discipline gives the child a sense of security and, at the same time, of freedom. The child is aware of limits placed upon his behavior which, if accepted by him, assure him of the reward of emotional security. Within these limits the child is free to express himself, gain certain gratifications, and not jeopardize his basic relationships. It assures him further that he is protected by those limitations from carrying out impulses which might destroy what he wants to preserve.*

---

* Reprinted by permission of the author and the Family Service Association of America.

GUIDANCE WHICH HELPS MEET THE OBJECTIVES OF DISCIPLINE

The Child Needs Limits That Are Geared to His Capacity to Tolerate Frustration. The selection of the limits and the *feelings* and *attitudes* which come into play when they are taught and enforced are important factors in personality development. *The child needs parents and nurses who analyze the requirements they place upon him from his point of view as well as from their own.* They need to appraise the child's capacity to tolerate restrictions and to know the limits of their own patience and tolerance. They need to ask themselves the following questions and then structure the child's environment accordingly: "Is the rule or limit made with sufficient consideration of the child's needs and ability to meet the frustration involved in it? Is it essential for the child's welfare and the welfare and comfort of others within his environment? Will it help him to become more self-reliant and independent and maintain his feelings of self-esteem?" If the answers to these questions are in the affirmative, the child needs help in learning to obey the rule or to meet the demand being placed upon him. If the answers are in the negative, the adult needs to ask himself another question: "Why am I making this rule?"

Many rules are made to meet the adults need to dominate, restrict or punish. Such rules do not teach the child respect for authority; they merely serve to give him the feeling that adults are inhibiting and controlling rather than friendly, wise teachers.

Every pediatric ward must have rules to help the children know the limits of their environment. It is important for the children's security and protection and necessary for the comfort of the personnel in the ward. However, the rules must be made carefully and taught with kindness and understanding. The hospital environment is new to children. Unless they have had previous experiences they do not know those things forbidden by hospital personnel. They do not know what is expected of them in the hospital ward, and they need and want to know.

In a ward where there are children of all ages and in various stages of illness, the personnel need freedom to modify rules and limits in accordance with the needs of their individual patients. Modifying rules to meet the needs of a particular child requires thoughtfulness, a knowledge of one's self and intuitiveness to sense the capacity of the child to tolerate frustration and meet demands.

Each child's capacity to tolerate frustration will be different and will be determined by his present circumstances and all that he has experienced before coming into the hospital. The age of the child is but one criterion for estimating his capacity to tolerate frustration. The majority of children in a hospital ward cannot function up to their age level. They are ill, separated from all that has given them security before and confronted with activities that in most instances are totally unfamiliar to them.

No two children come into the hospital ward with the same background of home experience. Some have been overindulged; others have been grossly and strikingly inhibited and deprived; others have been respected as individuals and guided with thoughtfulness and deep understanding of their developmental needs. Some have been handled with understanding in most areas of guidance but in other areas their parents have had problems which prevented them from accepting natural behavior. Probably the majority of children have had this latter type of experience, for no parents are perfect and they would not be human if they were. All these factors need consideration in providing individualized care for a child.

The Child Needs Consistent Support, Protection, Understanding and Teaching as His Horizons Broaden. When the child has learned to walk, he needs experience to gain mastery of his environment and guidance which helps him feel safe in his world. When the child has learned to walk he is ready to venture forth and to begin to discover more of the world about him. Confining the 8- to 24-month-old child in a play pen or crib limits his opportunities for physical and psychological growth. As Gesell[10] says, the child needs to explore and he cannot do so without traveling. *However, to explore, he needs the security of knowing that his mother is nearby and ready to protect and support him and to give him assistance whenever he feels the need for it.* Exploring a new environment is not approached with utter abandon. The child is unsure, wary and often frightened because he senses his inability to cope with the unfamiliar. He looks to his mother for help. He wants to know what he can do and what is unsafe and inappropriate for him at the moment.

It takes time and guidance for a child to develop the inner security that is necessary for him to feel safe enough to venture away from his mother. When a child is secure in his relationship with his mother, he can venture out of her sight. At first he will only go into the next room, but gradually, as he becomes assured of his own ability, he will broaden his horizons and feel safe away from the protective confines of a familiar and secure environment. Security comes from guidance which recognizes his needs for experiences that help him grow increasingly more assured of his own abilities. However, during the process of acquiring these abilities, he continues to have dependent needs that require satisfaction.

Mothers and nurses frequently ask the following questions: "How much should an adult play with a child? Shouldn't a child learn to play alone? When should I play with him? How can I help him to enjoy playing by himself?"

Security in knowing that his mother or nurse is nearby where he can get to her helps the child become assured of his own ability to get his needs fulfilled and to develop his capacities to play alone. The child will give the answers to the above questions if the mother or nurse observes and follows his lead. When he is contentedly playing alone, he does not need or want interference. When he gets lonely, afraid, bored or in need of his mother's reassurance or stimulation, he will scamper back to her and make his needs known. Perhaps it is only a smile he requires or reassurance that she is still there. Sometimes he experiments with a forbidden activity and then becomes frightened. To obtain reassurance that he is still loved, he goes in search of his mother. Sometimes he may wish to explore or experiment with something of which he is unsure. To obtain support in attempting a new project he may summon his mother for help. When his need is fulfilled and his security re-established, he can return to his play and concentrate upon it until a change in need arises.

When a convalescent toddler is confined to his crib in the hospital he has difficulty in playing, for he has no way of mastering his fear of separation through his own activity. He is as uncomfortable as the child who is kept confined to his play pen at home. It is anxiety which keeps a child crying instead of playing; it is anxiety which forces him to cling, demand and become impetuous whenever his source of security goes out of sight. He is not spoiled, ornery or a greedy little urchin; he is merely attempting to get what his infantile nature requires. When he gets it, and becomes assured he will not lose it again, his anxiety lessens and he has inner freedom to use his creative abilities in play.

The toddler who must be confined to his crib in the hospital needs a nurse who can feel with him and provide the security he needs to utilize his energies in tension-freeing constructive play experiences. The meaning of Mike's behavior was evident. Like all other 17-month-old children, he, too, needed freedom from fear and frustration to play and master the situation he was in.

Mike came into the hospital two days before a hernia operation was scheduled. He had a mild upper respiratory infection which necessitated limitations being placed upon his activity. He suffered acutely when he was separated from his mother and was confined to his bed. He screamed incessantly, clung to the side of the crib and was unable to play with anything that was given to him. Within five minutes after the toys were presented, he had cast them to the floor. He was placed in a high chair for feeding and would take fluids only from a bottle which was held by his nurse. When his nurse put his hands to the bottle in an attempt to show him he could do it independently, he complied with one hand. As he did so, however, he clutched the nurse's hand with the other. It was as if he needed to make sure he would continue to keep with him that which he felt he needed. The nurse stayed with him. Mike communicated his need and she met it.

After his feeding was completed, Mike went back into his crib willingly. He began to play with everything within reach and it was creative, organized activity. Periodically he would look up to make sure his nurse was still there. As long as she was, his play continued. The minute she went out of sight, his play ceased and he became disorganized, screamed and threw his play materials upon the floor. Anxiety overcame him and he was completely unable to function at his 17-month-old level.

Mike could not go in search of his nurse to master his fear of being alone for he was confined to his crib, which had sides that were too high for him to climb over. Since he could not master his fear through his own activity, his nurse kept herself in touch with him. She pulled his crib into the doorway, showed him where she was going and told him she would return. She did return frequently. If Mike was playing contentedly she stopped only long enough to let him know he was not alone. If he indicated he wanted her to stay, she did. Sometimes he needed only a change of play equipment. At other times a quick hug sufficed to give him renewed impetus to tackle a new play project. Gradually, he was able to tolerate longer and longer periods of separation, and through consistency in the nurse's care separation anxiety was minimized, and Mike was able to mobilize his energies for play.

Venturing forth with the use of newly acquired powers confronts the young child with dangers and temptations that he cannot withstand. Everything within his environment catches his attention. His impulses to investigate, sometimes even to destroy, are powerful and uncontrolled. It is natural for the child to reach or to climb up to get something from a table or the stove. His experience is too limited to know that a hot coffee pot or sharp knife is dangerous. Likewise he has no comprehension of the value of certain treasured objects.

The child must learn that there are many things that are dangerous and activities that are prohibited because they are unsafe or inappropriate for his purposes, but he needs to learn it gradually for his capacity to withstand frustration is limited. *In the process of learning he needs protection from excessive frustration and interference with his play.* To prevent excessive frustration, the young toddler needs an environment which is as free from dangerous and forbidden objects of interest as possible. Valued, breakable and dangerous objects can be put out of reach, and handles of saucepans can be turned inward on the stove to eliminate danger, temptation and constant prohibition.

There are further reasons why the child should be protected from too many environmental restrictions at this time. This is the time when he is busily engaged in adapting himself to toilet customs, learning to speak, acquiring motor control and developing his powers of sensory perception. In these experiences there is enough frustration to cope with—his ego is not sufficiently strong to cope with too many more simultaneously. In acquiring the above powers, frustration is involved but he also gets gratification. As he gains increased mastery of himself he obtains pleasure both from his parents' rewards and from his own activity and accomplishments. These accomplishments strengthen his ego and make it possible for him to tolerate larger doses of frustration.

Little by little the child can learn to handle his impulses to feel and to manipulate valued and breakable objects and to tolerate more restrictions upon his behavior. He will acquire tolerance for frustration if restrictions are introduced gradually and his basic emotional needs remain satisfied.

The child needs to learn safety precautions without becoming fearful and without feeling unduly thwarted. If the child's parents are perpetually fearful lest an accident occur, the child will become fearful also. There are children who are afraid to play because they have heard so many warnings of danger. Feelings of this kind restrict the child's opportunity for full self-expression and keep him in a constant state of apprehension lest danger befall him.

Children learn safety measures most easily through observing the parent or the nurse practicing them. Caution is taught by suggestions which help the child know what to do to keep himself and others protected from injury. It takes a great deal of supervision to teach this to the young child. One telling or one showing is not sufficient. Children forget and become overpowered with their aggressive feelings and their need to explore. The little child needs an adult consistently on hand to teach those lessons that are important for his safety.

Occasionally admonitions like "Don't do that" or "Stop that this very minute" are necessary to condition a child quickly when physical danger is involved, but there are other methods of teaching which are more successful when no immediate danger is involved. Admonitions like these do not teach caution; they frighten and anger the child and make him feel that adults are timid, restricting people who are always watching to curtail his pleasure. Some accidents are are inevitable; the majority of them are not serious, and most children do a great deal to protect themselves from injury because they instinctively avoid pain. A remark such as "You will hurt yourself with that stick" frightens the child and teaches him little that will help him to protect himself, but "Walk slowly when you are carrying a long stick" is a means of helping a child know how to do things safely. Children need to learn how to do hazardous things when the parent or nurse is there to teach him how to manage safely.

The above methods of teaching safety can be utilized in all situations where danger is involved. There are dangers in almost every situation the young child is in. Those who work with children must be aware of these dangers. They also need to be able to teach safe ways of doing things without limiting children's opportunities to express themselves freely in their play. If the mother or nurse asks herself the following questions, she will discover the learning that is required and will be able to present it in a way that teaches constructively: "What does the child need to know to keep himself and others free from injury? How can I teach him safety precautions without instilling fear, challenging him to defy me to prove his powers or making him feel he is being unfairly restricted?"

Elevators in hospital wards are often a source of danger for the child patients. Children are fascinated by elevators and often one sees groups of ambulatory children congregated about them. They like to observe the way they work. They enjoy watching people come and go and they know it is the apparatus that brings their parents to the ward. They often ring the bell and attempt to open the door when the elevator is forthcoming. Children need to know how elevators work but they also need to know where it is safe to stand when the door opens to unload people or hospital equipment.

Learning to cross streets is an example of an experience all parents must teach their children to do safely. Parents can do this best through example and verbal interpretation of the safe way to cross streets. If the child's mother stops before crossing the street, shows him the importance of looking both ways before advancing and says, "Now we will look both ways. If there are no cars coming we can cross," he will learn to imitate her behavior to keep himself safe.

In adapting to new social demands, the child continues to need substitute satisfactions that give him pleasure in the present. They help him to tolerate restrictions and to show recognition of his effort to refrain from a pleasurable, nonacceptable pursuit. The toddler cannot understand that his mother is preparing him for future life in a technologic society; he can comprehend only the present.[18] Therefore, the satisfaction that comes from a smile or an approving comment needs to come at the time he is struggling to meet her new demand. Menninger[18] says that children are frustrated more by deprivation of love than by the curbing of infantile pleasure and asocial traits. The child must learn to master the frustration and anxiety involved in restrictions. However, if demands are unreasonable or are made in anger, and if he is given nothing in return for his co-operative effort, he will respond with more than the natural amount of resistance and eventually will become filled with resentment and rage.[18]

Providing substitute satisfactions shows sensitivity to the child's need for understanding and emotional support throughout the socialization process. Children *want* to learn the ways of grown-ups. That urge is strong, but it can be kept alive and a driving force within them only if they feel loved and understood throughout the period they are learning. The following example illustrates the child's desire to know the right way of doing things:

> Walter, aged 3, was in the playroom with his nurse one day. Against the wall there were newly painted boards which were going to be used to construct a new bookcase. Walter took a board and dropped it carelessly to the floor. The nurse said, "Lay them down gently. They are newly painted. The carpenter will use them to build a bookcase."
>
> Walter looked up at the nurse and with seriousness and deep sincerity said, "I didn't *know*." Then the nurse said, "Of course you did not know. If I had told you before, I know you would have moved them gently." Walter completed his work and handled the boards with care because he had learned and wanted to please the person who had understood his needs.

When restrictions and limits are first introduced, one cannot expect a child to respond with complacency. He does not have the maturity to control himself to that degree. When restrictions are imposed, it is natural for a child to resist and to express his feelings of anger, negativism or disappointment.

The home and the hospital must be places where a child can express his true feelings, be they positive or negative. *The child needs his feelings understood.* As he begins to recognize himself as an individual, he expresses his feelings more freely and often with increased intensity. If his feelings are accepted he will continue to feel "good" and loved and deserving of his parents' affection. If a child is loved only when he is "good," he will have difficulty in learning to express his emotions in ways which are nondestructive to himself or to others within his society. When a child's feelings are not accepted and he repeatedly meets disapproval when he expresses the potent feelings within him, he will come to feel he is "bad" and undeserving of love.

A child needs to be loved as he is with his natural behavior being accepted as that which is characteristic of his age level. If his natural feelings and behavior are accepted he will feel secure even though he is little and uncontrolled. He will not have to repress drives, wishes and feelings. Nor will he have to struggle to conform to standards incompatible with his level of maturity to retain the love of the persons he is dependent upon. Feeling accepted by his parents is of primary importance for his feelings about himself are a reflection of those who guide him. If a child is in the hospital for a long period of time, his feelings about himself will also reflect the feelings his nurses have about him.

The understanding mother or nurse will be able to accept angry feelings or moments of resistant behavior without fear, anger or retaliation. She will know a child needs the most understanding when he feels angry and aggressive and is trying to meet his mother's or nurse's requirements. He needs the most love then because his negative feelings make him fearful.

When a new requirement is introduced, the understanding mother or nurse will wait patiently for the child's anger or resistance to abate and then help him to accept that which she knows is necessary for his growth. She will not get impatient and fearful lest he not comply for she will know her anxiety will be communicated to the child and will lessen his capacity to co-operate. She will wait for his anger to subside, then slowly, kindly and firmly she will reassure him she has faith in his ability to comply with her request and help him find ways to get satisfaction in an approved activity. In the process the child will learn what activities are prohibited without injury to his developing self-concept. He will also discover that temper tantrums or other expressions of negativism are unprofitable because they do not meet his immediate desires. Instead he will have discovered a way to handle his feelings which brings both approval and satisfaction of his drives. He will also know he is loved even though his behavior was not acceptable at the moment.

A child needs to know his parents or nurse will never turn against him but be constantly on hand to guide, redirect and thwart behavior which prevents him from learning those lessons he is ready to learn, which are required for emotional and social growth. It is reassuring to the child and gives him the security he requires. If the mother or nurse grows fearful or angry and withdraws or scolds rather than helps the child tolerate the frustration necessary to meet the requirement, he becomes deprived of a constructive learning experience. He does not get the help he needs and in all probability he will have discovered that expression of feelings is an effective method of controlling or punishing his mother.

The child needs a mother who can accept and guide him with consistency. Consistency and kind, friendly, imposed firmness teach the child the meaning of "This cannot be done but *this* is permissible." It takes time to teach a child the rules and restrictions required for harmonious living with others. He cannot learn the rules with one telling or through one experience which helps him to learn how to give vent to feelings or satisfy a drive in a socially acceptable way. He needs repeated teaching, and repeated redirection given with faith in his ability and desire to learn.

The child becomes perplexed when his behavior is restricted one day and permitted the next. Children have short memory spans, strong urges to practice their developing skills and insatiable curiosity about everything within their environment. When guidance is friendly and consistent the child feels secure—he feels loved, valued and protected. If there is no consistency in the mother's or nurse's guidance, the child never knows what is expected of him and can never anticipate the consequences of his acts.

Inconsistency in the mother or the nurse makes a child anxious for he cannot feel safe when her behavior is nonpredictable. Nor can he feel safe when there is no consistent warmth that he can depend upon. To be rejected one day and smothered with affection the next is a confusing emotional atmosphere for a child to live in. It provides no support, warmth and understanding of the child's need for the constancy of love which is the basis of all his security.

The language the adult uses and the way he speaks influences a child's behavior. A child becomes perplexed when he is shouted at one day and kindly guided the next. Pleasant, unhurried, positive suggestions bring the most desirable responses. Children can detect the adult's feeling in the tone of his voice and they react to it as much as they do to his words. A tone of expectancy and faith in his ability to comply helps the child to modify his behavior. If the adult is assured of the reasonableness of his restriction or demand and if he is confident of his ability to gain the child's co-operation, his voice will communicate his expectancy of reasonable behavior.

The adult reflects his feelings in his approach to a child. A nurse who has confidence in herself and the child will say, "Johnny, play time is over. It is time to wash your hands for dinner." An insecure nurse reflects her uncertainty not only in the tone of her voice but also in the way she phrases her words to communicate her wishes to a child. The inexperienced nurse or mother is prone to using questions when she really means to indicate what she is expecting from a child. Questions like "Johnny, do you want to wash your hands now?" leave the child wondering what is expected of him and fail to give him the help he needs in learning to manage himself more independently.

Whenever one's intent is to teach the child the ways of his world, statements that help him know what to do will be most helpful to him. If the adult's motive is to teach, the child will catch the helpfulness of her approach to him and respond appropriately. If her motive is to dominate and control, her tone of voice is apt to betray her inner feelings, and instead of co-operation the child may respond with determination that indicates his desire to do anything but what he is being directed to do.

Preparation for a new activity and explanations that tell him why interruption in play is necessary help the child to learn the routine of the day and to get ready to co-operate. Interpreting the routine in the following way gives him an opportunity to get himself ready to adapt to it. "Soon playtime will be over. When you have finished painting it will be time for temperatures and medicines. Dinner time is nearly here. You will want to be ready for it." Children resent having their engrossing play interrupted and many a temper outburst or display of negativism might be prevented if preparation preceded a change in activity. Perhaps the nurse can recall her feelings when her own work was interrupted abruptly by directions to take one of her patients to the classroom for a clinical demonstration or to the electro-encephalogram department. She did not have a temper tantrum but she probably had feelings and undoubtedly reacted to the interruption which interfered with her plans. The child has a temper outburst because he cannot withstand frustration and does not see any need for a change in activity as the reasonable adult can. As the child learns why interruptions are necessary, he grows more reasonable and more able to co-operate, just as adults do.

The child needs to incorporate permissive attitudes into his personality as well as to learn that which is socially unacceptable. Impulses cannot be dammed up without injury to the child's personality; they must find an outlet in constructive, socially accepted behavior. Helping the child find approved activities recognizes his wishes and his feelings and his need to express them. A child resents "Don't do that" just as the adult does. Perhaps the nurse can remember how much differently she felt when she had a supervisor who understood her feelings and need to learn and said, "You will get better results if you take Jimmy's temperature after his anger has subsided," instead of saying, "Don't handle that child that way."

The following situation illustrates a way of helping children incorporate permissive attitudes into their personality.

Thirty-month-old Ted had been returned to his bed after an experience in the ward treatment room. He was angry and needed to give vent to the feelings he could not express in words. He wanted to pound so he slid his arms through the bars of his bed, pulled the bedside table to him and took the soap dish from the drawer. He used it to pound the glass partition which enclosed his cubicle.

Ted grew angrier when the soap dish was removed from his hand and his bed was pulled away from the glass partition. The nurse understood his anger. She knew there was a reason for his behavior. She quickly got his pounding board from his toy bag and said, "I understand, Ted. You are angry. You need to pound. Here is your pounding board. You can use this. The needle hurt and it made you angry. All children feel that way when people hurt them."

The above kind of discipline indicated understanding of Ted's feelings and gave him assurance that he was accepted even though his thoughts and wishes were momentarily destructive. It also helped Ted recognize the feelings which prompted his behavior. Unless the child is aware of his anger he cannot learn to transform his aggressive energy into constructive sublimated activity.

This kind of guidance requires imagination and an ability to feel with or sympathize with children. The adult needs imagination to find socially acceptable outlets or substitute activities for the child. If she has not enough imagination to find them certainly she cannot expect little children to discover them independently. They cannot find them without help—their experience is too limited. They do not know which activities are permissible until the adults in their environment help them to discover them. This is also true of the inexperienced student nurse. She does not know the ways of a hospital ward and what is expected of her in a new and untried situation until her instructors give her the help she needs to learn.

The child's personality becomes shaped as he responds to restrictions upon his behavior and directives which help him to know acceptable ways of behaving. Gradually, through redirective experiences like the above one, the child learns to curtail the expression of his own impulses; he gets controls within himself. He incorporates these standards into his personality and makes them a part of himself. The child who is guided with thoughtfulness grows up with a less punishing conscience and as a result is a freer, more flexible and creative person.

One can observe the way the child learns to oppose his impulses in an attempt to master himself and meet his mother's requirements. He will reach toward a forbidden object or begin a disapproved activity and then frustrate his own desires by giving himself a command like the following: "Not the glass, Johnny. Use your pounding board." Ronnie's activity illustrates the above method of learning.

Ronnie was 30 months old when convulsive seizures necessitated study as a basis for medical treatment. When he was becoming adjusted to life in the ward, he vehemently resisted nap time. He would screech for a few minutes to express his feelings concerning interruption in his play. As he screamed, however, he showed his readiness and ability to tolerate the interruption of his play by removing his shoes in preparation for rest hour. Instead of giving negative commands the nurse helped him to know what was expected by saying, "Ronnie, it is time to lie down and close your eyes. This is resting time."

For several days Ronnie resisted rest hour in the same manner, but the nurse continued to help him in the above manner. On the fourth day Ronnie began the nap time preparation independently. He removed his shoes, pushed a chair beside the bed and climbed up onto it. As the nurse pulled up his crib side she heard Ronnie saying to himself, "Ronnie, it's resting time now. Close your eyes and go to sleep." And he did!

Self-imposed restrictions begin to be observable about the sixteenth to the twentieth month of life. In this period, however, parents and nurses cannot expect the self-imposed prohibition to function constantly. It will be a long time before the prohibition becomes a part of his conscience and functions automatically. Until it does, his ability to restrict his behavior will be determined by inner needs and outer circumstances. Sometimes the need for activity or the urge to investigate will be greater than his need for approval; at other times angry feelings may make it impossible for him to control the aggressive urges that well up within him.

Until the prohibition or control becomes an internalized part of the child's personality, the mother or the nurse caring for and guiding the child needs to function as his ego. It is the adult who must weigh values, interpret what is right for him and what is nonacceptable. It is the adult who must see that he does those things which are best for his welfare. The young child often sees no value in rest hour, going to bed at night, taking medicines or putting on his sweater when he goes out to play in cool weather. He does not have the judgment or the experience necessary to know the consequences of all his acts. He must acquire those capacities through a process of maturation and through experiences which help him to know and accept reality.

The adult caring for the child needs recognition of his immaturity and undeveloped powers of judgment so that she can function for him when he does not have the capacity to do so independently. As the adult takes on the functions of the ego, the child gradually adapts himself to them and takes them into himself, making them his own.

Ronnie's nurse was functioning as his ego in the above situation. He did not want to stop his play; he did not know how much he needed a period of complete relaxation. But his nurse knew the energy that he had expended during the morning and she recognized the signs which indicated extreme fatigue. She knew that he could not stop himself from play or anticipate the energy that he would need at his disposal for his afternoon activities. Instead of permitting Ronnie to do only that which he pleased at the moment, she showed him what she knew he needed and helped him to adapt himself to it. He could not have done it unaided.

Helping children between 1 to 3 years of age take medicines usually requires the same approach. They rarely can take them willingly and it is understandable why they cannot. To take bitter or unpleasant medicine requires self-discipline and ego strength which the young child has not yet acquired. To frustrate himself to the degree necessary to imbibe unpleasant tastes instead of pleasurable ones requires strength. The young child cannot comprehend the value of medicine. In most instances he cannot understand why he should even be subjected to anything as unpleasant as a dose of sulfonamide or aspirin.

In these instances the child needs a secure and kind nurse to show him the medicine is to be taken *now*. A dissertation to a 2-year-old on the values of the medicine is usually fruitless effort. Instead of helping the child, it only serves to prolong the agony and usually brings him to a state of frustration that is beyond his capacity to master. At first he may spit some of the medicine out and show anger at the person who presents it. This, too, is understandable. It is what the adult often wants to do, but his judgment and experience tell him the nurse is giving him something important for his welfare.

With the above kind of nursing the child learns that taking medicine is something which he must do. Gradually he accepts it and gains the strength to do it independently. Tommy, aged 2, acquired this ability by the end of his first week of hospitalization.

Tommy was in the hospital with leukemia. His medicines were bitter and distasteful even though they were mixed with corn syrup. He cried and resisted when they were presented. The nurse expected that he would and she understood the reason for his behavior. She also knew he would co-operate if she remained kind and free of impatience and anxiety. At the end of the week Tommy reached for his medicine and drank it down without any help from his nurse. As he returned the glass to his nurse, he smiled with self-appreciation and said, "Tommy drink 'mesin.' He did it himself." Tommy had mastered a difficult feat. He was proud of himself and wanted recognition from his nurse. Needless to say, he got it, for he was justly deserving of it.

There is further reason why the foregoing methods of discipline are superior to disapproval or physical punishment. In early life disapproval and physical punishment frighten the child. He fears he will be abandoned, hated or destroyed. Josselyn[14] gives the reason for these fears in the following statement:

> Disapproval by the parent has elements of real danger for the child. To the small child, anger and love cannot occupy the same space at the same time. When a small child loves, he loves; when he hates, he hates. He hates anything or anyone not complying with his expressed or unexpressed wish. He assumes the same lack of ambivalence on the part of the parent.*

The above statements describe the young child's emotional nature. He does not recognize the existence of ambivalent or contradictory feelings within himself. Nor has he had sufficient experience to know his mother loves him even though she sometimes feels angry as she inhibits and disapproves of some of the things he does.[14] Until he can recognize the existence of contradictory feelings within himself and has sufficient positive experiences to know that restrictions and thwartings do not mean loss of love, *the child needs protection from fear-provoking disciplinary measures.*

In early life the child becomes infuriated and destructive with toys that cannot do his bidding or satisfy the needs within him. However, eventually he will find the toys have other values than the one he desires that they have at the moment[14]—he discovers that they can be useful in other activities which give him pleasure.

When the child's mother thwarts him he has identical feelings.[14] He wants to destroy her as he attempted to destroy the toy which could not do his bidding. Josselyn[14] says that the danger lies in the fact that he thinks his mother is the possessor of similar wishes, attitudes and feelings. If she does possess them then he, like his toys, is also in danger of destruction or rejection.

Eventually, the child begins consciously to recognize that he has feelings of both love and hate for his mother. When he is aware and accepting of his ambivalent feelings and has had repeated experiences which bring neither rejection or destruction, he will know that his parents love him even when they disapprove of or are angry at the things he does.

Observation of little children at play and in situations where they do not comply and are scolded by angry adults will provide evidence to prove the above statements. Angry adults frighten young children. They show it in their faces and in their behavior. Some children pull away as though they expected physical retaliatory re-

---

* Reprinted by permission of the author and the Family Service Association of America.

sponses; others shrink in fear and whimper something like the following: "I be good. I not naughty any more."

Parents and nurses cannot be loving all the time. It is expected that they will feel angry and express their feelings overtly upon occasion. There are times when they are under excessive pressure and times when their frustration level has dropped below that which they normally possess. There are times, too, when a child's behavior *is* exasperating, unreasonable or downright impish. At such times the adult is justified in expressing his anger. It is better that it be expressed openly than held within where it creates tension, withdrawal and expression through subtle routes which are infinitely more disturbing to a child. However, if angry feelings are experienced repeatedly, it is important for the adult to evaluate his expectations and to determine why the child's natural tendencies create such a degree of emotion and tension within him. If the home and hospital ward atmosphere are predominantly loving and friendly, children can tolerate angry feelings occasionally. In this period, from 1 to 3 years of age, anger expressed in words is less injurious than is its physical expression. However, angrily spoken words will not be heard without some measure of anxiety.

Destructive aggressive feelings and a need for outlet do not arise without cause. Sometimes the reason is obvious, as in the case of Ted. However, at other times the reasons are hidden from both the child and those working with him, but they are there or he would not be acting hostile and destructive. The reasons can be found if one has the interest and the skill to search for them.

The hospitalized child has many reasons for feeling hostile, afraid and aggressive. One needs only to scrutinize his present situation and to analyze it from his point of view to discover a multitude of reasons why he might feel confused and anxious. Besides all the frustration hospitalization brings, the child is subjected to poking, probing, needling and oftentimes restraint. And often it is not from just one person but from many—nurses, residents, attending men and interns. The child's play is interrupted for tests, roentgenography and examinations in which he has little or no interest. Besides those reasons in his present situation, there are often those which come from past experiences in his home. Unless the causes can be found and eliminated and his goals attained through satisfying relationship experiences, the child's behavior will continue to be destructive rather than organized and satisfying.

In the hospital hostile aggressive feelings can be minimized if consideration is given to the emotional needs of the child. The sick child needs diagnostic tests and treatments, and many times pain cannot be eliminated. True explanations of what is to happen help the child prepare himself for the experience. In addition he needs kind support from a nurse he has come to trust. She needs to accept his fears and to permit him to handle them in any way he knows how. He cannot be brave and "a big boy." Forcing him to meet those standards is injurious to his mental health. The child is scared when he meets new experiences. He needs help in knowing it is the way all children feel in similar situations. Restraint can be done in a way which tells the child it is help and protection and not an attack or a punishing measure. If the nurse holding the child is free of anger and understands the child's natural response to a fear-provoking or painful treatment, he will feel the restraint as kind protection. A young child knows he cannot inhibit his impulses independently and he welcomes help from an understanding person. Barbara, aged 3 years, exemplified the above response to restraint.

Barbara had an infection in her genito-urinary tract and her doctor wanted a catheterized specimen of urine sent to the laboratory. To obtain the urine, it was necessary to pass a small rubber catheter into the passageway which leads to her bladder. Barbara was shown the catheter and the procedure was explained to her. She was told the nurse would use cotton and soap to wash her genitals and then pass the tube slowly into the place from which her urine flows.

After Barbara had scrutinized the tray of equipment, she climbed upon the treatment table independently. But when there she remained sitting bolt upright. Instead of lying down when the suggestion was made, she became rigid and set her jaw resistantly. She could not seem to make herself lie down and it was obvious her anxiety and tension were mounting. She did not cry but she bit her lips and clung to the sides of the table fearfully. Kindly the nurse said, "Barb, I am going to help you lie down. Then Miss Smith can get the urine and the treatment will be over. I know it is hard for you to lie down. And it's hard to lie still, too. I will help you so it can be over quickly."

The urine was obtained. When the nurse said, "It is all over. The tube is out and your urine is in the pan," Barbara jumped up and put her arms around the nurse's neck and laid her face against hers. The nurse who restrained Barbara was not the nurse who gave her daily care. She knew Barbara by sight and had spoken to her daily from her doorway. Barbara, however, had never returned the greeting. Her interest was concentrated on her nurse or the activity at hand and she seemed to have no desire to become acquainted with a new person.

When the treatment was over Barbara went back to her room. A few minutes later the nurse who had restrained her for the treatment passed by her door. This time her response was different. She called, "Nurse, don't you want to see my books? Come in. I'll show them to you."

When a painful treatment has been completed, the child needs permission to give vent to his feelings with words and in play. The nurse needs to anticipate the child's reactions to painful and frightening experiences and to develop the capacity to accept them. "I hate you" or "You are a naughty nurse," is a normal response to a painful treatment. It should not hurt one's dignity or pride to permit a child to express what he really feels. It will not hurt one's pride if his restraint or treatment was carried out in a nonhostile way.

When a child's behavior makes a nurse angry, it is difficult for her to restrain him or to carry out a treatment nonaggressively. If the nurse was angered because the child could not or would not co-operate and she did carry out the treatment with seething feelings within her, the child's verbal expression of hostility is often intolerable to her. Instead of giving him permission to vent his feelings, she often seeks reassurance for herself by saying something like the following: "It didn't hurt, did it, Jerry?"

When a child is confronted with a question like that, he is in a dilemma; he is in conflict and afraid. He has aggressive feelings which clamor for expression but simultaneously he has a need for acceptance and security. His aggressive behavior has already brought hostility. If he responds in anger and says, "Yes, it did," he may become the recipient of further aggression. This he senses both from the nurse's words and from the manner in which she handled him. His fear of retaliation or rejection often forces him to deny his feelings. Instead of expressing his true feelings, he inhibits his impulse to strike out against one who has hurt, and responds with silence or "No, it didn't hurt."

The above behavior usually brings the nurse's forgiveness, but the child is left with negative feelings within him. If he has ambulatory privileges he may express his feelings in play with toys or in aggressive play with children. This will provide outlet for his feelings and be a constructive way for him to handle his problem unless it gets him into difficulties with playmates or with personnel in the ward. If he is a bed patient and has no opportunities to drain off his feelings or to channelize them in active play, he may "swallow" or repress his feelings, which is unhealthy for him personally.

The child needs to express his feelings of anger. It is as important for his mental health as the treatment is for his physical health. A young child feels no gratitude for treatments and it cannot be expected that he should. Even if he could appreciate the fact that the nurse or doctor is trying to help him get well, he would still feel scared and resent the pain inflicted upon him.

The child needs opportunities to master his anger and fear in play. Some children cannot express their angry feelings in words but they can in their play. Because children in the hospital have many reasons to feel frustrated, afraid, hostile and aggressive, those who supervise play need to be able to tolerate a great deal of activity and to permit freedom of expression. They will also need to know how to help children channelize their feelings in play so they can master their fears and find aggressive outlets which are safe for themselves and their playmates. Further discussion of the values of play will appear subsequently and in other chapters of the book.

If a child does not react to painful treatments or situations, he is not showing a healthy response. He is making life easier for the personnel in the ward but he is injuring his mental health in doing so. The docile, submissive, nonreacting patient is a disturbed child. He is repressing his aggression because past and present experiences have taught him that expression was dangerous. Through experience he has discovered that expression of aggression brought loss of love rather than understanding. Unless he can be assured that angry feelings and aggressive play are acceptable, his energy will go into defenses which keep his feelings under rigid control rather than into achieving recuperation from disease or surgery.

GUIDANCE WHICH HELPS THE CHILD DISCOVER HIMSELF AND RECOGNIZES HIS RIGHT TO INDEPENDENCE

The Child Asserts Himself with Negativism. In the period from 1 to 3 years of age, the child discovers himself. In this period he is possessive, aggressive, self-centered and desirous of asserting himself and attaining his goals. He struts and is proud of his being! He is merely showing us he is an individual with powers, feelings and wishes that are his very own. This behavior is natural. He is in the egocentric phase of development and beginning to desire a greater degree of self-expression, freedom and independence.

In this period the child has new powers within himself and he is aware that he has a mind of his own and a capacity to assert it. Jung once said the child reaches the "no" stage when he discovers his soul. It is an easy way of asserting one's self and the child delights in the use of the word. He has come by its use naturally for it is often the way his mother asserts herself to him. However, expression of negativistic feelings makes him uncomfortable for he is unsure of his mother's response to his behavior. The kind of parental response the child's negativism elicits will further influence the concept he formulates of himself and will affect the way in which he will assert himself throughout his lifetime.

Negativism is a sign of maturation; it marks the end of babyhood and the beginning of a period filled with self-interest and new discoveries concerning his own capacities. It is an interesting and challenging phase of development if it is understood and viewed as a period of need for self-discovery and expression.

When negativism first appears, the child's expression of the word "No" is usually followed by compliance to whatever suggestion has been made to him. He says "No" to "Time to go inside now, Billy," and then proceeds to follow his mother's directions. His "No" does not signify an intent to refuse; it is impulsive and he does not understand its full meaning or from whence it comes.

The use of negativism comes from the child's need to be powerful and self-assertive, and how important it is for the little child to feel this way! The child's world is made up of big, powerful and many times dominating people. He is surrounded with things that are frightening, mysterious and infinitely bigger than himself. When he goes outside his home he sees speeding cars, elevators that whisk people away, crowds of strange people and a myriad of sights to which he has not grown accustomed. His sense of reality is undeveloped; he does not know what is safe and what is to be legitimately feared. Unless he loves himself, is helped to discover, develop and use his strength, he will feel inadequate, weak and fearful.

In early childhood the child's security and strength come from his parents; in adulthood his security must come from his accomplishments and the knowledge that he has inner resources of his own to cope with his world. It is during childhood that he must acquire inner resources of his own, for without them he cannot become an independent self-reliant adult.

Mothers and nurses need to know that a period of negativism and self-discovery is as natural and purposeful as sucking or walking; they need to have insight into its developmental implications so they can recognize it as growth rather than stubbornness or obstinacy. If his negativism is welcomed and accepted calmly, he will go through this phase with ease. He has acquired the capacity to assert his independence and he wants to practice those things he is capable of doing. In this phase of development the child is overpowered with his accomplishments. He reaches out for new experiences and says "Me do it" when tasks are taken over by others. He has a real zest for living, doing, learning and acquiring self-mastery; his enthusiastic spirit and belief in himself must be preserved.

If the child's "No's," "I won'ts" and "I don't want to's" are anticipated and accepted casually and he is taken gently and firmly by the hand to show him what is expected, he will co-operate. For a moment, he may display a bit of hesitancy or resistance, which is his new-found way of asserting his own mind. In that moment he appraises his mother's reaction. He wants both power and his mother's love and the choice is often a difficult one for him to make.

In all guidance one wants the child to acquire a *realistic* concept of his strengths and a knowledge of the limits of his power. If his "No's" and "I won'ts" make him the ruler of his universe, he will feel omnipotent and tyrannize his parents with his resistance and demands for self-expression. One wants the child to feel his 1-, 2-, or 3-year-old power and to respect his own capabilities—that realization is essential for emotional health. However, if his negativism and self-assertiveness give him power over his parents, he will acquire an unrealistic concept of himself, not recognize his limitations and be deprived of experiences he needs for growth. In addition he will be without the strength that should be coming from his parents.

The child needs help in using his new-found powers in constructive, socially acceptable ways. He needs help in knowing *how* to use his powers in becoming a more successful, self-reliant and secure little person. He does not get this help when his mother or nurse is frightened or angered by his "No" and withdraws from her guidance responsibilities. In addition to permission to express himself, he needs help in discovering that co-operation can be both pleasurable and fun. A child's "No's" frighten many adults. They interpret them as an expression of unfriendliness and become fearful lest following through with their suggestion will alienate them from him. It will not alienate him for he wants direction and has more security when the adult helps him to know the limits of his power.

At the moment the child is appraising his mother's response and vacillating between power and co-operative activity, he needs help in making a decision. If his mother or his nurse indicates ways he can use his powers independently, he will obtain satisfaction for his need of both self-expression and love. The following situation exemplifies the use of this principle.

Sally was 3½ years old and in the hospital with nephritis. Her nurse brought her medicine in to her and said, "Sally, here is your medicine. It is time to take it now." Sally looked up, made a face at the nurse and said, "No. I don't want it. Take it away. I want to play now." The nurse smiled, waited a moment and said, "Here's a spoon, Sally. You can use it to stir it up. Here's a straw, too. You can use either the straw or the spoon to get your medicine from the glass. You tell me when you want me to hand you the water." Sally reached for the tray, mixed up the medicine, and drew it into her mouth with the straw.

Sally's nurse was not frightened or angered by her negativism. She recognized the child's need to assert herself and knew she would delight in determining the way the medicine should be taken. The nurse's approach told the child what was expected of her and guided her in learning ways she could use her newly discovered powers.

Another way of helping the child in this period of negativism is to give him experience in learning to make choices. They lessen negativistic responses and give him pleasure in asserting himself. The following suggests one way this might be done: "Susie, it is time to go to bed now. Would you like to walk to your bed or shall I give you a piggy-back ride over to it?" When a child is given a legitimate opportunity to assert himself, he will have less need for "No's" and "I won'ts." By 3 years of age most children can make single choices and they like to feel they have a voice in matters which concern them.

There are many ways one can permit freedom of choice in a home or hospital ward. The child can choose between two suits, the toys he would like to take with him to the hospital or the operating room, the side he would like to lie on when his temperature is taken or the method he would like to use in getting up onto his bed at nap time. He will co-operate much more willingly if his need to express himself is taken into account for he will feel infinitely less dominated.

If a child is given a choice in ways of doing things, the adult needs to take the child's capacity in the realm of choosing into consideration and be ready to accept his selection. If the nurse says, "Susie, do you want to go to bed now or shall I go in to your room without you?" she must be certain she is capable of making a decision concerning her need for rest and be willing to accept "No" for an answer if it is forthcoming. A 30-month-old child is not capable of deciding the above question but he is able to decide how he would like to go to bed or what toy he would like to take with him. If the child is tired and shows a need for rest, this will need to be implied in the adult's question. The nurse's statement to Sally indicated what was expected of her and gave her experience in making choices.

When a child has made a choice, it is important that he be helped to hold to his decision. If he is encouraged to hold to his decision, he will discover the consequences of his action and learn that it is wise to think before he makes a choice.

Reality demands co-operation and consideration for the needs of others. Learning to adapt to the requirements of others is a long process that must be achieved a step at a time. Learning to handle one's self-assertiveness constructively is one of the first steps a child must take. The above kind of guidance not only helps the child to live in harmony with his parents, it also prepares him for social experiences with playmates, or peers as they are often called.

The child who rules at home or is subjected to adult or older sibling domination will have difficulties in his social relationships with teachers and peers. The child who rules at home expects that he shall be able to do the same thing with playmates. But he cannot. Playmates will not tolerate it and rebuff is inevitable.

Commands and domination increase negativism and stimulate stubborn resistance which brings relationship problems with both parents and playmates. Instead of learning that co-operation can be fun, the child's longings to assert himself become intensified. Instead of enjoying the things he ought to do, he wants to do only those things he is told he must not do. Eventually, to retain love he may acquiesce to his mother's domination, but the wish to assert himself will remain within him and will motivate his behavior throughout his lifetime.

With playmates the dominated child tends to be either submissive or a controlling little tyrant. The tyrant or bully has felt too weak to express himself with powerful parents or older siblings but in a group of children his own size he dares to exercise the power he has never been able to exercise at home. Both the submissive child and the bully are at a disadvantage with playmates. They feel weak, are little pleasure to themselves and have little preparation which helps them to relate successfully to others. Both types of children need help in acquiring security, belief in and respect for themselves and the ability to express themselves in ways that are satisfying both to themselves and to others.

The Child Uses Rituals to Express Himself and to Gain Security. As the child develops increased capacity to do things by himself, he demands this right. And what is more, he demands that he be allowed to do things in a certain way. He also demands that his mother or his nurse do things in a designated way and *he* wants to be the dictator. Temporarily, he becomes a ritualist. The period is short if it is understood and if his rituals are accepted and utilized advantageously.

The child begins to show characteristics of ritualism around 2 years of age. The period is at its height at 30 months of age and if he is guided wisely he will be infinitely less ritualistic by 3. Gesell[11] says that the child is in a transition period at this stage of development; he acts this way because his developmental state compels him to do so. He has achieved a certain degree of independence and acquired understanding of a great many things, yet he is far from capable of mastering himself or his environment. He feels safer when activities are carried out in a prescribed manner for it gives him a feeling that he is master of himself and of the situation. Then he is sure of what to expect, is able to master himself and is comfortable.

Respecting the child's ritualistic behavior is not spoiling him; it is meeting his need for security and at this stage of development he requires it. Using his self-made rituals also gives him a feeling of importance. This does not mean that he is going to grow up into a self-centered bigot. It serves rather to encourage the development of the reverse type of personality, for self-mastery and respect are necessary for love and respect of others.

Setting reasonable limits which give the child opportunity to execute his own rituals gives the child the security he needs and keeps the concept of his power a realistic one. It should not hurt one's dignity to accept a certain amount of direction from a 30-month-old child. It is true that one cannot let him completely dominate her for the reasons already cited and because it can so easily get out of bounds and become intolerable for the adult and depriving to the child. If the child is given complete freedom to dominate the adult, he will soon reach the limits of the adult's tolerance and an outburst of anger or rejection will be inevitable. This is frightening for the child and he will feel little security in an atmosphere of uncertainty.

One can respect a child's need for his bath ritual, for instance, and still help him know there are certain things designated by his mother which must be done. Using his rituals in this phase of development saves the mother or nurse time and energy. If his leads are followed, working with him will be much more pleasurable, for he can co-operate much more easily when he is familiar with the details of a routine. If we do not use his rituals, resistance is inevitable for he becomes uncertain of what is going to happen and his self-mastery becomes threatened. Jim's behavior illustrates this characteristic.

Jim, aged 30 months, has designed a getting-out-of-the-tub ritual. He wrung out the washcloth, placed it on the rack above the tub, carefully dried his water toys and placed them on the upper shelf of the cabinet which stood beside the tub and *then* pulled out the plug. When his mother permitted this ritual, bath time was a completely enjoyable experience for Jim and herself. But when she was in a hurry and attempted to rush the procedure and do those things Jim ordinarily did himself, he became resistant, and instead of shortening bath time it was prolonged and became a disappointing experience for both of them.

When the child must be hospitalized when he is in the ritualistic phase of development, unfamiliar routines will be a source of great concern to him. At home he has acquired a ritualistic way of bathing, dressing, toileting, eating and sleeping. He has acquired a routine way of doing things either because his mother has followed a patterned way of doing things or because she has planned routines in a way that meets his specific requirements. When a child is confronted with temperature, weighing, medicine, bed bath and a new kind of toileting, meal, nap and bedtime routine, he has a completely new regimen with which to cope. He cannot anticipate what is coming next and he has no idea of what is expected of him. Aside from the new routines, there is the inevitable unexpected trip to the roentgen-ray or the electro-encephalogram department which makes it necessary for him to be transported through unfamiliar territory. Is it any wonder the young child is overwhelmed with the admission procedure and life in a ward during the earliest days of his hospitalization? Is it not logical to conclude that he is in need of his mother when he is forced to adapt himself to so many new things all at once?

If the mother is not permitted to stay with her child during the period he is becoming familiar with a nurse and ward routines, the nurse needs to know the home rituals which gave the child security. Simulating his rituals in the hospital will help him feel more at home there and more a master of the situation. When a child is ill his powers of adaptation become threatened. It brings a great deal of concern to many children for they dislike losing the self-mastery which has given them feelings of pride, security and accomplishment.

A child will adapt to the hospital most readily if he is helped to become familiar with ward routines through consistently carried out experiences and through opportunities to make reasonable alterations in the way he would like things done. He will show us the adjustments he would like us to make. If the nurse is flexible and desirous of meeting her patient's needs, she will observe the cues which tell her what he has been accustomed to at home.

To see cues the nurse's interest needs to be focused on the child rather than on routines and procedures. Between 1 and 3 years of age the child cannot say, "Nurse, don't you know? At home I always play with Teddy before naptime. If I could have Teddy and be allowed to do things as I've been accustomed to doing them, I *could* rest." But he will show us his need in his behavior. We can learn to interpret his behavior if we have a genuine desire to bring emotional comfort to our patients. A nurse cannot help but know when she has interpreted a need correctly and responded to it appropriately. Anxiety lessens and the child's equilibrium becomes restored.

Children need nurses who have imagination and the emotional freedom to adapt procedures and routines to the needs of their patients. Nurses cannot do this if they are threatened by supervision which demands adherence to the lines of every procedure. The nurse needs to know the principles of the procedure so she allows only those adaptations which are safe for her patients. Aside from utilizing the principles of the procedure, the nurse needs freedom to use her creative imagination in meeting the needs of her patients. Without freedom to bring comfort to her patients, the nurse's work is not creative; it is technical, mechanized and unfeeling. When it is, neither nurse nor child can grow and get satisfaction from their experiences together.

To exemplify a way of helping children master their fears through the use of ritualistic behavior, a situation with 34-month-old Joey is cited.

Joey had a burned foot and wet dressings were required 3 times daily. Joey had been helped to master his fear of the experience through preparation and encouragement of his interest in helping with the procedure. Joey had his own nurse and together they worked out a way of doing things which was safe from a bacteriologic standpoint and acceptable to Joey. Each morning when the tray of equipment was brought in, Joey knew exactly what was going to happen and knew what he was going to do.

The first time the nurse did Joey's dressing she placed the equipment on the foot of his bed and waited for Joey to give her some signs of how he would like her to proceed. The sterile equipment was, of course, covered but there was equipment he could touch. There were scissors, bandages and a basin for waste. He reached for the scissors, eyed them carefully and looked at the nurse. "Yes, you can use them, Joey. I'll show you how," the nurse said. Joey was taught how to slip the scissor beneath the bandage on his foot and together they cut through it. Joey began to remove it. First, however, he looked at the nurse to appraise her feelings concerning his activity. "Here's a basin, Joey. You can use this to put the bandages in," the nurse said, to help him find ways of helping.

The nurse had brought two pairs of forceps with her. One pair she gave to Joey and showed him how they were used. "You can use your pair to put these pieces of gauze in your basin. I'll use my pair to take the dressings from your foot. It will hurt a little but I'll be very careful. Here are some bandages, Joey. While I take the dressings off, you can get the paper off the roll," the nurse continued.

While the dressings were removed, Joey's interest was divided between the nurse's work and his own. Once he winced and whimpered a bit. "You tell me when it hurts, Joey. I know it's scary and it hurts sometimes," the nurse said to assure him that expression of feeling was acceptable. His nurse completed the dressing and covered it with sterilized waterproof material. Joey knew the purpose of the bandage and handed it to the nurse. "Thanks, Joey. Now I'll show you how you can help to put it on," the nurse said. Joey did help and was proud that his nurse could see he was able to do so. Each time his nurse did the dressing, Joey's dressing ritual was followed. Through utilizing his ritual, Joey became master of his fear.

The first dressing utilized an hour of Joey's nurse's time and an abundance of her imagination in finding a way to keep Joey secure and comfortable. Had she been concerned only with carrying out an order for wet dressings to a foot, Joey's emotional needs would have remained unsatisfied. The dressing might have been completed in 15 minutes, but the help of a second nurse would have been required then and whenever the experience was repeated. However, more important than this was the fact that Joey's relationship with his nurse was maintained at a positive constructive level. Had Joey not been helped to meet the original frightening experience, dressing time would have become a nightmare. Instead of anticipating a dreaded experience, Joey knew what was going to happen and he knew it was something he could master. In between dressings he was free from anxiety, and his energy was available for play and the recuperation process.

Resistance to sleep is comparatively common during this ritualistic phase of development. Up until the fifteenth or sixteenth month of life the child usually accepts resting periods and going to bed at night amicably. Then a change in behavior is apt to occur. He resents stopping his engrossing play, and when he gets into bed he thinks up innumerable ways to keep his mother nearby or to bring her back to him. Often he needs to play for a while after getting into bed. Sometimes it is quiet play but more often it is active play which he seems to need to get release from tension.

When these changes in behavior are anticipated, the mother can prevent serious sleep disturbance by giving the child an opportunity to satisfy his newly developed needs. When his mother understands him she can kindly and firmly tuck him under the covers and help him to know that time for resting has come *now*.

When a child is unduly fatigued or keyed up from an active morning or afternoon of play, he often needs help in relaxing. His mother or nurse can help him learn to relax by sitting with him for a few minutes if she is relaxed herself. Some children relax quickly if their mother or nurse puts a hand on the arm or leg which is moving and softly says something like the following: "I'll help you keep your arm still, Sandy. You can do it, I know you can." Other children become more tense when this teaching devise is used. If increased tenseness is observed, it is better to tuck the child in bed with an affectionate kiss and to say something like this: "I'll see you in the morning, Sandy. Tomorrow play time will come again."

During this phase of development wakefulness during the night is not an uncommon characteristic and there are many reasons why a child might experience it. If one reviews the events occurring in the life of the 1- to 3-year old child, one can find reasons why he might dread the night and reasons why he often wakes up in a fearful state of mind. In this period he is discovering himself and his world. He feels powerful in many ways but in other ways he feels helpless and afraid. He is struggling to gain mastery of his body and experiencing many new events which he cannot quite understand.

Darkness separates the child from his mother, and he is left alone to cope with the anxiety he has not been able to master during his waking hours. Fraiberg[5] says, "Darkness and sleep are the toddler's enemies." She explains the reasons for her statement in the following paragraphs:

These two rob him of his newly discovered world and his new-found sense of *himself* as a being separate and different. At night his much-needed parents and his familiar possessions disappear and he, Peter, the "I" of this world, feels threatened with extinction too.

In sleep he encounters another world, a world he re-creates from the events of the day—but in a form tangled, distorted and disarranged. For Peter, this dream world is as real as the "real world." Sometimes it isn't bad. A lost lollipop may be found, a smiling mother bends over him. But the dream isn't always so merciful. The big dog that barked and the doctor who hurt come back again in the dream. A roaring vacuum chases Peter through the rooms of a dark house. Sometimes he calls out in his sleep, "No! No! No!" to attackers from this dream world. Finally when they get too much for him he wakes crying.

Peter fears the night for still other reasons. In the dream world he faces dangers all alone. This is frightening so he calls for his mother. She comes; she assures him he is safe. And *now* will he go back to sleep? "No!" Because if he goes back to sleep the bad dog will surely come again.

It is not unusual to see young children in the hospital resisting resting time, fighting sleep and having nightmares. The daytime events in the life of a hospitalized child are infinitely more difficult to handle than those the child at home experiences. Some hospitalized children refuse to lie down; they give in to their need for sleep only when they are at the point of exhaustion. Neither is it unusual to see a child in the hospital awakening from sleep in a state of terror.

The child who awakens from sleep in fear or terror needs a nurse at his bedside immediately to orient him to his surroundings, to comfort him and to assure him that she will protect him from harm. If he awakens fearfully at night, he also shows a need for more help during the day. He needs opportunities to master more of his anxiety through play and experiences which provide opportunity for him to participate in his own care. He also shows his need for a person to depend upon—someone who can help him know the ways of the hospital ward, who can assist him in discovering that the reality of his new world is not so dangerous as he imagines it to be.

A Child Dawdles in the Process of Discovering and Learning to Master Himself. Dawdling is another characteristic commonly observed in children between the eighteenth and forty-eighth months of life. The child has learned that there are certain prohibitions, but his ability to inhibit certain action is still very weak.[11] There are also many things he has not learned. He is still unsure of himself because he has little control within himself and cannot distinguish right from wrong. To expect that he should is to expect the impossible. Because he is unsure of what to do, he dawdles.

Gesell[11] says that the child under 3 years of age is incapable of making a single choice, so he makes two. His nurse calls him from the playroom and tells him it is tub bath time. He does not just come; he dawdles and comes and goes. He runs toward the nurse, arrives at his destination, and rushes away again; or it may happen that he does it in reverse order.

The young child who dawdles is not being obstinate; he is only experimenting with conflicting feelings and trying to discover a solution that will bring pleasure. When his nurse waits patiently and then says, "That's right, Billy. When I call tub bath time, it is time to come," he learns what is right and expected of him. If she sees his behavior as obstinacy and becomes exasperated with his dawdling he will not learn what is right and expected of him. Instead, he probably will discover a wonderful way to get attention and to tease his nurse. The situation described below exemplifies Steve's reaction to conflicting feelings and the method his mother used to help him make a decision.

Steve was 18 months old. His mother had gone to get him from a neighbor's play yard and he came willingly but dawdled about 50 yards behind. When his mother reached her yard she turned around and saw Steve with three boys who were dressed in cowboy suits. Steve was entranced watching them and then proceeded to join them as they progressed in the opposite direction to his home.

His mother called, "Steve, come this way." Steve continued to follow the boys but he also looked back at his mother. She called again but did not run to him because she knew it would retard his learning. Again he looked back and went forward. Then he walked a few feet closer to his mother and twirled himself in the middle of the sidewalk. He was undoubtedly in conflict. The fancily dressed boys intrigued him but he also needed his mother's approval. After he had twirled for a minute or two he came to his mother. She said, "When I call you, it means come home."

When a child does not get all the legitimate attention he needs and discovers that his dawdling brings what he is longing for, he may continue to be a vacillating, slow child because he finds it is a successful way of getting what he needs. Dawdling is characteristic in a period when the child is requiring less physical care than formerly but is continuing to need the companionship of his mother. If he fails to get his requirements for attention and recognition met in legitimate ways he may continue to dawdle beyond the period when it is developmentally required. Later he may use dawdling to express hostility. Especially is this true if he finds his dawdling is irritating to his mother and he has a need to punish her in some manner.

Excessive dawdling is frequently used by children whose mothers have inhibited their early aggression and signs of verbal negativism. Their "No's" and "I won'ts" and signs of natural aggression having been punished instead of being understood, their dawdling becomes an expression of resistance and serves a purpose for aggressively inhibited children. They punish their mothers and gain power and control with their slowness and their passive resistance.

Dawdling rarely brings deprivation of love, especially if the child uses it at mealtimes; instead it brings pleasure. During mealtime the dawdler usually becomes the center of attention and rarely is he deprived of his food even when the other members of the family have completed their meal.

Prolonged and excessive dawdling is a symptom and often indicates the child's need for socially acceptable aggressive and self-assertive outlets. Dawdling as an expression of hostility brings less disapproval than overt expression but it is not a constructive way to express one's feelings. It may be acceptable to the child's mother but it may meet with disapproval and limit his opportunities for growth-producing experiences later in life. When a dawdling child is given freedom to express his feelings in more active ways, his need for dawdling usually lessens. Scolding or nagging aggravates the problem; it intensifies his need to resist and punish. The example which follows illustrates a child's use of dawdling and a way which helped her to get attention in legitimate ways and express herself in ways which met her needs more fully.

Lucia was 3½ years of age and in the hospital with edema of unknown etiology. She had spent her life in foster homes because her mother was unable to provide care for her.

Lucia was a Negro child with flashing black eyes, a superficial smile for everyone and a submissive pattern of behavior. She never cried when diagnostic tests were done and she accepted routines like an automaton. For hours of the day she sat in a highchair in her doorway smiling at everyone who passed. When a hammer and peg board were given to her, she reached toward it but withdrew her hands immediately.

At mealtimes Lucia dawdled excessively and ate very little. She would take one half teaspoonful of food and hold it in her mouth while she observed her universe. When a nurse tried to feed her, she closed her mouth resistantly.

When Lucia was permitted freedom to be out of her room, she did not play or show interest in the other children. After two weeks she began to relate herself to her nurse, but her submissive behavior, dawdling and poor appetite continued.

A new plan of feeding was instituted. Lucia ate at a table with two other children and a nurse. Minute quantities of food were served to her with the comment, "Lucia, when you are ready for more, you tell me. You can help yourself from the bowls of food."

Lucia finished what was on her plate in a jiffy and said in a near to inaudible tone, "More meat." Lucia helped herself not once but four times and each time the helping she took got bigger. She poured her own milk, fed herself and smiled a "deep" smile of satisfaction as she was permitted to help herself.

Lucia also needed help in learning to play. She could do nothing without permission, and it was several weeks before she felt safe enough to do anything as aggressive as throwing a ball or pounding.

Lucia also needed help in expressing her anger. One day after she had submitted to a jugular puncture without any outward reaction the nurse said, "Children get angry when people hold them down and put needles into them. Some children tell us when they are angry." Like a flash, Lucia leaned over and hit the sleeve of the doctor's coat. His response showed understanding and brought changes in Lucia's behavior which were important for her mental health. The doctor said, "I'm glad you can tell me how you feel, Lucia. Needles do hurt and it's good when children tell us about it."

For the next hour Lucia played doctor to her doll in a way she had not done before. She used an applicator and stuck her doll and then spanked her, saying, "Naughty girl." The nurse said, "I wonder why the doll is naughty." Lucia said, "She's bad." The nurse said, "She's not bad. The needle hurt her and she hit before she knew it. When she is bigger she can tell her doctors and nurses how angry she feels." Lucia looked at the nurse and said, "She not bad?" Then the nurse said, "No, Lucia, the doll isn't bad. She's like all children. She could not say 'That hurts, I don't like you when you do that,' so she hit. But some day she will be able to say it. It did not hurt the doctor. Let's go find him. You will see he isn't cross. He knew it hurt you."

Promoting Independence Gives the Child Opportunities to Express and Master Himself and His Environment. *The child needs help in becoming increasingly more independent and capable of assuming responsibility.* Previously it was stated that the little child defies authority because he feels he is no longer a baby and wants to try out his own ways of doing things. Infantilization limits his opportunities to learn and to express himself. When he is recuperating from an illness he will want to do things for himself and he should be given this privilege. The more he is taught to do things independently, the less need he will have to assert himself in negativistic and nonconstructive ways.

One of the first things the child can learn to do independently is to feed himself. In the process of being fed the 8- to 12-month-old baby reaches out and clutches his food in his fists. At first his purpose is not to feed himself; it is to satisfy his potent impulse to smear and mess.[9] It is the time when it is natural for the baby to discover his body and its excretory products. However, his impulses to smear are wisely curtailed by his mother's care in pinning his diapers snugly. When his impulses to smear with feces are curtailed, he transfers them to his food, which is similar in feeling, temperature and consistency.[9] When the child is permitted this substitute pleasure, it is obvious that his enjoyment of food is greatly enhanced.

Gradually with experience the baby's messiness with food develops into the constructive activity of self-feeding and he begins to get the idea that food should go into his mouth and be eaten. At first he is messy and he does get food onto his face, bib, high-chair and oftentimes even into his hair and onto the floor as well. Restricting the child's natural impulses to feel and to manipulate his food usually brings anger and loss of appetite. If his mother is patient, he will gradually develop interest in using the spoon, and with experience he will develop the co-ordination necessary to keep the spoon upright and to get food into his mouth.

The child will acquire self-feeding capacity earlier if his natural interests are encouraged and his mother is able to tolerate untidiness at mealtimes. A large bib and newspapers upon the floor should catch the drippings and make it possible for the child to learn without having his messiness disapproved. Often the child is not skillful enough to feed himself the entire meal, but he resents it if his mother or nurse does not permit him to do the parts he is capable and desirous of doing. Instead of taking the spoon from his hand, it is wiser to assist him with another. If his natural interests are encouraged, he will have acquired proficiency by 16 to 24 months of age and be capable of feeding himself independently. However, if he is unduly tired or ill he may still be needful of help at intervals.

During the period the child is learning to feed himself he needs to have distractions kept at a minimum. Feeding himself requires concentration. If his mother or nurse talks to him a great deal during the meal hour he is distracted from the important business of learning to eat. When he has mastered the skills necessary for self-feeding, sociability will become an important part of the mealtime experience. Manners are a part of the distant future. He will acquire them later when he becomes ready to imitate his parents' table behavior. Nagging and criticism impede progress in acquiring the ways of our culture. Children want to be like the grown-ups they admire, and as their ability to co-ordinate develops, they will imitate their technics of eating.

In the early part of this period, the child shows food preferences; they need respect and understanding. Sometimes his dislike of certain foods is intense. In this period it is not unusual to see a child showing strong aversion to foods he formerly accepted with pleasure. Nothing is gained by forcing him to eat foods which distress him, and unhappiness and feeding problems occur when mealtime becomes a battle. If his choice of food is tolerated, the aversion probably will be only temporary. Later he will accept the temporarily unwanted foods as eagerly as he did on former occasions.

In the hospital, convalescent children enjoy sitting at a table for mealtime. They need to be comfortable in chairs which bring them to the right height for self-feeding and far enough apart to prevent them from interfering with one another. They will, of course, need adult supervision and guidance. Some will need help in learning to eat, and the entire group will need the security which comes from a person who is there to guide them.

A group of four 1- to 3-year-old children is as large as one nurse can supervise adequately. If the nurse eats with the children, she will be there to give them the security and the help they need to discover that eating together can be a happy experience. If the servings are small and in proportion to the individual child's appetite, the nurse will be less tempted to urge the children to eat.

There are no psychological formulae which can be used to help those children who are feeding problems. Each child will require individual study and guidance appropriate to meet his emotional needs. Unless the child has a physical disorder which brings loss of appetite (or anorexia, as it is often called), a feeding problem is symptomatic of a disturbance in interpersonal relationships. Unless the cause is found and rectified, changes in eating habits cannot be expected. When children are physically healthy, secure and happy in their relationships with those who are important to them, feeding problems are nonexistent.

In the hospital as in the home the morning and evening care procedures can be ones for learning and enjoyment of satisfying relationships with the child's mother or his nurse. He will enjoy pulling off his clothing and assisting with the bath procedure. If the bath basin is placed on the bed in front of the convalescent child and the nurse waits to discover the child's interests and abilities, she will give the child no end of pleasure. Instead of using her time to bathe the child, she can use it in teaching him the fun of a co-operative enterprise. He will love rubbing the soap on his stomach and his legs and will revel in the opportunity to squeeze the wet washcloth between his hands. He will enjoy putting his arms into his shirt sleeves and pulling the buttons through the holes. He will delight in putting the linen into the laundry bag and catching the soap to place it in his soapdish. And how understood he will feel when his nurse recognizes his ability and his need to play in water and to do some of the things adults can do!

The above kind of nursing meets the child's emotional requirements but it deprives some nurses of finding gratification for their own dependency needs. Through identification with the child some nurses obtain vicarious satisfaction of their own dependency needs. Nurses who do often fail to see the child's interest in wanting to do things for himself. If the nurse develops her skill in teaching and sees the results of her guidance in the pleasure and opportunity for learning that she gives the child, her own needs will be less frustrated and she will have a substitute satisfaction which will be infinitely more gratifying.

Learning to assume responsibility gives the child a feeling of importance and independence. His first responsibilities should be concerned with toileting, dressing and undressing, feeding, bathing and toothbrushing.

Some of the children the nurse will be caring for in the hospital will be physically handicapped in one way or another. There will be those who are blind and those who are crippled with such conditions as cerebral palsy, poliomyelitis or rheumatoid arthritis. There will be many things these children cannot do but many they can do if they are taught patiently and given time to do those things they are capable of doing.

A crippled child is as desirous and needful of mastering himself and his environment as is the normal child. He wants to do those things others do. Accomplishment and success are as necessary for his ego growth as they are for the ego growth of the nonhandicapped child. Unless he can be helped to gain inner resources and satisfactions from self-mastery, he will be forever dependent upon his parents for the gratification of his needs and never have the opportunity to develop socially and emotionally. Eventually he will want experiences with those outside his home. He will want independence, and every human being has a right to it. It is his parents and his nurses who need to recognize his growth requirements and it is they who must provide the experiences from which he can grow emotionally, socially and spiritually as well as physically.

Providing the crippled child with the kind of environment he needs for total growth is a difficult feat. It requires parental maturity, creative imagination and the selflessness necessary to see the child as a person with drives, wishes and feelings of his very own. In her story of Karen, Killilea[17] not only portrays the child's quest for increasing independence, self-realization and maturity, but also describes the way in which a family can function to provide the experiences and emotional support a handicapped child needs for growth. It is a beautiful and inspiring story of the way human love can be expressed. It brought self-realization and independence to Karen. After she had mastered the skill necessary to write, she expressed what accomplishment meant to her. She said, "I can walk. I can talk. I can read. I can write. Mom, Pom, I can do anything!"[17]

When the child has learned to assume responsibility in the areas of care already mentioned, he begins to show interest in learning to care for his clothing and toys and in doing simple household tasks. Clothes hooks, towel racks and shelves which are within the child's reach facilitate learning. In this period of development the child wants to help his mother, father and older siblings. If he is in the hospital, chores which are within his capacity will delight him and help him to feel important and accomplished. As the child grows in his ability to assume responsibility as a family member, it should be given to him, for self-reliance and an ability to enjoy co-operative living are basic requirements for sound personality growth. A situation observed at a refreshment counter in a downtown store illustrates the feelings of pride which come when a child is given responsibility.

A young lad of about 5 came into the five-and-ten-cent store with his mother for refreshments. In his arms was a package. He got onto the stool, put the package on the shelf under the counter and said, "Thank you, Mother, for letting me carry this package." To appreciate the full meaning of this to the child, one would need to have seen and heard him, for it was not only his words but also his feelings and facial expression which showed the thrill of accomplishment he felt when his mother trusted him with one of her purchases.

If a child's interest in helping is not recognized or is rebuffed by a mother or nurse who does not want to bother with a child's assistance, the adult runs the risk of difficulty in helping him to assume responsibility at a later date. The 2-year-old child enjoys dusting, washing dishes, pulling up the sheets on his crib, picking up toys, putting his clothes away and carrying silver to the table; the 6-year-old child resents the same activities if earlier interest in the same pursuits was thwarted.

Guidance Includes Recognition of the Child's Need for Toys, Raw Materials and Supervision in His Play. In this period of development the child needs toys and play equipment which promote large muscle development and growth in sensory perception, stimulate mental functioning and provide opportunities for self-expression in dramatic and creative play.

The toddler requires toys that help him to learn to differentiate colors, weights, shapes and sizes. When he has a variety of toys his powers of perception will develop through experience. In the course of experimentation, he will discover that small objects are sometimes heavy and sometimes light, and learn that large objects will not fit into small places. This type of knowledge comes only through experimentation with objects and through play. Therefore the choice of toys and the method of supervision are of educational significance for the child.[16]

A small wagon, baby carriage or animals and vehicles on wheels provide experience in pushing and pulling. Large balls, pounding boards, toy work benches and sand toys are examples of the kind of toys the 1- to 3-year-old child uses to great advantage. Dolls, animals, blocks, household equipment, cars, airplanes, fire engines, trains, etc., are also important for the child to possess.

Dramatic house and community play serves a useful purpose if the child is given freedom to use materials in his own individual way. He enjoys imitating his mother's activities not only because it makes him feel grown-up but also because activity is pleasurable and he enjoys learning. Play also prepares him for his future adult role and provides opportunities to master the feelings and the conflicts which his daily life experiences create within him. The child will need but little direction in the use of his toys. One only needs to present them and to give him permission to play. He will discover their properties and use them in a way that will meet his individual requirements. In the process of playing, he may discover, for instance, that blocks can be thrown as well as used for building. It is then that the adult enters in—not to restrict his play or to suppress the feelings that prompted the activity but to help him know where they may be thrown. The child will benefit as much from throwing them into a box or tin can as beneath his bed if his mother or nurse is there to help him have fun in the experience.

In all supervision of play, the child needs encouragement to develop his powers of reasoning in the solution of his problems. If the adult enters in and solves his problems for him, he will miss experiences which contribute to ego growth. The child learns through trial and error and through finding success. The adult's task is to help the child discover ways of achieving success. He does not achieve it when the adult solves his problem; he achieves it when he is helped to find a solution of his own. Each success strengthens the child's ego and helps him to feel, "I can do—I know I can." The following situation illustrates a method of helping children grow more capable of solving their own problems.

Thad, aged 26 months, was in the hospital playroom finger painting. His paint was drying and he needed water to moisten it. He had observed the nurse getting it and he knew she used one of the paper cups on the table beside him. He took the cup and went to the sink for water. When he could not reach the faucets, he looked at the nurse as if to say, "And what do I do now?" Instead of getting the water for him the nurse said, "Thad, look around. See if you can find something that will help you get the water by yourself." Thad looked around the room but began to lose interest because he needed further help. "Thad, I'll help you look. I'm sure you can find something to stand upon," the nurse encouraged. Then Thad's face lighted up in a smile. He saw the big blocks against the wall and ran over to them. He pulled one out, pushed it to the sink, and climbed up to get the water he needed. He succeeded and his facial expression evidenced his feelings of accomplishment.

The child needs raw materials like sand, large blocks, paper, crayons, paste, clay, easel and finger paint and supervision in learning to use them constructively and in his way and at his own speed. Play is not just purposeless diversion; it is experience which gives the child opportunity to know and to master himself and his environment, to express himself creatively, to gain release from tension and to find socially acceptable outlets for his feelings.

A child can be taught the general use of clay, finger or easel paint by simple demonstration with the nurse's or mother's own materials. The adult's objective in supervision is to teach the child the use of the material and the limits within which they may be used. She does not supervise to show him how to paint a picture or mold an art object; she supervises to give the child opportunity for spontaneous creative expression within the limits of the paper fastened onto the easel or the clay which is on the molding board. Setting a pattern of adult performance stifles the child's creativeness, for he recognizes his incapacity to measure up to the standards the adult is inadvertently setting for him. The child needs his own materials and they should remain his own. A child's spontaneous expression is inhibited and he experiences no self-realization when adults take over to direct or to reconstruct his products according to their own standards of attractiveness.

The child needs to have his productions appreciated. If the 18-month-old child's scribbles are viewed in terms of his level of development, the adult will see that they are as valuable and as artistic as the adolescent's intricate designs. In this period, from 1 to 3 years of age, the child's play with raw materials is largely manipulative. He is learning to use materials, and pleasure is derived from the activity itself. As yet he is not attempting to make anything—that will come later when he has learned the properties of the material and has developed increased muscle co-ordination.

Asking a child what he is making perplexes him and inhibits freedom of expression. Later, when he becomes as interested in his products as he is in the process, comments like the following will give him opportunity to talk about his creation if he so desires and provide the adult with increased insight into the feelings and the thoughts that are motivating his behavior: "Johnny, I'd like to hear about your picture if you'd care to tell me about it."

In this period of development the child's interest in books and stories develops, and he is stimulated to enjoy books through pleasant, shared experiences with his parents. Books with pictures of familiar objects are the first ones that will catch his interest. He enjoys looking at the pictures, turning the pages and learning new words which come in response to his pointing or to one of his earliest questions, "What's this?" As the child associates happy shared experiences with books, he will come to treasure them as his parents do. If books are given to the child as playthings and he never experiences the pleasure which comes from mother and the book when he is read to, the true value of books may never become appreciated.

Children in this period love stories that contain repetition, rhyme and sounds that can be dramatized and experiences with which they are familiar. One- to 4-year-old children delight in books about houses, boats, airplanes, buses, trains, adults and children like themselves. They revel in nursery rhymes, not because they comprehend the meaning of the verse but because the rhythm delights them. They love to hear the adult dramatize the words that symbolize sound and action. If the words, "Then I'll huff and I'll puff and I'll blow your house in," are read or said in a monotone, children are deprived of some of the pleasure of the story. Repetition in a story may be boring to the adult but it is often the part children enjoy the most. It is the repetition in books like "The Three Little Pigs" and "Ask Mr. Bear" which makes them classics and children's favorites.

When the child has learned more about people and his environment, he will begin to enjoy stories with simple plots and humor expressed in verse or line. When his vocabulary and experience widen, he develops the capacity to detect and to appreciate absurdities in the things story characters do and say. In this period the child profits most from books which increase his knowledge of people, activities and things within his world. Until a child can distinguish fact from fancy, fanciful stories and fairy tales need to be kept at a minimum.

Books need to be appealing to the child's interests rather than to the adult's. Pictures and stories which delight the adult are often totally uninteresting and inappropriate for the child. He enjoys large, realistic and artistic pictures, a narrative that is written in short, simple, uninvolved sentences and printed in large type. Those stories children ask to have repeated again and again are the ones which contain the characteristics that are appealing to children.

When a child is ill, he enjoys stories that revive early memories of comforting experiences with his mother. The sick child's attention span shortens and his mental functioning is often not up to his usual capacity. In selecting books for sick children the above factors need consideration.

Children greatly enjoy story periods. They like stories read to them, but even more they enjoy having the adult tell them stories which come from books or from their own childhood experiences. Story periods in the hospital ward help to make the children's days more meaningful. They provide a period of relaxation for them and are a social and educational experience they need.

Play activities are as necessary for children in the hospital as they are necessary for children in their homes. There are children in the hospital between 12 months and 3 years of age who are not ill enough to be confined to their beds. If the child is kept in bed when his physical condition does not require it, not only has he insufficient activity, but also his opportunities for gratification and learning become limited. The crib sides and possibly a restraint jacket in addition prevent him from seeking the satisfaction and experience he requires. He does not have the capacity to say, "I am bored, lonesome and afraid," or "This bed is limiting my opportunities for developing independence. It gives me no chance to run and play and get to the person who could give me comfort. I am tired of these measley little blocks, trains and spools. I need something new to explore." Because he cannot verbalize his wishes and feelings, he often acts them out by screaming, throwing away his toys or destroying the equipment which cannot satisfy his longing and need for activity.

Ambulatory privileges give the children opportunity for muscular and exploratory activity and contact with their nurses, but they also confront them with many threatening situations. They venture into isolated units and into areas dangerous for them to be in. They also run into adults who do not seem to realize they are too young to be familiar with hospital regulations or that they are only in search of satisfaction for their emotional and physical needs. Many times they are scolded or punished by being put back to bed. Such unreasonable management merely increases their frustration and intensifies their need for tensional outlets and comfort.

Ambulatory children need a place to explore, playthings appropriate for their use and supervision which meets their physical and emotional requirements. Toys and space are not enough to keep them secure, active and learning. They need supervision not only to learn where they are to play and the use of materials, but also to give them security, protection and emotional warmth. If the playroom is in the ward and without a gate and there is no kind, protective, thoughtful adult with them, they will not confine their activities there. This will be true even when the room is amply supplied with play equipment which ordinarily interests children at this level of development. They will leave the playroom and search for security, for without an adult usually they are anxious and unable to play.

Children in this period and the next need adult supervision to protect them from their own impulses and from those of others. They cannot control many of their impulses independently. This is as true in play as it is in other situations which have already been cited. Until children have acquired inner controls which check overt expression of their impulses, they need an adult to function for them, This fact can be verified readily in the hospital playroom or in any play group of preschool children. As long as the familiar "play lady," nurse or teacher remains within the group, happiness and constructive play usually prevail. But if the adult leaves and her return is not immediate, the character of the play period quickly changes. Temporarily, some may fight, snatch or throw. However, very soon the group will disband and the children will go in search of protection. The absence of the adult frightens them for they know instinctively that neither they nor the others can control their aggressive and possessive impulses.

Children are social creatures; they are interested in other children but they need their mothers or their substitutes close by to give them security and physical protection. They reach out for experiences with other children but at first they see them only as objects to explore. The 2-year-old youngster is beginning to want friends but he has not yet learned how to make and keep them. Usually his social approaches are aggressive instead of the friendly verbal variety characteristically used by 4- to 5-year-old children. *The young child needs help in learning how to approach other children but first he needs to discover that being with others is comfortable and pleasant.* When he finds there are advantages in being with other children, he will want to learn how to make friends and how to play co-operatively with them.

One- to 2-year-old children enjoy being together if there is an adult with them to provide emotional support and physical safety, but they are not ready to participate in co-operative play. They may sit opposite each other manipulating clay or stringing large heads, but this is not co-operative activity; it is what is known as *parallel* play.

Before children are ready to share and plan and execute projects co-operatively, they must first experience feelings of possession and learn how to do things independently. The adult who supervises 1- to 3-year old children in play needs the ability to plan the experiences so that it is possible for every child in the group to find satisfaction in playing independently and in being near others. Unless each child discovers that being with others is pleasurable and constructive, it will not be an experience which furthers good social relationships.

It takes a long time for children to acquire the social and the emotional maturity necessary to make it possible for them to engage in co-operative play with others. It will be a longer time before they have acquired sufficient independence from their mothers to be able to play with others without adult supervision. In the school age period children should be ready for some unsupervised social experiences. In the period which is to follow, growth and guidance must prepare them to meet the social requirements of their teacher and their peers.

Questions to Guide Observation

1. How would you determine a child's readiness for learning bowel control? Learning bladder control?

2. How does "training" for bowel and bladder control influence the development of personality?

3. How will you use the knowledge you acquired in relation to toilet traning in working with mothers in well-baby conferences?

4. How does illness change established patterns of excretory activity?

5. Select one of your patients who is in the training period of personality development. Describe his excretory behavior. What does he do and say when he eliminates? How has his behavior changed during his illness? Had his mother begun helping him to learn control prior to illness? What methods did she use? Do you think he is ready to develop control? What makes you think so? How will you assist him in gaining control of excretory functioning?

6. How do you feel about discipline? What does "disciplining" a child mean to you? How were you disciplined as a child? How did you feel about it? What determines the type of discipline a mother uses in guiding her children? What factors influence the way a nurse disciplines her patients?

7. What are your objectives of discipline? How did you determine them?

8. How do personal-social factors condition a parent's attitudes toward discipline? In what ways does a child's personality patterns reflect the type of authority he experienced at home?

9. How do you feel when a child does something you asked him not to do? Describe a situation when this occurred. What did you do? What was the child's response to your guidance?

10. How does the child develop a concept of himself as a person? Of what importance to the child is a good concept of himself? How do adults influence the child's feelings about himself?

11. Describe a child who demonstrates negativistic behavior. When does he use negativism? For what purpose does he use it? How do you feel when a child responds to you with negativism? What was your response to the child's negativism?

12. Describe a pattern of ritualistic behavior you have observed in one of your patients. How did you use it? What value had it for the child?

13. How do you feel when a child dawdles? Describe a situation where you observed dawdling. How old was the child? Why do you think he dawdled? How did you respond to it? How do you feel

when a head nurse hurries you? How do you respond to her disapproval?

14. How can a nurse help her patients to develop increased independence? Of what value is it to the child if the nurse helps him to increase his independence rather than infantilizing him?

15. Describe a situation in which you taught a child to bathe, dress or feed himself. How did you feel about it? How did you do it? What was the child's response? Did you enjoy it as much as if you had done it for him?

16. Observe a nursery school teacher or play therapist supervising a period of painting or clay activity. Describe what you saw. Did she stimulate creative expression? Of what value was it? How can you use what you learned in the hospital ward?

17. Select a book for a normal 3-year-old child. Explain why you selected it. What helped you in making your selection? What are the criteria for selecting books for preschool children?

18. Select three toys for a 2-year-old child who is restrained on a Bradford frame. What influenced your choice? Use these three toys and describe how you observed the child using them.

19. Observe several 2-year-old children together. How did they approach one another? What guidance do 2-year-old children need in learning to approach one another?

20. Describe a group situation you observed in the ward that you felt needed adult supervision. Why did you feel it required supervision? What were the children doing and saying? What precipitated the behavior you observed? What do you feel needed to be done? How would you have handled it if you had been the head nurse?

21. Observe several 1- to 3-year-old children in a playroom. Describe the situation generally. Then describe the play of two children. What did they do? What were they attempting to accomplish? What problems did they meet? How did they solve them? What help did they receive? Was it constructive or destructive? Why did you think so? Of what value was the experience to them? Of what value was the observational experience to you?

REFERENCES

1. Alexander, Franz: Gastro-intestinal disturbances, Chapter 9, p. 85, in Psychosomatic Medicine, New York, Norton, 1950.
2. Benedek, Therese: Personality development, Chapter 4, p. 63, in Dynamic psychiatry, Chicago, Univ. Chicago Press, 1952.
3. Bornstein, Berta: Phobia in a two-and-a-half year old child, The Psychoanalytic Study of the Child, Vol. 4, New York, Internat. Univ. Press, 1949.

4. English, O. S. and Pearson, G. H.: The psychosexual development of the child, Chapter 2, p. 18, in Common Neuroses of Children and Adults, New York, Norton, 1937.
5. Fraiberg, Selma: What are they afraid of?, Woman's Home Companion, p. 13, 1953, January.
6. Freud, Anna: Infantile amnesia and the Oedipus complex, Lecture 1, p. 11, in Psychoanalysis for Teachers and Parents, New York, Emerson, 1947.
7. ———: The Ego and the Mechanisms of Defence, New York, Internat. Univ. Press, 1946.
8. ———: The latency period, Lecture 3, p. 64, in Psychoanalysis for Teachers and Parents, New York, Emerson, 1947.
9. ———: The psychoanalytic study of infantile feeding disturbances, p. 119, in The Psychoanalytic Study of the Child, Vol. 2, New York, Internat. Univ. Press, 1947.
10. Gesell, Arnold, et al.: Eighteen months, Chapter 15, p. 141, in The Infant and Child in the Culture of Today, New York, Harper, 1943.
11. ——— et al.: Two-and-a-half years old, Chapter 17, p. 177, in The Infant and Child in the Culture of Today, New York, Harper, 1943.
12. Huschka, Mabel: The child's response to coercive bowel training, Psychosomat. Med. 4:301, 1942.
13. Hymes, James: Understanding Your Child, New York, Prentice-Hall, 1952.
14. Josselyn, Irene: The training period, Chapter 6, p. 47, in Psychosocial Development of Children, New York, Family Service Association of America, 1948.
15. ———: The latency period, Chapter 8, p. 75, in Psychosocial Development of Children, New York, Family Service Association of America, 1948.
16. Kawin, Ethel: The Wise Choice of Toys, 2d ed., Chicago, University of Chicago Press, 1938.
17. Killilea, Marie: Karen, New York, Prentice-Hall, 1952.
18. Menninger, Karl: Love Against Hate, New York, Harcourt, Brace, 1942.
19. Saul, Leon J.: The Bases of Human Behavior, Philadelphia, Lippincott, 1951.
20. Spitz, Rene: Steps to maturity: what it means to grow up, Child Study, 28:3, 1950-1951.
21. Spock, Benjamin: Toilet training, p. 193, in Common Sense Book of Baby and Child Care, New York, Duell, Sloan and Pearce, 1945.
22. Trainham, Genevieve, and Montgomery, J. C.: Development factors in learning bowel and bladder control, Am. J. Nursing, 46:841, 1946.
23. Weiss, Edward, and English, O. S.: Personality development and psychopathology, Chapter 2, p. 21, in Psychosomat. Med., Philadelphia, Saunders, 1949.

6

Development and Care During the Early Period of Socialization (3 to 6 Years)

THE EXPANSION OF CURIOSITY

SEX EDUCATION

CHANGES IN FAMILY INTERPERSONAL RELATIONSHIPS

SIBLING AND PEER RIVALRY

FACTORS INFLUENCING THE CHILD'S ADJUSTMENT IN NEW SITUATIONS
WHICH BRING SEPARATION FROM FAMILY AND HOME

During the preceding stages of development, the child has been absorbed in discovering himself and in acquiring increased mastery of his person and his environment in a way which will give him pleasure as well as security in the affection of his mother.

At 3 years of age, the child's curiosity becomes heightened; he sees, hears, feels and questions. The emotional and the verbal responses he receives to his inquiries influence his attitudes and his feelings toward himself, his parents and siblings, religion, sex, school, hospitals and the world of events about him.

In this period from 3 to 6 years of age, the child's capacity to give love is greater than it was in preceding years. Earlier, his energy was being consumed in learning and in adapting to reality situations. He mastered many things, and experience should have given him trust and security in those closest to him. Now he can give more love both because he has received it and because he has surplus energy available for loving.

In this period changes in his relationship to his parents occur. Earlier, the child's mother was the most important person in his world. Her capacity to give to her child was determined by her childhood experiences and by the degree of emotional support she received from her husband and others in her family and community. Indirectly in this way as well as in many others, the child was also receiving from his father. In earlier periods the child enjoyed his relationship with his father and it was imperative that he have his acceptance, but it was his mother who was his primary source of

211

comfort, his protector and his teacher. However, in this period the father's importance becomes heightened for both the boy and the girl.

The developmental tasks of this period are very difficult ones for the child. If his past experiences with both his mother and his father have been good ones, he will find less difficulty in surmounting the tasks inherent in this phase of personality development. The adults who guide the child in this period need understanding of the child's problems and fears so that they can provide him with the comfort and the experience he requires for physical and psychosocial development.

The child's adjustment in this period determines his acceptance of himself as a boy or a girl and the kind of relationships he will have with both sexes throughout his lifetime. *In this period the child needs to discover and to accept his sexuality and his place within his family and to come to find satisfaction in play and in his relationships with children outside his family. He needs to find answers to the many questions which perplex him and to develop wholesome attitudes toward all things concerning his personal development. He also needs to acquire increased self-dependence which will prepare him to make a good adjustment to experiences outside his home, for it is in this period that his life at school begins.*

THE EXPANSION OF CURIOSITY

INCREASE OF THE CHILD'S CAPACITY TO QUESTION

Children are keen observers and have a great need for information to solve their problems, for they are poor interpreters of what they see. When their curiosity is aroused, they attempt to find explanation for the things that perplex and give them concern. Before they can verbally question, they demonstrate their desire to know by their facial expressions and by investigative activity. Much of the young child's behavior which is labeled destructiveness is really a quest for knowledge.

Between 2 and 6 years of age the child's vocabulary increases at a rapid rate. During this period the average child acquires understanding of approximately 500 new words per year. By 3 years of age the child's sentences are longer, and his ability to put his thoughts together into complex, compound sentences is evident. By 6 years of age the average child utilizes every kind of sentence structure. When he is in emotional equilibrium, he uses language freely to express wishes and feelings and to gain his goals and to socialize with both adults and playmates.

By 3 years of age most children can verbally communicate their need to know and to understand. When they acquire this ability, questioning seems to be incessant. "What?", "What for?" and "What are you doing?" are usually the child's first questions and he uses them to learn the names of things and activities, to get reassurance and to acquire understanding of the people in his environment. Then he formulates where, why and how questions and uses them to search for answers to the many things which go on around him but are not yet understood.

COMING OF THE CHILD'S QUESTIONS IN RESPONSE TO NEEDS

The child's questions are not a purposeless play of words; they are asked to obtain satisfaction for a variety of desires and needs. They are an invaluable source of information about him as a person. They reflect his thinking, tell us of his desires and concerns and show us wherein he needs help in finding increased peace of mind.

The child's questions merit respect and need to be handled in a way which gives him security and the help he needs to become increasingly more able to think and to find solutions to his own problems. When questions come, the adult needs to pause, think and ask himself the following questions: "What is this child attempting to tell me? What is the object of his question? Of what is he uncertain? How can I help him become less fearful?" Too often the adult gives a quick answer without discovering what the child was really seeking to know.

Some of the child's questions reflect his need for socialization. It is the way many adults approach him and it is natural that he imitate their form of socialization. Little children cannot say, "I am lonely and miss my mother terribly. Please come and play with me." But they can communicate their feelings of loneliness and desire for company in questions like the following: "What's your name? What are you doing?" If the child is seeking a social response, his questions require more than literal answers; they require a conversational response and a relationship experience. If the adult ignores his need and answers, "I am Miss Jones. I am passing medicines now," the child's need will remain unfulfilled and he will continue his quest for companionship until his need is satisfied or until he gives up in despair.

There are other reasons why children question. Some questions are asked to discover how things go, of what they are made or to find out how to proceed with a project he wants to continue. His question may be to find out the whereabouts of one of his beloved parents or to gain assurance that they will return. Questions may express anxiety concerning a dreaded event or indicate a desire to put off something he is reluctant or unable to do. Karen's question indicated dread of a coming event. From her question and behavior it seemed evident that she needed help in becoming prepared for it and assurance that she would be given support when the time came for her to meet it.

Karen, aged 4½ years, was standing in the ward looking forlorn, frightened and near to tears. On her dress dangled a sign which said, "Nothing by mouth," to indicate she was going to surgery that day. The nurse took her on her lap and immediately a flood of tears flowed from the child's eyes. "Is it time to go yet?" she sobbed.

Karen knew about the impending operation. She had been to surgery the year before and she knew what the sign on her dress meant. She had also been prepared for the experience, but her behavior and questions indicated she was fearful of meeting it. First the nurse discovered Karen's interpretation of the verbal preparation she had been given. Karen had understood every detail of the preparation, and her interpretation was completely realistic. To give the child support the nurse said, "I will go with you, Karen, and stay close by you while you go to sleep. And I'll be right beside you when you wake up." Karen's verbal and behavioral response proved the experience brought relief from discomfort. She said: "This time I won't be all alone, will I?"

NEED OF THOUGHTFUL AND TRUTHFUL ANSWERS TO A CHILD'S QUESTIONS

When a child is seeking information to gain relief from fear or to gain understanding of what he sees or hears going on around him, he needs truthful and sincere answers to his queries to maintain his trust in those who care for him. A child loses faith in his parents, nurses and teacher and gets no relief from anxiety when he is told untruths or is considered to be too young to know.

A child's anxiety is increased when his questions make the adult angry, afraid or embarrassed. When a child seeks help with a perplexing problem and his questions are met with silence, anger or shaming, he feels that the subject is one he should not talk about. Silence, evasiveness and shaming reflect the adult's feelings and communicate attitudes which teach more profoundly than words. When a child is told with words or attitudes that he should not question a specific subject he feels he does not dare think about it, either. This brings further perplexity and weights his questions with anxiety.

When a child gets no relief from his anxiety and discovers his queries are taboo, he has to utilize his energy to bring himself comfort. In such instances the child either represses his questions and the feelings he has caught from his parents because he feels thinking about them is "bad" or he becomes preoccupied with the subject and attempts to find the answers through experimentation and thinking, or fantasy, as it is often called. If he fantasies answers to his questions they will remain with him and become reflected in his behavior the rest of his life. They will become the basis of his feelings and attitudes about a subject and influence his later ability to assimilate truths.

In the period from 3 to 6 years of age the child needs answers to his questions pertaining to religion, religious ceremonies and holidays. As he meets new experiences his interest in understanding them becomes aroused. The answers and feelings he acquires will form the basis of his future religious beliefs and the foundation of his philosophy of life just as the answers and feelings his parents acquired in their childhood determined theirs.

The answers the child receives will reflect the adult's attitudes and beliefs and the meaning which religion has to him personally. Religious beliefs and feelings are personal and meaningful. It would be impossible to suggest answers to these important questions. This is not the writer's intent. The way the child's questions are answered will depend upon the adult's personal beliefs and the feelings and attitudes he or she has associated with them. *The child needs answers which reflect the adult's faith in and respect for the ideas he is sharing with his child.*

Some of the child's questions will be perplexing and difficult to answer because they are emotionally charged; others may arouse anxiety and embarrassment because the adult has not formulated his own answers to the questions the child is pondering over in his own mind.

Parents who have a religious faith and accept it without question have little or no difficulty in giving their child knowledge concerning their beliefs. They have found a faith which satisfies their emotional longings and they are ready to share it with their children. They may find it difficult to interpret their faith simply enough for the child to understand and in a way which prevents fear but they have no conflict concerning the truth or correctness of their answers. Parents who are not sure what they believe or parents who have faith in their own beliefs but want their child to grow up free to find a religion which meets his own needs are the parents who leave the child wondering and oftentimes much bewildered. Some parents avoid the issue, refusing to solve their own perplexities and rationalize them away by saying children are too young to understand, anyway. But children do understand and they feel, and whether parents will it or not, their children will grow up believing and feeling as they do. When they grow up, they will be free to select any religious faith or philosophy they choose but their choice will be influenced by the attitudes, prejudices and emotional needs they have acquired in the process of growing up within their own families.

The child needs parents who are ready to interpret life and its events to them. Parents and adults working with children need to think through their attitudes and feelings concerning religion, death, nature, sex, birth, etc. They need to know what they believe and be capable of expressing it in simple, understandable language. Only then can they give the child confidence and security in knowing that it is the truth as far as the person knows it.

Many parents will have to say "I don't know" to some of their children's questions, but that is better than attempting to enlighten a child about something of which they are uncertain. Sometimes it is valuable for the child to know that there are people who believe one way and others who believe another. To this answer, there are children who will say, "But, Mother, I want to know what *you* believe." The uncertain mother will have no alternative but to say, "Johnny, I wish I could tell you, but I can't. There are so many ideas, I just don't know what to believe. Let's think and talk about it together."

The capacity for spiritual growth is within the child at birth; the way it develops is determined by the quality of love and the kind of acceptance and guidance the child receives during the earliest periods of his life. Answers to questions pertaining to religion are not the only factors which form the foundation for continuous spiritual growth. Of greater importance is the child's relationship with his parents and his siblings.

Religion is more than a set of beliefs and a knowledge of religious doctrines; it is a way of feeling about one's fellowmen—a way of life—and one's spiritual self determines the quality of one's interpersonal relationships. To acquire Faith, Hope and Love, the child needs to feel them in all his relationships with his parents. These spiritual qualities need to come from within and be an integral part of the individual's total personality; they cannot be grafted on to a basically asocial character.

In this period and in future ones the child has experiences which make him mull over the meaning of death just as he ponders over other things which mystify him. The child is not born with emotional feelings concerning death; they are communicated to him by those who care for and guide him. In his home and community the child hears the words death and dying. He hears his parents talk of funerals, passing away, last rites or the grief a friend is experiencing when death separates him from a loved one. If a relative or close friend of his parents dies the child feels the impact of the experience upon him. In addition he has hostile thoughts which provoke fear and he worries about his safety and the safety of those he loves and is dependent upon. Eventually questions pertaining to death will arise. He may ask "Will you die?" or he may express feelings which evidence concern for himself.

When a child asks questions to relieve his anxiety or to discover the meaning of death he needs help in understanding that which is a natural part of life. He needs truthful answers about death just as he needs them concerning other events which touch him or his parents personally. He also needs the security of knowing he and his parents are safe and that hostile thoughts and wishes cannot destroy and deprive him of those he loves.

A child's first experience with death may come in a hospital ward. Children in a hospital ward or room are aware of all that is happening there. They hear what the personnel do not intend them to hear and they see and feel apprehension and concern in those who are caring for them. Uncannily, they seem to know when there is a dying child in the ward. When his bed becomes empty, they suspect what has happened to him. If one observes hospitalized children closely, one will see apprehension reflected in their faces and behavior when there is a dying child in the ward. The situation which follows is an example of what one observes in a ward when children hear and see things they cannot understand.

Billy was 5 years old and in the hospital because he had asthmatic attacks. In the next room to his, one of his ward mates was dying. Her mother was beside herself with grief and expressing it in shrieks of anguish which could be heard throughout the entire corridor.

Billy was on his chair in his room, picking his fingers and looking panic-stricken. When the nurse went into his room he said, "Why is Martha's mother screaming like that? What's the matter? Stay with me. I am scared." The nurse said, "Martha is very, very sick. Her mother feels very badly because she loves Martha and wants her to get well. She knows Martha cannot get well and she is screaming because she is unhappy." Billy stopped picking his fingers and the apprehension in his face lessened. He said, "I didn't know. Stay and play with me, will ya?"

When a child in the ward dies and his ward mates ask, "Did he die?" or "Where did Jerry go?", they need to know the truth, for there is nothing much worse for children than losing faith in those who care for them. The child who asks is worried; he needs help in handling the feelings that arise when he becomes aware of what is happening in the ward. He may well be wondering if he is going to die also. If a ward mate dies, he thinks it can also happen to him. With his questions he may be seeking assurance that his sickness is different and curable.

Many school-age children with rheumatic heart disease and other chronic diseases like diabetes and epilepsy fear death, and it is understandable why they do. The child with heart disease has heard radio broadcasts which tell of its death rate. In addition, such children undoubtedly have anxious parents who are concerned about their prognosis for recovery and future adjustment to life. The child with diabetes has heard of the dire results his disease can bring and he has experienced the feelings which come with insulin reactions and high blood-sugar levels. Such feelings are fear-provoking for they bring loss of control and uncertainty. The child with epilepsy loses consciousness completely or has moments when he blacks out and returns to his world foggy and bewildered. Oftentimes he sees anxious people on return to consciousness and listens to their comments concerning his previous convulsive state. The situation which is cited subsequently exemplifies children's concern with their illness, death and the things happening in a children's ward.

Susan, an 8-year-old child with rheumatic fever, asked the following questions one morning while she was having her bath: "Nurse, do you know a boy on the third floor who is going to die in 3 weeks? He has a bug in his throat and when they give him blood, the bug eats it all up." At this point Susan paused. She looked anxious, thoughtful and quizzical. Then she turned her head, looked searchingly into her nurse's face and asked, "Nurse, do you know any kids in this ward that have what I got?" The nurse said, "Susan, I wonder what is troubling you." Then Susan told her nurse the following story: "I've got a bug in my throat, too. That is why the nurses and doctors wear gowns and masks when they come in here. The nurse told me so. What is a bug, nurse? Why do I have it and will it eat my blood up, too?"

Susan's nurse sat down and told her about bacteria and explained the reason why intramuscular injections of penicillin were being given to her. Susan needed to know that the boy up-stairs had an incurable disease that the doctors could not treat. She also needed to know that her disease was different and curable and the reason why she was being kept in bed and treated in the hospital. It eased her anxiety to know her nurse had cared for other children who had had rheumatic fever and had regained their health and gone home. Had the nurse not discovered Susan's fantasies about her illness, the child would not have had the help she needed to ease her troubled mind.

In the hospital ward there are children who must meet death before they have hardly begun to live and they appear to be experiencing feelings which seem to forewarn them that death is a reality which they must prepare themselves to meet. The critically ill child cannot help but observe the attitudes of his parents and the personnel. Nor can he escape being apprehensive as he feels his vitality dwindling or his pain increasing to an intolerable degree. He cannot help but react to changes in his body and the changes in treatment which come as his condition becomes increasingly more serious. Many children never verbally express their concern about their physical condition. Some are too young to express it in words but do so in their behavior. Some deny the reality of their illness and others seem to sense that their questions are the kind that would never be answered. However, there are some children who express their fear verbally and ask, "Am I going to die?"

There will always be differences of opinion as to how the question "Am I going to die?" should be answered when it is known that the child will die. There are those who believe that the child should never be told the truth even though death is imminent and there is nothing further that science can do to restore him to health. However, there are others who believe that the child is seeking relief from fear of the unknown when he asks, "Am I going to die?" They believe that the child's questions should be answered truthfully and in a way which gives him reassurance and support in meeting it fearlessly. Some parents have been able to support their dying child during the last hours of his life in the following way: "Yes, Jerry, you are going to die. You won't have pain any more and you will be happy. You will not be alone and you will always be cared for. Mother and Daddy will never forget you, Jerry. You will always be very close and dear to us." However, support of this kind can be given only by those who have faced the inevitable themselves and sincerely feel and believe that it is honest, true and what the child is seeking to discover.

The dying child needs more than words; he needs the support of a serene, comforting adult who recognizes his fear and is able to give him security in meeting the unknown. A dying child needs someone with him whether he asks for it or not. Many children who cannot express their fears in words communicate their inner anxiety in words like the following: "Stay with me," "Don't leave me alone," "Say a prayer with me," or "Please stay and sing to me" or "Tell me a story." Often as they say these words, they reach out for their mother's or their nurse's hand and cling to it for reassurance that they are not alone. This behavior discloses the child's need for continuing support and closeness with someone he has learned to trust.

Most parents will need the understanding and the support of doctors and nurses before they are able to maintain the composure their critically ill child requires. Often the nurse gropes for ways to support parents in these situations. She feels she must verbally express her sympathy and say something which will bring them comfort. The nurse does not need words at her fingertips. If she brings the child maximum comfort, keeps the parents informed about his progress and understands what they are experiencing, she will communicate her sympathetic feelings. Some parents have a great need to talk about their child and their own feelings and seek comfort from the nurse they have come to trust. When they do the nurse needs to be ready to understand.

"What is dying?" is an equally trying question and one which comes unless the child senses the anxiety his questions arouse in his parents, nurse or doctor. This is a difficult question for many adults to hear and answer in a non-fear-provoking way. The question is one that arouses anxiety unless the adult received help when he was a child and acquired inner security and faith in his ability to meet the unknown.

The answer the adult will give to the above question will depend upon the meaning which death has to him personally and upon the feelings which are aroused at the time the question is asked. Death means different things to different people. Some believe it is the beginning of a new and more perfect life in Heaven; others believe it is something to fear or the end of everything which could possibly be desired. Still others anticipate death because they believe it will relieve them of the discomfort they are experiencing on earth. There are adults who cannot think of death. They are terrified of the thought, are loath to think or speak about it and deny that it will ever come to them. The adult who accepts death as an eventual reality which must be faced with serenity will convey these feelings and attitudes to children and help them to accept it as a natural part of life.

There is no one way which is the only way to answer the above questions pertaining to death. Each person will need to think through his philosophy and find a way to keep children from becoming fearful when they hear and see things that arouse feelings of uncertainty. To help the reader think through possible ways of helping children understand death, the following explanation is given. It is simple and understandable to the child who has the mental capacity to verbalize his question. "When a person dies he lies very still. He does not breathe or eat or feel pain. He just lies still for he is not living any more. When people die, they are put into coffins where their bodies are kept. Then they are buried in the earth near to others. They are always loved even though they are not with us any more."

SEX EDUCATION

ACQUISITION OF SEX EDUCATION THROUGH RELATIONSHIPS IN THE HOME

The child acquires sex education not merely from answers to his questions, but also from the kind of life experiences he has felt within his own family group. Sex education consists of far more than the acquisition of biologic facts; it consists of feelings, ideas and attitudes the child absorbs from the emotional atmosphere existent in his home. The child learns from his parents constantly. This learning comes not only from verbal communication but also from the feelings that constantly are being conveyed to one another in their behavior. If his parents love and respect each other and if they accept and respect their child's unique individuality, he will grow up with a feeling of his own worth, be able to accept his sexuality, his respective sexual role and his limitations and utilize his strengths for the benefit of himself, his family and society.

The child's sex education begins long before he asks his first question; it begins at birth with the closeness he experiences with his mother and is influenced by his parents' feelings about him, toward themselves and each other and the love and care they provide for him while he is growing up.

The child needs parents whose ultimate objective of guidance is preparation for marriage and parenthood. To be a successful husband or wife and parent the individual needs more than answers to his questions; he needs a healthy personality which gives him freedom to give and to receive love. Personality does not develop by chance; it is the outgrowth of all the interpersonal relationships the individual experiences during the formative periods of his life. His adult sexual behavior will be determined by the personality structure he develops in the process of growth. As an adult he will love or hate not because he was born that way but because he was made that way. The child learns to love or to hate from his parents; he has no other models by which to fashion himself.

The child's questions pertaining to sex are originally no different from those pertaining to objects or activities. He sees and wonders about something and his questions concerning sex are no more charged emotionally than are his queries concerning the activity of the moment.

The child needs a home atmosphere which makes it easy for him to reveal what is giving him concern. Only then will he feel that the subject is one that is right to think and talk about, get the information he needs when he needs it and acquire the emotional feelings and attitudes which make for wholesome personality growth.

Providing the above kind of home atmosphere is not an easy task for the vast majority of parents. Although the child's questions are not charged emotionally for him, they are for most parents, and they cannot expect themselves to react casually to their children's questions. They can accept their child's curiosity and feelings with understanding and appreciate his need for help in understanding themselves and others, but they cannot be casual about a subject which arouses deep feelings within them.

Sex is not a subject; it is a powerful drive which cannot be treated with intellectualization or casualness. It can be expressed constructively or destructively. When this potent and creative emotion is expressed constructively it brings the highest forms of productivity; when its expression is blocked or distorted it brings unhappiness to the individual and destruction to society. The child needs help in accepting himself as a creative person; he needs understanding of his body and the motives which bring people of the opposite sex together. He also needs to acquire the feeling that sex is wholesome, beautiful and a drive which needs to be expressed constructively for the benefit of society as well as for himself.

It is difficult to understand that little children have sexual drives, fantasies and wishes, but it has been proved over and over again that they have. For many of us this fact seems unbelievable, for we have forgotten the early experiences which brought fear, anger, perplexity and frustrated wishes. It takes long periods of observation and living with children to detect behavior which is motivated by sexual feelings and wishes. Children express their feelings and wishes in words; they also express them in their behavior. When they cannot communicate them in words, they act them out in their relationships with their parents and with play materials and playmates. The theory presented in this chapter comes from observation of children's behavior in their homes, from their play and the words and feelings which accompany it. It also comes from the revived memories of adults who have experienced psychoanalytic therapy.

NEED OF THE CHILD FOR SEX EDUCATION GEARED TO HIS NEEDS

The child is a receptive, sensitive, observant and avidly curious being who is aware that there is a sexual side of life for it is a part of him as well as of every other person he contacts. To deny it is to exclude a very important element in his personality.

The child needs preparation for marriage, parenthood and family life given a little at a time when he shows readiness for it. When a child asks he is ready to know, for his questions or expression of ideas show he has been pondering about the subject previously. Sex education cannot be given in one dissertation; too much is entailed in it, and the child can only assimilate one idea at a time. If he fails to understand he will return again and again with the same or similar question. It does not indicate he is preoccupied with sex; it merely shows the struggle he is having in trying to piece his ideas together in a way which will bring him comfort and help him to understand himself and life in a bisexual world.

The important point for adults is to try to discover the child's feelings and thoughts at the moment by giving him undivided attention and encouraging him to talk about the subject which is perplexing him. It is not unusual to discover that the child's fantasies are the products of his imagination or the result of misinformation he has picked up from his friends. Often they are totally without basis in reality and therefore serve no constructive purpose for personality development. The child needs to ventilate his misconceptions to become ready to assimilate that which is true. A technic like the following often helps to discover the fantasies the child has pertaining to his inquiry: "That's something all children think and wonder about. All children tell themselves stories about the way babies begin to grow or about the part daddies play in starting babies to grow" (if that is the subject he is seeking to know about). "I wonder what stories you have told yourself. You tell me your stories and then I'll tell you mine."

When the parent discovers his child's fantasies are without bases in reality, he can correct them and then proceed to give him what he needs to know simply, truthfully, sincerely and in a way which leaves him with the feeling that he can return for more help whenever a need arises. This is not done with words alone; it is communicated in one's behavior if the child's natural curiosity is accepted, and he feels the sexual relationship is wholesome, beautiful and something to be desired. In writing of sex education for parents English and Foster[4] say:

For years we have been reaping a tragic harvest of unhappy homes in which to rear children, irritable, tense, impatient parents, frigid wives and impotent husbands because we have been afraid to admit that there is ecstasy in loving and being loved, great beauty in the human body and the way it is made, high dignity and reverence in the expression of our sexual powers. It is high time that we stopped and asked ourselves how we honestly feel about these matters of life, love and birth, marrying and coming together. Unless we ourselves are without shame and can say in the love words of the old English marriage service, "With my body I thee worship," we cannot possibly hope to give any sex education to our children that is adequate for their needs, no matter what we say or how hard we try.

Stimulation of the Child's Curiosity by His Observation of Sex Differences

When the child becomes aware of his body he compares himself with others and develops interest in the differences between boys and girls and men and women. The body and its functions holds great interest for the child, and his curiosity pertaining to it is the forerunner of his lifelong thirst for knowledge. Long before the child can verbally question, observation shows that he is interested in sex differences. Milton could not verbally question but his behavior expressed wonderment and the feelings he had about his own body.

Milton was 14 months old when a baby sister arrived. For 6 weeks he observed the baby as his mother cared for it. When he was 16 months old, he began to put his hands to the baby's genital region when he stood watching his mother diaper his sister. He'd touch her vulva and immediately put his hand to his own genitals. Then he would strut away looking proud and pleased with himself.

In Chapter 2 the girl's feelings upon discovery of the boy's anatomic structure were cited. Her pride often becomes injured when she observes that boys have something which she does not have and she becomes envious and competitive unless she has help in accepting herself as she is.

Shirley and Jimmy were both 5-year-olds. They were finger painting in the ward playroom. Jimmy enjoyed the experience and reveled in his own productions. His interest was centered on his own work, which was sharply in contrast with Shirley's response to the experience. Shirley was trying to make the biggest and the best painting. She kept watching Jimmy and whenever he made a circle, she made what she called a bigger and a better one. To this Jimmy made no comments. He continued his work and showed no signs of being threatened by Shirley's bragging and display of superior competence. The nurse said, "Both of you are painting lovely pictures. Jimmy likes his painting and Shirley likes hers." Shirley's response to this comment was full of feeling and unrelated to the painting experience. With dramatic gestures she cocked her head, put her hands to her fashionably dressed, beribboned hair and said with emphasis, "Well, I've got a 'horse's tail.' "

What were the feelings which motivated the behavior recorded above? Why didn't Shirley go ahead and finger paint as Jimmy did? What made her so concerned about herself and why did she need to point out that she had something which Jimmy did not have?

Her nurse knew she had more hair than Jimmy—what were the reasons for Shirley's behavior? What was she saying to her nurse in her behavior?

When the preschool girl first discovers she is made differently from boys, feelings and fantasies are stimulated which become expressed both verbally and nonverbally. Many girls wonder if they once had a penis and what happened to it. They wonder if they have damaged themselves or been punished for their naughtiness. One child disclosed her feelings and fantasy in the following way: "When I was a little boy and had a penis, I used to stand up to go to the toilet." It is not unusual for the little girl to feel deprived and direct her anger at her mother, nor is it unusual for little girls to tell their mothers they feel boys have everything. When they do they are usually speaking not of material possessions—they are trying to express a lack which has deeper meaning to them.

When the girl questions either verbally or through curiosity expressed in looking or investigating, she needs help in learning about her body and in accepting her femininity. She needs to know that boys are made differently and have penises like their daddies. She also needs to know that she was born with a vulva, a vagina and a uterus because she is feminine like her mother. Her organs are inside and cannot be seen but they are equally as important as sources of pleasure and pride as the organs the boy possesses. Giving children the correct names of their organs increases their pride in their own possessions and makes later teaching an easier process.

The mother who accepts her femininity will give her daughter the feeling that the way she is made is desirable and "right" because she is a girl. She will also give her daughter the feeling that being a girl is something of which to be proud. She does this not in words but in behavior which stems from pride and acceptance of her own femininity. Education like the following given a little bit at a time helps the girl accept her femininity and alleviates her anxiety about herself: "When you grow up, you will have breasts and hair on your body just like mommy. When you are a woman you will have a husband just as I have. Then you and your husband will have babies, too. You have an organ inside your body where babies can grow just as I have."

If the girl's mother accepts her own femininity and her father respects himself and esteems his wife's womanly qualities, and if both of her parents have made her feel accepted as a girl, she will be unthreatened by her feminine status. She will be proud of herself and demonstrate it in all of her behavior. She will not have to compete with boys, become their doormats or berate her own feminine qualities.

In this phase of development the girl wants to compete with her mother and "grow" a baby. When the girl renounces her wish for a penis, it is replaced by a wish for a child. If one observes children one will see girls acting their wishes out in their play with dolls and their younger siblings or playmates. Their dolls and younger children become "their babies," and in fantasy they are their mothers and their daddies are their fathers. If one watches children at play and listens to the verbal expressions of their fantasies, one will begin to see evidence which will verify the reality of the above statements.

The child whose mother cannot accept her feminine child or her feminine role, whose father is harsh, unloving and critical has problems unknown to the child who is accepted by parents who love and respect one another. If the girl's parents do not accept themselves and their child no words she hears will counteract the feelings she acquires through her interpretation of what she sees and feels going on around her.

If a girl's mother has not been able to accept her because she is feminine, she may attribute her mother's nonacceptance to the fact that she is without a penis. When a child feels rejected, she searches for a reason. If the girl compares herself to her more highly esteemed brother in an attempt to discover the reason why she is being rejected, she may conclude that the only difference is anatomic. To get acceptance and love she may feel she needs to strive to be like her brother. It will make her envious of her brother, and if he receives more love than she, she will hate him as well. It is circumstances like these which foster the development of pathologic personality patterns and prevent children from attaining full self-realization. This is the reason why acceptance of the child as he is, be he male or female, is of such paramount importance for personality development.

In this period of personality development the boy is equally concerned when he first observes the girl's anatomic structure. He does not feel envious but he wonders what has happened to the girl and is fearful lest he experience a similar plight. He imagines she was injured or punished for masturbation or "naughty" thoughts, and his anxiety is heightened because he has destructive fantasies concerning his father. The little boy may ask, "Where's Peggy's penis?" or "Peggy hurt?" Or he may just gaze with a facial expression that denotes utter perplexity.

Like the girl, the boy needs help in learning about his body and in accepting his appropriate sexual role. *He needs to know that he was born with a penis and will always have one because he is a boy, and boys are made differently from girls.* He also needs to know that he will grow up and be big like his daddy. When the boy learns that girls and women are made differently because they "grow" babies, *he will need to know that men share in the process of creating a child.* If he fails to get this knowledge, he may grow up feeling envious of women's capacity to bear children and reflect it in his relationship with his wife and all other women. The boy also has a desire to "grow" babies. He has to renounce his wish to "grow" babies, as the girl must give up her wish for a penis.

When children's questions remain unanswered or are evaded because of adult embarrassment, they sometimes investigate in an attempt to solve their curiosity. It is not uncommon to observe a little boy picking up a girl's clothing. He is not being naughty or shameful; he is merely attempting to find answers to questions his parents should have helped him to solve earlier. Nor is it abnormal for a child to peer under the skirt or look down into the neckline of his mother's or nurse's dress.

When a child experiments or investigates, he is communicating his need for reassurance. If a child peeks into the neckline of his mother's dress, a question like the following will restrict unacceptable behavior but give the child an opportunity to express his need and obtain the information he requires: "What is it you want to know?"

Many learning problems have their origin in this phase of development. Unanswered questions keep children preoccupied with sex and utilize energy which should go into learning the many other things they need to learn. Josselyn[20] explains the way some learning problems develop in the following statement:

> Normally, sexual curiosity expands to related aspects of life and develops into an eagerness to learn about many things. If the sexual curiosity is repressed before this expansion occurs, the desire to learn is also repressed. Learning in any area is then a forbidden pleasure.*

DEVELOPMENT OF THE CHILD'S CURIOSITY CONCERNING HIS ORIGIN

As the child begins to relate himself to his parents as persons of the opposite sex, and as he becomes more aware that his parents have an intimate relationship from which he is excluded, he begins to wonder where he came from and how he grew. These questions are further stimulated by the changes occurring within him and in his relationship to his parents. The child searches to discover facts about himself.

---

* Reprinted by permission of the author and the Family Service Association of America.

If the child's quest for information was satisfied and he felt accepted when his first questions were asked, he will turn to his parents when he wonders where he came from. "You grew inside Mother in a special place which kept you safe and warm," is a truthful answer which the child needs. He will love hearing about himself when he was in utero and when he was a tiny baby unable to walk, talk or play. To relate stories concerning the pleasure his parents experienced when he was born, learned to smile, feed himself or talk will delight the preschool child and increase his sense of belongingness. No other stories are as fascinating as those he hears about himself. In this period his interest is in himself and learning about himself is his birthright!

Drawing a picture of a woman's body to show the child where he grew is a useful method of helping the child visualize anatomic structures and understand the body. When the child asks, "Where did I grow?" the following answer is understandable to the 3- to 5-year-old child: "Mothers have a uterus where babies can grow." When he asks, "But how did I get out?" a simple response like the following will increase his understanding: "When you were big enough to live outside my body, you left it through a special passage. It is called the vagina." Many mothers find it easier to help their children learn with a simple diagram because the child's interest is centered on the drawing rather than on the face of the narrator.

DEVELOPMENT OF THE CHILD'S CURIOSITY CONCERNING BIRTH AND THE FATHER'S PART IN REPRODUCTION

The answer and the feelings and attitudes which are communicated when the child asks, "Did it hurt you when I was born?" will influence the way the child will eventually accept pregnancy in herself or his mate and approach the labor experience. This question often follows the one cited above or it may not come until months or years have passed. But it is something the child will eventually want to know. In the future the child of today will be facing labor and delivery as an expectant father or mother. The way he or she will approach it will be greatly influenced by the feelings and attitudes which he acquired during this period of his development.

If the girl's mother has accepted childbirth as a natural feminine function for which she is well prepared, the child will grow up desiring fulfillment of her feminine role because she has had the opportunity of identifying herself with a mother who accepted her femininity and wanted to fulfill her role. The mother who accepts her role and is unafraid of childbirth will convey her feelings in her behavior and words. She will be able to say with full sincerity: "Yes, Mary, having a baby does hurt. It takes hard work to give birth to a child. That is why having a baby is called labor. But I want babies, Mary, and I am ready to work to have them. When the time comes for the baby to be born, the muscles of the mother's uterus begin to work. That hurts, but the mother knows it will help to bring her baby out of her body. When she feels her uterus beginning to work, she goes to the hospital. There the doctors and nurses help her to bring her baby into the world. By the time the baby comes, the mother is tired but she is also very happy. She is joyful because she can see her baby and begin taking care of it outside her body."

It will probably be a long time before the child begins to wonder what made the baby begin to grow inside his mother. When the inquiry comes he will need to know that it grew from an ovum which is as small as a speck, alive, and a part of the mother's body. Queries which show the child's perplexity concerning the father's role in reproduction usually come later. He will probably be 5 to 8 years of age before he asks, "But how do babies start to grow?" or "How do daddies help babies to grow?" This is usually the most difficult of all questions for a parent to answer for it is the one which is most highly charged emotionally. If the child's parents learned the answer to the above question from a parent who was unashamed of the way he expressed his or her love for his mate, he will have less difficulty in giving the child wholesome feelings concerning the father's role in reproduction.

It can be written simply. To convey it to a child involves more than the thinking and the feeling of the person who communicates it to another; it involves an interpersonal relationship with a child who is depending upon us to give him healthy attitudes which are necessary for his emotional growth. In writing it can be stated as simply as this: "When daddies and mothers love each other they want to come close to one another. Daddies have special cells in their bodies just as mothers do. The daddy's cells are in a bag behind his penis. The bag is called a scrotum. The daddy's cells must meet the ovum in the mother's body where the baby will grow. The cells leave the father's body through his penis. He uses his penis to place the cells in the mother's vagina. The father's cells are called sperm cells and the mother's are called ova. The fluid the daddy places in his wife's body is called semen. Although he places only a small amount (about one teaspoonful) of semen in the mother's vagina, there are millions of male cells in it. The father's sperm cells can move. When a sperm cell reaches the mother's ovum and joins it, fertilization has taken place and a baby begins to grow."

Children acquire respect for their parents and themselves and are proud of their knowledge when their parents share the facts of life with them. Louise felt proud of herself and was un-self-conscious when she was able to contribute knowledge to her friends in the nursery school. This is the way children need to feel about it for it is the healthy way to feel about sex.

Louise was 4 years old and a nursery school student who was listening to stories with a group of children. After the teacher finished reading the nursery rhyme which reads as follows, "And what are little boys made of? Frogs and snails and puppy dog tails! And what are little girls made of? Sugar and spice and everything nice," Louise spoke up and said with pride, "But that isn't *really* the way babies are made. They grow inside their mothers and when they are born, they come out right through the vagina."

Louise's tone of voice and manner of speaking was no different from the way she would have said, "My mother is a wonderful woman. She went to the store today and bought me a new doll." She stated a fact and was proud of knowing it. She said it with emphasis and enthusiasm but there was no evidence that she felt it was a subject that was not right and natural to think and talk about.

DEVELOPMENT OF THE CHILD'S CURIOSITY CONCERNING THE CHANGES HE ANTICIPATES IN HIS OWN BODY AND THE THINGS HE LEARNS ABOUT LIFE IN A BISEXUAL-WORLD

In the school-age period the child needs understanding of the changes that will occur eventually in his own body. At this time his sexual feelings are more dormant and he can assimilate biologic facts more easily because he is less emotionally involved in his own sexual development. He sees the bodies of his older friends growing and changing, and it would be a dull child who would not anticipate that similar changes would sometime come to himself. In the preadolescent period of development children rebuff their parents' attempt to prepare them for biologic changes and seek answers to their problems from age mates. For these reasons early education is indicated.

Knowledge about menstruation can be given to children at the time they want to know about fertilization or it can be given when the child demonstrates interest in growing-up or in details pertaining to family life. Both boys and girls need to know about menstruation. They see advertisements for sanitary products, and it is the rare child who does not discover his mother's supply in his own home and ask questions pertaining to its use.

If the child's foregoing questions were answered and he was able to assimilate his parent's explanation, he will be able to understand a simple description of the menstrual cycle. Simple drawings facilitate teaching and give the child more realistic understanding of female anatomy and physiology. Menstruation can be described in the following way: "Each month the woman's body becomes prepared to begin a new life. A female cell or ovum moves down from one of her ovaries into a tube. If there is a male cell or sperm in the mother's body and it unites with her ovum, fertilization takes place. Then the fertilized ovum moves into the uterus, becomes implanted there and grows into a baby. To nourish a new baby the lining of the uterus becomes gradually supplied with blood each month. When fertilization does not take place, the lining of the woman's uterus loosens and leaves her body through the vagina. This is called the menstrual flow. When women are menstruating they wear sanitary pads or vaginal tampons to absorb the flow. Sometimes girls begin to menstruate at 10 years of age, sometimes not until they are 14 or 15. All girls grow up in their own way. Some begin to mature early and some later, just as some girls grow tall earlier than do others."

As the girl approaches adolescence she will need more details to prepare her for the onset of her own menstruation. She will need to have her own supplies so she can feel prepared whenever menstruation begins. She will also need to know the approximate length of the period and the facts pertaining to the irregularity characteristic during the early period of adolescence and to be helped to anticipate menstruation as a natural function.

Children need to know that seminal emissions mark the beginning of the boy's progress toward maturity. They need to know that involuntary discharges of semen from the penis occur during sleep in conjunction with sexual dreams and are as natural for boys as menstruation is for girls. Unless boys are prepared for seminal emissions, they are frightened and often miscorrectly attribute them to masturbation or disease. When boys and girls learn of menstruation they usually ask, "And what about boys? You said girls and women menstruate. Do boys and men do anything like that?"[26] When questions come, the child needs the above understanding. Seminal emissions require acceptance as do his changing voice, his growth of a beard and the spurt in physical growth. To prevent the boy from worrying, he, too, needs to know that there are wide variations in the time when maturity begins.

The above questions and answers by no means complete the child's sex education; it is infinitely less simple than that. As the child learns biologic and social facts at school, from newspapers, magazines, radio broadcasts and his friends, his thinking and feeling will become stimulated and he will bring more questions and ideas for discussion. If his parents have given him support before adolescence, he will seek further help from them when sexual feelings are reawakened and he feels a need for help in his relationships with friends of the opposite sex.

How the Nurse Can Assist Mothers in Becoming Prepared to Meet Their Children's Needs

Nurses in prenatal and well baby clinics, maternity units and the field of public health nursing have many opportunities to help mothers become prepared to give their children help in understanding the sexual side of family life.

In helping primiparous women to become prepared for labor and the care of their babies, the nurse can help them to become familiar with the names of the organs of the reproductive tract and the way their bodies function. Ignorance about the facts of anatomy and physiology is commonly encountered in laywomen. They need explanations to help them understand the physiologic changes that come with pregnancy and the mechanisms of labor. They need knowledge for themselves and to become prepared to help their children when they are ready for it.

The primiparous woman is often confused, curious and desirous of an opportunity to learn what she really wanted to know years ago. Sometimes primiparous women talk about their early fantastic notions pertaining to the origin and birth of babies. If they do, a comment like the following may guide them in thinking about children's need for knowledge: "Children get ideas like that when their parents do not realize they have questions which are giving them concern. All children wonder where babies come from, how they grow and how they are born just as you wondered when you were a little girl. Children need to know. If they fail to get the knowledge they need, they imagine all sorts of things which are not really true."

Nurses can also help expectant mothers become prepared to help their older children become ready for the coming of the new baby. Many mothers feel that children are too young to learn, and others because of their own childhood experiences fail to interpret the behavior which indicates a child's awakening curiosity.

Children are *not* too young to observe. They note changes in their mothers' bodies and in their behavior and they need to know what is bringing these changes. Even though the child cannot verbalize his queries, he will feel respected and reassured if he is included in the event which is absorbing his parents' interest at the moment. Permitting a mother to talk about her feelings concerning sex education often relieves her tension and makes it possible for her to prepare herself to help her child when his questions come. In the process of talking, she may recall how her questions were received and how she felt when she was shamed or reprimanded. It may help her to see the desirability of giving her child a different kind of experience.

Repeatedly, the nurse in maternity units discovers mothers who have been unable to prepare their older child for the coming of the new baby. When labor is over many of these mothers begin to wonder what effect their new babies will have on their older children. They may anticipate questions like, "Where did the baby come from?", "Why did you leave me home?" or "Why is your tummy so much smaller?" If the new baby's sex is unlike her older child's, the mother may wonder what she will say if her child comments on differences in anatomic structure. Here again the nurse has an opportunity to help mothers with their problems. If she has established herself with her patient and the mother has discovered she is a helpful person, she will talk about her problem and the nurse can help her discover ways she can meet her child's needs at home.

How the Nurse Can Help Hospitalized Children with Their Problems

Nurses in the hosptal are often confronted with children's verbal and nonverbal questions pertaining to sex differences, the origin of babies, birth, menstruation and anatomy and physiology. Nurses need to be prepared to help children handle their natural curiosity. Sometimes the child's first experience in seeing a child of the opposite sex occurs in the hospital ward. Children in the hospital hear and see many things which stimulate their curiosity, and it is not unusual for them to question their nurses about things which perplex them.

Because some parents prefer that their children be kept in ignorance, it is important that hospital policy sanction the giving of information to children who indicate a need for it. There are parents who would be irate enough to sue a hospital if their children received information they were unable to impart themselves. For this reason it is imperative that the pediatric staff's policy be known and accepted.

When a hospitalized child questions and he has been relieved of his anxiety through talking with his nurse, it is important that the nurse discuss the experience with his mother the next time she comes into the ward. The mother should know the child's thoughts and questions and how the nurse helped the child to handle his perplexities. She needs to know this as she needs to know about other things that are happening to her child. If the nurse has become acquainted with her patient's mother previously and has told her of other experiences with her child, the imparting of additional knowledge can be done in a way which can be accepted by the mother.

An experience of the above kind can be a real learning opportunity for the mother. In discussing the experience with the child's mother, the nurse will have an opportunity to observe the mother's reaction to her child's curiosity and the help which he was given. Many times mothers are relieved because the child's questions have been answered. In the course of talking some may become motivated to want to prepare themselves to help their children later when further curiosity evidences itself.

When sex play is observed in the hospital ward or home, the children need understanding, acceptance and help to find answers to their problems and more constructive play experiences. It is unwise to reprimand them for it makes them feel they are "bad" and shameful. Their sexual drives and interests are not shameful; they are natural, wholesome and the outcome of their development. *Children need help in directing their interests into constructive channels.* When their curiosity is satisfied and they have plenty of gratifying play activity with friends and happy, comfortable experiences in their home or hospital environment, sex exploration will be minimal and easily redirected with a story or a suggestion for a new activity.

CHANGES IN FAMILY INTERPERSONAL RELATIONSHIPS

DEVELOPMENT OF CHANGES IN FAMILY RELATIONSHIPS AS A NATURAL PART OF GROWTH

Between 3 and 4 years of age children begin to demonstrate changes in their behavior. The little girl acts as if she feels more like a girl and the boy behaves in ways which are characteristic of males. In this phase of development the girl becomes more aware of her appearance and strives to look and act like her mother. The boy begins to imitate his father's behavior when formerly his identification was with his mother. The cause of these changes in behavior is as yet unknown. Whether they arise from biologic changes or from psychological experiences within the home has not been proved scientifically.

In this phase of development the child's interest turns to the parent of the opposite sex with great intensity, bringing conflict, disappointment, anger and fear. Earlier the child experienced emotional distress when he discovered he had to share his mother's love with a sibling. However, the conflict at that stage of development was of minor intensity in comparison to the conflict he must face and solve between the ages of 3 and 6.[8] Now the child discovers that his parent of the same sex is a more powerful rival than his older sibling.[8] In this stage of development the child becomes competitive, jealous and aggressive toward his parent of the same sex and has destructive wishes which make him feel guilty and afraid. At the same time he loves his parent of the same sex, is dependent upon him and wants to be like him. He loves and esteems a parent he also hates.[8] He hates him because he prevents him from having what he most desires—the sole possession of the parent of the opposite sex.

The above thoughts and feelings are frightening to little children because they are powerful and incomprehensible and because of their belief in what Josselyn[21] calls the "magical power of thought." The little child has insufficient experience to know that his wishes and destructive thoughts are natural but that they cannot destroy. He also has had insufficient experience to know that wishes cannot deprive him of the person whose protection, support and love he is dependent upon. Whenever the child has these thoughts he grows afraid, not only because he fears they might destroy the person he needs and loves but also because he thinks there is also the possibility that that person might know what he is thinking and retaliate and bring injury to him.[19]

The Child's Need of Thoughtful Guidance to Solve His Problems

In this phase of personality development, the child needs help in handling his sexual feelings, in renouncing his desire for his parent of the opposite sex, in maintaining tender feelings for both parents and in finding gratification with playmates outside his family. Guidance in this period will determine his relationships first to boys and girls and later to men and women. It is sex education for it contributes to personality development and prepares the child for marriage and parenthood.

To succeed in accomplishing the above tasks the child needs the help of both his parents. He needs a parent of the opposite sex who understands his dilemma and accepts his awakening sexuality but firmly and kindly rejects the child as a love object and helps him turn his interest to children within his environment. He also needs a parent of the same sex who can maintain his affection and respect through acceptance of his intense love for his or her mate and the hostility which is directed at him or her. The mother, for example, needs to know that her daughter is not rejecting her completely but loves her even when she says, "Mother, I hate you," or "I love Daddy more than you and some day I am going to marry him," or "I wish you would go away and never come back. I don't love you any more." Unless her mother understands the developmental significance of her behavior and guides her wisely, it will be a trying period for all members of the family.

It is important that the parent of the same sex maintain the child's love, for it is with this parent that the child needs to identify himself. It is through identification (imitative copying) with the parent of the same sex that the child comes to accept his appropriate sexual role in the process of growing into a mature man or woman. The situation cited below exemplifies the way children disclose their feelings, fantasies and wishes in their behavior.

Joan was in this phase of psychosocial development. She dearly loved her daddy and had voiced her desire to marry him even though she had not yet become fully aware of what marriage really meant. Often she expressed hostility to her mother and made overtures to her father in her mother's presence.

In house play, Joan would send her mother doll to grandma's house to live, and leave her girl and father doll in the play house together. [Why did Joan send the mother doll away and leave the little doll in the house with her father? This never happened in reality. From whence did the idea come? Could it have reflected her wish to take her mother's place in her home? If so, what need was she seeking to satisfy in her play?]

One day Joan's mother was going out for the afternoon. Joan wept and clung to her mother like a leech. Her mother had insight into the basis of her anxiety and knew she needed experiences which would help her to learn that fantasies and wishes were natural and nondestructive. On the other hand she did not want to invade the child's fantasy world for she knew children resented and feared interpretations given by their parents. To reassure Joan she said, "You are wondering if I am coming back. I am coming back, Joan, and I will always be here to love and take care of you." Joan's response was quick and it reinforced her mother's assumption concerning the cause of her daughter's fear. Joan gasped, "You won't come back. I know you won't."

Joan's response showed her belief in the "magical power of thought." She feared her wishes would become fulfilled and deprive her of her mother whom she deeply loved and hated simultaneously. She had not had sufficient reality experiences to learn that wishes cannot eliminate a person she momentarily wanted abolished from her environment. Joan's mother reassured her in the following way, "I know you are scared, Joan, but I *am* coming back. I used to feel angry at my mother and used to get scared too. Sometimes I would be angry at her but I loved her, too, and wanted her to come back whenever she went out in the afternoon. I am coming back to take care of you." Reassurance of this kind helps the child know that her ambivalent feelings are acceptable and that destructive wishes do not really destroy.

The child needs a parent of the opposite sex who can help him accept the incest taboo inherent in his nature without feeling ashamed of his sexuality, inadequate or rejected as a child. The child needs to be loved by the parent of the opposite sex but he needs the kind of love which is appropriate for a child. He needs protection from fear of his rival parent's retaliation and from sexual stimulation which has no opportunity for release and gratification. When the child is loved, protected and accepted by the parent of the opposite sex, he will feel less frustration, inadequacy and resentment. He will also have pleasant memories of their relationship, be happy in the acceptance of his sexuality and eventually seek a love object as a substitute for the one originally desired.

In this period the child needs protection from overstimulation and help to find his place in his family. It is not unusual for boys to want to sleep with their mothers and girls to get into bed beside their fathers. Sometimes children show evidence of wanting to separate their parents and crawl into bed *between* them. If the child's parents permit this behavior, they are not protecting the child from overstimulation or helping him find his place and accept the fact that his parents have an intimate relationship which cannot be shared with him regardless of how much he is loved. The child's desires need understanding and acceptance but they must be thwarted even though it disappoints and angers him. Guidance which expresses the following feelings helps the boy find his place without feeling guilty about his natural desires: "I know you are angry. Children often get angry when their mothers and daddies want to be alone together. Some day you will have a wife just as your father has and you will know why there are times that we want to be together."

The child needs happily adjusted parents to make a healthy solution to his relationship problems. His parents' personal adjustment and their adjustment to one another determine the way he will solve the conflicts of this period. If the child's parents are happy in their relationship with each other, the child will have the protection and support he needs for growth. He will experience disappointment and frustration because his parent of the opposite sex does not respond as he wishes he would, but frustration is necessary for emotional growth and less injurious than fear of retaliation, guilt or a love relationship with a parent who fails to recognize his child's need to find a love object outside his family which will bring growth and eventual fulfillment.

The child whose sexuality is unacceptable to one or both parents is confronted with problems which may lead to pathologic solutions of one kind or another. If loving the parent of the opposite sex brings disapproval from the parent of the same sex, the child may find it safer to identify with the parent of the opposite sex. In so doing he will develop characteristics belonging to the opposite sex rather than characteristics belonging to his own. The girl, for example, may feel her mother's dislike of her affection for her father. To obtain approval and relieve herself of the anxiety she feels from disapproval, she may aspire to be like her father, feeling perhaps it may possibly bring her the love she needs and desires. This is another reason why the child needs the concept of his sexuality accepted by his parents. Unless they have emotional understanding of it, the child is without the support he needs.

The child who loses a parent through any of the circumstances of separation such as illness, death, war or divorce needs careful guidance to prevent emotional disturbances from arising. If a child loses his parent of the opposite sex, the remaining parent needs to be able to appreciate the grief the child experiences and help him or her to find comfort. If it is the parent of the same sex who dies or becomes separated, the child will require wise and careful guidance. When a child loses his parent of the same sex he will experience both grief and fear for his feelings about his parent have been ambivalent. He has had destructive wishes and thoughts. He has also had feelings of love and dependency. He has needed his affection, protection and support, and when it is taken from him, overwhelming anxiety will be inevitable. Unless his problems are understood and he receives support and help to accept the *real* causes of his parent's death or separation, he may go through life feeling he was in some way responsible for his death or leave taking.

When a child loses a beloved parent, relative or friend, he needs help to express his grief with another person and experiences which ease his fear and loneliness. When a child loses someone he loves he grieves, feels lonely and temporarily lost just as an adult does. Parental attempts to protect the child from their own expressions of emotion often increase the child's feelings of loneliness and indirectly tell him that overt expressions of grief are nonacceptable. Controlling one's feelings brings withdrawal and leaves the child alone with his feelings of loss. Both parent and child are experiencing loss. Both must face it but the child has too few inner resources to do it alone. Death of a loved one brings fear and perplexities. The child needs opportunities to express his grief overtly and fears and help to understand death and to rid his mind of fear.

When a dependent child loses a parent he needs repeated reassurance that the remaining parent will continue to be with him. He cannot help but wonder, "And who will take care of me now? If Mother dies is it not possible Father may die also?" The child needs reassurance with words; he also needs it from repeated experiences which restore the child's feelings of security and trust. If the child asks, "Will you die, too?" the following explanation will help to give him the reassurance he is probably seeking: "Yes, some day I will die, Skipper, but I hope it will not be for a long, long time. When people get to be old men and women they die. But they are ready to die then. By the time I am ready to die you will be grown-up and able to take care of yourself. By that time you will have a wife and family and you won't be alone."

How the Child Solves His Problem Through Identification with the Parent of the Same Sex

In the course of normal development, the child solves his relationship problems with his parents by repressing the sexual feelings he has for the parent of the opposite sex and the anger he feels toward the parent of the same sex and supplanting them with tender, affectionate ones. If his expressions of anger and competitive feelings have been accepted by his parent of the same sex, he will have less hostility to repress and more love for him. However, all hostility is rarely, if ever, expressed. The child represses that which his ego cannot accept and permits only the tender, loving feelings to remain in his conscious thoughts. In this way the child defends himself against anxiety and makes it possible for himself to go on loving both of his parents.

To maintain his security the child changes his goal from wanting to be the parent of the same sex to a desire to be *like* that parent. The girl changes her goal not only because she is afraid she will lose her mother's love but also because she loves her parents, wants to please them and knows they expect her to accept her place within the family. The boy changes his goal because he fears his father and wants his continued love. It is *safer* for the child to be like the parent of the same sex for then he can be assured of both his parents' love, acceptance and approval.

Through the process of identifying with the parent of the same sex, the child's conscience becomes a part of his psychic structure. Training during earlier periods of development affected the formation of his conscience, but it is not until the end of this period that parental standards become internalized within the personality structure.

Internalized standards or the conscience become a powerful influence on the child's behavior in the periods of development which are to come. Internalized standards keep the child doing what he has discovered to be "right" and prohibit him from doing what he has learned to be "wrong." Because the standards have become internalized, they direct his behavior even when his parents are not with him. In later phases of personality development, his conscience will become modified to a degree as he meets and adapts himself to the codes of his group, those of his teachers and counsellors and eventually the standards and conventions of the community in which he lives.

How the Child Handles His Conflict and Feelings by Masturbating

During the two earlier periods of personality development the parents' interest in the child encouraged his interest in himself, his body and its functioning. As the 9- to 12-month old infant learns to use his hands he discovers the various parts of his body. He finds his eyes, nose, mouth and genitals and discovers there is pleasure in handling them. He also finds that there are areas of his body that are more pleasurable to touch than others. This is natural and as important for him to discover that he is the possessor of genital organs as it is for him to learn that he has hands, feet and the capacity to use them in obtaining experience and gratification. If his discovery of self is not shamed or punished and if his emotional and exploratory needs remain satisfied, he will not handle himself often to obtain pleasure.

At the end of the training period, the child's energy becomes directed away from the excretory organs to the genitals.[5] He has obtained control of his excretory apparatus and physiologic and psychological changes bring genitalization of sexual feelings.[5] The child's fantasies bring tension and longings to be near his parent of the opposite sex.[12] Through experience he discovers he can get relief from tension and loneliness by being near his parent or by masturbating. The situation which is cited below is an example of one boy's longing for contact with his mother's body. He did not ask for a blanket; he asked to have his mother's coat put over him. He did not do it by chance; it arose from an inner need.

Peter, a 5-year-old, was in the hospital because he had a brain tumor. He had been operated upon and was miserably uncomfortable, tense and afraid. His mother went to lunch and left her coat at his bedside. In her absence he became restless and asked that her coat be placed over him. "Put the shiny side next to me," Peter said. The coat was placed over him. As the soft lining contacted his bare skin he moved his hand to his penis and his restlessness ceased.

Masturbation is as normal in childhood as is the child's pleasure in gross motor activity or in sucking during the earliest phases of personality development. It is not injurious and serves a useful purpose. As the child masturbates he has fantasies which are guilt-provoking and cause him concern. If he is shamed or threatened with punishment or rejection, his guilt and fear of injury will be intensified. It is these feelings, not the act, which increase his anxiety and need to masturbate and injure his personality development. If a child never masturbates he is probably scared and would not dare to have sexual gratification. In the process of growing up the individual first finds pleasure in himself. Later in life when maturity is reached he will transfer to an object of love and share the experience with his or her mate. The child who is afraid to masturbate because he has been shamed or punished will have difficulties in expressing himself sexually in later life. If the child is happy and has satisfying relationships with others and interest in the world about him there is no cause for concern, for he will not need to seek comfort from himself very often.

Masturbation tends to occur less frequently when sexual stimulation is kept at a minimum. If the child's desire for independence was utilized in the preceding period, and he learned to bathe and dress himself and be less dependent upon physical demonstrations of love, he will be protected from overstimulation. It is not unusual for the boy of preschool years to show indications of wanting his mother to bathe and caress him. If he has already attained independence his mother can say, "You can bathe yourself, Jimmy. I will be right here, and when you are finished, we will play games together."

If masturbation occurs to the extent that the child has little interest in the world about him, it indicates that he is in need of reassurance and increased satisfactions in his interpersonal relationships. A child who masturbates excessively is turning to himself for solace and comfort, for he is not experiencing sufficient pleasure from others. He needs to know his parents love him. If they ignore his masturbation and do not give him equivalent satisfactions he is apt to feel that no one cares. In addition he will experience excessive sexual excitation which he cannot master and which consequently brings anxiety. To protect and support him the child needs *kindly* given help. If his mother says, "I think you can have as much fun playing with these toys," and stays with him to give him an equivalent pleasure, he will not feel he is being punished; he will feel there is someone who cares and wants to help him to learn to enjoy other people and things.

When children in the hospital masturbate, it is usually because they are in need of comfort and reassurance that their bodies have not been injured. The reasons for their unhappiness and fear of injury should be sought and rectified. Unless they are the children will have to resort to obtaining pleasure from themselves.

It is not unusual to see a preschool or school-age boy clutching his penis; he usually does so to reassure himself that it is still there and uninjured. He values his penis and fears injury. In this period he has destructive wishes toward his father and they make him suspect that his father has similar destructive wishes toward him. When he becomes assured that no harm will befall him, his need to clutch his penis will become nonexistent.

Nurses can anticipate masturbatory activity for parents and help them to understand its purpose and developmental significance. When parents know it is a universal characteristic, they will be more able to understand it and to remain free of fear when they observe it. However, some parents and nurses, too, will be unable to accept emotionally the theory of its origin and purpose. If they have been shamed, restricted or rejected, they have incorporated their parents' standards into their personalities and the sight of masturbation in another activates feelings of repulsion and compels them to do to children what has been done to them. Scolding the child meets their own needs but threatens the child's security. Understanding of its universality often helps the adult gain control over the expression of his impulse to scold, punish or reject.

NIGHT TERRORS AN INDICATION OF A CHILD'S NEED FOR REASSURANCE

Night terrors are common and natural between 3 and 6 years of age for a number of reasons. In this period the child fears abandonment and punishment. He also experiences feelings of disappointment and inadequacy. His impulses are strong and overpowering and his ego is too weak to keep them in check without the help of his mother. His hostile thoughts and impulses are frightening because he is learning to distinguish right from wrong. For these reasons it is natural for children to have dreams which symbolically express their wishes and their struggle to gain mastery of their fear of aggression.

Night terrors indicate a child's need for reassurance and support. The child awakens and needs comforting but it is better given in his own bed than where he often seeks it—in his parent's bed. Fear of the dark begins in the preceding period and often continues into this period. Darkness makes a child feel lonely, and loneliness is threatening in any phase of development.[21] Leaving a light on often alleviates the child's fears and lessens the occurrence of night terrors. However, more important in the prevention of fears is the recognition of the reality of his anxiety and the understanding and help he receives from his parents.

The child's fears are real, potent and frightening and because they are he needs reassurance which helps him to know he is safe and loved and will be given the help he needs in learning to master his aggressive impulses. Explaining the irrationality of the fear to the child is of little value. His fears are not irrational in his eyes. Security comes only when he feels loved and discovers his mother or nurse is there to help him keep from doing those things he knows to be wrong. When he masters his fears and feels competent his night terrors will subside.

HOW THE CHILD HANDLES HIS CONFLICT THROUGH SATISFYING AND CONSTRUCTIVE PLAY EXPERIENCES

Fantasy and Play Help the Child Tolerate Frustration and Anxiety. Becoming a man like the father and a woman like the mother is a long process which must be accomplished a step at a time.[7] It will be many years before the child reaches maturity and has opportunities for direct gratification of his drive to be a mate and parent. In childhood the child must learn to handle his drives and become prepared for his future adult role within his own family. He accomplishes these tasks partly through identification with his parent of the same sex and partly through the use of fantasy which denies his childishness and inadequacies.[7]

The child's desire to be like the parent of the same sex provides the impetus for learning but it also brings frustration and anxiety because he discovers he cannot do all the things he sees his parent doing. The boy loves to work with his father in the garden, for instance, and observation will show that he imitates everything his father does. However, many of the things his parent can do the child cannot do no matter how hard he tries or how keen his desire is to learn. He cannot, for instance, go to the office, drive a car, have babies or a mate. Nor can he do the family shopping, pay the bills or go out with his mother to the office dance. This brings disappointment, feelings of futility and anxiety.

The child cannot tolerate feelings of futility and anxiety and grow emotionally; he must defend himself to keep himself comfortable and to protect his growth potentials. To defend himself from anxiety, the child uses the ego defenses Freud calls *denial in fantasy*[9] and *denial in word and act*.[10] His fantasies and play make life bearable; they make it possible for him to tolerate the frustration that comes when he must give up immediate gratification and wait for greater satisfactions which will be attainable when he is a man like his father or a woman like her mother.[7] French[7] explains the purpose of the above ego defense mechanisms in the following statement:

The discrepancy between child and adult is so great that were it not possible to fill in the gaps by means of fantasy, the incentive to become like the parent would be confronted with insuperable obstacles. . . . If it were necessary for the child to make this identification all in one step, the task would be so utterly hopeless that the only possible solutions would be either complete resignation or intense frustrated envy. By means of fantasy, however, the child is permitted to grow up by shorter steps that are within the range of its capacity. Urged on by the pressing need to be like his parents the child copies what it can and fills in the rest with fantasy. The urge to emulate the parents becomes thus an incentive for a continuous learning process rather than the source of hopeless frustration.

The child's play is not imitative and random; it is his way of learning, withstanding the pressures of his immediate desires and serving to help him understand the people around him. Play as father or mother gives the child a feeling of power. In play he *is* the father, engineer or doctor; he *is* grown-up, adequate and powerful. The child's use of fantasy in solving his problems is evident in his play. In fantasy, Joan, Peter and David were not preschool children; they were grown-ups experiencing things they were unable to enjoy in reality.

Joan, Peter and David were all 4-year-old children in the nursery school. Peter asked Joan to go with him to the office dance. She accepted with childish graciousness and the two children scampered off and climbed into the nursery school truck on the playground. Peter helped Joan into the truck and took his place behind the wheel. Just as they were about to drive off in fantasy, David ran to the truck, jumped onto the running board and gave the following command to Peter: "Don't you kiss my wife. She wouldn't like it if you did."

Although the child's play is only a temporary state of experiencing what he longs to experience in reality, it gives him pleasure and helps him to master the reality demands of his world, which is what he needs for emotional growth. In play the child can have a mate and babies, and he can shop, drive a car and go off to the office dance with the person he loves. If he has had pleasure in play during the day, he is better prepared to tolerate it when his parents leave him behind to go to the office dance. Through repetition of his play he gradually works through his conflicts, masters his frustration and grows emotionally.

Children need adults who can empathize or feel with them. If they can, they will provide opportunities for play and give them freedom to work out their problems in their own way. They will not laugh at their fantasies, direct their play or impose restrictions which limit their opportunities for growth. They will watch and listen to gain increased understanding of them as persons and stand by to support and help them attain their goals and find satisfactions. Observation is essential to gain understanding of children. Isaacs[15] says:

But by patient listening to the talk of even little children, and watching what they do, with the one purpose of understanding them, we can imaginatively feel their fears and angers, their bewilderments and triumphs; we can wish their wishes, see their pictures and think their thoughts.*

A Nursery School Experience Promotes Personality Growth. In the nursery school environment the child can express the positive and negative feelings that he did not dare to express at home and can learn to handle them. The nursery school environment is a safer place to express certain of his feelings than is his home for his relationship to the teacher is less emotionally involved than is his relationship to his mother.[23] His teacher can be more objective, and the child more free in expressing the feelings within him.[23]

As the child's intense love for the parent of the opposite sex is thwarted, he needs playmates to solve the painful conflict with his parents. Through his relationship with the nursery school teacher, the child's capacities for socialization can unfold. She can help him turn to playmates to find outlet for his affections and substitute satisfactions. Making friends and learning to enjoy them helps him to become less dependent upon his parents for affection. When relationships with playmates are happy ones, the disappointment he experienced with his parents becomes more tolerable.

* From *The Nursery Years* by Susan Isaacs. By permission of the publisher, the Vanguard Press, Inc.

At first the child may play alone in the nursery school but gradually he will learn to share, to take turns and eventually to plan and execute play projects with other children. Many children just watch when they first enter a nursery school. They need to observe the children and the teacher and to acclimate themselves to new surroundings in a passive rather than an active way. When they have found they are comfortable and safe within the group, they will be ready to learn to approach others, share, take turns and find outlets for their aggression and need for self-expression in constructive play with others. Others rush into the new situation as though they were overpowered with a desire to explore and test out everything they have never experienced before.

Children need guidance to make friends with other children and to learn technics of co-operative social play; they acquire the capacity to share and to take turns through their desire to please their mothers, teachers or "play nurses" and to remain loved and accepted by them.[25] It is their relationship with the adult which makes it possible for them to give up their desire to monopolize toys or to do only those things they wish to do. One- to 6-year-old children are impulsive, self-centered and undeveloped socially and emotionally. They acquire attitudes of consideration and generosity because they want their teacher's acceptance, not because they comprehend the needs of their playmates.[25] If the supervising adult is a warm, kind, understanding person, the children will want to please her and win her love. However, if they do not value her friendship, they will have little incentive to please her for they know that they will get nothing from her in return for the sacrifices they make.

In learning to play with other children, the child will need his teacher's help in learning to express his angry feelings constructively. A child who is learning to play with other children meets many situations which frustrate and provoke him to anger. The cause of his outburst may be evident to the adult who is observing or it may arise from inner feelings which had their origin in his home before he came to school that morning. If the child's background experiences are known and the situation he is experiencing within his group is studied, ways can be found to help him get the satisfaction he requires in more constructive ways than through the use of temper outbursts. Sometimes the child having the outburst will need to be separated from the group until his anger subsides and he regains his equilibrium. However, prolonged isolation does not help the child learn constructive socialized ways of behaving. He needs experiences with others and help; his unsocialized behavior is his language. He is telling the adult that he has feelings within him that are making him miserably uncomfortable.

When the child acquires increased language facility, the nursery school teacher helps him to talk about his angry feelings and to solve his problems with words rather than with temper outbursts or physical fighting. An ability to express hostile feelings verbally shows growth; it is a maturer way of giving vent to one's feelings. Children need an outlet for their feelings; they need permission to talk about their angry feelings. The situation which follows subsequently shows one way of applying this principle.

Tom was riding a tricycle in the nursery school yard. Joe approached Tom, stopped him and attempted to push him off his bike. Tom had a temper outburst and hit Joe, and the resulting battle became one that needed adult guidance. The teacher restricted their physical response and said, "Tom, you can tell Joe that you are angry. You can tell him you aren't through using the tricycle." Tom was not able to verbalize his feelings at the moment, but the teacher's words gave him an idea he could use another time when he had grown capable of expressing his anger in other than physical ways. Joe did not grab for Tom's tricycle because he was mean or domineering; he grabbed it because he wanted it and he had not learned to wait—he had not learned to function according to the reality principle.

Joe needed help. He was the aggressor and he needed to learn to ask for a turn instead of grabbing what he wanted at the moment and to tolerate the frustration necessary to wait for its use. The teacher did not scold. Instead she said, "Joe, Tom isn't through using the tricycle. If you tell Tom you want a turn on the tricycle, I think he will tell you when he is finished with it." Joe turned to Tom and said, "You finished. Then me ride. Yes?" To help Joe learn to tolerate waiting for something he wanted at the moment, the teacher said, "Come, Joe. Let's find something else you can use while you are waiting."

Through play the child gains mastery of his fears and relief from the tension they create within him. Adults talk about their fearful experiences as a way of handling the emotional tension which the experience precipitated. The child in the early part of this period cannot verbalize many of his fears. Instead he expresses them in his play. Experiences a child is forced to accept passively are usually reproduced in his play. The child who has been hospitalized will frequently spend hours in hospital play. In this play he identifies with the person inflicting the discomfort and actively relives the experience to gain active control of what he had to endure passively. In his play he utilizes the ego defense that Freud calls *identification with the aggressor.*[11]

If the hospitalized child is given opportunity to play, he will not have to wait until he returns home or to the nursery school to begin to master his fears. Ideally, the ward playroom should be equipped with doll beds, soft rubber dolls, small bedside tables and such accessory equipment as tongue depressors, emesis basins, bandage, adhesive tape and "play" stethoscopes, thermometers, syringes and needles. When there is a nurse in attendance to supervise the play, a real syringe and needle can be used with great value to the child. The following situations exemplify the way children can master their fears through supervised play experiences.

Carol was 5 years old when she required hospitalization for treatment of cardiac disease. She had had intramuscular injections of a digitalis preparation daily for a period of 1 week. During morning care her anxiety pertaining to the anticipated hypodermic mounted. She could hardly eat breakfast and her restlessness was obvious. When the nurse arrived with the hypodermic tray she shrieked in horror. She needed help to keep her leg still and the ordeal left her trembling, fatigued and unable to play.

One day her nurse taught her how to fill a syringe and how to inject a needle into her doll. At first she was hesitant, saying she was afraid her doll would be angry. Gradually she became less fearful and gave her doll not one injection but a succession of them. For days she asked to have the hypodermic tray, and over and over again she played nurse to her doll.

Carol's fear at hypodermic time gradually lessened. First she asked to cleanse the area that was to be used for her injection and then came the day when she said, "I give dolly a shot and I'm not scared any more. I can hold my leg still. Put it in fast and it will be all over." Carol had mastered her fear through her own power and from then on she had more energy available for recuperation.

Bobby, aged 3, had tubercular glands in one side of his neck. In the operating room, he had a cervical gland removed, and the incision extended part way to his shoulder. When the dressing was changed, large scissors were used to remove the outer bandage. Bobby screamed in terror and clutched the doctor's hands.

When the dressing was reapplied, Bobby said, "Me do Dolly's dressing." The doll was placed in his lap. On a low table beside him there were scissors, applicators, bandages and dressings. He covered the doll's forehead with bandage and when the scissors were passed to him, he grabbed them eagerly. "You can cut, Bobby. I'll show you how," the nurse said. Bobby cut through the bandage. His anxiety vanished as if by magic, and his face lighted up with a smile. "I tut it— I tut it," he shrieked in delight. Then Bobby picked up the applicator, cleansed the doll's postauricular area, placed a dressing over it and again began to place the bandage. But he never got the bandage on. Instead, he placed it and cut, and repeated this action over and over again. When subsequent dressings were done, he showed no evidence of anxiety when the scissors were used.

In the nursery school there is appropriate equipment and space, and the child's ego can become strengthened through the acquisition of skills. In the nursery school there are opportunities for gross motor activity that are unavailable in the home situation. Children need this kind of activity not only to develop the large muscles of their body but also to use their excess energy and to get release from tension. And what ego strength the child gains as he learns the skills which make him more self-sufficient and capable of competing favorably with his new friends!

In the nursery school the child can also develop his small muscles and become increasingly more skillful in using paint, clay, brushes, scissors and paper. Little children enjoy and profit from learning to cut, paste, put pegs into boards and string beads. However, they cannot attend to activities which require fine muscle coordination for long, but they are excellent activities to introduce to alleviate the fatigue or tension which come after a period of active play within a large group of children. They are excellent activities for bedridden hospitalized children; they provide relief from tension and give the child an opportunity to feel proud of himself.

In the nursery school the teacher guides the child so his attention span can increase. She helps him learn to listen and participate in music and story periods. In play periods she helps the child discover the many things he can do with blocks, clay, sand and doll corner materials. When the child discovers the properties of his materials his attention span lengthens and he spends increasingly longer periods at one activity. At the 2-year level, the child flits from object to object, spending only a few minutes with each. By 5 years of age his attention span has increased and he is able to center his interest in one thing or on one activity for a longer period of time. He has developed a longer attention span not only because he has grown in years but also because his teacher has helped him to develop his interest and powers of concentration through story, music and play periods.

In nursery school the child not only learns the use of materials for his work and play but also learns to do things for himself and for others, gaining ego strength in the process. He is helped to find ways of contributing to the group and helped to see that his contributions are worth while. He has his own locker where he hangs his clothing and he is encouraged to do all those things he is interested in and capable of doing. He learns to put away his toys, manage himself independently in the bathroom and feed himself with expertness. Besides this he learns to adjust to a situation other than home. If the atmosphere of his home is warm and understanding, he will discover that adults outside his home are friendly, helpful and responsive to his needs.

Preschool children in a hospital ward need the same opportunities for psychological growth as normal children in the community. Play, social experiences and opportunities to become increasingly more self-assured and reliant and free of fear are in reality more important for the child in a pediatric ward for he has infinitely more problems than the child at home. Study of the nursery school program, educational philosophy and methods of guidance and experience there will give nurses the knowledge, attitudes and skills they need to make hospital wards more appropriate places for their child patients. Of necessity, there will need to be certain changes in the routine because the children are ill or recuperating from disease, but study will disclose that there are many principles of nursery school education that can be adapted to the hospital ward.

Preparation for nursery school is of vital importance to the child. The factors involved in preparation are nearly as important for the child entering school as they are if he must become hospitalized. In a subsequent section the child's adjustment to experiences which bring separation from family and home will be considered.

SIBLING AND PEER RIVALRY

NECESSITY OF ADJUSTMENT TO A NEW SIBLING IN THIS PERIOD OF DEVELOPMENT

The child's fear of losing his mother's love manifests itself again when a new baby is expected within his family. All children fear the possibility of having a rival brother or sister. When they see or learn their playmate has a newly born sibling they suspect that it could also happen to them. Many children want a sibling but at the same time they sense that his coming will bring changes which will have a direct effect upon him.

A knowledge of the mother's pregnancy arouses mixed feelings in a child and creates needs requiring satisfaction to alleviate his anxiety. When a child first learns he is going to have a sibling, his feelings probably will be mixed ones. He may be overjoyed temporarily because he has been desiring a playmate. He will also be fearful of how the new baby will affect his relationship with his mother. He will wonder what will happen to him, and will dread the baby's arrival lest it monopolize his mother and leave him without the care and love he knows he requires. Unless the child has seen little babies and knows their characteristics, it will be difficult for him to know that a sibling will be both a pleasure and an annoyance which he will need help in meeting. *Before the baby arrives the child needs to know that the baby will be little and helpless and needful of his mother's care because he cries and is unhappy unless he has food and love when he needs it. He also needs to know that his mother will have time to take care of him because she knows he will need it as much as he needs it now.*

As the time for the baby's arrival draws nearer, the child may become fearful lest he be unable to control his feelings and behavior. Ann, aged 5 years, evidenced this fear in her behavior.

Ann was artistically gifted and showed her fear in her drawings and in her panic lest she fall downstairs. One day she drew a mother, a father and a baby tiger and enclosed them in a cage which had bars very close together. Her mother was with her and commented, "How close the bars are. I wonder if you are afraid the animals are going to get out." Ann's quick response was, "No, I'm afraid of falling down the stairs."

Ann's mother suspected that her fear of falling downstairs was connected with her concern about her pregnancy. She thought it was a reflection of her fear of what was going to happen to her when the new baby arrived. She also suspected that Ann was worried lest she might hurt the baby and be punished by her parents if she did.

Ann's mother knew she needed assurance to alleviate her anxiety. She said, "When children are going to have a new baby in their homes they worry about what is going to happen to them. Sometimes they are scared they will get angry at the baby and hurt it. They are scared because they do not know the baby will be little and sleep a lot for a long, long time. They don't know their mothers will understand when they get angry because the baby cries a lot and needs their mother's attention. Nor do they know their mothers won't let them hurt the baby when they wish it was not there. Even though mothers have little babies, they always have time to love and take care of their bigger children too. I will have time, too, and will love you just as much as I do now. Sometimes I will be busy with a crying, hungry baby but when it is fed and asleep you and I will have lots of time to be together just as we do now."

Ann could not express her feelings of relief in words but she showed her appreciation of her mother's understanding and preparation in her behavior. She dropped her crayons, went to her mother and with the tenderest of feelings caressed her cheek and then returned to her play.

Ann used the ego defense mechanism called projection to handle her anxiety. She was afraid of her own feelings of aggression toward her parents and the new baby. These feelings threatened her with possible loss of love. To master her anxiety, she projected her own angry feelings onto others. It was as if she were saying, "It is not I who wants to hurt my parents and the baby, it is Mother, Father and the baby who will hurt me."

The child needs preparation for his mother's hospitalization and opportunity to become adjusted to the person who will give him care during his mother's absence. He needs to know where his mother is going and why she must be separated from him, and assured that she will return to take care of him. If he has not had an opportunity to develop a relationship with the person who is to care for him in his mother's absence, he needs this experience while his mother is with him. Whatever rearrangements must be made in the home must be made prior to the infant's arrival and with the child's help in making and carrying out of the plans. Then he will feel that his needs are being considered for he is given the privilege of sharing in the experience.

Preparation in advance of the event gives the child an opportunity to prepare himself and to gain some mastery of the fears it brings. In his play he will portray his feelings, discharge uncomfortable tension and attempt to master his fears pertaining to the oncoming experience. He cannot completely master his feelings prior to the sibling's arrival but he can prepare himself for the event. To master his feelings completely he must meet the experience in reality and discover that he is still loved although he sometimes feels and behaves aggressively.

The arrival of a new sibling into the family is a time of crisis for the child. Its arrival may destroy the foundation of his security and his zest for living or it may bring increased security and a happier life of shared pleasure. Regardless of how well prepared the child is, he will be jealous, hostile and afraid although his feelings may be unrecognized by the untrained observer. The child who does not have a sibling never discovers through experience that he can maintain his special place with his parents even though another child arrives and is loved.[16]

Determination of the Kind of Adjustment the Child Will Make by Past Experiences and Guidance Before and After the Sibling Is Born

The child's adjustment to a new sibling will depend upon the quality of the early relationships he has already experienced within his home. A child of 3 years is usually more ready to adapt himself to a new sibling than is the child of 12 to 18 months. But more important than age is the degree of ego strength the child possesses for the adjustment. The child who has acquired trust from repeated experiences of fulfillment and inner resources for independent activity which bring pleasure will be less threatened by the new arrival than will the child who has been deprived, infantilized with maternal overprotection or handled with inconsistency in emotional expression.

The child's adjustment to a new sibling will also depend upon the quality of guidance he receives at the time the sibling arrives. *During the adjustment period the child will need parents who can see the experience through his eyes and have empathy with him, who are able to permit expression of his feeling and give him the assurance he needs to know that he continues to have a very special place in their affections.*

EARLY MANIFESTATIONS OF SIBLING RIVALRY

A child's response to a new sibling will depend upon the intensity of his feelings and the patterns of behavior he has utilized to handle previous situations which involved conflict and anxiety. If he has been permitted to express his feelings about other painful experiences, he will be able to express them overtly now. If his earlier overt expressions of anger and fear met with parental disapproval and he repressed his feelings, he will probably respond similarly when he is threatened again.

Regression is a common and natural response during the time the child is adapting himself to a new sibling. Regression occurs when a child is anxious and has insufficient ego strength to master it. The child sees the baby getting care because of its helplessness. To attain the attention he needs either because anxiety has brought regression and a need for more dependent care or because he needs reassurance that his mother continues to love him, the child may demand more physical attention, ask for the bottle or become less capable of controlling his urges than he was before.

Some children become hostile and aggressive and show resentment toward their mother who produced the baby; others direct their hostility toward the baby and hurt it if the baby is not given sufficient protection; other children withdraw, become depressed and show changes in their physical status. The children who withdraw often have eating and sleep disturbances, excessive fatigue, exaggerated fearfulness and lack of interest in activities which formerly brought them joy. These children are angry, disappointed children but they are unable to express their anger overtly because early expression of it brought punishment or withdrawal of love. These children "swallow" their anger and disappointment or symbolically incorporate the object of their hatred. Their depression is a defense against fear of their own aggression. It brings changes in their physical status and in their relationships with their mothers. Unless the child is helped, his opportunities for growth may become jeopardized.

Then there is the child who becomes overwhelmed with fear because he sees the baby as a positive sign that he was not as good as he should have been. Somehow he feels as if he had failed to please his mother.[16] He feels guilty, remorseful, inferior and convinced that his mother would never have wanted another child if he had been a better child and lived up to her expectations.[16] His anxiety brings him discomfort, making him irritable and prone to outbursts. His irritability shows how really badly he feels inside. He needs reassurance and love, not condemnation, for that merely serves to prove he has not been good enough to win his mother's love.

In their play children reveal the feelings they cannot verbally express or direct toward the real object of their anger. If the child has dolls and household play equipment, he will utilize them in an attempt to work through his problem and master it. Observation of his play will help the adult gain insight into the child's feelings concerning his sibling and his present status with his parents. By observing play we can often find the reason for behavior that was formerly unexplainable. We can discover the child's fears and wishes and take steps to meet the needs he is attempting to communicate to us in his behavior.

The following situation occurred in the nurse's office within a nursery school and serves to exemplify the way children disclose their feelings in their behavior. Joan, Jimmy and Larry had reason to feel aggressive. Had they not had aggressive feelings within them, they would have spent their time in the nurse's office differently. Their activity relieved their tension and brought reassurance, for they discovered that the nurse accepted the feelings within them.

Joan, Larry and Jimmy were among a group of children waiting for their daily examination. When the nurse finished her examination, Joan went to the cupboard, picked up a rubber doll and tossed it into the wastebasket, saying, "There, that's where *you* belong, you naughty doll." Jimmy saw her and went to the basket, stamped his foot on the doll and said, "There, that's what *you* get." Larry, who had been watching the two children intently, ran over, joined the group and with intense feeling said, "If I had some cinders, I'd throw them in and *grind* them into her."

All three children had had new siblings within the past two months. It took little speculation to surmise the content of the fantasies that accompanied their acts and words of violence.

GUIDANCE WHICH HELPS THE CHILD MASTER HIS FEELINGS

First and foremost in importance are the recognition and the acceptance of the fact that the child will be anxious until he becomes assured that he has not been displaced by what he feels to be an intruder. Every child wants to be the most loved; that is his nature and he cannot feel otherwise until he has mastered his fear through discovering he is loved, cared for and protected. This takes time, energy and thoughtful guidance.

The mother's arrival home from the hospital with a new baby needs to be planned so that the older child has an opportunity for a happy reunion with her. This is a crucial period for the older child. He undoubtedly has suffered during his mother's absence and it will take time and skill on the part of the mother to re-establish their former relationship. The more casual the father can be about the new baby, the easier it will be for the older child, although his fears are usually in relation to his mother.

The nursing situation is usually the hardest one for the older child to experience, and signs of regression are often most pronounced at this time. The child needs his regressive behavior understood or his anxiety will mount and increase his need for infantile care. When he becomes assured that his needs will be met, his anxiety will lessen and he will have energy to use in mastering his present situation.

The child needs acceptance when he feels hostile, protection from his urge to injure the persons who bring him discomfort and reassurance that he is loved. When a child attacks his younger sibling, he is showing his need for acceptance and reassurance. Hating someone one feels he should love is frightening. The child does not know that acceptance of a sibling cannot come at once; he does not know that all children are scared and angry when they are uncertain of their mother's love. This kind of guidance is best given through acts which strengthen the child's ego to the point where he can master his feelings. The situation which follows shows application of this principle.

Mrs. J. had two children. Ned was 5 years old and Sally was 1 when this situation was observed. Sally had been irritable all day and required a great deal of her mother's time. Ned played outside with a friend all afternoon but when he came in he was tired, irritable and needful of his mother's attention. His sister was on the floor playing when he approached her and grabbed the toys from her hands. He was about ready to hit her when his mother intervened to protect Sally from physical injury and Ned from expressing his feelings directly and feeling guilty and afraid.

Mrs. J. gently took Ned's hands and said, "I am not going to let you hurt Sally. She needs her toys. She cannot do all the things you are able to do. I've been watching you from the window and I saw the wonderful building you and Jim made. Sally cannot do those things. Let's you and I go over to the davenport and talk about the things you did this afternoon. You have had a hard time today because

I have been so busy with Sally. I know because I used to have hard times when my mother had to take care of my baby sister."

Ned went with his mother and in a few minutes he had regained his composure and chatted with enthusiasm. His mother showed her pride when he told her about the things he and Jim had been doing and it seemed as though he became aware that he and his mother could share things which Sally was not old enough to enjoy. One couldn't help but surmise this for after Ned had felt his mother's interest, he went to Sally and played with her tenderly.

Mrs. J. recognized Ned's feelings and helped him to handle them. She did not shame or punish him. As a result Ned did not have to bury his feelings in his unconscious. His mother did not make him feel wicked or bad; she gave him reassurance that he was loved as he was. She knew his feelings were natural and was aware that Ned was communicating his need for reassurance in the only way he knew how to do it. She knew the meaning of his behavior. His behavior was saying, "I am uncomfortable inside. I haven't had enough from you today and I'm scared lest you don't love me as much as you did. If that little sister weren't here I wouldn't be feeling like this. She is to blame for my discomfort and though I love her most of the time, I've a powerful urge to hit that I can't control."

To protect the child's personality growth, he needs opportunities to express his feelings in words and in socially acceptable forms of aggressiveness. The more outlet the child has in words and acceptable forms of aggressiveness in doll play or in activities like pounding, running or playing kick the ball, the less need he will have to attack physically the persons who have brought him discomfort. The preschool child will need help to find these outlets. If he is shamed or made to feel guilty for his feelings or behavior instead of wisely guided, he will be forced to utilize his precious vital energy in repressing feelings to avoid punishment and anxiety. When he is forced to repress hostility into his unconscious, he develops opposite characteristics to hide his angry rivalrous feelings. Instead of hating outwardly, he seems to love, though beneath the surface there are currents of intense emotion which bring guilt and tension and disturb his feelings about himself and his relationships with others. One cannot hate and be at peace with himself or the world!

A child who represses his hostility maintains his security with his mother but the price he pays for it is tremendous. A child who represses his hostility is usually oversolicitous and protective of his sibling. He shares too much and constantly wants to take care of the baby. He may also curtail his aggressiveness and become submissive with other children or he may use another defense called *displacement* and displace his hostility onto peers and do to them what he would like to do to his sibling. Being hostile to peers safeguards his relationship with his mother but it keeps him dependent upon her because his aggressiveness with playmates prevents him from being accepted by them.

The overly good and depressed child needs more help than the child who can express his feelings overtly. If his "goodness" is misinterpreted, he will undoubtedly be praised for it, and that makes him need to hide his feelings even deeper. Instead of praise he needs permission to be less attentive to the baby and to express his feelings. Such permission needs to be given by word and deed before the child feels safe enough to express himself. A mother might say, "Sometimes you must wish the baby did not cry so much. Some children feel more like scolding their mothers rather than taking care of their baby brother or sister. Lots of children are angry and tell their mothers they are." If the child is able to express his feelings with this kind of help, he needs reassurance to know he *really is* accepted. If the following feelings can be expressed in behavior, the child will feel secure and comforted: "I'm glad you can tell Mother how angry you are. It *is* hard having a little baby in the house. Every child feels that way for a long, long time. There are lots of things you like to do and you don't need to take care of the baby so much. Come on, let's you and I go and do a puzzle together."

When the child's natural responses to the new baby are met with acceptance and he learns he is not going to be deprived of love, it will be possible for him to perceive values in having a sibling. However, this cannot happen overnight. Gradually he will learn that he is not going to be deprived of love. If the parents share the baby and permit him to feel it is his baby, too, he will gradually develop protective feelings toward him. He will begin to show interest in the baby and request that his mother let him participate in his care. When he develops readiness to help, he needs permission to do so, although the mother will always need to be in attendance to protect and help him should an uncontrollable urge to hurt arise when he is doing his level best to help and handle his feelings.

Gradually, as the child's anxiety is relieved through happy experiences that tell him his worst fears are unfounded in reality, he will regain self-esteem and self-confidence. If his need for companionship with his parents has been fulfilled, he will see that he is superior to the baby in that he can enjoy experiences the baby is too young to appreciate. When he perceives this, he can love the baby, although for months and sometimes for years there will be an ambivalent quality in his relationship to him.

Both girls and boys master their problem by assuming a mother role in the care of the baby. In being "bigger" and "stronger," their feelings of inferiority and fear vanish and become replaced with feelings of protectiveness and affection. Although this is the healthy solution for the child to make to his problem, he should not be forced into helping with the baby through fear of deprivation. He will resolve his problem if his parents are patient, just and impartial in their respect and love for each of their children.

How Nurses Can Help Mothers Understand Their Children's Problem

Nurses can interpret the child's dilemma and help mothers develop empathy for their child who is fearful lest he not keep his place in the sun. Many parents are not aware of the emotional turmoil a child experiences when a new sibling arrives. Many do not know that a child needs preparation for its arrival and support during the time he is getting used to sharing his parents' love with another. The nurse can interpret the inevitable changes that come to children during the adjustment period while mothers are in the prenatal clinic or in the maternity ward. In so doing she will help prepare parents to meet behavior change in a way which gives their children the security and reassurance they need.

The Nurse's Role in Helping Hospitalized Children Handle Their Feelings of Rivalry

Understanding of a Child's Early Experiences Aids the Nurse in Providing Individualized Care. Nurses as well as mothers and teachers need to be aware of children's feelings and capable of helping them deal with the emotions that are aroused in close interpersonal relationships. They also need to be aware of their own feelings toward the patients for whom they are caring, for children sense favoritism in the ward as well as in the home. It is true that a functional method of assigning duties to nurses in a ward would eliminate rivalrous feelings, but what help a child toward maturity are close personal relationships and guidance to aid him in handling his feelings and to become increasingly more able to share with others. Nurses can assist children in acquiring these abilities by helping them to feel secure in their relationships with them.

Without the above kind of relationship experiences in their home, school, clubs and hospital ward children will remain infantile, self-centered and unable to enjoy the pleasures involved in mature give-and-take adult relationships. Unless the child can resolve his rivalry during childhood, he will continue to be insecure and rivalrous throughout his lifetime. Not only will it influence the kind of relationships he will have with his siblings, it will also interfere with his interpersonal relationships with others as well.

The nurse needs to know the child's background of experience with his parents and his siblings for this knowledge gives her the insight she needs to understand his behavior in the hospital. Knowledge of his home experiences will guide her observation and the care she gives the child. The nurse's need for information concerning the child's background of home experience is illustrated by some incidents which occurred in the nursing care of Martha.

Martha, aged 5, came into the hospital with acute glomerular nephritis or "Bright's disease." Martha had two brothers, aged 4 and 2 years, and two sisters, aged 3 years and 6 months. Martha's parents reported she was a well-adjusted child with no problem behavior. They said she responded amicably to her siblings, feeding, toilet training and the disciplinary regime they used to help her learn to become co-operative and generous.

Martha brought toys and an album of pictures of herself and her four siblings with her into the hospital. Everyone who entered Martha's room was greeted with the following remark: "I've got pictures of my brothers and sisters. Do you want to see them?" Her interest in her siblings seemed exaggerated for a 5-year-old child. [What was the meaning of Martha's behavior? Why did she need to show the pictures to every nurse who entered her room? Those were the questions Martha's nurse needed answered.]

When Martha first came into the ward, she screamed when she had treatments. However, in a few days her behavior changed. She never cried, moved or expressed anger when treatments were done. When her blood pressure was high, she showed signs of irritability but the symptoms were mild. She talked little, dawdled excessively at meal times and played with slight interest or enthusiasm. She seemed to have little confidence in herself and needed someone to help her with her play. In play with an adult she would say, "Which one shall I cut out? How should I do this? You do it, I can't."

After a nurse had cared for Martha for 10 days her behavior began to change. During this period the nurse met her demands. She assisted her at bath and meal times and followed her directions in the long period of play they had together. On the tenth day, Martha began to show anger whenever her nurse prepared her for her leave taking. She threw toys on the floor with gusto, said "No" to every suggestion and pouted. However, she rarely raised her voice but began to dawdle in everything she did. When a second child was brought into her room to give her company at meal time, Martha showed resentment toward the intruder. It was obvious she did not want 3-year-old Peggy in her room. Whenever Peggy touched her toys, she would say, "That's mine. I don't want Peggy to have my doll. Tell her not to touch those things."

One day at rest hour Martha saw her nurse through the glass partitions of her room. Martha was standing up in her crib looking longingly at those who were outside her door. It was not possible for her nurse to go to her at once. When she did five minutes later, Martha's bed was soaked with urine for the first time since admission.

[Martha's mother had said she was compliant and without problems at home. Why was her behavior changing now? Was it because she was ill and separated from those she loved? If this was true, why had she not displayed her reactions to separation at the time she was most anxious—when she was acutely ill and first admitted into the hospital? Why wasn't Martha able to express her hostility and rivalry at home? Was it because her security was dependent on compliance and submissiveness? Was she daring to express her hostility now because she was less dependent on her nurse than on her mother or was it because of some changes in her physical condition? Those were the questions her nurse had when she began to observe the changes in Martha's behavior. She wanted to understand her so she could maintain a constructive relationship with her and through it help Martha to become more at ease with herself.]

Martha's physical condition improved but her resistance and expressions of anger became intensified. In the meantime she seemed surer of her nurse. Her nurse did not like her less because she threw things, dawdled and expressed her anger. Instead, she seemed to like her more for she was learning about the real Martha and was discovering the reasons for her submissiveness and lack of spontaneity.

Her nurse spent more time with Martha and found ways for her to redirect her aggressiveness in constructive and pleasurable ways. She painted, manipulated clay and used the pounding board. When Martha's anger mounted as her nurse said, "Martha, it's time for me to go and take care of Sally now," her nurse understood it. To reassure Martha the nurse said the following, "You want me to stay here with you. I know because all children get lonely when their nurses leave. Sally needs her bath now and I must take care of her, too. I won't forget you while I am gone. You are my patient, too, and I will come back when you need me. Do you want to use the pounding board while I am gone or would you rather I'd send Peggy in to play with you? If you need me while I am gone, you call loudly and I'll come."

Understanding of the Dynamics of Group Interaction Is Necessary to Help Children Handle Their Feelings.

When children have become convinced that they are loved although their mothers love others, too, they relinquish their desire for exclusive love, accept sharing her but simultaneously demand that others in the group, be it family, school or hospital ward, do the same.[25] They demand that no other child receive more or be given privileges denied to them.[25] If the mother or the nurse gives more to one child than another, it is deeply resented, and sibling or peer rivalry becomes grossly intensified. If one child usurps the attention of the mother, the nurse or the teacher, the children show him that it is not permitted. If they share, they expect others to do the same thing.

Between 2 and 6 years of age children observe each other very closely and tattle when they see other children getting more than they. Peller[25] has written extensively on the meaning of this behavior and shows its developmental significance. Tattling is prevalent in both hospital wards and homes. In tattling the child is saying, "Jim is getting more than I am and if he gets it I have a right to have it, too." Larry demonstrated this feeling in the ward one afternoon.

Several children were having midafternoon juice and crackers around a table in the playroom. The children knew two crackers apiece were permitted at one time. Jim took four crackers, and Larry turned to the nurse who was at the table supervising the activity and said, "Jim took four crackers." The nurse's response was, "Just two crackers at a time, Jim." Larry turned to Jim and said, "Just two crackers, Jim. That's all you can have."

Sometimes children tattle for other reasons than the one cited above. Sometimes what sounds like tattling is really the child's attempt to reassure himself that he should not carry out an impulse he really wishes to gratify.[25] He is not tattling in the true sense of the word; he is asking for help in controlling an impulse that is clamoring for satisfaction. This need was vividly illustrated in Terry's behavior.

Chad, Joy, Terry and Bob were in the hospital playroom. Joy, aged 1 year, was playing with blocks and kitchenware on the floor. Chad, aged 4, went over and grabbed Joy's toys. Terry saw him do it. Quickly he ran to the nurse and said, "Chad took all Joy's toys." The nurse recognized Terry's need to be reassured that it was something which should not be done, and said, "Chad should not take Joy's toys. She needs them. Come, I'll help you find some other toys that you will enjoy playing with."

If the nurse had scolded Terry for tattling his need would have remained unmet and he would have felt that his telling the nurse was something which was "bad." What Terry probably was trying to say was: "Chad is doing something I want very much to do. I don't want to do it but I'm very much tempted to do the same thing. Please help me refrain from doing something I know to be wrong."

Some children solve their rivalry problem with exaggerated competitiveness. They must always win, jump the farthest or make the biggest house in the playroom. These children are attempting to prove to themselves that they *are* good. Their parents have not helped them feel accepted and secure. Their need to convince themselves that they are good demonstrates itself in compensatory competitiveness which utilizes much of their energy but never brings them any measure of real satisfaction. By their behavior they are saying, "I am good. I am not really the 'bad' child my parents think I am. I really surpass others."

The child who repeatedly "shows off" needs help, not criticism and remonstrance. He is handling his problem in the only way he knows how. The child needs an adult who can lessen his need to show off. This can be accomplished by giving him the feeling that he is loved and accepted just as he is.

When children's ages are widely divergent, rivalry within the group may be more exaggerated. The little child often wants the privileges and the possessions he sees his older sibling receiving and yet in most instances he is unready for them. Unless the older child experiences advantages and can see values in being his age, he, too, may be rivalrous with what his younger sibling is receiving. He may resist growing up to get the attention he longs for.

When each child within the home, nursery school or hospital is guided in accordance with his specific requirements, rivalry will be considerably lessened. Treating two children alike in that they are given the same presents and the same amount and kind of parental attention is not being impartial. Each child is different. They are different in age and different in that their needs cannot be satisfied in the same way. If the 6-year-old child's relationship with his parents is like the one his 18-month-old brother has with them, both children will miss experiences they need to learn to accept each other.

The nurse is often confronted with the above situation in the hospital ward. She may be assigned to several children who are different in age and different in that their requirements for nursing care show wide variation. Instead of observing to discover the specific needs of each child, the nurse often budgets her time and plans to spend equal time with each patient. Many times she does this to ease her conscience. If she prefers one child to another and cannot accept this feeling in herself, she may handle it by equalizing the time she spends with each patient.

It is not time which counts; it is the quality of interpersonal relationships that has meaning for the child. Care and guidance must be individualized to meet children's requirements for growth. If care is based on the procedures which are to be done, the children's needs become frustrated and problem behavior ensues. Children need to have their nurses aware of their needs and capable of appraising those which need attention at the time. Children are understanding persons! If plans are shared with them and they recognize their nurse's faith in their ability to understand, they get the help they need to make it possible for them to tolerate temporary frustration. The following situation highlights the nurse's role in helping children to share.

Miss J. was taking care of 1-year-old Johnny and 4-year-old Cecilia. Before planning her morning's work she observed both children and discovered that Johnny was acting as though he were very hungry. He was crying and twirling his hair, and as the nurse approached him he put out his arms to be picked up. Cecilia was chatting with her neighbor in the cubicle next to hers. As the nurse approached, Cecilia said, "Hi, bath time now?"

After greeting Cecilia, the nurse said, "Johnny is all alone in his room, and he is very hungry and lonesome this morning. How would it be if I get John's breakfast first so he can start eating? Then I'll come back and help you with your bath. You and Sally can visit until I return. Here's a book. Maybe Sally would like to read to you while I am gone. I'll pull your beds closer together so you can see the pictures while she is reading. I'll be back as soon as Johnny gets what he needs. He is a little boy and he can't wait very long for his food."

Cecilia's response showed her acceptance. When her bed was moved close to Sally's, she expressed her joy with her whole body. She jumped up, clapped her hands and said, "Goody, goody, gumdrop, now we can really play together."

Through observation and planning the nurse can keep in touch with all her patients. With thoughtfulness she can help all her patients to feel considered and secure. Miss J. did not give only to Johnny; she gave to Sally and Cecilia as well. She met Johnny's need for food and Sally's need to grow increasingly more able to tolerate the frustration she felt when she had to be separated from her nurse.

FACTORS INFLUENCING THE CHILD'S ADJUSTMENT IN NEW SITUATIONS WHICH BRING SEPARATION FROM FAMILY AND HOME

Between 3 and 6 years of age many children are confronted with the difficult task of mastering a new experience in a nursery school, kindergarten or hospital. Adjusting to a new situation which brings separation from family and home brings the child new problems which he will need help in surmounting.

There are many factors that will influence the kind of adjustment the child will make. The most important of these factors are as follows: (1) the degree of anxiety with which the child must cope, (2) the meaning which the experience has for him personally,

(3) the child's chronologic age, his past experiences and ego strength, (4) the child's and the mother's preparation for the new experience and (5) the quality of the relationships the child and his parents experience in the new situation.

Influence of the Degree of Anxiety with Which the Child Must Cope on His Adjustment in New Situations

The Child Requires Freedom from Fear to Make a Healthy Adjustment to Situations that Bring Separation from Family and Home. *The child needs freedom from fears which prevent him from mastering new experiences and from achieving optimal physical and mental health.* The child's need for freedom from fear has been existent from birth and ways of providing security have been cited in the foregoing material. As the factors which influence a child's adjustment in new situations are discussed, it will become more evident why the child needs a background of security to handle the fears characteristic of this period of development. It will also be evident why the child needs security as preparation for the broader social experiences that come during this period. Fears are crippling. They injure physical health and rob the child of the security (peace of mind) he requires to participate in the new experiences and the adventures necessary for social and emotional growth. A child cannot enjoy nursery school, kindergarten or play in his friend's back yard if he is afraid and insecure concerning his parents' affection.

There are many children in our society who have experienced little freedom from fear and as a result their adjustment in new situations is precarious and dependent upon the help they receive when they are confronted with new situations. Hospital personnel, nurses in doctors' offices and teachers need understanding of the genesis of fears, a capacity for empathy and the desire to give children comfort in times of stress.

The Child Acquires Fears from Adults and Experiences Which Are Painful. Before a child enters school or hospital he has already acquired attitudes and feelings about the institution that will come into play and will influence his adjustment in the new reality situation. If his attitudes and feelings are wholesome ones, he will be more prepared to master the problems which are an inevitable part of any new experience. If they are unwholesome, he will have more problems to overcome before he can feel safe in an unfamiliar and untried situation.

Many fears are unconsciously communicated to children by adults in their environment. If parents are fearful the child cannot help but feel and absorb their anxiety even though they never put it into words. The child's parents are his strength. When they are uneasy about their child, his support is weakened and he responds with apprehension. An anxious nurse precipitates a similar reaction in her patients. If she approaches a child in the admitting room with trepidation lest she be unsuccessful in helping him co-operate with the routine admission procedure, his fear of the experience will be intensified.

The child may also acquire fear through what is called verbal association. Directives like the following make children fearful lest injury befall them: "Don't talk to strangers; they might hurt you," or "Don't touch that. You will burn yourself." If there was nothing of which to be afraid the adult would not forewarn or offer reassurances. This the child senses from the uneasy feelings which are communicated with such words.

Many children have been threatened with punishment and sometimes even coerced into obeying through fear of the teacher, the doctor, the nurse, illness, surgery and sometimes even abandonment. Later when they are expected to adjust themselves to school or to a hospital experience, they feel fearful instead of safe. Parents have said, "If you touch matches again, you will get burned and have to go to the hospital," or "If you touch yourself again, I'll take you to the hospital and have the doctor cut off your 'wee wee.'" When a child is threatened with comments like these, he is made fearful of hospitals and their personnel. He is also made fearful lest his body become injured. Instead of learning that hospitals are places that heal and comfort people, the child acquires the concept that hospitals and their personnel punish and injure.

Many of the children who come into the hospital have already acquired the above concept and it is understandable why they react to hospital personnel and the experiences they meet there with fear and mistrust. Behavior which seems unreasonable would be explainable if we could but know the content of the child's fantasies!

It is the degree of anxiety the child has within him which will determine his behavior and influence his ability to master the new situation. If he is overwhelmed with anxiety, his adjustment will be precarious, and his need for help will be urgent and of paramount importance to him both physically and emotionally. An experience with Mike illustrates the foregoing points.

Mike, aged 8, spent seven miserable days in the hospital while he was being studied to determine the treatment he required for convulsive seizures. He did not master his hospital experience. He was withdrawn and unable to enter into ward activities with his age mates. When diagnostic procedures were done he was apprehensive. Preparation never seemed to lessen his wariness concerning his welfare. His appetite was poor and he rarely talked except to say that he could not wait until he could return home again.

The day Mike was to be discharged from the hospital, his mother came for the first time since he had been admitted. Before she greeted Mike, she said to the nurse who was with him, "You know, before Mike came here I got very mad at him one day and told him I would take him to the hospital where the doctors and nurses would make him behave. I also told him I would not come to visit him, either. I should not have said it but I did. I just could not get here to see him before. I've been too busy at home."

The look of relief which came into Mike's face when he saw his mother and heard her comments was striking. It is little wonder Mike had such problems in trying to master his hospital experience. Certainly he must have expected severity of discipline; he may also have wondered if his mother would really come to take him home. Mike's behavior was not only a response to the reality experience of hospitalization, it was also a response to all that had gone before.

Professional and nonprofessional personnel in hospitals have also been guilty of making children fearful and thereby increasing their difficulties in mastering their problems in relation to their illness and treatment. All those who work in hospitals have at one time or another heard a member of the staff say, "Johnny, if you do not drink more water, I will give you needles." Such remarks are understandable. When people are frightened because a child is not getting enough fluids and frustrated in their attempts to get him to cooperate, they say things to meet their own needs but they do not go unheard. If clysis or intravenous therapy becomes a necessity, the child who has been threatened with a remark like the above is panicky. Instead of believing that the treatment is given to help him become restored to health, he sees it as punishment. It was obvious 2½-year-old Suzy felt that way. When the intravenous therapy equipment was brought to her bedside she wailed: "I be good. Me sorry. Me not do it any more."

The child also acquires fears from experiences which bring him discomfort. When a child becomes secure enough to venture away from his mother, he meets experiences which are fear-provoking and painful. He does not know what is dangerous and what is safe. He does not know, for instance, that dogs may snap at him if he approaches them too roughly. He approaches a dog because it interests him. He wants to know what it is like and what it can do. If the dog snaps and barks as he touches it, the child may acquire fear through direct conditioning. He can acquire fear of new places in exactly the same way. If he is taken to a clinic, a dentist or doctor's office, a nursery school or a hospital psychologically unready, and if he experiences anxiety he is unable to master or is hurt physically, he will acquire fears that are extremely difficult to dispel. The following situation is presented to illustrate the way in which thoughtless guidance evokes emotional responses which negatively condition a child to an experience which he needs to master instead of fear.

Peter, aged 6, experienced pain for which he was unprepared. His reaction to it brought a physical and psychological response which clearly demonstrated the way mind and body function together as a unit.

Peter came to the clinic for a camp examination and was accompanied there by his 7-year-old brother and his mother. Peter was acutely anxious as he waited for a blood count. His face was contorted with furrows in his brow and around his mouth. He was trying not to cry even though he was panicky at the thought of going into the next room to have his finger pricked.

Peter's mother was also anxious. She talked incessantly, and tried to goad Peter into being a big boy. She told him that it would not hurt and there was nothing of which he need be afraid. Peter was not listening; he was too scared. Besides he knew better for he had heard screams coming from the next room. Peter ran to the door and peered into the room where another child was having a blood count. He would peek and run away again. He did this over and over again. It seemed as if he were trying to prepare himself to go in there when his turn came.

The nurse said, "Peter, it's scary being in the clinic for a blood count. All children are scared. I wonder if you would like to know exactly what the lady is going to do to you?" "Am I next? Will it hurt?" Peter said, in tones which disclosed the height of his anxiety. "Yes, it will hurt, Peter. Come, I will tell you all about it and I will help you when it is time to go in," the nurse assured him.

By the time Peter was ready to listen, there was a boy in the chair whose mother had prepared him well for the experience. He had mastered his fear and was able to show interest in what the technician was doing. "Let's watch, Peter. I'll tell you about everything the lady is doing," the nurse suggested. During the preparation Peter began to evidence signs of increased composure.

When Peter's turn came to get into the chair, he was in equilibrium and handled himself amazingly well. Peter could not yell "ouch" when the needle was thrust into his finger although he was given permission to do so. When he did not yell it, the nurse did it for him, and his first response to completion of the needle insertion was to laugh and say, "She said 'ouch' for me." His older brother was there watching, and while the children were exchanging words concerning the experience, the technician quickly thrust the needle into Peter's finger again without his awareness of what she was going to do. For this extra needle insertion Peter was totally unprepared. He could not yell or say, "You old meany! Why didn't you forewarn me of what was to come? I think you are the meanest creature I have ever encountered." Instead of fighting, Peter withdrew just as he had done from the doorway as he was trying to get ready to meet a painful situation.

Peter's response to a painful, physical and psychological experience affected his entire body. Instantly his face grew white, perspiration appeared on his brow and in a faint voice he said, "My stomach is wiggling. I am dizzy." Then he looked blank, and for a minute the nurse thought he was going to have a convulsive seizure. Then his body grew limp and he was unable to utter a sound. His head was lowered and in a few instants he pulled himself into a sitting position and got to his feet. He staggered and followed his mother to get a drink, but he continued to be speechless.

Peter had had an experience which might easily have been prevented. In the future when Peter must have other blood counts, feelings concerning the original situation will become reactivated and influence his adjustment to it. Unless the next technician Peter meets understands that behavior is not only a response to what is happening in the present but is related to all that has gone before, she will probably have thoughts something like the following: "What is wrong with this child? He certainly does not act his age. I wonder why his mother never taught him to be brave."

Hospital experiences during the first three years of a child's life can also negatively condition a child to hospitals and their personnel. If a child must experience hospitalization without his mother during the earliest years of his life, feelings pertaining to the experience will become reactivated each time he enters a hospital.

The Child Acquires Fears from Experiences Which Are a Part of Growth. In the process of growth the child has destructive feelings and wishes that bring fear of punishment and desertion and create a need for repeated experiences which teach him that his thoughts cannot bring injury to him. The conflicts that develop as the child is torn between his own desires and his fear of loss of love have been discussed. Many times the child feels destructive and his wishes are like the acts themselves. The child from 3 to 6 years of age has not lived long enough to discover that his wishes and thoughts are not the same as deeds. Nor has he lived long enough to know that his parents will always love him even though he sometimes does forbidden things and they sometimes need to thwart and punish him. Until he learns this through repeated experiences which prove he is consistently loved and safe, he is fearful lest he be deserted or injured.

In this period increased mental functioning heightens the child's capacity for fantasy and influences his feelings and responses. He hears and sees things he cannot understand. They make him anxious, and his fantasies pertaining to situations are often most unrealistic. However, his fantasies are real to him and often they make him fearful in situations which are in reality safe and painless.

The above are some of the reasons why preschool children are fearful when their mothers are out of sight and why they react emotionally to the slightest injury which befalls them. Even minor injuries like a cut finger bring concern to the young child. His body is precious to him, and injuries and illness are a source of great anxiety.

Unconsciously many older children and adults continue to fear bodily injury and to express it in their behavior. Something in their early life experiences prevented them from mastering their fears. When these children or adults are confronted with illness or surgery, their behavior seems unreasonable and inappropriate to the situation they are experiencing. But it is not unreasonable—it is very real to them. To us it may seem as though there was nothing to be afraid of, but in the person there is uncertainty or he would respond with composure rather than with withdrawal or tempestuous behavior. The mother knows, for instance, that there is nothing within the nursery school environment which is dangerous but many times the child does not. Likewise the nurse knows that an x-ray examination is painless, but many children have not had sufficient experience to convince themselves that it is a safe procedure. Bob's nurse knew that the needle and the amount of penicillin she had prepared was the same as that she had used previously, but Bob, however, was not convinced that it was.

Bob was 8 years old and had had surgery to repair undescended testicles. Each day he groaned and his eyes flashed as he looked at the hypodermic needle and syringe and exclaimed in anguish, "It's bigger than it was yesterday." When the nurse who was unable to understand his anxiety said, "No, it isn't," Bob said, "But it *is*. I can see that it is. It is getting bigger and bigger every day."

The child's behavior is a clue to his feelings and his fantasies and cannot be ignored for it has purpose and requires understanding. The young child has insufficient language to communicate his feelings to us in words but he shows us his feelings in his behavior. When a child responds in a way which seems inappropriate to the situation, the child needs a nurse who searches for answers to the following questions in an attempt to understand and to relieve his anxiety: "Why is this child responding as he is? What could make him feel this way? What does he imagine is going to happen to him here? Does he imagine something unreal and impossible? If he does, how can I correct his misconception, support and help him feel less afraid? What is this child's background of experience with his parents? What can I learn from them that will give me increased understanding of him in this new situation?"

Indiscriminate reassurance is rarely effective, for unless the nature of the fear is known reassurance rarely touches the real anxiety and relieves a person's fears. Some older preschool children and most school-age children can tell us what they are afraid of and they will if they feel we are really interested in understanding them. The frightened child needs to get his fear into the open and to talk about it. If his fear is irrational, and in most instances it is, the doctor and the nurse can correct it and bring him comfort.

The frightened child needs a great deal of support. He needs a nurse who is able to accept unreasonable behavior and to remain understanding even though he is demanding, clinging, fractious and unappreciative of all she is doing for him. He needs patient support and experiences which prove the irrationality of his fear. The following example illustrates the application of this principle.

Marjorie was 5 years old when she went into the hospital with leukemia. She was acutely ill, miserable, uncomfortable and afraid of everything that was done to her. Her mother knew the child's prognosis and was unable to control expressions of anxiety when she was with her child. One morning an x-ray examination was ordered. When Marjorie was prepared for it she screamed, "I don't want to go, I am scared."

Marjorie could not tell her nurse what she was afraid of but it was obvious she was panicky, for her emotional reaction to preparation was grossly exaggerated. "All children are scared when they go to a new place for an examination. I am going with you and I will tell you about everything as we go," her nurse said, to reassure her of her support. En route to the x-ray department, the nurse stopped at each door to let Marjorie look inside. After she had peered through six doorways, her anxiety began to subside and she whimpered, "Stay with me. I'm scared."

Before she was taken into the elevator, the nurse told her about the lights she could watch which would indicate that she was moving upward to the floor where the roentgenogram would be taken. Her bed was pushed into the x-ray room. Before she had to be removed from her bed, she had an opportunity to watch another patient experiencing what she had been prepared for. She looked at the patient, then quickly turned her head back to the nurse. Over and over again she repeated this. She wanted to look but at the same time she was fearful and needed to withdraw. It also seemed as though she needed to reassure herself that her nurse was continuing to remain at her bedside.

When Marjorie's turn came to sit on a stool against the x-ray machine, she was able to co-operate even though signs of anxiety continued to be evident. She had heard the noise of the x-ray machine, had seen it move toward the patient's body and had witnessed her safety throughout the procedure. As a result of this experience she did not need to be forced into a fearful experience; she was able to help herself.

On her return trip to the ward, the nurse again stopped at each doorway. Many hospital personnel in the rooms smiled at her. Some exchanged words with her, and the trip gave her not only reassurance but pleasure as well. At the end of the trip her anxiety had lessened and with words she showed a need to repeat the experience to gain further mastery of her fears. She said, "Let's go again."

Signs of disturbing anxiety which cannot be relieved with the above kind of supportive nursing should be reported to the doctor. There will be some doctors who will ignore symptoms of anxiety. However, others will want the information the nurse has observed as she has given his patient nursing care. They will recognize the patient's need, appraise the seriousness of the symptoms and determine the kind of treatment the patient requires. Sometimes the doctor will discover he can alleviate the patient's anxiety. In other instances he may seek the assistance of the social worker or a doctor who is trained in the theory and technics of psychiatric treatment.

Influence of the Meaning Which the New Experience Has for the Child on the Kind of Adjustment He Will Make to It

The way the child interprets the new experience will be one of the most potent factors which influence his adjustment to it. Unless he knows why he has been placed in a nursery school or hospital, he may interpret it as abandonment or punishment. Jessner and Kaplan[17] say it may also mean the possibility of bodily injury and danger from an external power, and in some instances, where deep insecurity exists in a child, it may represent potential disaster for him. The meaning a new experience has for a child will depend upon his past experiences in his home and therefore will vary in different children.

If a young child has not been prepared for a new experience or if he has been unable to utilize the preparation constructively, either because he was too young or because his past experiences were such that he could not anticipate fulfillment from others, his thoughts, wishes and feelings may well be like the following: "Why did my mother leave me here? Doesn't she know I am scared when she is not with me? What is going to happen to me? Who is going to take care of me? I cannot take care of myself—doesn't she know that? Who will tell me what I can do and what I can't do? Doesn't my mother know I need her to know how to behave? Will my mother ever come back, or has she left me here because she doesn't want me any more? What have I done to deserve this? It must be because I was bad. Mother told me not to be naughty but sometimes I couldn't help doing those things she told me not to do. I hate her because she did this to me. I hate her so much I'd like to chew her up or smear paint all over her. But if I did that I would not have her any more and I need her. I love her, too, and want her here to comfort, guide and protect me. I am all mixed up. I am angry, miserable and scared, but I love my mother and want to go home. What shall I do?"

Current situations in the home and the problems of conflict that the child is coping with at the time of separation will also influence his thoughts and his feelings and determine the meaning which the new experience will have for him. If there is a new sibling in his home, the child may wonder if his mother sent him away because she loves the baby more and wants more time to spend with him. The little girl may feel she is being abandoned by her mother because she suspects her of having hostile wishes and a desire to have her daddy all to herself.

Thoughts, feelings and wishes like the above bring agony, grief, despair and panic which manifest themselves in nonconstructive and oftentimes destructive behavior of one kind or another. If his mother does not come to see him for a week after admission, and he experiences painful treatments without preparation and support, the child has no opportunity to get relief from his fears and anger. Instead, they are reinforced and deepened.

The way the child will respond to his feelings will depend upon the way he has responded to former stressful situations. He may scream and fight or withdraw and develop symptoms of depression like Mike. Or he may resort to rocking his body, masturbation or thumbsucking to relieve himself of anxiety and to bring himself comfort. Fighting is a healthier response and potentially less dangerous for him personally unless hospital personnel scold or withdraw from him and leave him unsupported. Any of the foregoing behavior is symptomatic of deep emotional distress and indicates that the child is unable to master the situation he is in.

It is not unusual to find children in hospital wards who believe that they are there because they have done something that makes them deserving of punishment. When a child does something he has been warned against doing and he becomes sick or injured, anxiety and feelings of guilt are inevitable.

A case which illustrates the above point is that of Sammy, who had been burned in a bonfire that he had set. He needed to atone for his "sins," and was seeing his hospital experience as punishment. He needed to have his fear and guilt relieved. After all, all boys do things they are told not to do and because he did, it did

not mean that he was wicked, needful of punishment and undeserving of love and care. Children have to disobey and defy their
parents sometimes. If they did not, many children would never learn,
nor would some children ever emancipate themselves from their parents. It is tragic that some children have to play with hazardous
objects and substances and do daring things to prove they can master
themselves and that they are powerful. Those who do need our
understanding. They should not be punished for something others
have made necessary.

Sammy, aged 12 years, felt he was deserving of punishment when
he came to the city for skin grafts. He had already spent a month in
his home-town hospital; but when his burned legs did not heal, his
family physician recommended that he be moved into a city hospital.
On admission to the hospital Sam was withdrawn, apathetic and
regressed. The least change in care made him apprehensive. He acted
as though he expected the worst to happen every minute of the day.
After a nurse had become acquainted with Sammy she discovered
he felt responsible for his burns. He said, "My mother told me never
to play with matches because she didn't like it. She said if I did this
would happen to me." Sam not only felt guilty because he disobeyed,
he also felt guilty because his hospitalization was costing his parents so
much money.
It was a long time before Sammy began to recuperate. Each trip
to surgery was a nightmare for him. When he awakened, the first
thing he would say would be, "What did they do to me now?" Gradually
he became more comfortable with his nurse and he began to tell her of
his activities at home. He was a Boy Scout, and it was obvious from his
conversation that he delighted in the Scouts' outdoor activities. He loved
to hike, fish and play baseball.
One day as he was talking his face changed. He looked sad and
anxious. Then as if he could hold it in no longer, he said, "I know I
will never be able to do those things again." During the preceding
weeks Sammy had suppressed the fears within him. Now when he was
reassured by both his doctor and his nurse that his fears were unfounded
in reality, he began to improve and participate in the ward activities.
Weeks later when Sammy was ready to go home his facial expression
and behavior were totally different from what they had been in the
early period of his hospitalization. The day he left the hospital the nurse
said, "Sammy, you look wonderful. You are happy; I can see you are.
I would hardly know you were the same boy I knew two months ago."
Sammy smiled. It was a smile which came from his heart, not just from
his face. He said, "I didn't think I was ever going to walk again,
did I? *Gosh,* was I scared! But you were right, I *can* walk. Just look
and I'll show you what I can do."

Nurses who have imaginative insight into possible meanings
which a situation might have for a child will observe and listen in
an attempt to discover the specific meaning which it has for a particular child. When nurses have intuitive insight they can see and

feel with the child and through this understanding they will be more sensitive to his total needs. If nurses cannot appreciate what separation, illness, surgery and uncertainty mean to children, they cannot possibly help them to become secure and comfortable in a new and threatening situation.

Security frees energy for healing! Can one doubt that relieving fear is an important part of a healing art? Would Sammy have had energy for healing two seriously burned legs and for mastering his hospital experience if he had kept his fears inside him? Should we have been contented to heal Sam's body at the expense of his mental health? What if Sam had spent the rest of his life feeling guilty? Would it have limited his opportunities for growth? If so, how? How would it have affected his adjustment in adolescence?

INFLUENCE OF THE CHILD'S CHRONOLOGIC AGE, HIS PAST EXPERIENCES AND HIS EGO STRENGTH ON HIS ADJUSTMENT IN A NEW SITUATION

Age is an important factor in the child's adjustment. The affects of maternal deprivation on the infant and the young child and their requirements in situations which necessitate separation have been cited in Chapter 1. The school-age child has a background of experience which helps him appraise situations more realistically. He can anticipate the time his mother will arrive and understand verbal explanations, and has within himself a degree of self-mastery which the younger child has not yet acquired. In children between 5 and 8 years of age, Bowlby's[1] study of clinical research indicated that a warm, secure, mother-child relationship eased the child's adjustment in new situations. He says:

> Contrary to what obtains in the younger age-groups, for children of this age the better their relation to their mothers the better can they tolerate separation. A happy child, secure in his mother's love, is not pathologically anxious; the insecure child, apprehensive of his mother's good feelings towards him, may easily misinterpret events.

To make a good adjustment to a hospital experience the child needs to have sufficient ego strength and emotional freedom to transfer his positive feelings from his mother to his nurse or doctor, to relate himself to other children, to find satisfaction in play activities and to express his feelings overtly.[17] These strengths are equally essential for good adjustment in a nursery school.

Mike, whose behavior was cited previously, came into the hospital unsure of his mother's good feelings toward him. As a result he did not have sufficient emotional freedom to transfer his positive feelings from his mother to his nurse; he was constantly worried about his relationship with her. In addition he misinterpreted every event he experienced. Explanations did not relieve his anxiety—he viewed each experience as a potential punishment. He could not verbalize his fears. As a result reassurance and support did him little good.

Children of school age and over who have not had experiences which have helped them develop the ego strength necessary to master difficult situations need help, not condemnation. They are incapable of mastering the situation not because they are "spoiled" in the way the lay person interprets spoiling but because they have not been given sufficient help to develop a greater degree of independence, trust and confidence in themselves and others. Deprivation comes from both too little care and guidance and too much of an unwholesome quality. Deprivation, inconsistency and prolonged unrestricted freedom keep a child dependent, demanding, unsure of his own abilities and unable to tolerate the degree of frustration the maturely loved and guided child learns to withstand.

If separation is necessary because of illness, the severity of the disease will be another determining factor in the kind of adjustment a child is able to make. Physical health is a great asset to the ego. If the child's illness is severe, his energy will go into combating the disease, and he will have little surplus energy available for adaptation to new people and a strange environment. If, in addition to illness, the child's ego must cope with excessive anxiety, severe regression or disorganization will be inevitable and the imprint of the experience will remain with him forever.

Preparation for a new experience supports the child's ego. If he is old enough to be prepared and is assured that separation is for legitimate reasons and not because he has been "naughty" or is unwanted, he will have less anxiety and more energy available for mastering his situation and combating disease.

When separation must of necessity be abrupt, the child needs his mother with him until he can be prepared adequately for the experience and her leave taking and until he has discovered through experience that there is someone who will take care of him in her absence. Emergencies are rare in comparison with the times when separation is anticipated. Even when there is an emergency illness, children need to be told where they are going and why going is a necessity.

If emergency surgery is necessary it is understandable why the child responds tempestuously when he awakens from anesthesia. He is confronted with a situation for which he is totally unprepared. He has had no time to become acquainted with ward personnel or the activities which are a part of any hospital experience. In many instances he does not see the ward until he awakens from anesthesia. Could anything be much more fear-provoking for a child than awakening from surgery and finding he is alone in a ward among a group of unfamiliar people? Is there any wonder he screams in terror, pulls out the intravenous needles and fights everyone who comes within his reach? If he does not fight and withdraws instead, it is an ominous sign that portrays his feelings about the world he is in.

Perhaps some day in the future, hospital personnel will see the the child's need for his mother at the time he is being anesthetized and when he awakens and is becoming familiar with his new environment. Some mothers could not tolerate this experience; others could be quickly prepared to function in a supportive way. If they were gowned and capped, the danger of operating room contamination would be no more than it is from clerks, technicians, orderlies and maids, who frequent the operating room in laboratory coats and aprons and whose presence is never questioned. Perhaps some day, too, hospital personnel will see the child's need to have his mother with him when he awakens from the anesthesia and during the period he is adjusting to new people and surroundings.

Meeting the above needs would not be catering to a child; it would be meeting his need for emotional security. In such situations the presence of the mother is as important to his health as drugs, surgery or intravenous therapy. To neglect his need for his mother is as hazardous as neglecting his need for surgical intervention when there is acute abdominal pathology. It is true that it will not bring death but it may injure the mother-child relationship on which the child's emotional health depends. It will require more initial nursing hours because mothers will need help in handling their feelings, but might not hours be saved because the child will be able to regain his physical health and emotional equilibrium more rapidly? In the process might we not also prevent emotional suffering and bring comfort to those who are in need of our help?

INFLUENCE OF THE CHILD'S AND THE MOTHER'S PREPARATION FOR THE NEW EXPERIENCE ON HIS ADJUSTMENT IN A NEW SITUATION

Preparation for a New School Experience. *When entrance into school is anticipated, the child needs verbal preparation and physical and psychological readiness to master the situation.* There are many things a child needs to know before he goes off to nursery school. First he needs to know why he is going to be separated from his mother and placed in a new situation. He must realize that it is because his parents feel he is ready to learn to do things which they know he will enjoy. If the child feels he is being sent to school, he will resent it and wonder why his mother feels it is necessary to send him away.[3] He needs to know who will take care of him there and to be helped to know he can go to his teacher whenever he needs her.

In the better nursery schools, parents are requested to bring their children to school before they are admitted as students because the faculty believe that anxiety is allayed when children see that school is a pleasant and a safe place for them to be. This gives the children an opportunity to become acquainted with the physical environment of the school, to observe the children enjoying the experience and to meet the teachers who will satisfy their needs during the period they are separated from their mothers.

Until the child becomes comfortable in the nursery school and develops the capacity to go to the teacher for protection and help, the mother is encouraged to stay in the nursery school to give the child the security he needs to make a healthy and comfortable transition from home to school. The length of time the mother stays with her child is dependent upon the child's ability to transfer his positive feelings to the teacher. Gradually, through experiences which help him feel safe and happy in school, he acquires the ability to remain for the entire school period without his mother being with him.

Adapting to kindergarten or first grade is a more difficult task, requiring increased emotional preparedness to make a healthy adjustment to it. The kindergarten and first grade environments are less flexible than is the nursery school situation. Mothers are not usually permitted to remain with their children and a greater degree of control is needed to master a situation where there are fewer teachers, a larger number of children and more rigid requirements to meet. *To ensure good adjustment in primary school, the child needs to be secure in his parents' love and to have learned to adapt himself to separation from home and parent. He also needs to be independent in toileting, dressing and undressing, to be able to tolerate reasonable frustration, to take care of his possessions, to share his teacher's love and to play co-operatively with other children.* When a child has accomplished these tasks, one can say he is *emotionally* ready for a school experience.

Because it takes courage for the child to go off to school, he needs a mother who is proud of his ability to go and able to control her feelings of loss or sadness. Many mothers have ambivalent feelings when the time arrives for their children to start school. They feel lost when they think that "their babies" are old enough to begin their careers at school. At the same time they are proud and hopeful that their children will achieve well in school. It is better that children do not know their mothers' feelings of loss or sadness for they tend to burden them and make them feel that their mothers would rather they stay at home with them.

In going to school the child will experience new pleasure but he will also be deprived of some of the satsfactions he enjoyed previously. When the time comes for him to go to school, he will have less time to play and to be with his mother and in most instances he will have less freedom to choose what he wants to do.

The child starting school needs to know what is expected of him at school. He needs to know that there will be story periods when the children must sit still and listen as quietly as possible.[13] He needs to know that the teacher will be like a mother and request that he do certain things at certain times.[13] He needs to know that his teacher will expect him to take care of his possessions and his own toilet needs.

All children need to go to school fully prepared to go and to return home independently and safely and for what they are expected to do when school is over. It is the parents' responsibility to teach the child safety precautions in crossing streets, and the safety precautions necessary to protect himself from emotionally sick individuals who molest little children. If the mother wishes her child to come home after school to tell her where he is going to play, the child should know her expectations.

The child also needs *physical* readiness for his new school experience. The child who is in optimal health will be able to make a better adjustment and have more resistance to the organisms he will be exposed to in a crowded school situation.

The nurse can contribute to preventive health programs in our society. Preparation for adjustment away from home begins at birth. The nurse is helping parents get their children ready to adjust outside the home whenever she gives them help in understanding their children's physical and psychological requirements. The more completely his early needs are gratified, the more able is the child to develop the kind of ego strength that makes it possible for him to bear pain and the frustration, conflicts and anxiety inherent in every new and trying life experience he will have to meet.

If the nurse knows the criteria for appraising emotional and physical readiness for school, she will find many opportunities to help mothers gain insight into their children's needs for preparation and support in meeting it. She can motivate them to see a need to continue having medical supervision for their children during preschool years. She can also observe children to detect physical and emotional deviations from normality which indicate a need for medical or psychological treatment. She can help parents know how to keep their children healthy with adequate nutrition, immunizations and a home regimen that promotes optimal physical and mental health.

Preparation for a Hospital Experience. There are further factors than those already cited which need to be considered when a child is being prepared for hospitalization, a clinic visit or a trip to the pediatrician's or the dentist's office. Preparing a child for these experiences is a much more difficult task than preparing him for school because physical pain may be an inevitable part of the experience. If hospitalization is required, preparation for longer periods of separation is a necessity from the child's standpoint. Ideally, the child should receive preparation from his parents, for in them he has his greatest trust. However, many parents will need a great deal of help in learning how to prepare their children for hospitalization, and for surgery if that is going to be a part of the experience.

There will be many parents who will need help in seeing their children's need for preparation. Some parents deceive their children. They say they believe children should be protected from anxiety. They have little insight into what hospitalization might mean to their children and cannot conceive of the agony they will experience if they are deceived or unprepared for what they are to meet. Some parents want to save themselves the difficulty of enlightening their children and meeting the responses they anticipate when their children learn what is going to happen to them. Some are afraid lest an explanation will arouse their children's anger; others harbor guilt feelings concerning their children or their illness and are therefore unable to prepare them adequately.

There will be frightened and grief-stricken mothers who will need help before they are able to help their children. Some mothers are so frightened of hospitals, their personnel and their procedures that they are unable to use their mental faculties to think through their children's requirements. Some are grief-stricken. They see their child's illness or deformity as injury and frustration to themselves. These feelings blind them to the needs of their children. If they are immature in their way of responding to their child's illness or deformity it is not because they are ignorant, neglectful or unfeeling—it is because they have met deprivation themselves and are therefore unable to respond with mature feelings, insight and understanding.

The mother's feelings about the child's illness or deformity and need for hospitalization will also influence the way he will approach and adapt himself to it. The child interprets his illness or surgery and hospitalization in the light of his past experiences; he also interprets them in the light of his current situation. If his mother is anxious and fearful of all that is going to happen, the child will feel that he is about to meet an ominous situation. If his mother feels it is a tragedy and something to be dreaded, her child will feel likewise. His mother's anxiety will color his fantasies, which in all probability will be infinitely more gruesome than what the child will have to meet in reality.

When hospitalization or a trip to the clinic or the dentist is necessary, many parents need someone with whom they can talk. The clinic and the office nurse can be of real service if she gives parents an opportunity to express their fears and feelings and to question ways of helping their children to become prepared for the experience. Many times it is the public health nurse who is in a key position to help parents prepare themselves to do this important preventive work.

The mother needs relief from fear before she can help her child. If the nurse can gain the mother's confidence through sympathetic listening and through giving her understanding of what hospital and clinic procedures entail, she will feel less anxious, more able to see her child's need for dental or medical care and more ready to give her child security and strength when he must meet the forthcoming event.

Both mother and child need a nurse who is sensitive to their need to be separated from each other when impending hospitalization is being discussed by the doctor or a second nurse. The mother needs an opportunity to express her feelings and questions without the restriction that comes when the child remains in the examining room. If the nurse has been able to help the child feel she is a friendly person, she will be able to take him from the conference room and interest him in some play activity. It will protect the child from hearing his case discussed and from the impact of the emotional experience upon his mother. It will also give the child an opportunity to discover that nurses are kind, understanding people. Although the experience with her will probably be a short one, it may influence his feelings toward other nurses when the time for admission arrives.

Entailed in his preparation for hospitalization the child needs a simple, truthful explanation of his sickness or abnormality and the reasons why hospitalization is necessary. When his illness or abnormality is explained in a way that he can understand, he is helped to accept it in a realistic way. He will not feel that he is being punished and sent off to the hospital because he is unloved. If the child has a congenital defect, for instance, and its cause is shrouded in mystery because his parents feel guilty or ashamed of the deformity, the child will have difficulty in accepting himself as he is. He will also have difficulty in accepting his need for surgery. The child with a deformity needs explanations as he discovers he is different from others. He needs them from his parents before his differences stimulate the curiosity and the whispering of his playmates.

Hypospadias is an example of a deformity about which an afflicted boy needs realistic knowledge. Hypospadias is the medical term used to describe a defect which interferes with the passage of urine from the bladder through the urethra, which normally extends to the tip of the penis. In hypospadias the urethra opens beneath the penis, and surgery is necessary to correct the anomaly.

When a child with hypospadias develops curiosity concerning the origin and the growth of babies, he can *begin* to learn something of the intricate process that takes place when the ovum and the sperm fuse and begin the formation of a new individual. Later when further questions come, the facts that follow can be given gradually until the child has gained understanding of his body and his need for surgery: "When you were growing in mother's body, one of the parts of your body did not grow together. The urethra is the passageway which brings urine from inside your body to the outside. When you were growing in my body, this passageway did not grow together. That is why your urine comes from an opening beneath your penis. Usually it comes from an opening at the tip of the penis. But it can be fixed, and when it is you will urinate just as other boys do. You will need to go to the hospital to have it fixed. There the doctor will first make your penis straight. Then he will close the opening beneath your penis. When he does that he will put a rubber tube into your bladder. He will put the tube through your tummy wall. The doctor does this so your urine will not run over the part he has fixed. Instead, your urine will run through the tube into a bottle that will hang beneath your hospital bed. Then later the doctor will make the passageway longer. When your body is all healed, the doctor will remove the tube and close the opening. Then your urine will come from your bladder through the passageway which will end at the tip of your penis."

Previous to the time the child enters the hospital the child needs to know when his parents will visit him. If the child is sure of his parents' love and the trustworthiness of their words, he will believe them when they tell him that they will come and visit him each day or on Tuesday and Sundays if those are the hospital's visiting days. However, when he gets into the hospital, he will need reassurance again when his parents leave him. In all instances it is important that the child be told the truth. Otherwise he will lose trust and become so concerned he will have little energy with which to adjust.

Because the preschool child's perception of time is limited, the time of his parents' arrival will need to be interpreted in relation to hospital activities. If visiting hours are from 2 to 3 P.M. each afternoon, the mother can say, "Every day after dinner, children in the hospital take naps. When they wake up it is time for mothers and daddies to come." That his mother will come and take him home as soon as he is well, or as soon as the tests are completed if that is why hospitalization is necessary, is reassurance that probably will need to be repeated several times in the interim before he is hospitalized.

The child also needs information pertaining to the experiences he will meet at the time of admission to a clinic or a hospital. If it is a public health nurse who is assisting the mother, she needs to know the admission procedures used in the hospital where the child is going. The mother will need to have the admission procedures explained in a way which gives her security in knowing what is going to happen. If she is secure in knowing this she will be more able to prepare her child. The nurse can also tell the mother that she knows the admission experience will be difficult for both the child and herself. If the mother knows that nurses do not expect complete compliance at the time of admission, she will feel easier and less threatened when she meets it.

How much more secure the child would feel and how much more ready to master hospitalization he would be if hospital policy permitted his mother to convey the following feelings to her child: "Billy, I will be there with you when the nurse is weighing you and taking your temperature. The nurse will let me help her get you ready to go to the room where your bed will be. She will give you a special gown to put on. Then she will take you to your bed in a wheelchair or a stretcher, as the case may be. I will go with you and stay until you are comfortable and until you get acquainted with the nurse, who will see that you are taken care of when I cannot be there. The nurse will tell you where you may keep your toys and what the children do in the hospital when they need to eat, go to the toilet or play. She will introduce you to the other

children and see that you have things to play with while you are
getting well. You be thinking about what toys you would like to
take with you. Together we will pack your suitcase when it is
time to go."

*The child needs preparation for the painful parts of the hospital
experience as well as the less painful ones.* "Billy, they will take
some blood from your arm. It will hurt a little but the nurse will
help you hold your arm still," will assist the child in preparing himself for the experience and will help him know that there will be
someone to help him meet it.

If the child is going to have surgery performed in the hospital
he will need detailed preparation for it. Preparation is a preventive
measure. In the following statement Vander Veer[31] expresses the
possible effects of surgery on children: "The frequency of fears
of death after general anaesthesia, and of acute anxiety states after
tonsillectomy, testifies to the potential catastrophic effect on children of even minor operative procedures."

Vander Veer[31] further emphasizes the child's need for preparation when he says, "Each child should go to the operating room
with full knowledge of everything he will consciously experience
before and after operation." Experience has demonstrated that children profit from a trip to the operating room prior to the time
surgery is going to be performed. On this trip they have an opportunity to familiarize themselves with what they have heard called
the operating room. They see the garb of the operating room personnel and the room where the anesthesia will be given. If a trip
of this nature cannot be arranged, the child will need to know how
he will be taken from his room to the operating room and what he
will see upon arrival there.

The child who is going to face surgery will need to know that
he may have a hypodermic of medicine before he leaves the ward
and be given something to smell which will put him to sleep so that
he does not feel any pain during the operation. Something like the
following will prepare the child for the experience: "Billy, the medicine the doctor uses to put you to sleep will not smell very good
and you won't like it. He puts you to sleep so you will not feel
any pain. He will put a dampened piece of cloth over your eyes
and a little cap over your nose. The nurses will hold your hands or
tie them down to the table. They do that to help you lie real still.
After the doctor has put the little cap over your nose, he will drop
medicine on it and tell you to breathe deeply like this. When you
breathe like I showed you, you will soon go to sleep. When you

awaken you will be in your own hospital bed. I will be beside you when you return to your own room."

The child also needs to know what is going to be done in the operating room, what he will experience postoperatively and why the operation and treatments are necessary. Unless the child will be able to see that a part of his body has been removed, it is better if the words "removed" or "take out" are not used. This is because children are fearful of losing a part of their body. This is as true of girls as it is of boys—sometimes little girls think they have already lost a part of their body. If they do they will be very frightened if they are not prepared adequately for surgery. If the operation entails abdominal surgery, and the removal of an organ is a necessity, an explanation something like the following will help to allay fear and also will prepare the child for what he will feel and see after the operation has been completed: "The doctor will fix the part of you that is making you feel sick. That part is called the appendix. You will be asleep and you will not feel it. When you wake up, your tummy will hurt. You will have a big bandage over your tummy. On your tummy there will be stitches or clips. After a few days the doctor will take the stitches or clips out. That will hurt a little but the nurse will be there to help you. When the stitches are out, you will be almost ready to come home." If the child will need to be restrained for any reason following surgery, or if intravenous therapy may be deemed necessary, this, too, should be anticipated for him. The reason for restraint or special therapy should also be stated so that he can understand the purpose of the procedure and master it.

Because a tonsillectomy is so universally spoken of as "Having your tonsils taken out," the following explanation will prepare the child who is about to face this operative procedure and lessen his fear concerning the loss of a part of his body: "Tim, your tonsils are making you have sore throats. The doctor is going to take them out. You do not need them. He is just going to take your tonsils. He would not take anything you need. When you wake up your throat will be sore. At first it will hurt to drink water but if you keep trying a little at a time, it will become easier. Sometimes you may vomit and spit up some blood. That almost always happens but it will not last long."

When an adult is faced with the necessity of meeting an unknown situation and he feels uncertain of what it holds for him, he experiences anxiety. One need only look within oneself to discover what he does when he knows he is to be confronted with an experience of which he is unsure. When a student nurse knows she is going to a new ward or to the operating or the birthrooms for experience, she has fantasies about it. She wonders what it will be like. She visualizes herself in the situation and oftentimes questions her ability to meet its requirements. In addition she questions, and oftentimes her inquiries are like the following: "What kind of person is the head nurse? How does one get along with her? Is Dr. —————— easy to work with and what does he expect of the nurses in his ward? What do you do in the birth- or operating rooms? Would you take me there so I can see what it is like?"

Thinking and questioning help to prepare the individual for what he is to meet. Many times the individual is wondering if he or she will be accepted as a person. He wants to be successful in his relationships with the personnel and the patients. Through fantasy and obtaining information concerning the reality of the situation, the individual prepares himself to make as comfortable an adjustment as it is possible for him to make.

If the above kind of preparation for a new experience is necessary for the adult who has lived for years and adapted to many previous situations, is it not equally necessary for the child entering a hospital? In reality is it not more necessary for him? He has but little background of experience to draw upon. He has not the ego strength of the adult. Yet in comparison with the nurse's situation cited above, the child has the more difficult situation to meet. The child needs hospital personnel who are capable of thinking, feeling and understanding. Only then will they see things which are important to human beings and plan ways to provide them.

Giving children an opportunity to become prepared for hospitalization is a change which could be effected in many children's hospitals. Nurses could be prepared to do what nursery school teachers are doing to prepare children for admission to school. How much less apprehension a child would have at the time of admission if he could be taken to the ward where he will be hospitalized prior to the time he must stay there as a patient! If he could be taken to the ward before he is admitted to meet the head nurse, to see the physical environment and to see that children are happy in a hospital, he would have an opportunity to mobilize his energies in preparation for the oncoming experience.

Observation has proved that it is less frightening to face a known danger than one which is unknown.[31] If this were not true why would we always seek to discover that which is involved in any new experience we think to be potentially threatening? On such a preparatory trip to the ward the child would undoubtedly see some children crying or observe other situations which would distress him. It might seem that that would increase his anxiety rather than lessen it. Temporarily it does increase his anxiety but it gives him an opportunity to prepare himself to master a greater amount when he becomes a patient in the ward.

If a child is taken to the pediatric ward prior to his admission there, a reaction to the experience is inevitable, healthy and desirable for his welfare. In the ward he may question many of the things he sees there. The experience might even bring fears or a temper outburst. Some children may withdraw and temporarily refuse to go on the trip; others may cry and reject the nurse's offer of friendliness. None of these emotional reactions would be surprising or unnatural. Nor would any of these responses to a new experience be detrimental to him personally. Instead, he would be benefited. If he expressed fear in words or in his behavior, he could be given reassurance which would be helpful to him. It helps children to know that other children are also afraid and that it is acceptable to feel that way. The kind of help suggested in the following sentences would give the child the feeling that he was understood: "All children are scared when they first see the hospital, Billy. Everything here is different. That's why children are scared. When they know about the hospital, they are not so scared. Maybe you could tell me what seems the most scary to you. That is what the children do when they come here. Then I will tell you all about this place. Then you will know exactly what will happen here."

A preparatory trip to the ward prior to admission would give the child time to assimilate the experience and to master his feelings in preparation for mastering the situation when the time comes for him to go to the hospital. After a preparatory visit to the ward the child undoubtedly would re-enact the experience in play in an attempt to master the feelings and the anxiety the trip precipitated. In play the child will accomplish what the adult achieves through preparatory thinking, questioning and planning.

Unless children are provided with information and experiences which give them an opportunity to become ready for admission and the experiences entailed in hospitalization, hospital personnel will continue to see confused, frightened and tempestuous children in admitting rooms and in hospital wards. And unless children are intelligently and understandingly prepared for hospitalization and guided through it, we will continue to see in our communities those who have been traumatized by experiences they were unprepared to master.

Conducting preparatory trips to the ward would take time, skill and additional personnel. However, would they not save time, protect children's mental health and give their parents an opportunity to become acquainted with the personnel in the ward? Would it really cost more to do this? Have we studied the time it takes to help frightened children at the time of admission to the hospital? Have we studied what it costs to treat children who have been traumatized in a hospital? A preparatory trip is not the only answer, however; of equal importance is the quality of care he and his parents receive throughout the period of hospitalization.

INFLUENCE OF THE QUALITY OF THE RELATIONSHIPS THE CHILD AND HIS PARENTS EXPERIENCE IN THE NEW SITUATION ON HIS ADJUSTMENT TO IT

What the child experiences in the new situation will affect his adjustment in school, his future relationships with his parents, his feelings about himself, schools, hospitals and their personnel. Verbal preparation and observing the nursery school prior to admission cannot completely prepare the child. He will need time to adapt himself to it because life is different there from what it is at home. If in the nursery school or kindergarten the child finds he does have someone to protect, understand and guide him, and discovers that there are opportunities for pleasurable activities, he will master and profit from the experience. He will need time to build up a sense of security with his teacher, the children and the physical environment, but he will accomplish the tasks if he is well prepared for the experience and meets warmth and understanding in his new environment.

In helping a child adjust to a new hospital experience, relationships are equally important. An experience in the hospital can serve to help a child physically and psychologically, or it can traumatize him in a way which can injure his emotional life. Positive relationship experiences help a child develop good attitudes toward himself, his illness, treatment, hospitals and their personnel; negative ones produce feelings which are destructive to his well-being. Relationship experiences in the hospital can jeopardize his relationships with his parents or they can serve to bring the family closer to full understanding of one another.

Of maximum importance is the *quality* of the interpersonal relationships both the child and his parents experience within the hospital. Involved in these relationships is the recognition of the child's total needs and sensitivity to the fact that his parents are not visitors but human beings and important persons to us, their child and the community in which they live.

It is not what hospital personnel do and say which is the most important; it is the way they *feel* about children, parents, co-workers and themselves that counts. It is the quality of their feelings which influences children's adjustments and determines the effect hospitalization will have on them personally.

As the nurse functions in a children's clinic, ward or convalescent home, she needs to think about her relationships with the children, their parents and her co-workers for it is her feelings as well as her knowledge which motivate what she does and how she does it, and they determine the quality of care she can provide for those within the hospital. As the nurse functions in the clinic or the ward she and her patients will profit from asking herself the following questions: "What kind of relationship have I with this specific child and his parents? What does the care of this child mean to me? Is he only gratifying my needs or am I seeing his needs and bringing satisfaction and comfort to him? How do I really feel about his parents? Am I enjoying my experience with the child's parents or am I finding them irritating, frustrating, threatening or a bore? Do I realize that many parents attack when they are anxious? Can I understand why they attack me and refrain from increasing their anxiety through an experience which communicates my acceptance of them as they are? Are my relationship experiences with the doctors, the nurses and the auxiliary workers affecting my capacity to give to the children? Am I getting enough satisfaction away from the hospital to be able to give while I am in the clinic or the ward? How do my own feelings prevent me from meeting the needs of the children and their parents?"

The child needs respect and an emotionally warm, comfortable and peaceful atmosphere in the hospital just as he needs it in his home. Children's wards need attractiveness, good equipment, a playroom and an ample supply of play materials. They also need personnel who understand their physical symptoms, are skilled in observing physical signs and symptoms and capable of providing them with skilled, scientific physical care, for these abilities are necessary to support the child physically so that he is able to surmount his current problem. However, of equal value to children and their parents is the emotional atmosphere which pervades the environment they are in. At home children need contented, well-adjusted parents who respect themselves and each other. They also need parents who respect them as persons who are in the process of growing and learning to live with themselves and others comfortably and harmoniously. Children in the hospital are dependent upon those who give them care. They sense the atmosphere of the ward and the attitudes the personnel have toward them and toward each other. They are sensitive to adult conflicts in the pediatric ward as they are sensitive to them in their homes.

The child in the hospital needs personnel who enjoy him and his parents and are able to establish and to maintain constructive relationships with others who work with them in restoring children to health. When a nurse enjoys a child and his parents and gets pleasure from seeing him get well and master his current situation, all individuals grow through their experiences together. When a nurse enjoys her relationships with doctors, social workers, auxiliary and nurse co-workers, she has more to contribute to the child for her energy is not being wasted in direct arguments, suppression of hostile feelings or searching for ways to relieve her own tension. Disgruntled, frustrated people cannot give children what they need during periods of illness or convalescence. Nor can they give the children's parents the consideration or understanding they require.

The child in the hospital ward needs personnel who are able to find gratification in their lives outside the hospital. One's personal life outside the hospital has a bearing upon the kind of relationships the individual establishes in the hospital clinic or the ward. If the personnel are not finding satisfaction in their social lives, they will have less to give to children and their parents and expect more from them than they are able or should be expected to give.

The child in the hospital needs a nurse who is aware of his need for a continuing relationship with his mother. It is understandable why the nurse working in a pediatric ward which has restricted visiting hours often forgets that the child belongs to a family and has a mother whom he needs to continue to love. When a nurse gives of herself to a child she cannot help but become involved in a meaningful relationship with him. It is an advantage for them both if the nurse remains objective and continues to see the importance of a continuing mother-child relationship. The nurse in the hospital is not her patient's mother. It is natural to wish she were, but if she plays this role she is apt to make demands upon the child, attempting to make of him what she desires in a child and to fail to see the child's mother as the important person she really is.

If the nurse thinks of the child as a part of a family and is aware that his hospital experience is but an episode in his life, she will achieve increased objectivity and prepare him to return to his family and to resume life there as before. She will keep the child in touch with his mother and his family and plan his care so the mother-child relationship is constructively maintained, for she will know these are two important objectives she needs to achieve. The following situation exemplifies the child's need to maintain his relationship with his mother and the difficulties he meets when those who care for him are unaware of its importance to him.

Jerry, aged 3 years, was in the hospital for diagnosis. He had congenital heart disease, and the possibility of surgery was being considered. Miss X. was assigned to give Jerry nursing care during the day hours.

One day she said with sadness in her face and voice, "I asked Jerry whose boy he was and he said, 'My Mommy's.'" The next day Miss X's. face and words were different. She was smiling and joyful and excitedly said to her supervisor, "Today Jerry is my boy. When I asked him whose boy he was, he said, 'Yours.'" Miss X. was elated with what she thought to be an accomplishment. However, what she was not aware of was the situation in which she had placed Jerry.

Of course Jerry was his mommy's boy. That is the way he needed to feel. But when he said, "I am my mommy's boy," he sensed his nurse's disappointment and perhaps even felt guilty and insecure because of it. [Why did he change and say, "Yours," when the question was repeated? What forced him to tell a lie and to deny his need for his mother? Was it because he sensed that his nurse could love him more if he said he was hers?]

Jerry's nurse gave the answer to the above questions. Jerry's perception was right—his nurse did love him more when he said, "I am your boy." It did not require guesswork to make this assumption for Jerry's nurse said she felt differently toward him when he reassured her of his affection for her. In addition to saying it, his nurse showed her change of feeling in her behavior.

The nurse can make a greater contribution to society and can gain more pleasure and feelings of success if she recognizes the child's need for a continuing relationship with his mother. If the nurse learns to do those things for children which mothers do for them, she will get the gratification which comes from the child's responsiveness and can feel valued and important in her role as a nurse. When a nurse helps a child to keep in touch with his mother and to discover that nurses are friendly giving persons who can relieve anxiety and help him master a painful experience, she has made a contribution not only to the child but also to society, and it is giving which is of inestimable value. It does not go unappreciated—it is never forgotten. The child cannot say, "Thank you for making life bearable while I could not have my mother," but he remembers and carries away from the hospital something that has become a part of him.

The child and his parents need positive relationship experiences from the time they enter the hospital door. So many times the child and his parents get everything but a consistent feeling relationship. The child gets the most scientific kind of physical care but is deprived of the personal interest which is the very heart of the nursing care of a child. The need for the case method of patient assignment has been cited in numerous instances before. It needs re-emphasis here, for without it the young child cannot master his hospital experience.

The child and his mother need a nurse who is interested in learning about him as a person. Wilkins[32] prepared a guide to use in obtaining data concerning the preschool child who is going to be a patient in the hospital. The child's mother can help nurses understand him. If the nurse knows something of his personality, she can establish a relationship with him much more quickly which will bring the child relief from discomfort and the nurse increased feelings of pride in her ability. His mother will be reassured when she sees that the staff is interested in those things that she has learned are important to her child. She will feel more secure and more comfortable when the time comes for her to part from her sick child. The guide Wilkins prepared follows.

Name of Hospital

Name_____Age____Date of Admission_____
Birthday_____
By what name does the child like to be called?_____
Are there other children in the family? Brothers: Ages_____
Sisters: Ages_____

Eating Habits:

How is the child usually fed? Bottle?_____Cup?_____Spoon?_____
Feed self independently?_____Feed self with help?_____
Food disliked?_____
Favorite foods?_____
What is his appetite like?_____

Elimination:

Is the child independent in toileting?_____To what degree?_____
What is the term used to refer to urination?_____
Bowel movement?_____
Is the child accustomed to a toilet chair?_____Bathroom?_____
What is the approximate time of daily bowel movement?_____
Is the child taken to the toilet at night?_____If so, at what time?_____

Sleeping Habits:

Does the child take a daily nap?_____What is his usual bedtime hour?

Does the child sleep alone?_____With whom?_____
Does the child sleep in a bed with sides?_____Adult bed?_____
Does the child have a prayer he says at bedtime?_____
Does the child have a special bedtime routine?_____If so, what is it?_____

Play Interests:

What type of play does the child like best?_____

Is the child accustomed to playing alone?_____With other children?_____

With adults?_____Does he have a favorite pet at home?_____

If so, state name and kind_____

Favorite type of toys?_____

Personal Habits:

Does the child brush his teeth?_____Comb his hair?_____

Bathe himself?_____Dress himself?_____

Miscellaneous:

Does the child know why he is being admitted to the hospital?_____

What information did you give him?_____

_____

_____

_____

How did he respond to it?_____

_____

_____

When was he told?_____

Has the child fears, such as fear of unfamiliar adults?_____

People in white uniforms?_____Needles?_____Surgery?_____

Other?_____

Do the parents live together?_____If not, divorced?_____

Deceased?_____At what age was the child when the parent died?_____

Have any new experiences occurred in the home recently such as birth

of a sibling?_____When?_____Other?_____

Has the child attended nursery school?_____Kindergarten?_____

Grade school?_____Sunday school?_____

Mother's Remarks:

[Record on the reverse side observations which describe the mother-child relationship, the child's response to admission, and the kind of adjustment he made in the ward.]

The child needs to be admitted to a nurse and not to a hospital room or ward. The child is not an independent being. Neither is the adult, but we often behave as if we expected a child to be. The child needs the assurance that there is someone who will take care of him and meet his basic needs when his mother is not able to be with him. This is the nurse's role! He needs to have her role interpreted to him not only in words but also in actions which provide him with experiences which prove to him that he is not alone and without the care which he requires to keep him comfortable, physically and psychologically. The child knows he needs help in controlling his inner drives and in meeting what is to come in a new situation. Unless he has someone to help him, mastery of himself and his environment will be an insurmountable task.

At the time of admission the child needs to have his nurse's interest centered in establishing a good relationship with him. If he is not acutely ill and in need of no immediate treatment or medication, he will welcome a chance to become familiar with her and his surroundings.

In the immediate adjustment period the child will be keenly sensitive to all that is happening around him. He will be observing his mother and the nurse and he will sense the attitudes and feelings they have toward each other. If he senses the nurse's respect for his mother and his mother's confidence in the nurse, he will feel safer and be more ready to put his trust in the person who will see that he is cared for in his mother's absence.

After the child has fully appraised his situation, he will begin to relate himself to the nurse in ways which are individual to him. He will indicate his needs and show her ways she can approach him. By waiting for the child to reach out toward her, the nurse can be more certain of giving him gratification in her first contacts with him.

To establish a relationship with the child, the nurse needs psychological readiness to meet whatever needs are existent within the child at the time she first meets him. She needs to be able to meet him at his current emotional level, make the fewest possible demands upon him, lessen his physical and emotional discomfort and provide the gratification he is seeking to have satisfied. This kind of care assures the child of his nurse's kindness and understanding. He will sense she has given him relief from discomfort and he will begin to develop positive feelings toward her. At first he may be overtly hostile and tempestuous or withdraw from her. In all probability he will be excessively demanding and dependent upon her, and it should be expected that he will, for it is the normal response to separation anxiety and fear of a new situation. The following situation illustrates the way children reach out for relationships and indicate their needs.

Jennifer was 4 years old when she came into the hospital with symptoms of a kidney infection. She was miserably unhappy in her room and was taken to the playroom with the hope that she would find life in the hospital more tolerable.

In the playroom Jennifer was equally morose. She was unable to enter into group activity and withdrew from the play director's overtures of friendliness. Jennifer spent each play period on the floor listening to the music which came from a musical chair whenever she pulled the string which set the instrument in motion.

It seemed obvious that Jennifer was not ready to share the play director with others or to enter into relationships with other children. Instead of a group experience it seemed evident that Jennifer was longing for and needing a relationship with someone who could meet her dependent needs.

A nurse was assigned to Jennifer, and her first objective was to establish contact with her. Jennifer was sitting on the floor just as she had been sitting there previously. She appeared to be in deep thought and completely withdrawn from all that was going on around her. As she listened to the music she sat motionless. Her face was immobile and expressionless. When the nurse introduced herself and told her she would like to play and take care of her, there was no response which indicated she even heard her words.

For 20 minutes Jennifer and her nurse sat together on the floor. When the music stopped, Jennifer again pulled the string. Occasionally she would look at the nurse, but immediately she would turn her face away. Finally she said in demanding tones, "Get Lizzie and bring her over here to listen to the music." The nurse complied, and when 16-month-old Lizzie began to sit on the musical chair, Jennifer raised her voice and said, "Sit here on the floor."

After a few more minutes of listening, Jennifer turned to the nurse and said, "This is where the music comes from." Then she picked up an airplane from the floor and said, "Fly this. Make it fly 'way up in the air." The nurse did as she was directed and flew it back to Jennifer when she requested that it be returned to her. Then Jennifer flew it, and when she wanted it sent back to her she said, "Hold it down here. Hold it just like I do." Then she used blocks and threw those and requested that the nurse do likewise.

At this point Lizzie entered into the play and began taking some of the blocks Jennifer seemed to feel she needed. "Don't let her take them," Jennifer shrieked. The nurse responded, "No, I won't let her, Jennifer. Those are yours. I'll find others that Lizzie can play with."

For an hour Jennifer played and began to relate herself to the nurse. Jennifer continued to make demands, and the nurse met each of her needs as they arose. Before the play period was over Jennifer was laughing and playing with more interest and enthusiasm than she had shown since being in the hospital.

The nurse took Jennifer back to her room and told her where she would be. Jennifer did not stay in her room. She walked up the hallway, returned and stood a short distance from the nurse. She would begin to come toward her and then withdraw. Because it seemed evident that Jennifer was longing for closeness but could not seek it independently, the nurse said, "I'm wondering if you want to sit on my lap. You can tell me if you do." Without saying a word, Jennifer ran to her and jumped upon her lap.

Later that day Jennifer's nurse learned that the child's mother had given birth to a daughter two days before. Jennifer had known that her mother was going to have a baby and she had had news of its arrival prior to the time the nurse observed her for the first time in the playroom.

It is interesting to speculate about the meaning of Jennifer's behavior. When the nurse met her demands and protected her interests when Lizzie was there, Jennifer's anxiety lessened and she had energy to relate to the nurse and to play. She talked more, playing vigorously and in a way she had not done before. She offered a hammer to the nurse and said, "Here's one for you. Now we can both play." Jennifer selected Lizzie, the youngest child in the room, to come and play with her. When she came she did not play with her. She needed her there for other reasons. She dominated her and demanded that the nurse protect her interests. Because her anxiety lessened when her interests were protected, it seemed logical to assume that Jennifer was attempting to master her fear lest the new baby receive all the attention and leave her without the care and the interest for which she longed.

Because the nurse had evidence which convinced her that Jennifer was worried about her future status at home, she proceeded to verify her assumption and give her more help if she showed a readiness for it. Later in the day when they were together the nurse said, "Jennifer, you have a new baby at your house. Some children get scared because they think their mothers won't have time to take care of them. I wonder if that is what you are worried about." Jennifer corroborated the nurse's assumption. She smiled and nodded her head and as she did so she snuggled more closely in the nurse's lap. After the nurse told her about new babies and assured her her mother could take care of two children, she was again able to play.

The child in the hospital needs a nurse who can maintain her relationship with him. When the nurse has established a positive relationship with a child and has relieved his anxiety and his tension through comforting experiences, she has begun to help him master the problems that illness and separation bring. When his illness subsides, she can help him become increasingly more independent and reach the level of adaptation he was capable of prior to hospitalization. To accomplish this, his nurse must maintain her relationship with him and his mother at a constructive level. The requirements necessary to maintain a constructive relationship with a child are cited on page 27.

Regardless of how well the nurse cares for a child there will be periods of anger which come when a child is left unsupported and alone. Nurses can meet many of the child's needs but not all of them, for there are many routine procedures and requirements unrelated to patient care which nurses seem forced to meet. When a child is left unsupported, he feels unloved and responds with anger.

It is not unnatural for him to react this way; it is the way human beings are made.

When a mature adult is hurt by another or is deprived of the love of the person for whom he cares most deeply he, too, responds with aggressive feelings, for it is the way he is made. Because he has a full-grown ego and controls within himself, he does not act his feelings out. The young child has no controls within himself, and his ego cannot handle excessive amounts of anxiety and hostility without crippling its potentialities for growth.

The child needs a nurse who can help his mother understand the responses that are the natural outcome of a period of hospitalization under our present-day regimen. If the nurse can help the child's mother understand the reasons why her child feels hostile and revengeful, she will be better prepared to feel with him and plan ways to give him what he needs to re-establish a friendly and trusting relationship with her.

QUESTIONS TO GUIDE OBSERVATION

1. How does care during the preceding period of development affect development during this period?

2. What are the needs of the child during this period of development?

3. How can guidance during this period of development arrest emotional growth?

4. Bring to class several of the questions you heard children asking in the ward recently. What needs do you think the children were seeking to satisfy in their questions? How did you meet their needs? How did the children respond to your interest in their questions?

5. What reactions did you have when one of your patients asked you where a deceased child had gone? What did you do when he asked? How did the child respond to your behavior?

6. What have you observed which shows evidence that children are interested in their bodies? How did you respond to their interest?

7. What family interpersonal relationships would adversely affect the child's progress through this stage of personality development?

8. What is sex education? How does a child obtain wholesome sex education? What determines whether or not the child will grow up with healthy attitudes toward sex and his own personal sexual role?

9. Think through the way in which you obtained your sex education. Were you satisfied with the education you obtained? What changes would you have liked to be made? In what ways does the kind of sex education you received influence your attitudes toward the expression of children's natural curiosity? Give an example, showing how your own education influenced your reaction to a child's question or display of sexual curiosity.

10. How did you feel when you went to the birthrooms for your experience? Did you anticipate it or approach it with dread? Did you feel sorry for the women in labor or did you feel that they were experiencing something which was a real privilege? Why do you suppose you felt the way you did? Could it reflect any early experiences you had? If so, how?

11. What guidance does the preschool child require to find and to accept his place within his family?

12. How do care and guidance during this period of personality development affect the child's future adjustment to marriage and parenthood?

13. How do you feel when you observe a child masturbating? Describe a situation you observed. Was the child having his need for an emotional relationship and play activities satisfied? What purpose do you think masturbation was serving for this child? What evidence do you have to support your assumption?

14. What do you think a child's concept of his world is like? Describe it in as great detail as you can. In this essay, describe how you think a 4-year-old child feels in a hospital ward.

15. Observe the play of one or two preschool children. Describe what you saw. What was each child attempting to do? What were their goals, desires or motives? Of what value do you think this play was to the children?

16. Describe a situation in the ward where rivalry was displayed. What precipitated the rivalrous feelings? How did the nurse respond to the children's expression of feeling? What were the children's responses to the adult handling the situation?

17. How can you help a child share you with other of your patients? Describe a situation where you helped a child accept sharing.

18. What are the factors which influence a child's ability to make a good adjustment to a nursery school experience? To a hospital experience?

19. What behavior characteristics in a child would lead you to believe a child was mastering his experiences in a pediatric ward? What would lead you to believe he was making a poor adjustment?

20. What knowledge of the child's nature should assist the nurse in knowing what he needs when he is coming into a hospital?

21. Observe a child as he is coming into a hospital ward. Describe what you saw and felt. How did the child react to the experience? How did the mother react to it? What do you think influenced the way the child responded to the new experience?

22. In what ways might a hospital experience affect a child adversely?

23. Describe a newly admitted child and tell how you developed a relationship with him.

24. If you were a nurse in a pediatric clinic and you heard the doctor tell the mother that her child, aged 5, had to be admitted to the hospital for an intravenous pyelogram, what would you observe and what would you do?

25. Johnny, aged 5, is going to be admitted to the pediatric ward for tonsillectomy on Friday. On Wednesday at 1:00 P.M. his mother is going to bring him to the ward to get him ready for the experience. If you were the head nurse in the ward, what would you do to help Johnny and his mother?

26. When is a child emotionally ready to enter first grade? How is emotional preparedness for school attained? What parental attitudes would prevent the development of emotional readiness for school?

27. How can nurses function to help children become ready for school experiences?

REFERENCES

1. Bowlby, John: Adverse effects of maternal deprivation, Part I, p. 16, in Maternal Care and Mental Health, Geneva, World Health Organization: Monograph *Series* No. 2, Palais Des Nations, 1951.
2. Campbell, Doris: How a child feels about entering a nursery school, (pamphlet), New York, New York Committee on Mental Hygiene of the State Charities Aid Association, 1946.
3. ———: What nursery school is like, (pamphlet), New York, New York Committee on Mental Hygiene of the State Charities Aid Association, 1946.
4. English, O. S., and Foster, Constance: Sex education for the school-age child, Parents' Magazine 25:36, May, 1950.
5. ———, and Pearson, G. H.: The pyschosexual development of the child, Chapter 2, p. 18, in Common Neuroses of Children and Adults, New York, Norton, 1937.
6. Frank, Ruth: Parents and the pediatric nurse, Am. J. Nursing 52:76, 1952.
7. French, Thomas: Defences and synthesis in the function of the ego, Psychoanalytic Quart. 7:537, 1938.

8. Freud, Anna: Infantile amnesia and the Oedipus complex, Chapter 1, p. 11, in Psychoanalysis for Teachers and Parents, New York, Emerson, 1947.

9. ———: Denial in phantasy, Chapter 6, p. 73, in The Ego and the Mechanisms of Defence, New York, International Universities Press, Inc., 1946.

10. ———: Denial in word and act, Chapter 7, p. 89, in The Ego and the Mechanisms of Defence, New York, International Universities Press, Inc., 1946.

11. ———: Identification with the aggressor, Chapter 9, p. 117, in The Ego and the Mechanisms of Defence, New York, International Universities Press, Inc., 1946.

12. Freud, Sigmund: Analysis of a phobia in a five-year-old, p. 149, in Collected Papers, Vol. 3, London, Hagarth, 1950.

13. Gabbard, H. F.: Preparing your child for school, (pamphlet), Washington, Federal Security Agency.

14. Gruenberg, Sidonie: The Wonderful Story of How You Were Born, Garden City, N. Y., Hanover House, 1952.

15. Isaacs, Susan: "Play and Growth," Chapter 2, p. 8, in The Nursery Years, New York, Vanguard, 1929.

16. ———: Two to six: the child and his parents, Chapter 6, p. 80, in The Nursery Years, New York, Vanguard, 1929.

17. Jessner, Lucie, and Kaplan, Samuel: Observations on the emotional reactions of children to tonsillectomy and adenoidectomy, p. 97, in Problems of Infancy and Childhood, New York, Josiah Macy Jr. Foundation, 1949.

18. Johnson, A. M. and Ross, Helen: Psychiatric interpretation of the growth process, (pamphlet), New York, Family Service Association of America, 192 Lexington Ave., New York City 16, 1949.

19. Josselyn, Irene: The oedipal period, Chapter 7, p. 64, in Psychosocial Development of Children, New York, Family Service Association of America, 1948.

20. ———: The latency period, Chapter 8, p. 75, in Psychosocial Development of Children, New York, Family Service Association of America, 1948.

21. ———: The training period, Chapter 6, p. 47, in Psychosocial Development of Children, New York, Family Service Association of America, 1948.

22. Levy, David: Psychic trauma of operation on children, Am. J. Dis. Child. 69:7, 1945.

23. McNaughton, Dorothy: The inner world of the preschool child, Child Study, 28:6, 1950-1951.

24. Pearson, Gerald: Effects of operative procedures on the emotional life of the child, Am. J. Dis. Child. 62:716, 1941.

25. Peller, L. E.: Character development in nursery school, Mental Hygiene 32:177, 1948.

26. Reid, Helen: A handbook on the sex education of children, Parents' Magazine 28:48, 1953.

27. Ross, Helen: Fears of children, (pamphlet), Chicago, Science Research Association, Inc., 1951.

28. Spock, Benjamin: Three to six, p. 294, in Common Sense Book of Baby and Child Care, New York, Duell, Sloan and Pearce, 1945.
29. Stevens, Marion: Parents are welcome on the pediatric ward, Am. J. Nursing 49:233, 1949.
30. Swift, E. H.: Step by Step in Sex Education, New York, Macmillan, 1946.
31. Vander Veer, Adrian: The psychopathology of physical illness and hospital residence, p. 50, in Personality Development and Its Implications for Nursing and Nursing Education, Springfield, Ill., Department of Public Health, 1949.
32. Wilkins, Gladys: The role of the nurse in the admission of pre-school children to hospitals, unpublished master's paper, University of Chicago, Department of Nursing Education, 1950.
33. The child's first days in nursery school, (pamphlet), New York, New York Committee on Mental Hygiene of the State Charities Aid Association, 1948.

7

Development and Care During the School-Age Period (6 to 10 Years)

ACQUISITION OF MENTAL SKILLS AND KNOWLEDGE AND THE CHILD'S RE-
SULTANT PLEASURE AND INCREASED CAPACITY TO SOLVE HIS PROB-
LEMS INDEPENDENTLY

EXPERIENCES IN HOME, SCHOOL AND COMMUNITY AND RESULTING OPPOR-
TUNITY FOR PERSONALITY GROWTH

THE SCHOOL-AGE CHILD'S NEED FOR STUDY AS A BASIS FOR GUIDANCE

During the first six years of life, the child's personality changes as he grows physically and adapts himself to his parents' guidance. At birth the child's personality was unformed and undifferentiated; it consisted of instinctual drives which were primitive, uncontrolled and striving for immediate gratification. But within the newborn there were innate potentialities for developing the power to modify the expression of his drives. With the assistance of understanding parents, he learned ways of expressing his needs and gaining gratification which were socially acceptable.

By the time the child reaches his sixth birthday, his personality has become structured. His ego has gained some degree of power over his aggressive and sexual drives and has resolved the conflicts which arose, and he has incorporated the standards of his society which his parents interpreted in all their relationships with him. By the beginning of the sixth year he should have surmounted his disappointment in his relationships with his parent of the opposite sex. This he should have accomplished through finding outlets for his affections in play with his peers and through identification with his parent of the same sex. By the beginning of the sixth year his conscience has become a part of his personality structure. His personality is no longer undifferentiated; it is structured. However, this does not mean that his personality development is at an end— it merely means that it has become differentiated into three distinct parts: the id, the ego and the conscience.

All the events of the earlier years have left their imprint on the child's personality. They have determined the way he will relate to boys, girls, men and women, the way he will obtain the gratification his nature requires and the way he will relate himself to the world.[22] Menninger[22] says that it is in the first six years of life that "basic character traits are initiated and patterns developed that largely determine the characteristics of that personality as an adult."

In this period and the two which follow personality growth will continue and bring changes in behavior. However, the changes that occur will only modify the child's basic personality structure; they will not produce a new one. The changes will influence the relationship the three parts of the child's personality will have to one another but they cannot create a new structure because to a large extent it is already fixed.[12]

If the child acquired the sex education that he needed and mastered the tasks of the earlier periods, his energy became freed for meeting the developmental tasks and demands of this period of personality development. The freed energy makes it possible for him to develop interest in learning more about the world in which he lives. In this period, his curiosity expands and he delights in new experiences which give him an opportunity to learn and to do things independently and with others. *In this period the child needs energy available for gaining skill in the use of his mind and his body, for developing stronger inner controls which help him to be more consistent in mastering himself and his environment and for developing his capacities for relationships with children and adults outside his family.* In this phase of growth his concept of himself will expand and through identification with members of his own sex he will acquire patterns of behavior which are appropriate for him.

ACQUISITION OF MENTAL SKILLS AND KNOWLEDGE AND THE CHILD'S RESULTANT PLEASURE AND INCREASED CAPACITY TO SOLVE HIS PROBLEMS MORE INDEPENDENTLY

DEPENDENCE OF SUCCESS IN LEARNING AND GROWING THROUGH SCHOOL ACTIVITIES ON THE CHILD'S PAST EXPERIENCES

In primary school the child will be confronted with frustrations, many experiences which require a moderate degree of ability to socialize and many demands that he has not been accustomed to at home or in the more flexible environment of the nursery school or kindergarten. If he has had a constructive nursery school and kindergarten experience, adjustment in first grade will be a more comfortable experience for him. However, it will not be a painless one for life in primary school is different from anything he has experienced before. Being one of a large group and adjusting oneself to a new person who is in authority and to new routines and rules are not easy tasks for the 6-year-old child—he will need help in making the adjustment.

The child needs time and support to make a good adjustment to school. Some children adjust rapidly; others require more time—sometimes a week, a month, and not infrequently a year or more. Temporarily, as the child is making the adjustment to school, he may feel he is losing his identity and becoming not so important as he formerly thought himself to be. For this reason and others the child going off to school needs an affectionate send-off and a warm greeting upon his return home from school. When a child comes home from school, he needs his mother there to welcome him after a long period at school; he needs her responsiveness, her interest and her warmth. He needs to feel that his mother is happy to see him again and ready to listen to all that has happened during the course of the day. Many times he will bring his mother a token, which should be received in the spirit it was given, for it indicates that the child has been thinking of her, missing her and putting forth effort to please her.

As the child progresses through the primary grades and into junior high school, emotional, social and intellectual requirements increase and require readiness to meet them. The child needs to be ready to meet the demands of his teachers and group and be able to obtain gratification from his accomplishments. Unless he can find satisfactions in school, his personality growth will be impeded, for successful mastery of the problems involved in this phase of development is dependent upon it. If, in earlier years, the child experienced deprivation or trauma, there will be obstacles which will increase his problems during the school-age period.

Problem behavior which often arises in this phase of development is directly related to the past. It stems from early deprivation or trauma and arises because the child is unprepared to cope with the problems involved in his present situation. The child who has been deprived has insufficient security and energy to relate himself well to the teacher, to become a part of his new social group and to learn from the experiences which are available to him.

The child needs sound physical health and emotional freedom to acquire knowledge and mental skills during the school-age period. If a physical defect or emotional unreadiness prevents the child from accomplishing in school, he will be handicapped not only at the moment but also throughout his lifetime as well. Opportunities to develop mental skills and to acquire knowledge come in middle childhood. Unless he acquires the basic skills during this period, surmounting the intellectual tasks required in junior and senior high school will be near to impossible.

The incidence of failure in school is high, and as frequently due to emotional disturbance as it is to mental retardation. Sometimes the failure is only in one area (like reading, for instance), but often there is general inability to master the subject matter being presented. Some investigators have estimated the incidence of reading failures in normally intelligent and superior grade-school children to be 8 to 10 per cent. Others estimate the incidence to be nearer 25 per cent. It is not unusual to find fourth- and fifth-grade children still struggling to master reading. Intelligence is a factor in learning but there are many superior children who become reading failures and many others who are unable to find satisfaction in school achievement. Kunst,[19] who has done intensive study and treatment of children with learning difficulties, estimates that reading difficulties occur 8 to 10 times more frequently in boys than in girls.

Emotional freedom to learn is as important for success in school as is innate intelligence. English and Pearson[7] say:

His success in school will depend not so much on his innate intelligence, important as this is, as on the degree of energy freed for the acquisition of knowledge by a successful solution of his conflict about his parents.

The child must be free enough to see and to listen and to remember what he has perceived. He must also be able to make connections between what he hears and sees and that knowledge he has already acquired. He must be able to make associations, conceptualize, draw conclusions and put thoughts together in a way which has meaning to him. Without emotional freedom he cannot utilize or develop the mental faculties with which he has been born.

A child who is overburdened with anxiety, feelings of disappointment and tension cannot concentrate even though a desire to learn and stand well with his classmates is existent. When a child feels he is failing, he becomes anxious, and often total failure becomes inevitable.

The causes of reading failure are usually multiple and difficult to discover and to eradicate. School failures are an expression of conflict and anxiety and stem from some quality in family interpersonal relationships which give the child insufficient emotional freedom to learn. Tutoring without consideration of the child's emotional needs rarely brings results because it does not eliminate the interpersonal relationship problems that are preventing him from using his mental faculties. Sometimes tutoring merely serves to aggravate the problem. Unless the causes are eliminated, the pressure involved in tutoring forces the child to deepen his defenses against his inner conflict. This is especially true when a parent selects himself to be the tutor. Through intensive study of the dynamics of learning difficulties in normal and superior children, Kunst[19] has found the following factors to be those which most commonly block children's capacities to learn.

Learning is both receiving and giving. The child knows that his parents want him to succeed and that they value success—they expect it as a gift from him. In the past they have also expected gifts of co-operation and affection from him. During the first six years of life a child has many problems to surmount and he requires constant supportive guidance to succeed. If one were to review the background histories of children with learning difficulties one would discover the reasons why they have come to this period unready for or resistant to giving. Some children have received little in the way of understanding and emotional satisfactions and as a result they have little incentive to give in return. The less ambivalence a child has concerning his desire to please his parents, the easier it will be for him to learn and to give his parents the sense of achievement they often avidly desire. In some instances failure to learn to read is an expression of negativism or a symbol of his desire to maintain his will against his parents.

Learning requires the use of aggressive energy; it also requires freedom to look, to discover the reasons for things and a desire to grow up and become increasingly more accomplished and successful. Reading or total school failure may stem from trauma which makes the child afraid to look and discover, or fearful that the aggressiveness required for learning will bring injury to himself or others. Sometimes failure in learning represents a regressive tendency in the child; he does not want to grow up for reasons which are deeply buried in his unconscious. There are children who fail because they fear success; they have to fail to keep themselves free of anxiety.

Despair is at the root of some children's reading difficulties. There is either no one who really cares whether he accomplishes or not, or those he wants to care never recognize his efforts and give him the praise and the acceptance he wants and needs to learn. Sometimes what he gives is never enough. No matter how hard he tries, his parents and teachers are never satisfied for they expect standards of achievement that are beyond his capacity to meet. Instead of praise and acceptance, he gets criticism, excessive nagging and needling which brings feelings of inadequacy, frustration, rebellion and sometimes even despair. When this happens his anxiety is increased. Anxiety not only lessens his ability to concentrate but also makes him angry and lessens his incentive to please and to give something of himself to his parents.

Some children demonstrate their unreadiness to leave home and meet the demands of the school situations in other ways than failure to learn.[31] Some children respond with gastro-intestinal disturbances, regression, stealing, resistance to going to school or truancy; others respond with bouts of overeating which lead to obesity, bringing ostracism from their schoolmates. Still others respond with loss of appetite which can lead to malnutrition and apathy. There may be a physical cause for the symptom, but more often emotional turmoil is at the root of the trouble. In the pediatric clinic Powers[29] found many school-age children who reacted to pressures at home and school with a somatic response. Unless these children receive the help that they need, their physical health and adjustment in school will be threatened.

The child who is failing in school or the child who is not adjusting socially to his new situation needs study and oftentimes medical or psychological treatment. It is important that the child be successful in his first years at school for what he meets there will influence his attitudes toward school, teachers and the experiences of learning. The child who is under par physically will have difficulty in applying himself sufficiently to master the subject matter of the curriculum and the social requirements of his group. The failing or poorly adjusting child may have a nervous system, eye, ear, glandular, or nutritional defect which prevents him from learning. Or there may be emotional problems which are blocking his interest or ability to learn.

When a child is showing symptoms which indicate he is not adjusting to school, the school nurse can study the home situation and bring observations which will increase the teacher's understanding of him. She can also help the child's mother find ways to lessen pressures upon him and to give her child more security at home. Oftentimes mothers do not appreciate what entrance into school means to their children. They have forgotten the discomfort they experienced when they felt unprotected in a strange and demanding situation. With insight many mothers and teachers can find ways to lessen a child's anxiety so he can feel more secure at school.

Some children may need medical treatment or the help of professional workers in a child guidance clinic. The nurse needs to know the resources of her community and to possess the capacity to interpret their value to parents in a way which makes it possible for them to accept their child's need for treatment. The therapist has special skills which enable him to help children and parents solve their problems. Parents need to have the functions of the therapist interpreted to them for it will influence his effectiveness should the parents recognize their need and seek his help. If there are no facilities in the community for the treatment of emotionally disturbed children, the nurse can work with other professional people to stimulate the citizens' interest so that they will be motivated to see their community's needs and to support plans to organize facilities that will meet them.

Dependence of Success in Learning and Growing Through School Activities on the School Environment

In 1945 a subcommittee was appointed at a meeting of representatives of the Federal governmental agencies to study and to suggest methods of implementing programs which would meet the health needs of the school-age child. This committee[34] defined the school-age child's health and fitness needs as follows:

1. *A safe, sanitary, healthful school environment*
This means:
Control of such environmental factors as heat, air, light, sunshine, buildings, grounds, noise, color, form, construction, water supply, sewage disposal, and play space so that they contribute to, rather than deter from, healthful school experiences.
An environment in which boys and girls are freed as far as possible from the conditions which produce unnecessary fear, anxieties, conflicts, and emotional stresses.

2. *Protection from infections and conditions which interfere with proper growth and development*
This means:
Adequate examination and inspection of pupils, teachers, and custodial personnel to detect communicable diseases as well as deviations which impair health.
An opportunity to receive necessary immunization and testing procedures.

3. *An opportunity to realize their potentialities of growth and development*
This means:
Adequate medical and dental care on the basis of individual needs as shown by examinations.

Adequate nutrition to assure well-nourished children.

Participation in a program of physical activity designed to develop organic power, strength, skill, agility, poise, and endurance, as well as ability to participate with others in games and sports which promote alertness, cooperation, respect for individuals and groups, initiative and a feeling of personal worth.

Participation in a recreational program designed to create interest in activities which develop talents making for wholesome living, and broadening the child's horizon of the world in which he lives.

A balance and rhythm in the child's daily life which is in keeping with his physical, mental, and emotional needs.

4. *To learn how to live healthfully*

This means:

An opportunity to learn and to make wise decisions, form health habits and attitudes based on scientific knowledge of health and disease.

An opportunity to make choices and assume increasing responsibility for one's own personal health.

An opportunity to acquire information and attitudes appropriate to the grade level about physical and emotional development, maturity, and patterns of social conduct which will contribute to the health of the individual and other citizens to insure wholesome family and community living.

5. *Teachers who are equipped by training, temperament, and health not only to give specific instruction but also to help children to mature emotionally*

This means:

Teachers not only prepared to teach but those who are also emotionally stable and adjusted, because the development of healthful personalities is dependent upon the relationships and attitudes which are built up between teacher and children.

The child needs teachers who recognize all his health needs if his full potentialities are to be utilized and developed to their fullest. The above recommendations consider both his physical and his psychological needs. From a psychological standpoint the child's teacher is the most important part of his school environment. However, what she can accomplish will be determined not only by her own personality and skills but also by the attitudes of his parents toward his work and life at school. It will also be influenced by parental attitudes toward the teacher.

The child needs parents and teachers who work together in his interest. The child needs to feel that his mother respects his teacher and that the teacher respects his mother. The child needs both his parents and his teacher. Both have their roles to play and both are very important to him personally. If parents and teachers misunderstand each other, usually the child is torn between people he needs to love and respect.

Many mothers have conflicting feelings which influence their relationships with teachers. Some of the ambivalent feelings some mothers experience when they anticipate their children's readiness for school have already been cited in Chapter 6. There are other feelings which bring disturbances in parent-teacher relationships. In many ways many mothers feel glad that the time for their children to go to school has arrived. It relieves them of some of their burdens and gives them more opportunity to do some of the things that they desire to do for themselves. It is natural for mothers to feel this way, but oftentimes they cannot accept the relief they feel for they think it conflicts with society's standards of motherhood.[21] Instead of facing and accepting their feelings, they repress them and experience feelings of guilt instead of relief.

There are other feelings which limit some mothers' opportunities for constructive relationships with teachers. Some mothers are rivalrous with teachers, fearing that they may alienate their children's affections and become more important to them than they. Feelings of jealousy bring resentment, and it is easy to see how such a situation would interfere with positive teacher-parent relationships. Other parents are in awe of teachers, and there are those who dread contact with teachers lest they criticize or demand something of them they are unable to provide.

Teachers are not without feelings; many of them have problems that interfere with their ability to understand parents. Some of them may be rivalrous with parents. Some may displace the hostility they feel toward their own mothers onto their pupil's mothers. Some may resent the mothers' interest in their own children and wish they would never visit the school. They cannot tolerate giving their pupils' mothers credit for their accomplishments in school, yet often they are quick to blame them if the children do not succeed.

When mothers bring their children into the hospital some of the above feelings of conflict may also become aroused. If they do, problems in mother-nurse relationships will be inevitable and need understanding for the benefit of mothers, patients and nurses. To ensure good relationships the nurse needs to think through her feelings toward mothers and to understand the meaning which the care of children has to her personally. When clashes in mother-nurse relationships come, the nurse needs to search for answers to the following questions: "Why do I react as I do to this mother? What has she done which distressed me? Are there reasons for her behavior? Has she cause to feel rivalrous with me? Have I accepted the child's need for closeness to his mother and done everything possible to help him respect her? What happens when I attack her as she has attacked me? Does it bring better understanding between us or does it block all avenues of communication with her?"

The objective of today's Parent-Teacher Associations is to bring increased understanding between the two groups of people who are most concerned with the welfare of children. The teacher needs to understand the feelings of conflict which parents experience. If she does she can maintain a greater degree of objectivity and a constructive relationship with them. Parents need increased understanding of the teacher and the role she plays in helping children to learn those things that they cannot learn at home. The child feels his parents' attitudes toward the teacher and the teacher's attitudes toward his parents. It is most important that he be able to sense mutual respect rather than antagonism, resentment or criticism. Would a Parent-Nurse Association be an inconceivable project in a community? Would it not bring increased understanding of one another and enhance the nurse's opportunities for satisfactions from her work? Would it not help parents understand the problems of nurses to a greater degree?

The kind of teacher the child meets in school will influence his attitudes toward school and the adjustment he will make. It is the teacher who must see that her pupil's environment is safe, hygienic and satisfying. It is the teacher who carries out the program of study and social experiences and provides the emotional nourishment on which the child continues to be dependent. She is the person who will help the child channelize his sexual and aggressive drives into learning and accomplishing. She is the one who must make the demands and help the child find gratification in meeting them. She does this by stimulating his interest in learning. She encourages his efforts and gives him freedom to develop his abilities in ways which are suited to him personally. The wise teacher knows that, "in order to learn, one must want something, notice something, do something, and get something."[23]

The mature teacher has faith in her pupils' desire and ability to learn and to meet the expectations and the requirements of the school situation. From her faith in them, the children gain strength and increased belief in themselves. It is the teacher's feelings about her pupils, and the attitudes she has toward them, which affect the children's attitudes not only toward themselves but also toward other children and adults as well.

The child can settle down and learn best when limits are set for him. His need for them in the home, nursery school and hospital has been cited previously. He also needs them in the school situation. Not only do they give him the security that he needs but also they give him the help he requires to transform, channelize or sublimate his infantile impulses into socially acceptable, learning activities which bring feelings of accomplishment and recognition.

Some children come to school unable to sublimate their aggressive drives into learning activities and need help if they are to be successful in learning. Children who cannot sublimate their aggressive energies have either had insufficient gratification or a laissez-faire type of guidance which failed to help them use their energies constructively. They will need guidance and a great deal of it, for unless they have help in channelizing their aggressive drives they will be unable to master the intellectual and psychosocial tasks necessary for continued growth.

The child needs warm, understanding, firm, fair and positive teachers who can provide him with pleasures and demands which assist him in learning. If there are too few demands made upon the child, he does not have the help he needs to sublimate his drives in studying and gaining the knowledge and skills he requires. On the other hand, if there are too many demands and he is unready to meet them, frustration and discouragement occur. In writing of the school-age child, Josselyn[17] makes the following statement which indicates the requirements that are essential in helping him adjust comfortably in school:

If he has had an opportunity for satisfying social contacts, if the demands made upon him at school are within his intellectual capacity, if the restrictions upon his behavior are reasonably geared to his capacity to tolerate frustration and to renounce his impulses, and if the total environment balances demands and frustrations with reasonable gratifications and recognition, the child during this period presents relatively few problems to his parents or to society.*

The primary school child needs school programs which are planned in accordance with his emotional and social requirements. First-grade children cannot adjust to rigid schedules or adapt themselves to long periods of concentrated study without strain and discomfort. Their attention spans have increased during the preschool years, but at 6 years of age they are still short and determined by their mental capacity, personality organization and interest in the subject matter. There are a large number of children in first grade who are struggling with problems for which they have not made successful solutions. When children are anxious and tense, they cannot remain quiet. They need frequent change in activity and opportunity to release tension and to express themselves in play, music and art experiences.

---

* Reprinted by permission of the author and the Family Service Association of America.

In first grade the child needs limited demands which are geared to his ability to endure frustrations. As the child develops increased capacity to get gratification from learning and becomes more comfortably adjusted to the group situation, he will have inner strength to tolerate increasingly more frustration. Then demands can be increased, and be of the kind which require more self-control and application.

The way the child relates himself to the teacher is determined by his past experiences; the way the teacher accepts the kind of relationship he makes with her is dependent upon the kind of personality she possesses. The teacher should be interested primarily in developing the personalities of her pupils. She needs to be sensitive and keenly aware of the significance of fundamental emotional factors in the growth of her pupils' personalities. She needs to know how emotional factors influence learning and be sensitive enough to detect those children who are in need of a special kind of help. She needs to be a mature person who is as capable of meeting the emotional and the social needs of her pupils as she is capable of meeting their needs for knowledge and intellectual skills.

Each child needs to be understood as an individual. The child needs a teacher who is capable of meeting her responsibility in providing him with the kind of dependable relationship he individually requires. If the teacher can accept the child as he is, be he dependent, dull, aggressive or self-reliant, controlled and bright, the child will feel safer. He will have more security and be able to adapt himself to an environment which is different from any he has ever experienced before.

The school-age child in the hospital ward and the convalescent home needs nurses who understand his needs and are capable of helping him have the experiences he requires for growth. The nurse needs the same personal characteristics as the teacher. Limits are as necessary in the ward as in the schoolroom, and the children need to be helped to meet the demands they are physically and psychologically capable of meeting. The children also need to have opportunities to gain satisfaction, for without them frustration will bring problem behavior and discomfort which will complicate their adjustment to their present situation and those they must meet in the future.

The convalescent, school-age child in the hospital needs school activities to learn and to gain satisfaction. When a child's mind is occupied with interesting projects which bring stimulation and relaxation, the body functions are released to restore it to normality. Children worry about keeping up with their classmates at school.

They want to learn, and there are many opportunities for satisfactions in the classroom. If the child's lessons are related to the activities of the world outside the hospital, he will not only learn but also have food for thought. This will help prepare him for the time when he returns to society and resumes life there as before.

The child who is resistant to going to the hospital classroom for work and group experience needs understanding and help to meet his responsibilities. When this occurs it is best if the nurse tries to discover the reasons for his lack of interest in school and works with the hospital schoolteacher to discover ways they can help him find increased satisfactions in the periods devoted to learning and group experience.

Children in the hospital need nurses and teachers who can collaborate in providing the kind of stimulating and productive environment they need for growth. The hospitalized child needs to feel that his nurses and teacher have respect for one another. Often the hospital schoolteacher is not kept informed of his medical progress and all too often she is excluded from the planning which would give her increased insight into his needs in the classroom. The hospital schoolteacher is part of the team which is working with the child, and the child needs her services utilized in implementing a plan of care for him.

The child comes to school with preconceived attitudes and feelings concerning the teacher and the school. Already he has made a generalization of what women are like and has developed personality traits in response to his parents' guidance. Observational studies show that the child transfers to the teacher the feelings he has about his parents, their authority, expectations and capacity for emotional warmth.[9]

The child goes to school anticipating the same reception he received from his mother in his home. If his mother has been warm and giving he will go to school anticipating a similar response from his teacher. He will be trusting, friendly and amenable to his teacher's guidance because past experiences have given him the feeling that women are kind, dependable and understanding people. However, if he has met harshness or deprivation at home, he will not anticipate kindness from his teacher. Instead, he will have little trust in others and expect harshness or deprivation and respond with the behavior patterns he has had to use previously. He may show suspiciousness and withdraw from fear. Or because he responded to previous harshness with counteraggressive behavior, he may come to school prepared and ready to fight.

The child perceives qualities of both parents in his teacher[7] and responds to her in light of his past experiences. The child will see his teacher as a person who is a protector and a giver if his mother has possessed those qualities and as a person who is the authority like the father. Because the child comes to school with preconceived attitudes about his teacher and the school activities, his response to the teacher may not be appropriate to her behavior toward him or to the situation he is in. Many times the teacher is warm, giving and sufficiently permissive in her attitudes, but instead of responding with behavior which denotes trust and inner security, the child responds with fear, suspicion and withdrawal or open rebellion.

Nurses in admitting rooms and in pediatric wards need understanding of the above phenomenon for they will meet similar experiences and need to be ready to handle children objectively. If they recognize from whence these feelings and attitudes come, they can be more understanding and objective, remain unthreatened and use the experience to observe and to help the child. Behavior which is an inappropriate response to a gesture of friendliness provides clues to the child's background of home experience and indicates something concerning his individual needs.

It takes a long time and repeated consistent experiences to modify a child's concept or generalization of what women are like. It cannot be done in one school year or in one experience with an understanding nurse. This knowledge is important to those who work with children. Without emotional acceptance of this knowledge teachers and nurses might cease their efforts to provide experiences which would help him to correct the generalizations he has made about adults before he had had sufficient corrective experiences to feel differently toward those within his environment.[16]

The child adjusts to first grade and to classmates through the relationship he forms with his teacher just as he did in earlier group experience. The child applies himself in learning to please his parents and his teacher.[7] That is his motive in school. If pleasing the teacher and his parents is not made difficult by impossible expectations and if he receives praise and encouragement, he will feel successful and get gratification from learning.

Recognition from his parents and his teacher influences the child's concept of himself and helps him to gain inner motivation to accomplish. When a child receives recognition, his pride and his self-esteem become heightened and he becomes motivated to seek further success. When increased motivation comes from within, he will be spurred on to master more and more difficult intellectual tasks. As he conquers them he will gain self-confidence and become increasingly more able to plan, make decisions and take responsibility for his own welfare.

The school-age child needs adults who recognize his developing powers of self-direction and give him opportunities to use the initiative, judgment and intellectual capacities he acquires through experience. Using his abilities and discovering he can choose and make decisions bolsters his confidence in himself. He needs to know he has abilities within himself; it gives him courage (ego strength) to face his world.

Growth and Resulting Preparedness for Learning Mental Skills

Learning the Three R's. Physical maturation and experiences in the home and the nursery school should bring the child to first grade ready to begin learning to read and write. Experience in preschool years has provided opportunities to learn the shapes of things, to develop a concept of numbers and to develop interest in letters and numbers. Prior to school entrance many children begin to show an interest in letters and numbers and attempt to make them as they draw or paint. If the child has had shared experiences in reading and looking at books with his parents, he will want to learn to read as they do. If he has had the opportunity to go on trips to such places as the zoo, the fire department, the dairy, the airport and the post office, his interest in learning about his environment will have been stimulated. The parents' task is to get the child ready to learn to read and write; most teachers want to do the rest.

By 6 to 7 years of age, the child's nervous system has developed markedly, and he is biologically ready to begin to learn to read and write. Before that time the neuromuscular system is not sufficiently developed to accomplish the tasks with ease. The child is far-sighted until the eighth year, and the fine muscle co-ordination necessary for reading does not develop much before that time.

When teachers understand and respect the developmental process, they plan their curricula in accordance with the child's needs. They do not emphasize learning to read and write in first grade for they know that physical and psychological readiness must be attained before children can learn comfortably. In some progressive schools, the speed of teaching is geared to the individual child's readiness to learn. In many private progressive schools there are fewer children per teacher, and more individualized teaching can be done.

Havinghurst[13] says that psychological studies have shown that reading, arithmetic, spelling and writing ability is acquired by the twelfth or thirteenth year and that it seldom improves after that period. However, he continues, comprehension may increase beyond that point if the individual continues to learn. Havinghurst[13] also says, "In general, the basic mental skills are acquired well enough by the age of 12 or 13 to enable a person to get through life at the lower class and perhaps the lower middle class level."

Acquiring Knowledge of His World. During the school-age period the child needs to acquire a multitude of concepts which will help him to think with clarity and to solve the problems with which he is faced.[13] This is not a difficult task for the well-adjusted child for he is avidly interested in every detail of life about him. During the first six years of life, the child's sensory perception developed markedly. In this period there are many other things that he must learn. To acquire knowledge and to learn to apply it, *the child needs concrete experiences which give him first-hand information about the world in which he lives.*

In the school-age period the child's interests expand and motivate him to want to explore learning opportunities away from his home. His home and back yard do not satisfy him any longer. Luckily his interests do expand for this characteristic meets his need to learn more about the world in which he lives. Interests outside the home also give the child opportunities to develop his capacities for solving more of his own problems independently. Gradually, with experience he gains self-reliance which enables him to broaden his horizons and to attempt the solving of increasingly more difficult tasks.

In this period the child wants to go to the woods and the lakes where he can hunt, swim, fish and explore to learn new skills and to acquire knowledge of plant and animal life. The urban child is often at a disadvantage because his opportunities to go on scouting expeditions are usually limited. However, in the city there are museums of natural history, science and industry, institutes of art, and organizations like the Y.M.C.A. which provide experiences for which the school-age child has a readiness. These institutions and organizations need to be utilized for they broaden children's interests and satisfy their longings to learn about their world.

A child who must spend his sixth year of life on a Bradford frame in a hospital ward will have erroneous concepts concerning life in a public school. He will not know what being one in a large group in school is like even though the hospital schoolteacher shows him pictures and describes activities common to the experience. He cannot develop realistic concepts about life in a public school until he has had experiences within one.

The child who must spend long periods in a hospital or a convalescent home needs concrete experiences from which to learn. There are many opportunities for teaching children in the hospital. Children find kitchens, telepage systems, storerooms and laboratories exceedingly interesting, and trips to them can be used for learning experiences. What an opportunity nurses have to help children learn about hospitals, prevention of disease and the mechanism of the human body! Their searching questions reveal their interest, but responses given by nurses are often unsatisfying. If children's questions were heeded because they were recognized as expression of need and answered in a way which was understandable to them, the children in our hospitals would get knowledge and in many instances they might also get relief from anxiety concerning their bodies or their illnesses. And might they not also acquire some wholesome attitudes about hospitals and their personnel and about their own bodies?

Hospital and convalescent home porches, back yards and environs could also be utilized to the children's advantage. They, too, would give the child a change of scenery and opportunities to learn. Physically handicapped children at the Illinois Hospital School in Chicago are taken on weekly outings. The director of this institution sees the children's need for excursions to learn about the world in which they live. They are taken to baseball games, circuses, beaches, movies and sometimes to restaurants for luncheon or dinner. At La Rabida Hospital in Chicago, the children who are convalescing from heart disease are taken to Jackson Park for picnics and have the opportunity of cooking and planning parties in their own building. The personnel in these institutions know that children need stimulation to keep their interest in learning and living alive. They know that children become bored, listless and withdrawn if they are not motivated to use the powers within them.

In hospitals that lack facilities for transporting children or in instances where the children's physical conditions forbid excursions, some of the outer world can be brought in to them and used for educational purposes. On returning from Florida one nurse brought a very beautiful array of seashells to the children in an orthopedic ward and spent an hour with them describing where they were found, what they originally held and how they got onto the shore from the sea. The children's questions revealed their interest and erroneous conceptions of what a sea and its animal life were like. Another way to bring the outside world to hospitalized children is through the use of educational movies. They are welcomed by children for they satisfy their curiosity and their need to learn, divert their interest away from themselves and give them food for thought and play.

The above activities take time and personnel, but are they not more important to children than some of the things we have become accustomed to think are necessary for children? At the present time hospitals have neither time nor personnel to take children on excursions. In many instances they barely have time to transport them to such places as the physiotherapy or occupational therapy departments. Some children have to remain in wards because personnel cannot find ways to take them to the play- or classroom. Volunteers are useful in pediatric wards and they can be taught how to assist in activity programs. There are also many things being done in pediatric wards which might be eliminated. If we studied our routines, policies and procedures, were convinced of children's need for constructive diversion and sought the co-operation of the medical staff, many changes might be made which would bring increased benefits to children.

Acquiring Facility in the Use of Language. From 6 to 10 years of age the child's vocabulary increases at a rapid rate. The average 6-year-old child has a vocabulary of approximately 2,500 words. By 12 years of age his vocabulary has increased to approximately 7,200 words.

In this period the child delights in learning and sharing his knowledge and experiences with others. He is reaching out for broader social experiences and is interested in acquiring vocabulary and discussing his knowledge with both children and adults. He revels in talking about what he has read and done, and the time his parents spend in listening and discussing knowledge and activities with him is time well spent.

In this period the child develops increased capacity to communicate his needs and his feelings with words, and he will be encouraged to do so if the adults in his environment give him the interest he longs for. School-age children in hospital wards long for interest in themselves and they need it from their nurses. In the hospital they have much to talk about. There are things about home, school and their activities outside the hospital that they need to express, and in addition there are the many new things which stimulate their interest and curiosity and bring them concern.

The child in the hospital reacts to his experiences, develops attitudes about his parents, the personnel and the experience and needs someone with whom he can share his feelings and problems. When an adult is in the hospital and subjected to an operation or other perplexing situations, he talks about them because he has a need to do so. In talking about them he gains perspective, and through another's help he often sees he has misinterpreted or exaggerated the events he experienced. The child needs to do the same thing not only because it brings relief from tension but also because he may need help to understand himself and his experiences or the persons who are providing him with care.

The hospitalized child needs a nurse who can help him master his anxiety through talking, assist him in understanding reality through learning his concept of what happened and correcting his interpretation of what happened to him and prevent him from suppressing or repressing the event and the feelings that were aroused. The following situation illustrates the application of these principles. Ken needed help to understand himself and others, and to channelize his feelings into constructive channels. Ken needed to talk to relieve his tension and to give his nurse understanding of the things that were bringing him concern.

Kenneth was 9 years of age and in the hospital with rheumatic fever. He had had intramuscular injections of penicillin twice daily and had not been told why they were necessary. Twice a day he had been subjected to "needling" which was done skillfully according to scientific standards but without utilization of the psychological priniciples necessary to prevent feelings of resentment.

When Kenneth's new nurse approached him to tell him it would soon be time to have his hypodermic in preparation for tooth extraction, she observed a child who was filled with rage as a result of previous experiences. He looked hostile and indignant as he nervously flipped the pages of his comic book, pretending to read its story. "They like to hurt people," he blurted with a trembling voice. The nurse waited but no more words came. Then to try to find the meaning of Ken's anger, the nurse said, "Nurses don't really like to hurt people. They give them medicine to help them get well." "Like fun they do. They like to hurt children. They jab that needle in as though they were running a sword through you," he continued. "They do hurt, Ken. And some nurses don't understand that children need to know why they are getting hypodermics. Some nurses don't know it makes children angry but I know they hurt and make them angry too. All children get scared when they have to have hypos," the nurse said, to encourage Ken to tell her more which would increase her understanding of him. "Yes, but they like to give them. I'll break the next one in half," he said angrily. As he listened and talked he rolled and unrolled his comic book and began to tear the corners from its cover. The nurse said, "I know it makes you angry and I am glad you can tell me how you feel about it. It helps to talk about things, Ken."

After Ken had finished expressing his feelings about former injections, the nurse told him more about his need for the one he was to receive prior to going to the dental clinic for a tooth extraction. "I'm not going to take it. You might as well not bring it in. If you do I'll smash it. How can it help my mouth when you give it clear down in my leg? Why can't I take a pill?" he continued.

After Ken had learned why he could have nothing by mouth, the nurse brought in a syringe, needle and empty vial. Ken was taught how to give a hypodermic. His anger and defiance vanished as he manipulated the syringe. "It's fun," he said as he pushed the needle in the doll. "It's not fun for me. I give them because I know they help children to get well and lessen their pain, but I know they are scary and I know they hurt," the nurse said. "Really?" he asked. "I thought nurses liked to give them. They act as if they do. They give them so fast and push them in so far. Gee, that doll looks mad! I'll bet she'd like to beat me up," he continued. "I'll bet she feels like she would like to. You know why?" the nurse asked. "No, why?" Ken said, as he played with the syringe, filling it and squirting it, and smiling with satisfaction as he did so. "Because that's just the way all children feel when things hurt, and they don't understand why they have to have them."

After Ken had manipulated the syringe and needle and given the doll a succession of shots, he was ready to go into the treatment room with the nurse. There he assisted the nurse in preparation and cleansed the area he selected for the needle insertion. "I'm a little scared but I can take it," Ken said. "It will hurt, Ken, but I will make it as easy as possible," the nurse assured him. "You won't stick the bone, will you? The other nurse did. She went like this," he said as he demonstrated the way a nurse had thrust the needle into his leg. "No, Ken. I won't. You tell me how you want it done and I will be careful," she said. "O. K. Do it slowly. I'm ready now," Ken said as he prepared himself for the moment of pain.

As the hypodermic was given Ken winced and said, "It does hurt some." "Of course it does, and most kids feel angry as the needle goes in. I'd understand even if you yelled 'ouch' or told me how mad you were. Lots of kids tell me that when I give them hypos," the nurse said, to give Ken permission to vent his feelings if he needed to another time. Then the nurse told him the reason why injections were often given rapidly instead of slowly. She also suggested that he tell the nurses that he preferred having them given more slowly even if it did bring more physical pain.

The nursing care cited in the above incident took time, but subsequent injections were readily accepted, and Ken was free from pent-up feelings which were consuming the energy he needed to recuperate from an acute attack of rheumatic fever. After this experience Ken was freer with his nurse and the children. He could play with them, when formerly his days were spent in fantasy. Why did Ken feel as he did? Were his feelings the result of the treatment he had received or was he projecting his angry feelings onto the nurses? From his comments concerning the doll's feelings, one knows they must have been a reflection of those which were within him. The doll could not talk but Ken made it speak with his thoughts and express what he felt. Through the experience Ken not only mastered his fear, he also found that his feelings were understood and that nurses were not the cruel individuals he had had to make them. No longer did Ken have to repress his feelings and project them onto others to hide them from himself. He had energy with which to master his current situation, and both he and his nurse grew through the experience.

In this period of personality development children devise codes and secret languages to experiment with words and to bring increased intimacy and secrecy into their peer group. They are intrigued with "pig-latin" and codes and delight in using languages which cannot be understood by adults. In this period they are developing interest in seeking increased independence, and the use of "pig-latin" seems more a gesture of this characteristic than a desire to learn a new type of language.

It is not unusual to hear children in hospital wards using specially devised codes to communicate with one another. They get together in little cliques and enjoy shutting out their nurses and their doctors with language that they cannot understand. One cannot help but wonder if they are using it to give the adults a taste of what they often experience, for often the medical jargon children hear in the hospital ward is as incomprehensible to them as their "pig-latin" is to the doctor and the nurse.

In the school-age period children use slang and objectionable words rather extravagantly. They hear them, and their use seems to give them a sense of power. They acquire sex vocabulary and slang from the children in the neighborhood and use them to communicate with one another. If one listens to a group of school-age youngsters on a playground unobtrusively, he will discover that the language they use is not typical of that one hears in "polite" society. But it is the school-age child's way of talking to his peers and he uses this method of communication because he has not lived long enough to learn to express himself with the social forms of language commonly used by adults.

Language which is common and acceptable to parents of the lower social classes is often very objectionable to the teacher or the nurse in the clinic or the hospital ward. The following example may arouse feelings of repugnance in the reader, and it is understandable why it will. He has undoubtedly learned that "shit" was a "bad" word, and when he hears it he cringes because of the feelings which have become associated with it. But it is what nurses are exposed to when they work with children.

Tim was 8 years old when he came into the hospital for a herniorrhaphy. His home was in the stockyard area of Chicago and he and his friends were from the lower economic class of society. After the admission procedure was completed, he turned to the nurse and said, "Say, where do the kids go to shit around here?"

The hospitalized child needs nurses who are able to accept the culture he reflects in all his behavior. He will reflect the cultural patterns of his parents not only in language; he will reflect them in all his behavior. Children are a product of their environments, and standards of the lower social class are different from those of the middle or the upper ones. The more the nurse knows about the cultural backgrounds from whence her patients come, the more she will be able to understand and to accept their behavior. If the nurse cannot accept the culture her patients reflect in their behavior, there will be barriers which prevent them from communicating with and understanding one another.

Swearing and the use of slang can be eliminated only through understanding and thoughtful guidance. Nagging and punishment make the child the center of attention, and that position is difficult for him to relinquish. Often the child uses swear words to shock the adult or to impress him with his "grown-upness." If his words fail to shock and bring no adult drama, he will get no pleasure and feel less need to use them. However, the words often slip out because it is the way he has been talking with his friends. If his parents rebuff or scold him, he will feel misunderstood, and a barrier will come between him and them. If his parents understand it is the group's way of talking and accept it in a friendly manner, the child will be able to utilize the following type of guidance: "You know, Bill, I know that's the way children talk, but there are some people who are bothered by the words you've just used to tell me about the things you and your friends have been doing. There are other words you can use which grown-ups won't mind." In this period the child delights in learning new words. If the adult uses his readiness to increase his vocabulary, he can help him find substitute words which will eliminate the objectionable ones and serve to enrich his vocabulary.

Most children go through a period of language experimentation and use such words as "dopey," "pooper," "stinker," "squirt," "rat," "sassy pants," etc. These expressions are used as commonly by school-age children as is the erudite language used by some college freshmen. Parents and nurses often call the child "fresh" or impudent when he uses words like the former. In most instances, he is not fresh; he is merely exercising his power to pick up new words and to use them in testing their effect upon adults and children in his group.

EXPERIENCES IN HOME, SCHOOL AND COMMUNITY AND RESULTING OPPORTUNITY FOR PERSONALITY GROWTH

The period from 6 to 10 years of age is a relatively peaceful time for the child in comparison with the earlier periods of his life. The strength of his instincts has lessened, and immediate gratification is less urgent than it was before. With growth in fine muscle co-ordination and intellectual capacities, he has new ways of obtaining gratification through his own independent activity or in play with others. As a result of these changes he has energy available for personality growth.

In this period of personality development the child needs opportunities in his home, school and community to develop ego strength. Guidance should assist the child in using his energy to acquire the ego strength he will need to master the problems of this period and those which follow. *In addition to educational experiences in school to gain ego strength the child needs (1) the guidance of his parents and his teachers and (2) opportunities to find his place within a group of peers and to enjoy and profit from experiences with them.*

SUPPORT TO THE CHILD'S EGO FROM PARENTAL AND TEACHER STANDARDS WHICH MAKES IT POSSIBLE FOR HIM TO BECOME INCREASINGLY MORE SELF-DIRECTING

In this period the child's relationship to his parents becomes different in quality. His relationship with them is less intense emotionally, and he is unsatisfied with exclusive attention from them. He wants a greater degree of independence and he struggles to obtain it. In preschool years the child endowed his parents with supernormal qualities which they did not have. He needed to idealize and to give them the strength he did not have within himself. In imaginatively endowing them with omnipotence, he received the strength which his helplessness required from them.

In the school-age period, the child begins to see his parents in a more realistic light and comes to recognize that there are others who can be right and possess qualities worthy of imitation. In preschool years mother and father are always right. One hears preschoolers discussing their parents. Each one thinks his parents are the best, the richest, the brightest and the most powerful of all. In the school-age period the same children are heard making comments like the following: "It is right. I *know* because my teacher says so," or "No, Mother, you are wrong. My camp counsellor said it was not like that at all."

In the middle of this period the child does not need to endow his parents with omnipotent powers for he has new ego strengths within himself. In the preschool period the child was impulsive, and his responses to frustration were immediate and overtly expressed. His angry feelings spilled out freely in aggressive behavior and eventually in words. The school-age child is more controlled. Instead of directly expressing his impulses, one sees he has adapted to his parents' standards with a variety of defense mechanisms. As a result it is possible for him to meet more demands and adapt to the realities of his new school world.

Some of the school-age child's impulses have become sublimated into constructive, acceptable activities; others he controls through the use of the ego defense which has been mentioned previously— the reaction formation. Instead of overtly expressing an impulse, he reacts against it, condemning its desirability. He represses the impulse and replaces it with a characteristic which is directly opposite to what the infantile part of his personality, the id, desires. Ross[30] describes some of the changes which come as the school-age child utilizes reaction formations and sublimations to control his impulses. She says:

Exhibitionistic tendencies have given way to modesty; messiness to cleanliness; uncontrolled aggression and cruelty to sympathy and a feeling for one's fellows; unbridled curiosity to sublimated investigative pursuits; greediness to cooperation and willingness to share.

The defenses the child's ego constructed to handle his conflicts between his parents' standards and his own desires become strengthened in this period of personality development. In the early part of this period the child's defenses are weak. When demands are too great and he has more disappointment and frustration than he can endure, his impulses break through into overt expression. This is observable in many 6- and 7-year-old hospitalized children. When illness robs them of energy and brings more frustration than they can withstand, their defenses break and they are unable to control the overt expression of their impulses and drives. When their illness subsides and they obtain gratification from satisfying relationships which prove that their environment is safer than they imagined, they again become capable of handling their impulsivity. It is also observable during the period the child is adjusting to a new school environment. It is for this reason the child's new school environment needs to be flexible and geared to his tolerance for frustration.

In this period the child's ego is supported by his conscience, and it is another reason why he is able to be more self-directing and controlled than he was formerly. He has incorporated his parents' standards and gained additional power to cope with his impulses. In this period he gains a certain degree of independence from his parents, but their standards have become a part of him and continue to exert their influence on his behavior indirectly through the functioning of his conscience. Now he has an inner voice or newly formed conscience which restrains impulsive behavior and brings feelings of guilt if he fails to meet its demands.

Feelings of guilt bring as much discomfort as his parents' expression of disapproval. In writing of the influence of the conscience or super-ego on the child's feelings and behavior, Freud[9] says:

> When the child does not obey it, he begins to "feel" his dissatisfaction as "inner dissatisfaction," and the sense of satisfaction when he acts in accordance with the will of this superego as "inner satisfaction." Thus the old relationship between the child and the parents continues within the child, and the severity or mildness with which the parents have treated the child is reflected in the attitude of the superego to the ego.*

During preschool years the child observes his parents' expectations, incorporates them into himself and formulates a self-ideal to remain secure in his parents' love. From experiences with his parents, the child discovers those traits of character they consider "good" or right to have and those they consider "bad" or wrong to have. From these experiences he formulates a picture of what he must be to be loved by his parents and to remain free from discomfort. The incorporated standards form the basis of his ideals and influence the development of his character.

The child's ego-ideal is not self-made; it is the outgrowth of all his experiences with his parents. His parents' ideals become his ideals and throughout his lifetime he will strive to attain the goals he acquired in childhood. Experiences outside his home will modify his goals, but his desires will always be influenced by the ideals he acquired in childhood.

In the school-age period feelings of guilt supplant the fear the child formerly had of his parents. As the child sees his parents less omnipotent than he did formerly, he fears them less, but that is not the end of his anxiety. He now experiences what Freud[10] calls *super-ego anxiety*. It is this anxiety and the increasingly higher standards set by parents and teachers which compel the child to strengthen his defenses against his infantile impulses.

One of the mechanisms of defense the school-age and preadolescent youngster utilizes to handle his anxiety is the compulsive use of

---

* Reprinted from *Psychoanalysis for Teachers and Parents* by permission of the author and Emerson Books, Inc.

self-devised ways of doing things.[31] He concocts "magic ways" in an attempt to ward off things he does not wish to happen or as penance for the thoughts and wishes he feels are "sinful."[31]

In preschool years he also had thoughts and feelings that he considered bad, but now they make him feel guilty because his conscience is becoming stricter.[31] His "magic ways" or compulsive gestures have purpose; they keep him free from anxiety and protect him from what he feels to be dangerous. All school-age children use these gestures in one way or another. They are normal unless they are used excessively and become so obsessive that the child has difficulty in functioning comfortably without them.[31]

Observation of school-age and preadolescent youngsters provides examples of their compulsive rituals. The most common of all compulsive acts can be observed by watching school-age children walking down the street. When they come to a crack, they skip over it. If you ask them why they do it, they will usually give the following answer: "Step on a crack and you will break your mother's back." They do not know why they do it, but their behavior has purpose or they would not feel compelled to exercise their rituals. They hold their breath as they ride by a cemetery, cross their fingers when they tell a fib, knock on wood to prevent undesirable things happening and mumble magic words when they get themselves into a predicament. Joan, aged 10 years, had many little compulsive mannerisms. The following situation exemplifies the type of thing she would do to relieve herself of anxiety.

Joan loved playing games with her nurse but she had an insatiable need to win every game she played with her. She would get panicky whenever her nurse got ahead of her to the slightest degree. Losing made her angry, but her conscience would not let her give vent to her feelings. Besides, her aggressive, competitive feelings were frightening. To protect herself from discomfort, she devised a system she hoped would keep her nurse from winning. If she believed the "magic" would work, her anxiety was relieved, and she could attend to the business of playing to win.

Every time Joan's nurse played with her, she noticed that she began the game by putting down scores, and the highest score was always under the nurse's name. To discover the meaning of this behavior the nurse said, "Joan, I haven't won those points yet. I wonder what makes you think I'll get them." Joan's response was revealing. It was, "I'm just putting them there to keep you from winning them."

GUIDANCE AND CARE PLANNED IN ACCORDANCE WITH THE CHILD'S CAPACITY FOR SELF-DIRECTION AND ITS EFFECT ON PERSONALITY DEVELOPMENT

The child needs his parents in this period of personality development equally as much as he needed them before. If parents are not aware of the new ways they can support their child's growth, both the child and his parents find this period a difficult one. His new interests take him away from his home, and his parents feel as if he needs them less than he did formerly. The school-age child can do more for himself and he resents the helping hand he formerly sought so frequently. It consoles many parents to learn that they are equally important to their child now as they were before. In this period he needs them in different ways than he did when he had little or no capacity within himself for self-care and self-direction.

As the child develops increased capacity for self-direction he needs guidance which encourages him to use the inner resources his parents helped him acquire in preschool years. Physical and mental growth and the guidance the child received from his parents brought changes within his personality. He is more independent and self-directing and often assumes an air which is interpreted as arrogance. In many ways he appears "all-knowing." He is proud of the new inner strength he feels within himself and he reflects it in his behavior. The 8- or 9-year-old who does not radiate feelings of inner security needs study, for a goodly degree of self-reliance should have been attained by that age. When he has acquired inner strength, he needs a new kind of guidance from the adults within his environment.

The school-age child needs nursing care which is based upon his physical and his psychological levels of development. Care which is needed by the child at the preschool level of psychosocial development is inappropriate for the school-age child unless he has regressed from illness or is immature because past experiences have not provided what he needed to reach the stage of maturity characteristic at this level of development. Unless his physical condition places limitations upon his activity, he should do for himself all those things he did for himself at home. It is depreciating to bathe, dress and feed a school-age child who does not require it physically, and he wants and needs protection from becoming infantile.

The school-age child has learned to enjoy and is proud of the independence that comes from being able to take care of himself and he needs understanding care when illness threatens his newly acquired self-mastery. He needs a nurse who is sensitive to the anxiety which comes when his newly acquired independence is threatened by her solicitude and care. If a child is acutely ill and must be bathed, dressed and fed, he will need a nurse who has the ingenuity necessary to help him accept it without giving in to infantilism or being threatened by his temporary loss of power.

There are many children who feel threatened by illness and dependent care even though they are acutely ill and need solicitude and care. The child who feels threatened by his illness and inactivity often manifests his anxiety by being demanding, directing and deaf to the doctor's instructions for limited activity. Instead of staying in bed, he gets up every time the nurse goes out of the room. Admonitions to stay in bed and rest prove ineffectual. Instead of bringing compliance, admonitions often intensify his drive for activity. It often seems as though he is driven to prove continually that he has power within himself and is capable of doing those things he had formerly been able to do. Many times the nature of his illness makes him fearful of losing his power, and this is threatening to many insecure children, and especially to the activity-loving school-age boy.

When a child shows evidence of being threatened by his illness, his inactivity and the dependent care his physical condition requires, the nurse's first task is to try to discover the nature of the child's fears and to correct the misconceptions which are bringing him anxiety. She will need to make friends with the child, increase his confidence in her, listen and watch in an attempt to discover the reason why he is driven to do those things which are injurious to his physical health.

There are other ways the nurse can help the child who is threatened by his illness and dependent care. The child who is scared needs help which will build up his confidence and bring reassurance to him. The nurse can permit him to help plan his schedule of care and to direct those parts he is capable of directing. She can encourage him to express his opinions concerning the program and events of the day. She can visit with him, letting him talk about his interests, the stories he has heard and the activities he formerly enjoyed. If the doctor permits, he should have periods of companionship with another child of his choosing. Later in this chapter the child's interest in making rules to govern himself will be discussed. If the threatened child's interest in rules is utilized, the nurse can help him formulate some of his own to use when he feels compelled to give in to his need for activity. As soon as he is physically able, he will welcome opportunities to give himself whatever bits of care he is able to do and to utilize his powers in creative activities which will bring him a feeling of power, increased self-esteem and confidence in his own ability. Together the child and the nurse can anticipate the things he will be able to do when he is well. This will help him to feel that regaining his power is a *reality* to which he can look forward. The more he understands his illness and the reality reasons why his activity is limited, the more rationally he will be able to view his fears.

In some instances the child's fears may be deeply buried within his unconscious and he will require psychiatric therapy to become aware of his fears and to obtain mastery over them. When the nursing care cited above does not bring relief from anxiety, the nurse's responsibility entails giving a detailed report of her observation and care to the doctor.

The well-adjusted convalescent school-age child needs less supportive care than does the younger child because he has controls within himself and does not need the direction that he did formerly. He can make more decisions and take responsibility, and he enjoys doing so. He responds with pleasure when his nurse or his parent expects him to be reliable in meeting the routine requirements of life in the ward or the home. The preschool child needed help to know what was expected of him; the school-age child knows what is expected of him at home and in school. He learns quickly what is expected of him in the hospital ward. He searches to find the limits of his new environment because he wants to please, to feel safe and to be self-directing.

The school-age child feels respected when his intelligence and his ability to assume responsibility are recognized. The school-age child resents the nurse who says, "Johnny, it is time for rest hour now." He knows very well it is time for rest hour unless he has just come into the hospital and has had no time to observe the routine which exists there. He will comply infinitely more readily if his nurse assumes that he knows and respects his intelligence and spirit of co-operation in such matters. He may sputter and grumble about the hospital regulation, but shortly his feelings will become dissipated and he will be ready to join the other children for rest hour.

EFFECT OF BROADENED SOCIAL EXPERIENCES ON PERSONALITY GROWTH

When the child becomes secure in the knowledge that he is successful in pleasing his parents, his teachers and his self-ideal, he will have energy available to tackle his next task—that of developing social relationships with his peers. As the child's social world expands *he needs group experiences (1) to develop his capacities for social relationships with peers, (2) to learn to adjust to society's laws and regulations and (3) to develop skills, to master his fears and to gain release from tension.*

Group Experiences Provide Opportunities to Develop Social Relationships with Peers. The way the child relates to his peers is influenced by the way he solved his conflict with his parents and handled his feelings toward his siblings. To relate well to his schoolmates, he must have achieved a certain degree of independence from his parents and have accepted his place within his family. Many times sibling rivalry has not been resolved successfully in the preceding periods of the child's life. When a child has not successfully mastered his rivalrous feelings (and this is more often the rule than the exception), he will transfer to his peers those feelings and attitudes he has toward his siblings.[9]

In this period of development the child continues to need help in handling his rivalry with his peers. Rivalry is apparent in every group of school-age children, be it school, hospital, club, church or playground. In group situations where the teacher, the nurse or the leader has insight and is a skillful person, children can be assisted in learning to handle their competitive feelings more constructively.

In this period when the child goes off to school and is separated from his parents for long periods each day, he needs to get gratification from the world of people outside his home—in the school, the church, the playground and the club. Unless he finds success and gratification in the outer world, he cannot venture away from his parents, their substitutes—the teacher and his home.

The school-age child continues to need and to love his parents, but he also needs and wants success and happiness in his relationships outside his home. The child feels a need to gain approval, acceptance and a feeling of belonging from those within his group. He knows instinctively that he can never gain the freedom of independence unless he finds satisfactions with those outside his family.[31]

The child needs both freedom to go forth and the assurance that he will obtain support and gratification when he finds life in his school world more difficult than he can endure. Life at school and in his community brings frustrations, disappointments and problems that he cannot surmount alone. When he meets disappointments and obtains the dependent gratification and support he needs, he will again be able to go forth and have the opportunities he needs to become related to those in his broadened social world.

A child's need for freedom to go forth and to develop relationships with his peers becomes thwarted when parents and teachers attempt to meet their own needs through children's scholastic achievement. Many parents and teachers feel that the acquisition of knowledge and the ability to use it are the only tasks of importance. They feel this way because of their own need to have their children or pupils excel. In their desire to meet their own needs, they hold up standards which inhibit children's opportunities for growth. When this occurs the children become anxious and tense and have little energy available to develop social skills and relationships with children. If a child's security depends upon high scholastic achievement, he may meet his parents' or his teacher's demands at the expense of making sacrifices which jeopardize his potentialities for personality growth.

Group Experiences Provide Opportunities to Learn to Adjust to Society's Laws and Regulations. The school-age child needs an environment which is a laboratory for learning and growing socially and emotionally as well as mentally. The school, the hospital and the convalescent home need to be places where children's personalities can develop. Hospitals and convalescent homes must do more than heal and repair diseased or handicapped bodies. This is a necessity for it is in this period that children need to develop the capacities which are required to adapt to the realities of the culture in which they live.

The school-age period is the time for the child to learn to adjust to more of our civilized way of life. It is then that he becomes keenly interested in group activity and is ready to learn those things it is necessary for him to know if he is to be an accepted member of his group. Physical growth slows down in this period,[31] and the child has energy available to learn those things which will help him to surmount the tasks of adolescence and to learn to live comfortably in our society.

To reach emotional maturity and live at peace in our culture, the child needs to gain control over his sexual and aggressive drives. When physical maturity is reached, the energy of the child's drives will be increased and he must be ready to handle them in ways which bring satisfaction to him and which meet the standards of the culture in which he lives. He also needs to learn the laws of his society and to develop the desire and the capacity to abide by them.[31] An uncontrolled individual cannot survive with comfort. He brings destruction to himself as well as to others in his society.

Acquiring the ability to adapt oneself to co-operative living and the capacity to assume responsibility as a member of society is a long and difficult process; it begins in infancy and continues throughout the period of growth. First the child must learn the pleasure of give-and-take relationships in his home. Then he must learn to assume increasingly more responsibility for his own behavior in play outside his home. Eventually he must acquire the capacity to found a home, to function with others to make their community a healthy place for its families and to learn to participate in national and international affairs. The basis for acquiring these capacities is in childhood. In this period of development the child is ready to learn and to profit from experiences which provide the opportunities he needs for growth. In writing of the meaning of this period in the personality growth of the child, Spock[31] says:

It seems as though the child's inborn nature, which is the accumulation of the evolutionary experience of the species, says to him when he is about 6 years old: "Whoa! You cannot be trusted with a full-grown body, with full-grown sexual and aggressive instincts in this close community life which man now leads, until you have spent years learning in advance how to control those instincts for social and idealistic purposes, until you have felt the importance of getting along with, becoming close to people outside your family, conforming socially to their standards, co-operating with them in the service of the community, learning eagerly the skills by which they make a living. You must also develop a strong conscience so that you will carry around with you after you have left your parents' roof their moral teachings, and so that you will accept also the morals and laws of your tribe or nation. In order to make this adjustment to the outside world you must free yourself of your dependence on, your consuming interest in your parents and other adults—rebelling against them if necessary—and turn your interest toward more abstract and idealistic things."

To be a successful member of a group the school-age child must be able to contribute something and to forego some of his own desires for the benefit of others. During earlier years he experienced many conflicts between his own desires and those of his parents. The anxiety these conflicts brought motivated him to tolerate frustration to maintian his parents' and his teacher's love. In the school-age period he experiences more conflicts; he wants both personal gratification and acceptance from his group. The anxiety that arises from conflict again becomes useful. It helps him to forego pleasure for the benefits arising from socialization.

Acquiring the control necessary to forego pleasure for the benefit of the group requires more than physical maturation; it requires ample opportunities for *learning* and *practicing* the social skills essential for getting along with others. First the child needs to discover that group activity provides pleasure and personal advantage. If he has learned this in preschool years, he will be ready to learn that group activity requires giving as well as taking. Each time the child discovers that pleasure comes from improved relationships within his group, his ego becomes strengthened and he has more power within himself to withstand greater degrees of frustration.

In the school-age period the child needs group experience to help him grow out of the egocentric stage of personality development and to find satisfaction in considering the wishes and the needs of others. In preschool years the child's social experiences broadened. He adapted himself to a small group of children but his interests were primarily selfish. He had not matured sufficiently to recognize the rights, the feelings and the needs of others. The child needs group experiences to learn to respect the rights of its members. In this phase of development he respects their rights because he wants and expects other members to respect his rights in the future as he has respected theirs now; it is not to gain approval and the love of his mother or teacher as it was in preschool years.[27]

To grow emotionally and socially the school-age child needs to learn the significance of fair play and of rules, and to learn to adapt himself to them. Rules interest children in this phase of development. If there are none, they make them, and each child begins to see the reason why he and the others in his group must obey them. Because he must work hard to obey them, he expects others in his group to do likewise. "What is fair for one is fair for all," becomes the motto of the school-age child.

Piaget[28] studied children's play with marbles as a means of determining their behavior in games. Through observation of children, he found that they played differently at each level of development. As he observed preschool children's play with marbles, he discovered that they experimented with marbles as they experiment with any other object. They rolled them, put them into containers, shook and dropped them. Next, they used them in imitative play. They observed other children using marbles and imitated the way they used them. They did not enter into co-operative play; they merely manipulated the marbles exactly as the others did. Piaget said each child felt that he was winning just because he was playing. The situation which follows exemplifies this characteristic.

Larry and Joe, both 4 years of age, were playing with a magnetic dart set in the hospital playroom. Larry threw the darts at a metal board that contained circles of different colors. Then he told Joe to do the same thing. When Joe threw his dart and it landed in a circle, he clapped his hands and shouted, "I winned. I winned. Hooray! Hooray!" Then he turned to Larry and asked, "Why don't you clap? You winned, too."

Earlier that day Larry and Joe had observed school-age children playing the same game. They had heard them exclaiming over winning, and Joe got the idea that winning and playing were synonymous.

Piaget observed changes in behavior after the seventh year of life. At 7 or 8 years of age the children saw each other as partners and were intent on each other's actions and in playing according to a common set of rules. They had learned that there could only be one winner of a game, and it was expected that he should receive recognition from the others who were playing. Piaget found that this stage of game playing lasts until about the tenth year of life. After that age, Piaget found children developing increased interest in rules.

About the tenth year of life children begin to show a need for organization in their play. They form clubs and compete with each other to obtain offices in them. They vote on passwords, secrets, rules and meeting places. They keep minutes of their meetings, pay dues and levy fines on those members who break the rules. This kind of play is not purposeless activity; it is preparation for social living in a society where respect for organization and adherence to law and order is necessary for survival. Piaget[28] referred to a description of children's play which exemplified children's interest in game rules and the way they organize themselves in their activities. He says:

We have described elsewhere the extraordinary behavior of eight boys of 10 to 11 who, in order to throw snow-balls at each other, began by wasting a good quarter-of-an-hour in electing a president, fixing the rules of voting, then in dividing themselves into two camps, in deciding upon the distances of the shots, and finally in foreseeing what would be the sanctions to be applied in cases of infringement of these laws.

Piaget[28] also observed children's play to determine their attitudes toward rules and found that they, too, changed as the children grew older and more experienced in group activities. When children first learn about game rules in their sixth or seventh year, he found that they regarded them as sacred and unchangeable and made by their fathers, the town council or God himself. They obeyed them because they felt that they would be "bad" if they did not. This is the age when children are beginning to show compulsive traits. They are compelled to do things according to the letter of the law because it helps them to gain mastery of their impulses. Later their consciences will become less rigid, and increased flexibility will become a part of their personality make-up.

At around 9 years of age Piaget found children changing their attitudes toward rules. At this age level they had ceased to believe that rules were made by adults in authority and had to be obeyed. Instead they had become aware that rules were necessary to prevent quarreling and to make the game more enjoyable for all. They realized that it was within their power to change the rules if they so desired. However, by this period they had learned to consider the needs of each other and to feel that it was imperative for each member to understand and to accept the newly formulated rules.

Nine- to 11-year-old children use their aggressive energy in play and feel the competitive spirit of the game. Their interests are changing; they want to win and they want the game to test their capacities in competition with others. As they master the game with one set of rules, they formulate elaborate new ones or change the old ones to make the game more interesting and more difficult to win.

Changing rules brings legislative activity into the group experience and shows children's developing capacity to govern themselves. In preschool years the adult had to set the limits of the children's environment. After 9 years of age, children can do a great deal in setting limits for themselves. They have learned through experience that greater freedom of expression and more fun can be had when there are limits and rules which everyone must obey. The following situation illustrates children's awareness of their need for rules and the way they function to meet it.

Sarah, Sally, Joan and Ann demonstrated their ability to govern themselves. They were 9- and 10-year-old children who occupied a four-bed unit in a pediatric ward. They found difficulties in rooming together and decided that rules were necessary to live happily together. They spent hours deciding upon them, and when they were finished they proudly showed them to the head nurse in the ward. When they were completed they hung them on the wall and began legislation to determine the penalties for breaking the "laws" of their temporary home. Making rules and levying penalties was a method of helping themselves keep controlled. Their selection of rules reflects their inner standards and the social niceties they considered important to achieve. The following are the rules they formulated for themselves:

1. To say please and thank you.
2. To say good morning and evening.
3. To share our things.
4. To not holler at each other.
5. To clean up after we get done.
6. To keep our room clean.
7. Do as the doctors and nurses say.
8. Say our prayers.
9. Do not take money from anyone you don't know.
10. Do not say naughty things.
11. Say Mr. and Mrs., Miss, etc.
12. To stay in bed when the nurse tells us to.

The child's personality grows through experiences like the one cited above. Legislative activity provides invaluable lessons in democratic living. Through it the child's conscience becomes modified by peer interaction. If a child does not have this kind of group experiences, he will lack the opportunities he needs to become a group participant. Instead of learning to be a part of a group, he will remain a blindly obedient follower who accepts rules and abides by them because his parents told him to do so. He will never learn that rules can be changed through co-operative effort, or that rules are made to bring benefits to all who participate in the game or in living together. Later in life he will be either his employer's blindly obedient slave or a tyrannizing autocrat who cannot permit his associates to have the freedom of expression he once desired.

There are many adults in our society today who never question rules or consider the possibility that there are many which need to be changed or made more flexible. Year in and year out they continue to do the same things in exactly the same way. New knowledge, changes in our society—these do not alter their thinking or feeling. When suggestions for changes are made to them, they are received with ears that cannot hear and emotions that cannot change because to such people change is a violation of tradition which has continued to assume "sacred" significance for them. They not only frustrate themselves and retard their own development but also stifle other individuals who want to experiment to find better solutions to their problems.

Group Experiences Provide Opportunities to Develop Skills, to Master Fears and to Gain Release from Tension. As the child grows socially and emotionally, he should become progressively more capable of adjusting himself to an increasingly larger group of associates. In first grade the child is an individualist, and his group of associates is small. At first children group themselves together and form cliques. They move freely from one group to another when their desires are not satisfied. However, as they grow older the cliques become larger and develop into clubs and gangs. Later when stability and organization begin to be evidenced, shifting from group to group becomes nonacceptable. If a child leaves a group because he wants his own way and he cannot get it, he is either ashamed, ridiculed or rejected.

Until 7 or 8 years of age boys and girls play happily together and accept those of the opposite sex quite amicably. However, after that age period changes in cliques and groups become apparent. Between 8 and 12 years of age children segregate themselves with members of their own sex. At this stage of development, children see little value in the opposite sex, and attempts to bring boys and girls together invariably end in failure. The years from 8 to 13 form the period referred to as the "gang" age. It is a period of marked social growth and a period for gaining increased acceptance of one's sexual role. Children in the "gang" age discover their sexual differences and strive to acquire the characteristics of their sex.

The above changes which take place in peer relationships have purpose and developmental significance. The child's intense love for his parent of the opposite sex has been thwarted and he turns his interests to those of his own sex. In relationships with children of his own sex, he dramatizes the unconscious feelings he has toward his parent of the same sex. In preschool years he experienced feelings of both love and hate toward his parent of the same sex. Because his feelings of hate were threatening to his peace of mind, he repressed them, but this did not eliminate them or end all the tension within him. In play with his peers, he drains off the energy of these feelings and wishes and relieves himself of some of the tension they create within him. This makes it possible for him to master his feelings more successfully and brings him comfort.

Fighting is common in this phase of development. One minute pals fight, ridicule and damn each other and swear they will never speak to their friend again. The next minute they become "blood brothers" and swear they will be friends forevermore. Boys' fighting is largely physical, but girls' quarreling, while more subtle, is equally as effective. Girls fight with their tongues, using sarcasm, ridicule and shaming. Usually they do not hurt each other physically, but the feelings which stimulate the tonguelashings are equally hostile and hurt as much as the fist fights and wrestling in which boys indulge.

The school-age child needs active outdoor play to work off hostility and aggression, of which children have plenty that needs outlet. They have it within them as a result of frustrating past experiences; they also have it as an outcome of experiences which happen during the course of each day. No matter how well they are guided by parents and teachers, they meet frustrations every hour of the day.

The child needs wide open spaces where he can run, jump, climb and "screech at the top of his lungs," to get release from tension. In school the child must keep his aggression under control, but as soon as the bell rings the need for control is gone and aggression comes forth like steam from a pressure cooker when the gauge is released. One only needs to observe just once at the door of a grade school at closing time to see this phenomenon at work. Before the bell rings the children are mobilized for action, and action comes the minute the teacher gives her signal to go. Like motors, they spring into action the second the current is turned on. They bolt through the door as if release were an utter necessity. And it is, or they would not respond as they do. If they do not have opportunities for release and escape from the stresses and the presures of the day, they will be unready to meet the demands of the day which is to come.

In this period of development the child needs to indulge in dramatic play to master his fears and to gain release of tension. Boys play war, cowboys, cops and robbers and spacemen with an enthusiasm that knows no bounds. They do it because they need to feel powerful and because there are feelings within them which require it. To suppress such play is hazardous, for without it the child cannot relieve himself of tension or gain control of his aggressive feelings and handle them constructively. The more the child's aggressive feelings can come out in active, constructive play, the greater is the possibility that he will gain the power he needs to control them. The following situation illustrates the way Jud used play in an attempt to gain mastery of his feelings.

Jud, aged 6, had many reasons to feel angry and aggressive but the feelings were frightening and he was trying desperately hard to get them under control. One day he was playing intently with soldiers, Indians, cowboys, airplanes and blocks. He constructed a building of blocks and placed the soldiers around it in strategic spots. He flew airplanes into the air, shot at them but always made sure they landed right side up and undemolished. He took two Indian figures and said, "These are *bad* men." Then he put the soldiers together and called them *good* men. He then excitedly said to the adult observing his play, "There are only two bad men and lots of good men. There *are* fewer bad men, aren't there?" "I wonder what you think, Jud?" the adult commented to his question. "I think there *are* only two bad men and lots and lots of good men. I am sure that's right," he answered. Jud pulled a pile of blocks over to him and said, "I've got to have blocks. I've got to block the bad men in so they can't get out."

Jud used blocks and built a wall imprisoning what he called the bad men within it. "Now those bad men can't get out, can they?" he asked. Without waiting for the adult's response he said, "If they do get out, these good men won't let them by. There are so many good ones, they won't let the bad ones out. See all the good ones! The bad ones haven't a chance. They will never let the bad men get by!"

Jud's play was more than idle diversion. A room full of toys and ample raw materials to use in less active kind of play were available, but at the moment he needed activity that would help him master the conflict and the ambivalent feelings within him. He had aggressive feelings within him, but they were frightening and his conscience told him that they were "bad." He also had positive feelings of love which were bigger and stronger and capable of keeping his "bad" feelings under control. In play he dramatized his conflict between his id and his conscience. In so doing he helped himself toward mastery of the drive which was threatening to express itself overtly.

In the *Encyclopaedia Britannica* film, "Fun on the Playground," a group of school-age children are playing Indians. They use sticks and shoot at the children who are impersonating wild buffalos, and then dance around the captured animals, beat on imaginary tomtoms and shout in wild exultation. What was the meaning of this play to the children? Why does this kind of play give children feelings of accomplishment and release from tension? Could it be that the imaginary wild buffalos symbolized their infantile aggressive feelings, and that through play they mastered their fear of them and released tension through the dance and the exuberant shouts that accompanied it? The play portrayed in the film was not unusual play; it was the kind one observes on playgrounds, in vacant lots, in backyards and in alleys. In active play, school-age children invariably have an enemy whom they are out to kill, capture or master. During the offensive they are intent and serious, but there is always a happy ending which invariably brings wild shouts and relaxation. They conquer the enemy, and through it acquire a feeling of power and increased mastery of themselves.

Reading comic books and listening to or watching murder and wild west stories, boxing matches or competitive sports on the radio or television serves a purpose which is similar to the play described above. They give some children vicarious outlets for their aggressive feelings and release of tension but they are not a substitute for what the child gains through active dramatic play, participation in competitive sports and creative activities. Children who have ample opportunities for exciting, adventuresome and creative activities with their pals have less need to listen to radio and television programs and to read comic books than do children who must lead restricted lives.[8]

In this period of development children need opportunities to develop physical skills. They need their parents' help in learning to ride bicycles, to skate and to play tennis, golf, hockey and baseball. They are desirous of perfecting their skills, acquiring new ones and putting them into opposition with others. They know that they are tasks of the school-age period. Physical skills are highly valued by children, and to obtain prestige and status in their group children need to have them. Especially is this true for boys. Girls can obtain status with a moderate degree of physical skill but boys cannot. The group punishes the boy who is un-co-ordinated, unskilled and incapable of competing favorably with others. Often the group labels him a "sissy," and without physical skills he is apt to feel inferior and weak.

Many boys do not channelize their aggression in the kind of active play described above because they feel it is unacceptable to their parents or they do not have the physical energy or the need to express themselves in that way or they have discovered other outlets which are more satisfying. Those boys who never participate in the above kind of play because they have discovered that active aggressive play is unacceptable to one or both parents may hide their feelings of inadequacy and obtain outlet for their aggression in excessive interest in study, unusual scholastic competition or by denying their wish to excel in physical activities. Outwardly they may seem to be uninterested in sports. However, psychological treatment of these boys usually uncovers their repressed longings to compete favorably with others. If they cannot compete with others in the realm of sports for physical or psychological reasons, they often imagine they are excelling, and to alleviate their feelings of inferiority they often concoct fantasies of being more powerful and mighty than any of their group.

There are other boys who never participate in the above kind of play because they have less need for such strenuous activities and find greater release and pleasure in other types of play. Sometimes they do not possess the physical strength or have a need to be the school's best fighter. These boys are often in conflict and troubled because they feel that they are not measuring up to parental or group standards or because they fail to get recognition from their group.

Our culture seems to give a stamp of approval to the athlete, the "strong" man, the "tough" guy. Many will say that this is not characteristic of American culture, but if it is not true why does the school-age boy feel such a need to be a "toughie," and why is he in conflict when his nature neither fits him for strenuous activity nor creates a great desire within him to be an Indian brave or a prize fighter?

The boy who feels troubled and inadequate because he is not a "toughie" needs help to accept himself as he is. If his parents and teachers accept him as he is, recognize the talent he does possess and help him to develop it to such a degree that his group sees that it merits recognition and is valuable to them, he, too, will accept himself and have energy available for extravertive activities.

Cultural factors and inner needs play a part in determining the school-age girl's play. On the whole girls' play is less active. They are expected to be ladylike, while most boys are given permission to be active, "wild little cowboys and Indians." Most girls enjoy sports, active games and outdoor activities but they spend more time in craft activities and in doll play. They continue to play house but it becomes more elaborate and creative as new skills are acquired.

Identification with the parent and friends of the same sex is outstanding in this period. Girls become interested in learning to cook, sew and play school and boys become motivated to acquire skills which are typically masculine.

Hospitalized convalescent school-age children need active play for the same reasons that normal children do. When children recuperate from illness, energy is released which must find an outlet. Opportunities of the kind suggested in the foregoing pages are not usually possible for children in a hospital ward. Many of the children are not physically capable of such activity because of illness or a physically handicapped body or because their normally active bodies are immobilized with casts, splints or traction apparatus. However, there are other children in the ward who are physically capable of activity.

When opportunities for release of aggression and tension are not provided for children in the hospital during the day hours, they find ways to meet their needs during the evening. During the daytime children keep themselves under control. There are doctors and nurses in the wards and they provide the controls the children need to keep themselves in check. After a day of frustrations many hospitalized school-age children are full of hostility and aggression to the point of exploding, and more often than not, they do.

Frustrated convalescent school-age children cannot bolt through the hospital door when 8 P.M. comes but they can find ways to meet their needs to obtain release from tension. It is usually the lone evening nurse who is confronted with children who cannot control their aggressive feelings any longer. They have pillow fights, wrestling matches and arguments and shoot paper wads in all directions. They release their feelings in any way they can devise, and their repertoire of tricks and activities often seems inexhaustible. Scolding increases the children's aggressive feelings, and rigid control forces them to dam up feelings which should be released in constructive activities.

Prevention is the only constructive method of handling the above problem. If the children are given opportunity to use their natural and normal aggression in constructive activities during the day, explosions will occur less frequently during the evening hours. If there is a playroom away from the ward, or an outdoor porch, it can be used to give children the activity they can physically tolerate and need. Children profit most from periods of self-directed group activity because they get the greatest release of tension and gratification when they can do the things that they feel a need to do. They will, of course, require supervision and leadership to plan, organize and carry out their play because they have not learned to handle all their problems independently.

When there is no space for active play, the convalescent child will need help in finding activities which will absorb his interest and meet his needs. School-age children delight in making things. They have little interest in manipulating materials as the preschool child has; they want to construct and to make things which are realistic and useful. They enjoy soap carving, sewing, jewelry making, plastic cord weaving, crêpe paper, papier-mâché, leather and pottery crafts. They like the small blocks they can use to construct garages, forts and houses, and will spend long periods constructing and painting airplanes, boats, space ships, trains and other vehicles.

Nurses who work with children and families need to know how to do handcrafts and to have the skill necessary to encourage children's interest in learning to do them. Unless the nurse enjoys creative actvities herself, she will probably have difficulty in stimulating children's interest in them. Mothers who have chronically ill or convalescent children at home often seek help from the visiting nurse to find ways of keeping their children constructively and happily occupied in bed. The nurse who is interested in crafts and has a knowledge of the things children enjoy doing will be able to give mothers suggestions which will help them solve their problems.

Hospitalized children vary in their capacity to do creative work. Many children will have ideas of their own that they would like to use in play periods. If they are provided with materials, they will do their own creating. The use of their own originality should, of course, be encouraged because children, like adults, get more feeling of accomplishment when their project has been entirely self-made. However, there will be other children who are impoverished from long periods of illness, discouragement and a dearth of the kind of experiences which normally stimulate children's creative imagination. There will be other children who have had their creativeness stifled because their parents and their teachers have held up standdards of perfection that they were unable to meet. There will be many children in hospital wards who will need a great deal of help in becoming motivated to try out their own abilities in doing crafts.

Discouraged children need nurses who are interested in helping them to find ways to express themselves and to develop feelings of confidence and courage. There are many discouraged children in hospital wards and convalescent homes. They are the ones who underestimate their own abilities because no one has helped them value themselves or develop their talents. Chronically ill and physically handicapped children are often discouraged and need help in developing faith in themselves. Feelings of pity do not help these children acquire faith in themselves; they need experiences which help them learn that they are capable of doing things of which they can be proud. If the adults in their environment have belief in their ability to do creative work, they will absorb their faith in them and begin to show signs which indicate that they have acquired increased feelings of self-esteem.

In helping the discouraged child develop increased self-esteem, the selection of the activity and the methods of helping him acquire courage to try out his own abilities are factors of great importance. The discouraged child rarely has any ideas of his own. He is too preoccupied with himself and has insufficient emotional freedom to utilize the creativeness which is existent in him. The nurse will need to select the project carefully, for if it is too difficult for him to master, his feelings of self-esteem will be lessened rather than increased. Many times samples of finished products will stimulate his interest in learning to create. If the nurse helps him to feel that she has confidence in his ability and is ready to help him learn to do the difficult parts, he will be encouraged to develop the project with his own color scheme or design variation. Often the completion of one object provides ideas for the development of a project of his own imagination. If the nurse encourages his suggestions and shows interest in his work, he will be motivated to try increasingly harder tasks and to develop his own originality. As he does he will obtain increased satisfaction and renewed confidence in his own abilities; he will have obtained increased ego strength, which is what the discouraged child needs as much as he needs bed rest, physiotherapy, school work or medicinal therapy. A case which showed the results of encouragement is the following:

Susan, aged 10, was a discouraged child. She had been in the hospital one month with rheumatic heart disease. She accepted invalidism without any healthy resistance and showed that she had little motivation to do things by herself. She was withdrawn, noncommunicative and uninterested in food or the activities of the ward. She spent hours of the day in fantasy. When she was asked what she would like to do she said, "Nothing." She listened to radio stories and read a comic occasionally but aside from this she did nothing which helped her feel she was competent and worthwhile.

The first day her nurse took her to the playroom, she made no comments indicating an interest in anything. After she was there half an hour, she wanted to go back to her room.

The next day her nurse showed her a clay ash tray. Susan held and scrutinized it and handed it back to the nurse saying, "I don't want to do anything." The nurse said, "Sometimes children don't want to do things because they are afraid that they cannot make anything they will like." Susan looked up at the nurse and said, "I couldn't make one like that. I'd rather go back to my room and listen to the radio." The nurse said, "I know you could make something out of clay. I'd love to show you how and I'll work along beside you to help you when you need it."

Susan did not object further, and the nurse worked with her until Susan had completed an ash tray similar to the sample the nurse had shown her. She was quiet during the project, but her tension lessened as she worked the clay into form. Her finished product merited praise. The nurse asked her what she thought about it and she said, "It's not very good. Other kids can make things which are better." The nurse helped her to see the good quality of her work. At that point Susan could not see anything good about herself or her work, so the nurse was careful not to overevaluate it. She knew that Susan would need much more personal interest before she had acquired the capacity to view herself as she really was.

In the next four weeks Susan's behavior changed. She not only became intensely interested in clay modeling and produced objects she began to see value in but also learned to make doll clothes, to paint, to do bead work and jewelry crafts and enjoyed the activity. During the first weeks, commendations were always received with responses similar to the following: "It's not very good. I didn't get the hem in this dress very well," or "It would have been better if I had used another color paint."

In the fourth week Susan was more relaxed and talked a great deal about her play activities. One day she made a clay head which was no better than those she had made previously. When the nurse commented on its attractiveness she said, "Gee, thanks! I kind of like it myself." Susan was beginning to absorb other people's feelings about herself.

In the fourth week Susan became less depressed, her appetite improved noticeably and she began to show interest in taking more care of herself. Instead of waiting for her nurse to comb her hair or to get the things out for her bath, she surprised her and had her care completely given by the time the nurse came into the ward in the morning. When the nurse said, "I knew you would want to do those things for yourself some day. Now I'll have more time to teach you new crafts," Susan smiled and said, "Let's try something new today."

Both preschool and school-age children enjoy collecting things. The collecting instinct reaches it height in this period of growth and continues through adolescence and sometimes even throughout a person's lifetime. It has been estimated that approximately 50 per cent of all children collect one thing or another during this period. They collect because possession gives them a sense of ownership and because the items have symbolic value to them personally. The objects that they collect have value for them but usually they are the only ones who appreciate them. They may collect sticks and stones, playing cards or marbles, or it may be insects and snakes which become the objects of their interest.

Children who are convalescing from acute illnesses or suffering from conditions which keep them bedridden enjoy collecting things in the hospital. Penicillin bottles, pill boxes, paper cups, greeting cards have often been collected by hospitalized children. Many school-age children enjoy collecting stamps and pictures of football and baseball stars, movie actors and actresses and television stars. When they have accumulated them, they like to put them into scrapbooks of their own making or trade them with their friends. Their collections are important to them and some children spend hours arranging and organizing them in their own special way. At intervals school-age children show a drive to systematize, to arrange and to put things in order.[31] They are beginning to feel a need to regulate their own lives to a greater extent, and they begin by organizing their own possessions.[31] Ted and Sam showed the above characteristics in their recreational activities.

When Ted and Sam were 12 years of age, they became interested in radios and the mechanism of Ted's television set. They went on jaunts through the alleys and discovered that radio shops disposed of their partially used tubes and electronic equipment. They began to collect tubes, and it developed into a hobby of great magnitude. Ted's father contributed a closet off his typing shop, and a year later these two boys had it fully equipped and magnificently organized and had developed an interest in electronics which was consuming much of their time and energy.

As Ted and Sam talked about their project, it was evident that it was serving a deep and important purpose for them. They were proud of their collection and fully informed about every tube in their possession. "If we had to buy these tubes new it would cost us $1,500," Ted said. Then Sam told how they had cataloged them, and added that monthly they made a complete listing of everything in their shop. "We're going to have a shop of our own some day. We have it all planned, and we are getting ready to set it up now," Ted said, with the confidence and the trust in his own ability and enthusiasm which is so characteristic of the well-adjusted 13-year-old boy.

They had sales books and together they practiced buying, selling and ordering. They already had a name for their store, "The Will Ful Radio and Tee Vee Service" and a rubber stamp that they used freely on every sales check and inventory sheet.

Children's interest in hobbies thrives with encouragement but wilts when adults attempt to force their interests on them or direct their projects in any way. If there is genuine interest and if the hobby meets their emotional needs, the child will have inner motivation to continue it. He will want people to be interested in it, but he will resent it if they direct it in any way. Ted's and Sam's interest was genuine. They appreciated their parents' interest in it and welcomed an opportunity to discuss it with their contemporaries and adult friends. But they needed no direction in developing their hobby. They were filled with ideas, and had plans as to how they were going to get the knowledge and the experience they needed to realize their dreams.

Children's interest in hobbies often leads to vocational choice. Already Ted had made plans for his education. He was going to a technical high school because he knew they taught what he wanted most to learn. "Then I am going to go two years to Illinois Institute of Technology and two years to Purdue. In that way I can get two points of view, and two theories of electronic engineering which will make me ready to open our shop," Ted said, with feelings which showed the depth of his interest in his hobby. Ted's and Sam's activities were more than a hobby—these boys had sublimated their aggressive and creative drives into a constructive activity which gave them pleasure, recognition and preparation for their masculine roles in society.

School-age children also enjoy puzzles and games like checkers, Sorry, Qubic, Monopoly, Winnie-the-Pooh, dominoes, flinch, Old Maid and the various games which can be played with standard packs of playing cards. Every ward needs a supply of puzzles and games because they are invaluable for getting groups of children together. They provide a constructive outlet for their competitive feelings and opportunities to develop their mental skills. Playing games with a newly admitted school-age child often helps to establish a positive nurse-child relationship. Through play the nurse and the child can become better acquainted, and the nurse can learn more about the child she is going to care for in the hospital. Later the nurse can help the child become acquainted with other children by inviting them to participate in the game. When he becomes acquainted with other children he will not need his nurse in the same ways that he needed her when he was becoming adjusted to life in the ward.

School-age children also need books available in the ward and the story periods to help them learn and get gratification and to give them opportunities to escape from the problems entailed in hospitalization. Some children prefer literature to comic books, and others will vary their reading if other books are made available to them. Story periods are usually welcomed by children at this level of development. Hospitalized children are cut off from the outside world and story hours can do much to give them periods of escape from what they must feel to be a humdrum and unexciting environment. Story periods can also help them forget their troubles temporarily and make it more possible for them to withstand physical pain and the frustrations that come to children when they spend long periods in bed.

At this level of development children begin to select the reading material which meets their individual needs. Those who are avid comic book readers need them or they would not select them. They may need to read them because their group expects them to be informed about the happenings of Superman or the Bat Man, or they may read them to master their fears or to satisfy some of their natural craving for excitement and adventure which is being denied to them at the time. Unless nurses and recreational therapists can provide substitute activities which fulfill a child's need for adventure, and provide opportunities to gain mastery of his fears and release of tension, absorption in comics, radio and television programs can be expected.

All school-age children go through a phase of intense interest in comic books, and it is understandable why they do. This is a period when children are struggling to get their aggressive drives under control. As stated previously, the comics give many children a comparatively constructive outlet for their aggressive feelings and uphold the standards they are attempting to incorporate within themselves. In most comic book stories, the "good" individual is saved; the villain is captured and "good triumphs over evil."[8] If school-age children's interest in comics is understood rather than criticized and if their parents provide them with good literature and encourage their interest in it through shared reading and visiting experiences, they will outgrow their need for comics naturally.

Most school-age children are ready for fairy tales, stories with longer and more complicated plots and stories of children who live in foreign lands. Most children in the first grade can distinguish fact from fancy, and it is the logical time to introduce the classic fairy tales. Their attention spans are longer and they enjoy stories which have an exciting plot. In this period children are interested in almost everything, although specialization in interest begins to be apparent by the end of this period. As their social imaginations grow and they begin to understand space and can appreciate the study of geography, they become interested in stories about children in other lands. The travel stories which emphasize the *likenesses* of all children, be they Oriental, European or South American, are preferable to those which dwell upon the differences in color, customs or religion. If children are going to develop wholesome attitudes toward those in foreign lands, they need to know that all people have the same needs and merit respect and understanding regardless of where they live, how they worship or what they look like.

Observation of the child's reactions to stories, radio and television programs provides clues which can increase the nurse's understanding of his needs. He will talk about them and disclose anxieties which they activate if he has an interested listener. Frank[8] quotes Blos who says that most children protect themselves by withdrawing from programs and movies which bring more excitement or fear than they can tolerate. When children cannot find their own level of tolerance, Blos says that parents must do it for them. In the hospital this responsibility is one which must be assumed by the nurse.

THE SCHOOL-AGE CHILD'S NEED FOR STUDY AS A BASIS FOR GUIDANCE

EFFECT OF EMOTIONAL UNPREPAREDNESS FOR SCHOOL AND ENVIRONMENTAL PRESSURES ON THE PHYSICAL AND THE MENTAL HEALTH OF THE SCHOOL-AGE CHILD

In every school and hospital ward there are some children who show evidence indicating that they are having difficulty in mastering their current life situations at home, in the hospital or in school. A review of the foregoing material should give the reader increased insight into the problems of the school-age child and the reasons why health problems often manifest themselves in this period of development.

When the child comes to the school-age period he faces new problems which are broader and more complex than he has ever faced before. To accomplish the tasks of the period he has to meet the demands of his parents, teacher and schoolmates. This is no easy task for a child even when he has been well prepared as a result of wholesome experiences with his parents and his siblings.

The child's teacher and parents expect him to be ready to adapt himself to the teacher's discipline and to learn from the curriculum she presents. To restrain impulses formerly expressed with abandon requires inner strength and the ability to handle considerable tension. The child who has been permitted to dissipate his feelings of anger and disappointment in words and active play comes to this period with a less punishing conscience and more tensional outlets at his disposal. However, many children come to this period unable to channelize their negative feelings in words and play because past experiences in their homes made it unsafe for them to do so. They may act them out in the classroom because they are less fearful of their teacher's response, or they may keep them under such rigid control that they have little energy to learn and too much tension to dissipate in ways that bring him no injury.

The child's classmates also make demands upon him which are difficult to meet. Previously the child's need for friends was cited. Acceptance by his group depends upon the personal assets he has to contribute to its members, his capacity to renounce many of his own wishes and the degree of freedom his parents permit in allowing him to become one of the "gang."

The child's drive to please his parents, his self-ideal and his teacher and to be successful in his relationships with his peers puts many pressures upon him which he must master if his personality is to grow. If in addition he is forced to handle pressures and tension because of conflict with his parents, teachers, nurses and peers, he will inevitably reflect his inner distress with symptoms of a physical, psychosomatic or emotional disorder.

Psychosomatic illnesses, nervousness, expressions of inner tension such as tics, ear pulling, thumbsucking, enuresis, stealing or nose picking are frequent in this period of development and those which follow. They reflect inner conflicts, repressions and anxiety which prevent many children from making a comfortable adjustment to the life situation they are in. There is other behavior which is symptomatic of emotional ill health and needs recognition by those who work with children in schools, hospitals, clubs and convalescent homes.

The unruly, acting-out aggressive child never goes unnoticed in either the classroom or the hospital ward. His attacks upon others which often seem to be without provocation disturb both adults and children. He may be cruel, destructive, dominating, inattentive and unable to apply himself to any task or group activity. He is an annoyance to the teacher or the head nurse and to his group as well. He frustrates the teacher's or the head nurse's goals and increases the tension within her. Because of her own frustration, she is often blind to the fact that the child is also annoying and destructive to himself and is being deprived of the positive pleasures which come from accomplishment and satisfying relationships with others. The gratification he gets from his impulsivity is minimal in comparison with what he would get if his relationships at home and school were constructive and satisfying. The unruly child is a child with problems which are as injurious to himself as to others. He acts the way he does because he has not had the emotional security and guidance that he needed to learn to act in ways which are socially acceptable and satisfying to himself. To bring changes in his behavior, he needs study to determine the factors which are producing his asocial, uncontrolled behavior and individualized guidance which satisfies his fundamental basic human needs.

However, the acting-out aggressive child is not the only one who requires study and special guidance suited to his particular needs; the quiet, withdrawn, asocial child is also in need of help. Because he presents no problems to the adults in his environment, he often goes unnoticed. But he, too, is an emotionally sick child and one who is uncomfortable, lonely and afraid. He shows little initiative, get discouraged easily and rarely questions or makes comments to anyone. He looks preoccupied and scared and cannot seem to enter into relationships with anyone. He is not impulsive and without inner controls; he is repressed, over-controlled and utilizing his energy in defenses which bring injury to himself rather than to others. His symptoms of emotional distress go unrecognized because he does not make any complaints and protects himself from conflicts with others by isolating himself from them. Often he lives in a world of fantasy because reality has brought pain instead of pleasure.

The school-age child who is not progressing in his relationships with other children needs help. If he reaches preadolescence unable to become a part of a group, he will be greatly handicapped. There are school-age children and preadolescents in schools, clubs, Sunday schools and hospital wards who cling to adults and never enter into group activities. These children are retarded emotionally and unready for the group experiences necessary for personality growth. Something in their life experiences has made them feel unlovable and has prevented them from gaining the parental security and the freedom they needed to become associated with a group of peers.

Today many teachers and club counsellors recognize the importance of finding what Moreno[24] calls the "isolate." Moreno[24] devised a sociometric technic to discover the associates with whom a child wished to live, work and go to school. He used his sociometric device in an institution for delinquent children which utilized the cottage system of organization.

In recent years Moreno's device has been used in schools to discover those children who need help in becoming increasingly more comfortable and accepted by those within their group. Each child in the schoolroom is instructed to name the three individuals he prefers or considers to be the most popular in his group or to designate those individuals he would choose to work with on a special project. After the children have indicated their choices, the results are diagramed on a chart. By this method the "isolates," or children who are not selected by anyone or who make no choices, are discovered. On the plotted sociogram what Moreno calls "islands" are also identified. "Islands" is the term used to designate pairs or small groups of children who do not become an integral part of the larger group formation.

When the teacher or club counsellor discovers the "isolates" and those children who make up an "island" through a sociometric technic like the one designed by Moreno or through a personal observational study of his group's interrelationships, he can plan ways to help them further their social adjustment with others. Some "isolates" may need the experience of a dependent relationship with an adult before they are able to feel safe enough to participate in group activities.[17] Others respond with less intensive individualized guidance which provides the support the youngsters need to develop their potentialities so they can obtain recognition from their group.

To help the child become accepted by his group the teacher finds his interests and special abilities and encourages him to want to do those things he is capable of doing. The teacher's acceptance of the "isolate" helps the group to perceive his special qualities and to recognize that he, too, has something of value to contribute to them. The teacher's interest in him and his problems often gives him the security he needs to lessen his dependence upon adults and to increase his interest in finding ways to become a part of the group. A case is presented to illustrate the way a child can be helped to find his place in a group of hospitalized children.

Joan, aged 10 years, was an "isolate" in the pediatric ward. She had experienced a degree of rejection because her mother was unable wholeheartedly to accept a child with a harelip. Joan was a pretty, blond haired, blue-eyed girl, but she could not appreciate the admirable qualities which she possessed.

Many years before, Joan's harelip had been repaired, but the cosmetic effect was not superior and Joan felt disfigured, unattractive and not likable. When she came into the ward, her nurse showed her the playroom, introduced her to the children and invited her to remain there and to participate in the group activities. But Joan did not wish to remain there. She had brought her radio with her into the hospital and she expressed a desire to return to her room so that she would not miss "her favorite story."

Joan was in the hospital a week before plastic surgery was performed on her lip. She stayed in her room listening to her radio and reading comic books. There she seemed to feel safe from ostracism and the questioning her mother said she had experienced many times before.

Joan's nurse observed her shyness and exaggerated interest in her radio and books. She also noticed that she was tense and suspected she was lonely, too. Each day she spent time with her trying to discover her interests and to find ways she could help her to be happier in the hospital. Together they discussed the comics and radio programs, and one day Joan told her nurse she was interested in painting. Together they planned a picture Joan could put on her room window with poster paints. Joan responded to the nurse's interest in her, became enthusiastic about the art project and began to produce an unusually attractive design upon her window.

It was not long before ambulatory children stopped by Joan's room; they were attracted by her talent. They entered into conversation, and Joan discovered she was accepted even though her face evidenced a deformity. Gradually friendships developed. The other children caught Joan's enthusiasm for painting and wanted to do some too. They invited her to the playroom and indicated they wanted her help in getting started. And Joan went. The change in the child was a revelation to see. After she had had surgery and was confined to her bed, the children called upon her and hopefully waited until she was well enough to rejoin them in their playroom activities.

OBSERVATION OF THE CHILD'S ADJUSTMENT AND INDIVIDUAL GUIDANCE IN SCHOOL

The school-age child needs periodical physical examinations and psychological study to evaluate his physical status and state of emotional health as a basis for care and guidance. Physical defects and disease need to be prevented for they, too, are prevalent in this age group. They affect not only the child's physical health but also his personality development as well. There is no question concerning the child's need for physical examinations and correction of physical defects. However, the physical examination is not the only answer to the child's health needs. In addition he needs study to evaluate his social and emotional adjustment at home, at school and in the hospital if he is a patient there. The earlier emotional problems are recognized and effort is expended to alleviate the pressures and the anxiety that produce them, the greater is the possibility of the child attaining the emotional freedom he needs to realize his potentialities.

Two decades ago the importance of the child's social and emotional needs were not considered to the degree that they are today. The White House Conference of 1950 centered its interest in the child's emotional, social and spiritual needs.[36] In the White House Conference of 1930 it was the child's physical development and needs that were studied. Today many teachers and administrators in primary, junior and senior high schools are attempting to discover those children who are having problems in adjustment and planning ways that they can supply the corrective experiences they require. Many of the better schools in our country have social workers or visiting teachers on their staff. Laabs[20] defines the func‹ tions of the school social worker in the following way:

1. To help the individual child find a personally satisfying and socially effective place in the school and in the community.

2. To consider and plan with the teacher and other school personnel how and to what extent the needs of the particular child can best be met in the classroom and in the entire school program.

3. To help parents understand the purpose and the program of the school; to assist the parents through their relationships with the child to facilitate his best use of the school; to promote understanding and acceptance between the parents and the school.

4. To procure the services of other social agencies in the community in assisting the child and his family; to promote understanding of the purpose and the program of the school among representatives of social agencies.

5. To stimulate the school and the community to recognize a responsibility to children for adequate facilities in education and other welfare services as needs become apparent from the school social worker's experience with individual children who are unable to make effective use of the school or whom the school is not able to help effectively because of lack of resources.

Other schools have consultants on their staff who function in an advisory capacity. The child with problems is studied, and all those who work with him meet with their consultant in an attempt to discover the factors that are preventing him from adjusting to the world in which he lives. The objective of the case conference is twofold. It not only brings understanding of the child and suggests guidance technics which can be used to help him become more comfortable and able to function in accordance with his innate potentialities but it also serves as an in-service training program for the entire school staff.

The school nurse is in a position to contribute to preventive mental health programs which have been organized in many of our schools. She can contribute observational material which will increase the consultant's and the school staff's understanding of the disturbed child's problems. She sees the child and his parents in a different setting and under different conditions than the teacher, the social worker or the school administrator.

The school nurse needs to be observant of the child's behavior and parental pressures and able to interpret his needs to his parents and teachers. It is as important for her to be as observant of the child's behavior in his relationship to her as she is of his body and the expression of his symptoms. When a school nurse makes home visits, she needs to be as sensitive to parental attitudes and feelings which may be putting undue pressures on the child as she is to the cleanliness of the home, the degree of the parents' interest in immunizations or their response to the suggestion that their child needs hospitalization or medical treatment to correct a defect. School nurses can interpret the school child's needs to parents. Unfulfilled social and emotional needs bring physical, psychosomatic and mental illness. The promotion of health is the nurse's job. She needs preparation to function in preventive mental health programs because the very nature of her work places her in a position which offers unique opportunities to be of real service to children and their parents.

OBSERVATION OF THE CHILD'S ADJUSTMENT AND INDIVIDUAL GUIDANCE IN THE HOSPITAL

When children are hospitalized for psychosomatic illnesses and emotional disturbances, the nurse needs to be able to observe their behavior and to have the capacity to record what she sees, feels and hears. This information is valuable to those who are treating the children medically and psychotherapeutically. It is also valuable to the nurses because they need knowledge of these children to provide them with the kind of nursing care they individually require.

If a child is having psychiatric therapy while he is a patient in the ward, his nurses will profit if they seek the guidance of his therapist. The therapist can help nurses understand his behavior and give them help in providing him with the kind of nursing care that he needs to regain his health.

Therapists are interested in knowing how their patients adapt themselves to their social environment. Details concerning his play activities in the ward, his choice of play materials, the use he makes of them and the verbalization that comes as he plays are important factors in gaining understanding of the child. Therapists are interested in learning about the child's social relationships with peers, doctors, nurses and other personnel in the ward. His responses to ward routines, treatments, school activities and the comings and goings of his parents also supply valuable information to those who are treating the patient medically and psychotherapeutically. They are also important to those who are providing him with nursing care.

Group conferences with physicians, therapists, social workers, recreational therapists, schoolteachers, aides and nurses would be invaluable for the child, bringing increased consistency in his care and giving all those working with him understanding of those factors which produced his illness. Every hospitalized child needs the concerted effort of every individual who is participating in his care. Everyone, including floor sweepers and kitchen maids, is influencing him, and each person needs to pool his efforts in providing the child with what he needs to become a healthier and a happier individual.

Group conferences would also be invaluable to the nurses caring for the child because understanding of children brings gratification which routinized care can never provide. Nurses who can observe behavior and describe what they see and feel will have material to contribute to the group conference, and they need to feel their responsibility in doing so. Nurses' observations provide additional material because they see the child functioning in a social setting, and often this opportunity is not available to the therapist or physician. Observing is the most vital part of nursing. Every nurse needs to see its value and to expend effort in increasing her skill in the utilization of this art, for it can bring satisfaction to her patients and to herself. Study of children will increase the nurse's interest in the child as a person. This is its objective, and unless it serves this purpose, its value is negligible. Peller[26] emphasizes this point when she says:

The ultimate goal of studying a child is to deepen our sympathies and to broaden our acceptance of children. Child study is a detour that leads through our heads, but it is meaningless unless it ends in our hearts.

The child with a physical disease or handicap in a pediatric or orthopedic ward also needs observation to evaluate his social and his emotional adjustment to the social environment he is in. Observation will give the nurse clues to know how to help him in his relationship to other children and in his adjustment to his illness and his hospitalization. During visiting hours the nurse can obtain valuable observational material which will serve to further her understanding of the child and the relationships he experiences with his parents.

Many hospitalized school-age children will show evidence of emotional immaturity for one or for several reasons. Arrest in development is often due to illness. During the acute stage of an illness, children regress emotionally, and many find gratification in dependency. Some children cling to this dependency either because they have experienced deprivation before and are attempting to get what they missed formerly or because their nurses do not recognize signs of emotional maturation and give them permission and the help that they need to socialize with children in the ward.

Giving verbal permission to be independent and to socialize with age mates is not enough for many children. In addition they need to know through experience that they will continue to have interest centered in them even though their friends and their activities with them become more important to them than their nurses. Many children also need their nurse's help to find their place within the group. However, one cannot or should not force a child into a group situation, because if he is not ready for it he will become frustrated, grow anxious and regress further. At first the child may be ready for only short periods of activity with another child, and while he has that experience he may require his nurse to be with him for emotional support. Gradually as he becomes more secure and finds acceptance from other children, he will spend increasingly more time with them if his security with his nurse remains unthreatened.

Some parents and nurses can only give to the immature, dependent infant or child. They keep their children and patients dependent upon them because they meet their own needs for affection, their need to have children dependent upon them or their need to dominate and to control. When a child recuperates from an illness and seeks to wean himself from dependence on his nurse, his nurse's needs may become frustrated. When this happens the child senses it more often than does the nurse, and unless he can continue to feel secure in his relationship to her he will be unable to obtain the experiences he desires and needs.

When a parent or nurse keeps a child dependent upon her, she increases the child's problems, for in addition to friends he needs adult acceptance and love. This incapacity is nothing of which the nurse needs to feel ashamed. It is infinitely more admirable to recognize and accept it and to limit one's work to the care of young children than to deny the existence of such feelings in oneself and to continue to meet one's own needs at the children's expense. If a nurse desires understanding of this problem within herself, and she wants to expand her capacities so that she can function more effectively with children in all age groups, she might consider seeking psychiatric guidance to gain increased understanding of herself and her relationships with others.

QUESTIONS TO GUIDE OBSERVATION

1. What developmental tasks does the child need to accomplish in the school-age period?

2. How does guidance during earlier periods of personality development affect the child's adjustment and growth in this period?

3. What kind of home environment helps the child to accomplish the tasks of this period? What parental attitudes prevent emo-

tional and social growth during the school-age period? What emotional problems produce learning difficulties?

4. What kind of school environment helps the child to accomplish the tasks of this period?

5. What character changes occur during this period of development?

6. How does nursing care of a child in this period differ from the care a preschool child requires?

7. Observe first-grade children in a public school. Describe what you saw and felt as you observed the situation. How did you feel on entering first grade? How do you imagine children feel? In the first grade you visited, were the demands made by the teacher excessive? How did the children respond to them? Did they get sufficient gratification to balance the demands which were made upon them? What gratification did the children receive?

8. Observe first grade in a progressive school. What differences did you observe between the public and the progressive school? What is progressive education? Which teacher met the children's needs most effectively? Why?

9. Is the intelligence quotient an index to accomplishment? Why? What are the factors which influence the degree of accomplishment the child attains in school?

10. What behavior would lead you to believe that a child was not making a good adjustment in first grade?

11. If you were a school nurse and a teacher reported to you that a certain child was not making a good adjustment in first grade, what would you do? What would you want to know about the child before you considered ways to help him?

12. What behavior in a school-age child would lead you to believe that he needed study and treatment?

13. Why do children need outlets for their aggressive feelings? From whence do aggressive feelings come?

14. Observe school-age children on a playground. Describe the behavior and the activities of the group. How did the children's behavior differ from the behavior you observed in preschool children? What do you think the children on the playground were trying to achieve? How did they do it?

15. Observe hospitalized school-age children's behavior from 8 to 10 P.M. some evening. Describe what you saw, heard and felt. How were the children's needs met during those hours? Were they satisfied and ready for sleep?

16. Observe the play of school-age children in the hospital playroom. How did it differ from the play you observed on the play-

ground? What accounted for the differences? Were the facilities for play adequate?

17. Why does a school-age child need to be a member of a group? Observe school-age children in the ward. Observe one child who does not enter into group activities. What does he do all day? What are his interests? What are possible reasons why he isolates himself? What could you do to help the child make friends in the ward?

18. Observe one of your patients with a psychosomatic illness. From a study of the child's history, what factors in his background might have influenced the development of his illness? Describe the behavior you have observed. How does he respond to his illness, to treatment, to hospitalization, to other children and to you? What have you observed in the mother-child, father-child relationships? Has the child said anything which gives you clues concerning his feelings toward his siblings and his parents?

REFERENCES

1. Abbate, G. M.: The "middle-aged" child steps out, Child Study 28:9, 1950-1951.
2. Alexson, Alfhild: The new child at school, Publ. Health Nursing 41:464, 1949.
3. Baumgartner, Leona: The new look in health for children of school-age, Publ. Health Nursing 40:444, 1948.
4. Beverly, Ira: The Psychology of Growth, New York, McGraw-Hill, 1947.
5. Breckenridge, M. E., and Vincent, E. L.: Child Development, ed. 2, Philadelphia, Saunders, 1947.
6. Buxbaum, Edith: A contribution to the psychoanalytic knowledge of the latency period: Workshop 1950, Am. J. Orthopsychiat. 21:182, 1951.
7. English, O. S., and Pearson, G. H.: Common Neurosis of Children, and Adults, New York, Norton, 1937.
8. Frank, Josette: Chills and thrills in radio, movies and comics, Child Study 26:6, 1948.
9. Freud, Anna: The latency period, lecture 3, p. 64, in Psychoanalysis for Teachers and Parents, New York, Emerson Books, 1947.
10. ————: Orientation of the process of defence according to the source of anxiety and danger, Chapter 5, p. 58, in The Ego and the Mechanisms of Defence, New York, International Universities Press, 1946.
11. Gesell, Arnold: The Child from Five to Ten, New York, Harpers, 1946.
12. Hartman, Heinz, Kris, Ernst, and Loewenstein, R. M.: Comments on the formation of the psychic structure, The Psychoanalytic Study of the Child, Vol. II, New York, International Universities Press, 1947.

13. Havinghurst, R. J.: Developmental Tasks and Education, New York, Longmans Green, 1948.
14. Hildreth, Gertrude: Child development and the school nurse, Publ. Health Nursing **39**:181, 1947.
15. Hubbard, Elizabeth: Your Child at School, New York, Day, 1942.
16. Hymes, J. L.: Teacher listen: the children speak, (pamphlet), New York, Committee on Mental Hygiene of the State Charities Aid Association, 1949.
17. Josselyn, Irene: The latency period, Chapter 8, p. 75, in Psychosocial Development of Children, New York, Family Service Association of America, 1948.
18. Kunst, Mary: Educational therapy, Home Life for Children **36**:7, 1949.
19. ———: Personal communication.
20. Laabs, Alma: When a school child is in trouble, The Child **12**:82, 1947.
21. Lemkau, Paul: The school period, Chapter 11, p. 173, in Mental Hygiene in Public Health, New York, McGraw-Hill, 1949.
22. Menninger, W. C.: Psychoanalytic psychiatry: its contribution to the understanding of behavior, Chapter 2, p. 50, in Psychiatry: Its Evolution and Present Status, Ithaca, New York, Cornell, 1948.
23. Miller, N. E., and Dollard, John: Social Learning and Imitation, New Haven, Yale, 1941.
24. Moreno, J. L.: Who shall survive? Washington, D. C., Nervous and Mental Disease Pub. Co., 1934.
25. Pearson, Gerald: A survey of learning difficulties in children, p. 322, in Psychoanalytic Study of the Child, Vol. 7, New York, Internat. Univ. Press, 1952.
26. Peller, L. E.: Significant symptoms in the behavior of young children: a check list for teachers, Mental Hygiene **30**:285, 1946.
27. ———: Character development in nursery school, Mental Hygiene **32**:177, 1948.
28. Piaget, Jean: The rules of the game, Chapter 1, p. 1, in The Moral Judgement of the Child, Glencoe, Ill., Free Press, 1948.
29. Powers, Grover: School health problems as seen in a pediatric clinic, Publ. Health Nursing **37**:7, 1945.
30. Ross, Helen: Psychology of pre-adolescent children in war time: III. Emotional forces in children as influenced by current events, Am. J. Orthopsychiat. **13**:502, 1943.
31. Spock, Benjamin: The middle-aged child, Penn. M. J. **50**:1045, 1947.
32. ———: Problems of the school child as encountered by the pediatrician, Am. J. Orthopsychiat. **11**:430, 1941.
33. Sylvester, Emmy, and Kunst, M. S.: Psychodynamic aspects of the reading problem, Am. J. Orthopsychiat. **13**:69, 1943.
34. Health needs of school-age children and recommendations for Implementation, School Life **28**:7, 1945.
35. Your child from 6-12, (pamphlet), Washington, Federal Security Administration, Children's Bureau, 1949.
36. Proceedings of the Midcentury White House Conference on Children and Youth, Raleigh, N. C., Health Publications Institute, 1951.

8

Development and Care During the Preadolescent Period (10 to 12 Years)

PSYCHOLOGICAL GROWTH AND RESULTING PERSONALITY CHANGES

GUIDANCE OF THE PREADOLESCENT

The preadolescent period of personality development is the two-year period preceding the onset of physical maturity. The beginning of the period will come earlier to some children than to others because there are wide variations in the rate at which children begin to mature sexually. Characteristics of preadolescent behavior extend into adolescence, and in some instances they may also continue throughout the individual's lifetime. Preadolescence will begin at a younger age in some girls than in boys for girls begin to mature sexually approximately two years earlier than do boys.

The preadolescent period of personality development is characterized by marked psychological change. Gesell[3] says that "growth is motion." In this period of development motion is a predominant characteristic. Since earliest infancy the urge to grow up and to become master of himself and his universe has been within the child. In this stage of development the urge becomes intensified and driving. Deutsch[1] calls this period prerevolutionary because the forces needed "to combat the sexual drives in puberty are prepared in prepuberty, the period of greatest freedom from sexual urges." Deutsch[1] continues by saying, "In this the human psyche is a wise government, forging its weapons before the aggressor appears."

During the school-age period the child's ego became strengthened through experiences in his home, school, church and community. *In preadolescence, the child needs experiences which further ego development and give him opportunities to acquire the psychological preparedness necessary to make healthy solutions to the conflicts of adolescence.*

In preadolescence the child is struggling with two potent forces within him: (1) A quantity of energy made available through successful solutions to earlier problems and (2) a powerful urge to master reality in preparation for the physiologic changes which are to come.[1] Before the end of this period hormonal activity begins to influence the child's physical growth. Hormonal activity brings an influx of energy to the individual[3] and changes the child's behavior patterns and responses to parents, teachers and friends within his environment.

Every child will respond to prepuberty in his own way. His response will depend upon the strength of his ego and the quality of his relationships with his parents and his siblings both before and at the time changes in behavior begin to manifest themselves. In this period, personality changes are marked and disquieting to adults if their psychological purposes are not understood.

PSYCHOLOGICAL GROWTH AND RESULTING PERSONALITY CHANGES

PURPOSE OF THE PERSONALITY CHANGES OF PREADOLESCENCE

During the school-age period of personality development the child acquired mastery of his sexual and aggressive drives and acquired intellectual, social and physical skills. Gradually in the years from 6 to 10 years of age, the child acquired mannerliness, a desire for cleanliness, empathy with others, self-reliance and an ability to meet the demands of his parents, teachers and group. He became increasingly more co-operative and developed a real capacity to apply himself to the tasks at hand.

As the child acquired increased mastery of himself and his environment, he gained status with his friends, his teachers and his peers, sensed a feeling of power in his achievements and freed his energy for new tasks. Accomplishing the tasks of the school-age period took energy because each conflict brought anxiety and the need for finding a satisfying solution to his problem. With the resolution of each conflict, more of the child's energy became freed for new growth experiences.

One of the commonest characteristics of the preadolescent is his abounding energy and need for activity. He cannot sit still and is "on the go" incessantly. During school hours preadolescents tap their feet, drum their fingers or their pencils on their desks and throw their gangling arms and legs in all directions. In after-school hours, they engage in competitive sports, club activities, play acting and the pursuit of their chosen hobbies. This is usually as true of girls as it is for boys, and it is not unusual to see girls engaging in so-called tomboy activities.

The preadolescent grows anxious and becomes preoccupied with himself as he senses that adolescence is approaching. His ability to concentrate wanes because his energy is being consumed in fantasy, physical activity and anxiety. As a result it is not unusual to see a decline in scholastic achievement. These children are preoccupied, and never seem to hear the things their parents and teachers want them to hear, yet conversely what adults want to have go unnoticed or unheard these youngsters never fail to perceive.

Personality changes come as the preadolescent grows and experiences life with his age mates. He seeks experiences with age mates because he needs affection, emotional strength and opportunities to meet reality situations without adult interference. Life within his group modifies the parental standards within him, and as a result his conscience becomes less effective in checking impulsive behavior than it was before. The preadolescent has anxiety, an abundance of instinctual energy at his disposal and a conscience which is becoming modified by peer interaction. They bring regression and increased unruliness. Old unresolved problems and interests characteristic of preschool years reappear with renewed intensity.[4]

Personality changes bring changes in behavior. Instead of mannerliness and perseverance, the preadolescent becomes uninterested in his appearance and in practicing the social graces. He becomes less controlled and has only fleeting interest in activities which formerly captured his wholehearted approval. In this phase of development, greediness, cruelty and exhibitionism reappear.[2] The preadolescent's appetite is apt to resemble the kind he had in his earliest years of rapid growth,[2] and his approach to food is similar to that observed in the young child. Table manners vanish, and he gorges with the same avidity he approaches all other reality situations. However, it is not unusual for preadolescents to be late to meals. They become engrossed in their own affairs or conveniently forget that their parents expect them to come home on time. Their interest in after-school chores dwindles, and each new task becomes a subject for argument.

Negativism and assertion of independence reappear in the preadolescent period of development, as marked as when these children first discovered that they were separate and powerful individuals.[1] They struggle endlessly with something that they know their parents could help them with, but often they are adamant in refusing their assistance. It seems as though the preadolescent's behavior were saying: "It is not true that I cannot do things for myself. I am not a child any longer. I am growing up. Can't you see that I am? If you cannot see it and understand my need to feel more independent, I'll prove it to you by showing you I can govern myself. I know I can, and what is more I will keep trying until I prove to you that I am a capable person."

The preadolescent period of personality development provides the child with another opportunity to resolve the problems which will be an obstacle to further growth. From an adult standpoint increased activity, regression and changes in parental standards brought about through association with a clique or a gang are disadvantageous. But for the preadolescent, these changes in character have purpose—*"disorganization,* not a permanent disorganization, of course, but a disorganization for future growth."[4] *The preadolescent needs a period to become ready for adolescence.* Redl[4] explains why disorganization is an important and necessary phase of growth. He says:

> This disorganization must occur, or else the higher organization cannot be achieved. In short, a child does not become an adult by becoming bigger and better. Simple "improvement" of a child's personality into that of an adult would only produce an oversized child, an infantile adult. "Growing" into an adult means leaving behind, or destroying some of what the child has been, and becoming something else in many ways.
>
> The real growth occurs during adolescence: pre-adolescence is the period of preliminary loosening up of the personality pattern in order that the change may take place. It is comparable to soaking the beans before you cook them.

NEED FOR IDENTIFICATION WITH A GROUP OF PEERS FOR GROWTH

The preadolescent needs to identify himself with a "gang"; he is not strong enough to stand alone and he cannot tolerate being dependent upon his parents. Redl[4] says, "In no other age do youngsters show such a deep need for *clique and gang formation* among themselves as in this one." They need to find their place within a group because they need the security which comes from the belongingness they find there. They have much that they can learn from one another and they have problems which they feel they need to share with others than their parents. Through group experience their concept of themselves changes, and they begin to see themselves as a member of a group as well as a member of a family.

The preadolescent needs parents who understand his need to grow away from them—to other adults, to age mates of the same sex and eventually to a heterosexual mate. It is natural and normal for children to detach themselves from their parents and to become identified with a group of age mates.[4] They begin to separate themselves from their parents in the school-age period but the separation which comes in preadolescence is more complete.

The preadolescent period of personality development is the *early* psychological weaning period, and one of great import for the individual. Final emancipation from parents comes at the end of adolescence, but it is in the preceding periods of development that he becomes prepared for the final personality reorganization which will determine his adult level of emotional maturity. Unless parents, teachers and nurses understand this fundamental need, the preadolescent will not get the preparation he needs to master the most difficult of all conflicts—those which are yet to come—those of adolescence.

The preadolescent needs a group within which he can experiment with his own powers of control, meet reality and prove to himself that he can manage himself more independently. Preadolescents resent adult intrusion upon their play, and rightfully so. Previously their parents resented their intrusion upon their private lives, and this was as it should be. Children cannot grow up without renouncing their desire for their parent of the opposite sex and accepting their place in their family. Their parents have been wise in helping them to accept substitutes for what they originally desired. The child must turn his interests to those outside his home or he will become deprived of the experiences he needs for social and emotional growth. When children find their place in a peer group, their parents must in turn respect their right to privacy and their desire for increased freedom to develop their own powers of self-direction and to discover the strengths and the weaknesses they have within them. The following situation illustrates the way preadolescents maneuver to bring modifications in their environments which meet their needs for growth.

Jackie, Madeleine, Caroline and Rose were preadolescents in a pediatric ward. They discovered each other in the hospital playroom and became bosom friends. They asked the head nurse if they could room together, and when they had completed moving, they arranged their four-bed unit into what they called "the girls' dormitory." They wanted privacy and a place where they would not be intruded upon by either younger children or hospital personnel. When they discovered that there was no privacy available in their hospital unit, they found an isolated area which was used to store stretchers and miscellaneous equipment. They rolled the stretchers out into the hallway and proceeded to set up a clubhouse.

In the hospital they found materials to use in furnishing their clubhouse. In the playroom they obtained material to make curtains and pictures that they could put upon the walls. They borrowed furniture and household equipment and set up a kitchen, bedroom and clubroom.

They spent hours each day keeping house and going to club meetings. One doll was ill, and they borrowed treatment room equipment which they deemed essential for her care. The nurses recognized their need for independent play and helped them get the equipment that they needed to carry out the projects the group had planned independently.

These four girls not only made it known that they wanted privacy, they also took steps to ensure it. They brought screens from the storeroom, and placed them in front of the door. In addition they hung a sign on one screen which said, "No admittance here. Please keep out."

These children desired privacy and their wish was respected. When they wanted adult guidance and company they sought it, and they knew that it was readily available. They gave parties and entertained interns and nurses and often called the head nurse in to help them decide issues that they were unable to decide independently. When they wanted to segregate themselves from others and to feel the joy of independence, they were permitted this freedom.

In cliques like the one described above, preadolescents reveal their sexual curiosity which becomes rearoused in this period of development. Preadolescent youngsters are intensely interested in their bodies and watch for and welcome signs which indicate oncoming maturity. In writing of the preadolescent girl's develop-ment, Deutsch[1] says:

Absorption in the functions of the sexual organs and their size, in the inside of their own bodies, in the development of their breasts, etc., now replaces their old interest in the difference between boys and girls.

Preadolescents reveal their feelings toward themselves and those of the opposite sex in their behavior. In this phase of development the boy's fear of bodily injury and the girl's envy of the masculine body become revived and expressed.[2] Sex antagonism increases, and they point up every frailty in the opposite sex that they can devise. They do not ignore the opposite sex, however; they are keenly aware of them. Their conversations are filled with discussions of what they have observed, but boys cover their interest in the opposite sex with expressions of scorn and girls cover theirs with a supercilious air of indifference. In this period they *seem* to be blind to the attributes of the opposite sex but they are not going unnoticed. The following example illustrates the way Bill expressed his interest in Peggy. If he had not been aware of her as a feminine person, his conversation would not have centered around Peggy. He talked about Peggy frequently, and his comments were always similar to the ones illustrated herewith.

Bill was a preadolescent who was hospitalized with a badly fractured leg. He met Peggy, aged 11, in the playroom. Peggy and Bill shared a nurse, and the three of them were often together. When Bill and his nurse were alone together he talked freely, and Peggy was often the subject of conversation. He said, "Peggy is *just* a girl. She is an awful gossip, just like all girls are. Girls are a bother. I can't see anything in them at all. I'm not going to marry. I'm going to be a bachelor." Bill seemed to think that liking girls was unmanly, yet he never missed an opportunity to observe and to make comments about them.

Preadolescents are observant, meddlesome, secretive, outwardly "all-knowing" and ready to share their thoughts and their knowledge with an age mate. They delight in enlightening each other about their own development and the things that they have learned through observation, reading or conversation with others. Again they become absorbed in adult activity. They observe, interpret, imagine and draw conclusions concerning all that they see and hear. They meddle in the affairs of their parents and older siblings and grow increasingly more interested in all that they do. However, simultaneously they withdraw from their parents and become secretive with them, rarely expressing their inner feelings and thoughts to them. Instead, they share their thoughts and perplexities with their age mates. They have secrets together, and each expects the others to keep them in utter secrecy.[1] They tell "naughty stories" and jokes[4] and play out their fantasies together.[1] The example cited below illustrates the way preadolescents rebuff their parents' desire to prepare them for adolescent changes. They assume an air of indifference, and often give the impression that they do not need their parents' guidance.

Laura was 11 years of age, and her mother felt she needed further preparation for menstruation. She knew about menstruation but her mother wanted to prepare her further because she recognized that she was nearing puberty. When her mother told her where she could find the sanitary supplies she had purchased for her, Laura said, "Let's talk about something else. I don't see why people take things so seriously. I certainly don't. Come on; let's finish lengthening my skirt. That's more important."

In this phase of development children continue to associate with members of their own sex and to grow through their experiences with them. There are advantages in the close interpersonal relationships with members of their own sex if they do not bind the youngsters to the preadolescent stage of emotional development. They help the youngsters get along with members of their own sex and give them opportunities to gain independence from their parents of the same sex. They also provide them with friends who will meet their need for affection, security and belongingness. Together they can face and solve their problems of growing-up physically and emotionally. This phase of development often continues through the period of early adolescence. Until the adolescent has developed security in his relationships with those of the opposite sex, he will continue to need a close relationship with a friend of his own sex.

Association with a group brings many pleasures and advantages for the preadolescent; it also brings trials, heartaches, fears and frustration that he feels he must surmount without his parents' aid. In the "gang age" the group's codes are strict,[4] and the preadolescent who cannot abide by them is ostracized by its members. Preadolescents are hard on one another. Every school-age child and preadolescent experiences moments of rejection by friends and by the group. Children over 6 years of age fear disapproval, failure and lack of acceptance and the ridicule of their age mates. In preschool years the child feared parental disapproval, but in the school-age and preadolescent phase of development group disapproval is a greater threat to his ego. To run home for solace now injures his self-esteem. Previously he could do it with abandon and accept his mother's comforting, but now, if he succumbs to his desire for parental protection, he feels weak, afraid and unsuccessful. He feels he *must* succeed; his desire for growth and freedom brings pressures from within.

The group's codes are unlike those the preadolescent's parents set for him.[4] They are often directly opposite to those his parents formulate for him. Parents, for instance, set standards of cleanliness and dress and are pleased when his teacher comments upon their youngster's appearance and physical hygiene. However, the peer codes often ridicule the well-groomed boy and label him a "sissy." Teacher approval merely designates him as "teacher's pet."

Peer codes also become formulated by children in pediatric wards. If a child seeks the approval of the head nurse rather than the approval of his peers, he will inevitably meet rejection to some degree. Janet missed opportunities for group experience because she became labeled "the head nurse's pet." A description of her behavior appears below.

Janet was 11 years old when she required a long period of hospitalization for neurodermatitis. She had met parental rejection, and her need for her mother's acceptance was reflected in her behavior. She clung to the head nurse, sought her approval constantly with affectionate overtures and expressions of flattery and exaggerated helpfulness and frequently brought tales concerning the children's infringement of ward rules. She obeyed hospital rules rather than peer rules but simultaneously received privileges from the head nurse which were not granted to other children in the ward. Before long, Janet became on "outsider," and her problems were increased rather than lessened.

Janet's behavior showed that she had an exaggerated need for the head nurse's approval. Had she received it in a way which protected her need for friends, she would have experienced less frustration and more opportunities for growth.

Learning to get along with one's gang brings conflict and anxiety. The codes of the group may conflict with the middle-class preadolescent's internalized parental standards and bring guilt and varying degrees of fear to some children. When this happens the child is torn between satisfying his conscience and being accepted by his group. The latter need is usually the strongest. Unless depriving past experiences have made him unduly dependent upon his parents, he usually accepts the standards of the group instead of those his parents select for him. In this way the superficial layers of his conscience again become modified, making him more ready to emancipate himself from his parents during adolescence.

IDENTIFICATION WITH ADULTS OUTSIDE HIS FAMILY AS AN AID TO THE PREADOLESCENT IN EMANCIPATING HIMSELF

The preadolescent needs an adult friend of the same sex to emulate and to idealize and from whom he can obtain emotional support and understanding. He gives up his identification with his parent of the same sex and finds a substitute with whom he can identify himself. In identifying himself with an adult outside his family, he takes another step in emancipating himself from dependence upon his parent. He cannot be without a substitute for his parent for that would leave him unprotected, frustrated and insecure. To wean herself from her mother, the girl selects an older girl or young woman, endows her with protective and affectionate qualities and berates her own mother.[1] In this period of development she cannot receive gratification of her dependent needs from her own mother for it threatens her grown-up, independent feelings about herself. Cynthia showed her need to feel independent when she said the following to her newly acquired adult woman friend: "I love my room. I keep it just the way I like it, and play that I live all alone. I like to have candy in my room. I don't like it but I like to have it to serve my friends when they come. It makes me feel grown-up, and as if I were alone in my own home."

Boys go through a similar phase of development but it is less intense and less observable in them for a number of reasons. Our society frowns upon strong masculine attachments and exhibitionistic expressions of affection. Another possible reason why boys have less need for attachments to men outside their family is that they have more opportunity to master their fear of dependence through constructive independent activities. It is in this period that many boys begin to take over paper routes, to act as delivery boys or to get odd jobs within the neighborhood. Even if there were opportunities, many parents would express disapproval if their daughters displayed interest in working away from home.

The preadolescent's behavior expresses the struggle he is having between his desire to remain a child and his urge to grow up. He is more critical of his parent of the same sex than he has ever been before. Outwardly he manifests no advantage in being a part of his family unit. He has little appreciation for what is given to or done for him.[4] Rarely are his desires satisfied, and he clings to the belief that other children have parents who are more generous, fashionable and infinitely more understanding than his own. Criticism and devaluation are expressions of his struggle to free himself from wanting to be a child and desiring all that has brought him comfort before.

The preadolescent needs parents who understand his conflict and need to devaluate their personal qualities. The preadolescent attitudes expressed above are difficult ones for parents to accept. Unless his parents understand the reasons why he must temporarily underestimate their assets and strengths, they will be hurt, withdraw or respond with counteraggression. If they do respond negatively, the preadolescent's conflict will be intensified and he will not have the energy he needs to master his problems. It often consoles parents to know that simultaneously with their youngster's expression of hostility and criticism, they are also recognizing that they have qualities within themselves that are like those of the parent with whom they have formerly identified themselves. The preadolescent does not hate the parent he depreciates. There are things about him he dislikes but he also loves him; he is merely trying to prove that he does not need him as much as he used to think he did. Parents need to understand this. When they do, they are less threatened by their youngster's display of independence and depreciation. Cynthia's behavior exemplified the foregoing characteristics.

Cynthia was 11 years old and in the hospital with acute sinusitis. When the infection subsided and she became convalescent, she demonstrated avid interest in creative activities. As she engaged in these activities, she chatted freely and disclosed feelings about herself and her relationship with her mother. Cynthia was absorbing some of the womanly characteristics of her mother. At the same time she was feeling markedly critical of the things that her mother said and did.

One day Cynthia was making a veil during play time in the ward. "It's going to be just like my mother's veil. I am going to wear it in the evening just like she does," she commented as she attached ribbons to hold the new style veil in place. "When I grow up I am going to have lots of hats just like my mother. I guess I am lots like my mother because she likes to dress herself up, too."

Just then Cynthia's mother arrived for visiting hours. Immediately Cynthia suggested that she would like to play a game of "Sorry" with her mother and nurse. During the course of playing Cynthia's mother made an unwise play. Like a flash Cynthia said, "How stupid of you! What kind of a mother have I got, anyway? I guess an awfully stupid one from the looks of things. Don't you see it would have been better to get one of your men out on the board?"

After visiting hour was over Cynthia's mother commented upon her daughter's increasing dissatisfaction with everything that she did. "I cannot seem to please her any more. Sometimes I think that she is trying to be as different from me as she can possibly be," she said.

The preadolescent needs to feel that he is different from his parent of the same sex because it brings strength to his ego. To feel independent is an absolute necessity; it lessens his anxiety, increases his self-esteem and brings him comfort. Cynthia's mother enjoyed playing games. It was relaxation for her. She did not feel a need to concentrate or to put forth an effort to win. Winning did not have the same meaning to her that it did for Cynthia. Cynthia needed to compete and wanted to be different from her mother. And in game play she was successful!

When a preadolescent girl is hospitalized for long periods of time, she should have a nurse who understands her psychological needs. If the girl identifies her nurse as a mother figure, she may displace the hostility that she feels toward her mother onto her. Or the nurse may become her ideal, and the person she uses to help her gain a measure of freedom from the attachment that she has to her mother.

It is important that nurses understand this phase of development. If they do the preadolescent can use her relationship with her to grow emotionally and socially. If the youngster is hostile sometimes, and the nurse recognizes the origin of her feelings, she will not be threatened and withdraw or respond with counteraggression. Instead, she will continue to support her with her friendliness and understanding. If the youngster makes her nurse her ideal, the nurse can meet her dependent needs by showing interest in her as a person and by helping her find increased satisfaction in her social relationships with age mates in the ward. The understanding nurse who has no need within herself to keep the child dependent upon her will find ways to give her both support and the freedom she needs for growth.

The preadolescent needs to have his choice of friends in the ward respected. Moving beds, bedside tables and personal belong-

ings is an arduous task but one which is important if we want to
promote social and emotional growth and bring increased happiness
to the children in our hospital wards. Children of the same age like
and need to be together. Occasionally children whose personalities are not compatible are placed together in a room. To subject them to each other's company can be painful and oftentimes
nonconstructive.

The head nurse in a pediatric ward needs to be sensitive to her
patient's psychological needs. She needs to be observant of peer relationships in the ward and try to place children with peers who can
become their friends. It is not unusual for children and preadolescents to change friends rather frequently. This can happen in the
hospital ward as well as in the community. Often the head nurse
can help youngsters straighten out their difficulties; at other times
a change in roommates may be the wisest solution to the problem.

GUIDANCE OF THE PREADOLESCENT

Disequilibrium from Personality Changes Which Frighten the Preadolescent

It is not difficult to understand what the foregoing personality
changes can mean to a child who has previously experienced a feeling of strength within himself. The prepubertal personality disorganization and the thought of oncoming adolescence are frightening. Previously, the child's inner voice kept his impulses under
control but now it has become weakened and does not protect him
as it did before. In preschool years, the child was aggressive,
impulsive and dependent, but his ego was weak and he had no
inner voice which chastised him if he leaned upon his parents for
strength and comfort.

The preadolescent needs a strong ego to handle the prepubertal
changes which are to come. The youngster who meets prepuberty
with a weak ego is faced with more problems than is the child
who comes to it with a goodly degree of self-reliance, trust in
the people of his world and trust in his own capacity to meet the
problems of growing-up.

*In addition to a strong ego, the preadolescent needs understand-
ing, tolerance, support and faith in his ability to work out constructive solutions to his problems.* The preadolescent is experiencing
conflict from within for his primitive impulses are again at war
with his ego and his conscience. If, in addition to inner conflict,
the preadolescent is forced to cope with parental, teacher or nurse
misunderstanding, his problems will increase and more intense disequilibrium will be inevitable.

The preadolescent whose natural behavior brings adult rejection or counteraggression is in a predicament which must be solved before growth can take place. Anxiety and anger intensify the power of his impulses and put strain upon his ego. If the strain is excessive, his ego will either yield to his impulses or tighten its defenses to an intolerable degree. Neither solution is a healthy one because neither prepares the youngster to meet and satisfactorily solve the developmental problems of adolescence. If he yields to his impulses, he will become delinquent; if he yields to his conscience, the changes which are important for growth cannot take place. To become an independent and emotionally mature individual, his conscience must become modified to a degree, and it is in preadolescence that it must begin. Gus's behavior demonstrated his inner conflict. Had his behavior been condemned, he would have felt misunderstood and been driven to repeat behavior which was injurious to his health.

Gus was 11 years of age and in the hospital with diabetes mellitus. He was receiving insulin twice daily and was on a restricted diet. One day he took a piece of cake from the food truck which was standing in his ward. When a staff nurse discovered it, she called the supervisor and expressed her angry feelings because Gus had "stolen" food which was not prepared for him.

The supervisor went to Gus to obtain understanding of his behavior. She found a youngster who was suffering as a result of his behavior. He was pacing up and down the ward with signs of anxiety on his face. She engaged Gus in conversation and waited until he was able to tell her of the experience. Finally he said, "I took some cake from the cart. I just couldn't help it. Something inside of me kept saying, 'Gus, go take the cake. You'll like it!' The minute I ate it, something inside of me said, 'Gus, you shouldn't have done it.' "

Gus's eyes were as big as saucers as he talked, and he was serious and scared. He was not fabricating; he was expressing in words the inner conflict he was experiencing. At the moment he craved the cake, his conscience was not strong enough to withstand the temptation, but the moment his craving was satisfied, his conscience took over to check further impulsivity.

Gus knew that he had done wrong. He did not need further punishment. Had he received it, he would have had increased difficulty in controlling his impulses. The nurse understood his conflict and said, "Gus, it is hard not to take things that you want so much. The next time that you feel tempted, come and tell me. We'll find a way for you to withstand the temptation. This happens to all boys sometimes. Let's talk to your doctor. Maybe he can help us plan a diet which you will enjoy more. Maybe he doesn't know how much you like sweet things once in a while."

PREADOLESCENTS' PARENTS' DISCOURAGEMENT FROM
PERSONALITY CHANGES

Many parents are perplexed with their child in the preadolescent level of personality development because they do not know his behavior is symptomatic of growth. They feel as if their efforts to help their child gain control of himself were of no avail. They become discouraged with themselves and with their child. Instead of recognizing his disorganization as a sign of growth, they feel frustrated, disappointed and angry. This emotional state creates anxiety in them all. Instead of feeling parental strength, the preadolescent becomes more fearful and has less power to combat the strength of his impulses. The example cited below serves to illustrate a common parental response to preadolescent personality changes.

Mrs. S. was anxious about Sally because her behavior had changed in recent months. She said, "I wonder if Sally will ever get hold of herself. Everything seems so futile, and I am utterly discouraged with her. Previously, Sally enjoyed her household responsibilities, was neat and orderly and in control of herself in almost every situation with which she was confronted. Now she is different. Everything she has gained previously seems to have become lost. Nothing I do is right, and she seems to be completely intolerant of frustration. As long as she isn't crossed in any way, she is amenable and composed, but the minute I ask her to do something she blows her top."

Feelings of frustration like those cited above are not unusual ones; they are almost universal unless the preadolescent's parents understand his need to experience a period of disorganization. Changes in the child are often sudden and marked. Often there is nothing in the current environment to explain them. But there is much within the child which can explain them, and if his parents search they may discover they are not quite ready to accept their child's need to begin breaking the emotional ties which bind him to them. A description of Sally, the child referred to in the above paragraph, serves to illustrate the way some children respond to their mother's discouragement.

Sally was a tall, gracefully built, brunette, preadolescent youngster. She was a sensitive, intelligent child who responded to people's feelings with an unusual degree of intensity. Sally was equally as anxious about herself as was her mother. She was discouraged, scared and occasionally felt as if she were being rejected. There were times she was near to despair because she doubted her ability to please her mother. Sally did feel hostile toward her mother many times, but she also longed for her acceptance. When her mother was critical of her, feelings of hostility and aggression seethed within her because she did not feel as if she were always completely at fault. She tried to be reasonable but there were times she just could not be no matter how hard she tried.

Sally knew her mother expected her to be self-directing, composed and compliant. Sally wanted to be that way herself but inner anxiety, tension and powerful inner needs made it impossible for her to control herself consistently as she had been able to do several months previously. There were times Sally felt she just *had* to assert her independence! She would keep her feelings under control as long as she could. Then they would gush forth like lava from an erupting crater! Usually the precipitating irritation was a minor one but it was one more than Sally could tolerate at the moment. When it was more than she could endure she "blew her top" just as her mother said she did.

Sally became tempestuous, demanding and very frightened. She needed presents constantly to reassure her that she was loved. She became scared because she did not have the controls that she had had formerly. Her inner voice responded with self-accusation, and she would become repentent and withdrawn and attempt to punish herself. Expression of hostility made her feel guilty, and she handled it with increased expression of affection for her mother and self-punishment.

Fortunately for Sally, her mother gained insight into her behavior as she began to talk about the changes which were occurring in her. She recalled some of her own childhood experiences and remembered the heartaches she had had in this phase of development. She began to understand Sally and saw some of the precipitating factors which were influencing her daughter's behavior. When she did, she was able to change the way she had been accustomed to respond to her behavior.

In preadolescence formerly repressed hostile feelings come to the surface and express themselves directly and indirectly. In preschool years the child has to repress many of his feelings. Like all preschool girls, Sally had also repressed her feelings of hostility toward her mother and supplanted them with feelings of tenderness, love and a desire to become like her. In preadolescence repressed feelings come to the surface and become directed at the real object of his hostility—the person closest to him—or they may be displaced to others outside the family. When Sally established a relationship with her nurse, she disclosed many of the feelings that she had toward her mother.

In the hospital Sally was often irritable with her nurse. Many times there were legitimate external reasons for her tempestuousness but at other times her irritability had its roots in her feelings about herself and her mother.

In game play Sally was extremely competitive and grew angry whenever she was not winning. Sally needed to win—she liked herself better when she did, and winning made her feel strong, adequate and independent. As long as she was winning, she was able to keep her angry feelings under control but whenever she was losing to the person she identified as her rival, she was threatened with intense feelings that she felt she needed to keep under control.

Sally knew the game of "Winnie the Pooh." Each player had an animal character that was moved on the board in accordance with the colored disk one drew from a bag. Some colors were advantageous to draw; other colors placed the player's animal character on a picture of a bench to await a further turn. Whenever Sally's turn came to take a colored disk from the bag, she peeked before she withdrew one. When she was skillful in peeking and drew a colored disk which gave her the lead in the game, she had increased assurance that she would win and could relax until her opponent had her turn.

Understanding Sally's need to win, the nurse suggested a change in rules. At first Sally could not concede to this; her inner voice undoubtedly said, "That isn't fair," and curtailed her acceptance of something she very much desired. When her nurse helped her to see that changing rules was acceptable to her, but undoubtedly not to her age mates, she was able to accept her opponent's giving. Sally discovered that her nurse was not competing with her and deliberately trying to defeat her. Children often feel that adults always have the advantage, and most often they do.

At times children need to feel that they, too, can have advantages and become master of the situation. In game play with adults, the child should be given a handicap because of his need to win. A child's cheating should not go unnoticed. It is far better to permit him to change the rules so he can have equal advantage. As his capacity to compete with the adult increases, he will lose his fear of competition and failing and withdraw the handicap on his own volition. Again it is a matter of following the child's cues. He will show us his needs, and we will meet them if we are emotionally free from competitive feelings ourselves. When Sally grew aware that her nurse was not trying to outwit her and she grew more secure in her relationship with her, her behavior in game play began to change.

Sally's feelings about losing manifested themselves one day when she said, "When I get into Pooh's garden [a disadvantageous spot to land in], it's just like my mother's punishment."

After Sally's nurse let her manipulate the rules so that she would have increased opportunity to win, Sally suggested a new rule which was designed to give her nurse an advantage. Gradually she altered the rules so that she had fewer and fewer advantages. Then came the day when she suggested that her rules be abandoned and the "legal" ones reinstated. Her expression of pride in achievement the day she won "legally," as she expressed it, was a revelation to see. She had mastered her fear of losing. Playing games with her nurse changed from an anxiety-ridden experience to one that was filled with pleasure. She relaxed; she did not need to concentrate as intently as she did before. The time spent in playing games became filled with lively, spontaneous chatter that had been completely nonexistent before.

NECESSITY OF UNDERSTANDING GUIDANCE TO SUSTAIN
GOOD ADULT-CHILD RELATIONSHIPS

The preadolescent's need for understanding guidance is urgent; he needs the lines of communication with his parents and other adults kept open. Sustaining good adult-child relationships throughout this crucial period of development is a difficult task, because the preadolescent is not easy to live with,[4] and working with him is not free of frustration by any means. However, his need for understanding is crucial; he needs his parents' approval more than he can possibly admit to himself.

The preadolescent needs democratic guidance which gives him status, security and the strength he needs to master his temporary impulsivity and resolve the old conflicts that he was unable to do before. Neither laissez-faire nor autocratic guidance meets the preadolescent's needs. Laissez-faire guidance provides no strength or security; autocratic guidance provides no freedom for growth.

The preadolescent needs freedom within limits and guidance which recognizes that he is a person who has grown and is therefore in need of a different kind of discipline and expression of love than he has ever known before. The preadolescent thoroughly dislikes overt demonstrations of love; it is too reminiscent of that which he enjoyed as a child. But he recognizes and can accept the love which is expressed in tolerance, freedom to be with his group and interest in his newly developed activities and hobbies when he shows a desire to share them with his parents, teachers or nurses. The preadolescent rebels when he is disciplined as he was when he was a child, and rightfully so. He loathes hearing about how good he used to be[4] and hates being compared to others in a derogatory manner. However, he wants limits to give him controls which he does not have within himself. The preadolescent can take punishment if it is the kind appropriate for his level of development and if he has done something that he knows is a punishable act or something that he feels has been injurious to himself or others.

The preadolescent needs parents, teachers and nurses who explain the reasons why they make the decisions they make. The preadolescent can understand explanations which motivate adult behavior and he needs them because they give him the knowledge he requires to be increasingly more self-directing. There will be times when he needs to be temporarily deprived of a possession or a privilege to learn that there are some things which are not permissible and acceptable at the time. If the deprivation fits the offensive act and he knows why his parents or other adults feel the way they do about it, he will recognize its fairness and have less need to retaliate or rebel at their choice of punishment.

Scolding and physical punishment are completely noneffective and only serve to give the adult release from his own tension. If the child's background of discipline included large measures of scolding, it will certainly fall upon deaf ears in preadolescence. Spanking is a punishment of the past; it merely serves to make the child infuriated with the person who inflicts it. It teaches nothing. It may clear the air but the punisher is as aggressive as he is telling his preadolescent youngster not to be.

The school-age child and the preadolescent recognize their need to right their errors and that it is the only fair thing to do. If they destroy something, they should pay for it if they have the money to do so. If they have no money on hand from their allowance, their parents need to help them find ways to earn it. If they have something within their possession which does not belong to them, they should return it. It is rare to find a preadolescent feeling resentful or picked upon if he is asked to rectify something that he really feels is wrong, unfair or childish.

However, the preadolescent cannot tolerate or accept punishment for behavior which is normal and a natural part of growth. If he is unreasonably punished it will not serve any useful purpose; it will merely make him resentful, hostile and in some instances afraid to grow up.

A youngster who does not misbehave, regress and rebel to some degree in this phase of development is a sick child who is in need of psychiatric treatment. Unless he asserts his independence and regresses occasionally, it indicates insecurity, a lack of confidence in his own worthiness, or insufficient motivation to become an accepted part of a group.

The youngster who loses all control and shows no positive response to understanding guidance, reasonable and kindly imposed limits, and constructive forms of guidance[4] is also an emotionally sick child. He, too, is in need of help before sexual maturity is reached. He is emotionally immature and needs guidance which motivates him to want to develop inner controls, and rewards his efforts to become a more socialized individual.

The preadolescent needs opportunities to let off steam,[4] and to utilize his increased energy in constructive, ego-strengthening pursuits. He needs activity and lots of it. The more he can direct his energy into constructive channels, the less aggressive he will be in his relationships with others. The preadolescent needs to assert his independence. If democratic leadership is available, the adult can help him use his drive for independence in activities which prove to him that he is growing up and that it is acceptable to his parents and teachers. He needs to discover that he *has* inner resources. It gives him inner strength that he can get in no other way. There will be times when his dependent longings will overpower his urge to grow up and to be independent. At such times, his wishes need to be gratified without resentment or recall of the times when he rejected the adult's offer of assistance or affection.

The preadolescent needs to have his irritating activities recognized as phasic behavior and tolerated with grace. The preadolescent's exuberance, insensitivity to the needs of grown-ups and displays of self-assertiveness and power will sometimes exasperate the most tolerant of parents, teachers and nurses. The preadolescent cannot be allowed to do everything that he pleases.[4] That degree of permissiveness would not provide the understanding and support that he requires. When the adult knows that his behavior stems from a drive to feel powerful and assertive, the wise and understanding adult will permit him to gratify his need. If his behavior is not tolerated, the adult and the preadolescent will become engulfed in a battle which will block the possibilities of ever learning to understand one another. To work with the preadolescent successfully, the adult needs to develop tolerance for the trivial annoyances which, if analyzed, will be seen to be nonconsequential and unimportant as far as the preadolescent's development is concerned.

The following example illustrates the application of this principle. Jim was irritating at the moment, but it was not characteristic of his general behavior. He was reasonable and constructive most of the time, but occasionally he was annoying with displays of self-importance. His parents understood his needs and refrained from making comments which would depreciate or lessen his feelings of self-esteem.

Jim returned from the store after buying favors and prizes for his eleventh birthday. On his return home he found a living room full of adult guests. He showed the guests his purchases and said, "These are to annoy my mother. The louder they crack the better I'll like it." At that point he cracked one of the favors in his mother's ear and gloried in his ability to startle her. His mother quickly regained her composure, and said, "Jim, show us the prizes you selected. The kids are going to love the favors even if I don't." She was not angered by Jim's behavior. It is true she did not enjoy his antics but she was able to control her feelings because there were so many things that Jim did which she loved.

From experience the preadolescent learns to size up people, recognize their strengths and sense their weaknesses. This is a quality of great value and one he will use throughout his lifetime. In pre-

adolescence he uses his understanding of people for his own purposes. Redl[4] says that adolescents have learned what behavior irritates their parents the most. They use this knowledge when their
need to assert their independence is the strongest. To prove how
independent and powerful they are, they do the very thing they
know will exasperate their parents the most. Redl[4] explains the
way that preadolescents acquire their knowledge of adult psychology. He says:

> Their skill in sizing us up and using our emotions and weaknesses
> for their own ends has reached a peak at this age. It took them eight
> to ten years to learn, but they have learned by thorough observation.
> While we were worrying about them, they were not worried about us,
> and they had ample time and leisure to study our psychology.

The child in the hospital is equally observant. It does not take
him a lifetime to size up the nurses in his ward. While the nurse
is concentrating on removing the wrinkles from his draw sheet and
on straightening the comic books on his bedside table, he is taking
inventory of her weaknesses and her strengths. He uses this knowledge for his own advantage—and why shouldn't he? That is what
his parents have probably done to him, and through experience he
has discovered its effect on one's feelings.

The bed-ridden preadolescent youngster also needs opportunities
to let off steam. He also needs his radio, his comics and plenty of
constructive activities to give him a feeling of accomplishment. It
takes little imagination to appreciate what a preadolescent experiences when his body must be encased in a cast and he is forced
to rely on others to do those things he wants most to do by himself.
The bed-ridden preadolescent who feels well wants to be experiencing adventure, growing in independence, and expanding his own
powers of adaptation to life. Is it any wonder immobilized preadolescents grow restless, un-co-operative and sometimes even bel-
ligerent or uncouth at times? They must feel threatened, inadequate
and disappointed many times during the course of each day. To
remain in bed when they are longing for experiences which give
them prestige and make them feel strong and capable is frustration
which takes superb ego strength to withstand. Under these conditions irritating behavior occasionally is justifiable and a healthy
response to a stress situation which cannot be alleviated in any
other way.

QUESTIONS TO GUIDE OBSERVATION

1. What physical changes appear in the preadolescent period of
personality development?

2. What changes in behavior occur in the period prior to the onset of puberty? What produces these changes?

3. How could you interpret these changes to parents?

4. What guidance does the preadolescent require?

5. What behavior in the preadolescent would signify emotional disturbances?

6. What is the child attempting to accomplish in this phase of personality development?

7. What may happen to the child if parental guidance prevents him from accomplishing the tasks of this period of development?

8. Observe one of your preadolescent patients in the ward. Describe his behavior. What does he do all day? Does he ever annoy you? If so, how? How do you feel about it? What do you do when he does annoy you? What reasons can you find for his behavior?

9. Observe fourth- and seventh-grade children in a public grade school and compare the two age groups. How is their behavior different? How did their teachers' guidance differ? Did the preadolescents' teacher give them opportunities to use their inner resources? How did she use their initiative in planning their program of study? How did the youngsters respond when she made an effort to let them participate in the planning of the day's program? What did you learn from this observational experience which will increase your skill in working with preadolescents in a hospital ward?

10. Observe a group of preadolescents in a hospital ward. Describe their activities. What was their response to the adults in the ward? Select one incident you observed, describe it and attempt to think through the reasons why they behaved as they did.

REFERENCES

1. Deutsch, Helene: Prepuberty, Chapter 1, p. 1, in Psychology of Women, vol. 1, New York, Grune & Stratton, 1944.
2. Freud, Anna: The Ego and the Mechanisms of Defence, New York, Internat. Univ. Press, 1946.
3. Gesell, Arnold, and Ilg, F. L.: The Child from Five to Ten, New York, Harper, 1946.
4. Redl, Fritz: Pre-adolescents: what makes them tick, Child Study, 21:44, 1943–1944.

9

Development and Guidance During Adolescence

Adolescence begins with the onset of physical maturity and ends when the individual has acquired crystallized patterns of adjustment to the conflicts of the period. Adolescence is a period of marked physical and psychological growth. It is a conflictful, trying phase of growth and brings stresses, frustrations and anxieties as well as potentialities for pleasure, accomplishment and self-realization.

Adolescence is a crucial period in the individual's life. In a few short years the adolescent must adapt himself to a rapidly changing body, intensified instinctual drives, new relationships, new responsibilities and a society which expects a great deal of its youth. However, his society simultaneously offers opportunities for a satisfying, democratic way of life. The adolescent has to resolve old conflicts, find solutions to new ones, develop mature attitudes and discover ways that he can get pleasure in socially acceptable ways. It is natural for the adolescent to be anxious and upset. He has many major problems to solve, and his future life is dependent upon the kind of adjustment he is able to make in the period prior to becoming a working adult member of his society.

The individual's response to adolescence, and the way he will adapt himself to its problems, will be determined by past experiences and the guidance that he receives throughout this period. The adolescent who comes to this phase of growth with belief in himself, trust in others, self-dependence and an ego which is strong enough to master the increased intensity of his instinctual drives will have little difficulty in surmounting the tasks of adolescence. He will experience strain and anxiety and have many new problems to solve, but he will have the inner resources necessary to find constructive solutions to his problems. The adolescent who has suffered traumas and repeated defeats and who has experienced relationships which did not fulfill his needs will approach the period with an excessive amount of anxiety and a weak ego, both of which will threaten his opportunities for growth.

The adolescent is in a process of growth; he is not an emotionally or socially mature individual. The emotionally mature adult's interests are outside of himself and he is able to obtain pleasure in working with and for other people. He knows who he is, what he believes in and what he wants to and is able to accomplish.[7] He is secure, free of the fetters which bind him to his parents, self-understanding and accepting, and emotionally free for independent, constructive, creative activities. He is free from exaggerated competitiveness, feelings of inferiority or egotism,[25] and as a result he can live comfortably with himself, tolerate the frailties existent in others and permit them to use their creative powers without feeling threatened or hostile.

The mature individual is discriminating, wise in his judgment and able to choose and stand by a mate, establish a home and rear a family. He feels parental and can provide his mate and children with the kind of environment that they need for growth. He can face and meet the responsibilities entailed in parenthood and social living with confidence and trust, and obtain pleasure from both independent and shared activities. He enjoys both recreation and responsibility and has the flexibility of character which is necessary to balance the two in a way which keeps him free from tension and productive. He is generous with his love and accepts and values the love and loyalty of others. He has a firm grasp of reality and has the capacity to adapt to changes within himself and those which come in the outer world. He has control over his aggressive and sexual drives,[7] is in harmony with his conscience and his infantile impulses,[25] and has inner resources to use when frustration and disappointment threaten his security and his peace of mind. He is master of himself and his universe! Yet he is humble and recognizes his own limitation and those of reality.

No one possesses all of the character traits cited above, for obtaining them is a lifelong task. As long as the individual lives, he will have problems to surmount. If the personality reorganization of adolescence leaves the individual with a strong ego and a flexible character, he can continue to grow with each new relationship and reality experience he meets. If he approaches adulthood with a restricting, rigid personality, he will have insufficient freedom and energy to experiment with new ways of solving problems. He will be encumbered with a character which limits his opportunities for continued growth throughout his lifetime.

The young adolescent has none of the above characteristics but he wants them and struggles to attain them. His personality is unorganized from the changes which occurred in preadolescence. Now he must master his unconscious wish to remain a child and become prepared to try his own wings in a world that is at strife, highly competitive and exacting. The adolescent wants independence, freedom to solve his problems in his own way, and the kind of security that gives him unshakable faith in his ability to meet life with all its responsibilities, inevitable changes, frustrations, disappointments and pleasures. The adolescent wants to achieve, realize his potentialities and contribute to society. Deep down inside himself he knows that real pleasure comes only from a balance of loving, giving, accomplishment, receiving and play.

Life in adolescence is serious, challenging and energy-consuming. The above goals are the adolescent's tasks. He feels the magnitude of his problems; he responds to them with fear, inadequacy and a state of indecisiveness. He is uncertain of his own status and powers and fearful lest he not measure up to all he and others expect of himself. *To reach adulthood emotionally, the adolescent needs to find and to accept himself and his sexual role, emancipate himself from his parents, establish his independence and select a vocation or career and prepare himself for it.*

The adolescent needs opportunities to explore and to meet real life situations which give him confidence, security and preparation for adult living. In writing on this topic Josselyn[17] says:

> The adolescent needs to experiment with his intensified drive toward maturation. He cannot be protected from all frustrations and dangers that lie in exploration. Only by trying his strength can he test his adequacy. Only by experiencing some of the frustrations and hazards of maturation can he learn to deal with the reality world as separate from his fantasies. Only by experiencing the satisfactions of independent activities can he resist the lure of permanent childhood.*

The individual cannot surmount the tasks of adolescence independently; he needs relationships with emotionally mature parents and professional workers who can guide him as he goes forth to tackle new experiences. The adolescent needs relationships from which he can gain strength, wise counsel and inspiraton. The adolescent must do his own growing but he needs guided experiences and support which provide what he needs to find satisfying, creative solutions to his own problems and a way of life which has deep

---

* Reprinted by permission of the author and the Family Service Association of America.

meaning and significance to him personally. Unless he has freedom
to explore and the emotional support and democratic leadership he
needs from his parents, teachers and other professional workers, mastering the tasks of adolescence can never become a reality.

The adolescent needs help to appraise his strengths and his immaturities. Growth comes through mastering difficult tasks. When
an adolescent surmounts a problem, he gains trust in himself and
self-esteem and is challenged to tackle more complex problems; he
gains ego strength which alleviates his anxiety. To attempt experiences for which he is unprepared brings fear and regression instead
of growth. To prohibit the adolescent from attempting tasks he is
psychologically prepared to master is equally as retarding to growth.
*The adolescent needs freedom when he is ready to utilize it creatively; he needs limits when he is emotionally unprepared to use
freedom for his own personal growth and the benefit of others in
his society.* The adults in the adolescent's world need the capacity
to appraise his strengths and to give him freedom to use the judgment he has acquired. They also need insight into his immaturity
and the strength to restrict activities which they know he needs protection from experiencing.

Anne Frank's[9] moving diary provides insight into the emotional
life of the adolescent. She wrote about her feelings as she developed self-awareness, adolescent relationships with her parents, her
sister, Margot, and the friends who shared the "Secret Annexe" in
which they had to live when the Nazis occupied Holland and made
it necessary for the Jewish citizens to flee from their homes. Anne's
diary tells of her trials, heartaches, loves, hates and triumphs. She
expressed her need for parental strength at the time she found
Peter, the adolescent who lived upstairs and desired her companionship. She said, "You can't coax me into not going upstairs;
either you forbid it, *or* you trust me through thick and thin, but
then leave me in peace as well!"[9]* She recognized that vacillating,
weak parents were of little value to her. She wanted strong parents
who had conviction and faith in their own judgment in relation to
her personal needs.

*In addition to opportunities for exploration, the adolescent
needs "the assurance of support when he becomes baffled, ineffective or frightened."*[17] In writing of the adolescent's use of a relationship, Josselyn[17] says:

---

* From Anne Frank: *The Diary of a Young Girl,* copyright, 1952, by Otto H. Frank,
reprinted by permission of Doubleday & Company, Inc.

He needs, therefore, people upon whom he can be dependent if he becomes frightened, but who will not demand continued dependency when he feels more assured and adequate in an independent role.*

The adolescent needs adults who understand his nature, enjoy him as a person and have the maturity which is necessary to recognize his individual needs for growth. The adolescent needs understanding and faith in himself more than anything else. If one knows his background of experience within his family, one can visualize the world through his eyes and have insight into the way his past relationships are motivating his present behavior and causing him to behave the way he does. To support the adolescent wisely, the adults in his environment also need understanding of the forces which produce his vacillating, unstable, aggressive and nonpredictable behavior. In addition, the adult who works with adolescents needs to have found satisfying solutions to his own problems and remained flexible enough to recognize each person's need to find a constructive pattern of adjustment which is self-made and his very own.[17] When an adolescent feels respected, understood and enjoyed as a person, he takes himself less seriously, feels loved and supported and has energy available to master his conflicts and to attain emotional maturity.

REQUIREMENT OF SELF-DISCOVERY,—UNDERSTANDING AND PERSONALITY REORGANIZATION FOR MATURITY

NEED OF THE ADOLESCENT TO FIND AND TO ACCEPT HIMSELF AND HIS SEXUAL ROLE

The increased hormonal activity which precedes the onset of pubertal changes affects the adolescent's total being. It not only brings physical changes in his body; it also affects his feelings about himself and brings emotional and social changes, conflicts, new interests, changed attitudes and marked changes in his behavior.

Hormonal Changes Brings Changes in the Body. The *physical* growth of the adolescent is rapid and affects all tissues of his body. The adolescent grows taller and broader and his body contours and organs change to adult proportions. His bones become larger, and muscular development is rapid. At 8 years of age, the muscles comprise 25 per cent of the individual's weight; at 16 years of age, 44 per cent of his body weight is muscle tissue.

Increased hormonal activity brings changes in the genital organs, skin, glands and hair. Breast development in girls, and increase in the size of the male sex organs are the first signs of oncoming phys-

---

* Reprinted by permission of the author and the Family Service Association of America.

ical maturity. Then pubic hair appears, and the sexual organs begin to function. After the onset of menstruation in the girl and seminal emissions in the boy, axillary hair begins to grow. Facial hair and voice changes appear later in the male and indicate that physical maturity has advanced to a considerable degree.[18] The sebaceous glands of the face, chest and back become more active, and if the pores of the skin are too small, the sebaceous material or sebum cannot escape. It collects beneath the skin and produces pimples or acne. Perspiration is increased, and vasomotor instability produces blushing.

The onset of menstruation and of seminal emissions marks the beginning of sexual maturity; it is not completed until the ovaries produce fertilizable ova and the testes produce mature spermatozoa.[18] Development of the testes and the ovaries continues throughout the period of adolescence. It is not until growth in height has ceased that growth of the testes and ovaries reaches maximum development.[18]

Pubertal Changes Bring Emotional Responses. The onset of menstruation brings emotional responses. In preadolescence the well-adjusted girl anticipates the growth of her body and looks forward to the time when she can label herself "grown-up." However, anticipating menstruation is different from experiencing it. Many girls feel embarrassed by the menstrual flow. They feel disgust, and are frightened lest their physical state be detected by others. Their disgust dates back to preschool years. Feces, urine, saliva and vomitus were labeled "bad," "unsightly" and "disgusting." At adolescence the girl's feelings about body discharges become reactivated, and she has to deal with the emotional feelings concerning them and the menstrual flow and all that it suggests to her personally.

When girls begin to menstruate, most of them have ambivalent feelings about it. They feel that menstruation is a burden and resent the fact that they must be encumbered with a body that is not completely controllable. However, simultaneously they welcome the manifest signs which indicate they have become women. The girl's response to menstruation reflects her feelings about growing up. Anne Frank's[9] reaction to physical maturity discloses ambivalent feelings, but her acceptance of her femininity and her pleasure in growing up is clearly evident in her writing. She says:

Each time I have a period—and that has only been three times—I have the feeling that in spite of all the pain, unpleasantness, and nastiness, I have a sweet secret, and that is why, although it is nothing but a nuisance to me in a way, I always long for the time that I shall feel that secret within me again.*

Many adolescent girls need help in accepting menstruation, for they do not see any advantages in the manifestations of their beginning signs of maturity. The label the young adolescent puts on menstruation discloses her feelings about her own physiologic functioning. Many girls call it "the curse" or "falling off the roof" because the use of the word "menstruation" is distasteful to them and is connotative of something they have not completely accepted. It takes time for many girls to accept menstruation and to feel comfortable and natural while they are experiencing it. The onset of menstruation brings anxiety to many girls because there are accompanying sexual feelings of which they have not yet become proud. *The girl needs opportunities to express her feelings about her body and to have her "coming of age" accepted by both her parents.* The physical changes of puberty enhance the girl's beauty. She welcomes her parents' approval, and when her father's admiration comes unsolicited, acceptance of her femininity is furthered.

Many boys need help in understanding the physical changes which come at puberty. The onset of seminal emissions is disquieting to the boy who has not had the parental help that he needed to anticipate the changes which would come in his body. He, too, may feel embarrassed and react to a body discharge as if it were something of which he should be ashamed. The changing of his voice may also bring him concern because it is observable to others, often laughed at and is a characteristic which is nonpredictable and beyond his control. Pubertal physical development does not enhance the boy's attractiveness. He has to accept a body which is unwieldy, awkward and less attractive than he has been accustomed to before. *He, too, needs his changing self accepted,* and his parents' admiration of his developing masculinity does not go unnoticed.

Physical Growth Brings Changes in Behavior. The onset of puberty brings *emotional* reactions which manifest themselves in changed behavior. The physical manifestations of adolescence bring self-consciousness, uncertainty and a generalized state of insecurity. The adolescent has a new self to which he must become oriented. His body is different, and his personality is in the process of change. He does not look like a child any longer; he is becoming a physically mature person, and it is this new self that he must become acquainted with and learn to understand. Until he does discover, understand and take himself and his capacities for granted, he will

---

* From Anne Frank: *The Diary of a Young Girl,* copyright, 1952, by Otto H. Frank, reprinted by permission of Doubleday & Company, Inc.

be preoccupied with himself and his own problems and have little surplus energy for giving, loving and creative accomplishment.[1]

The adolescent's preoccupation with himself has purpose; it helps him to identify and accept himself and to come to terms with his own individuality.[7] *His self-absorption is necessary for growth.* Without it he cannot discover his strengths, aspirations and hopes, and identify the problems and fears which are blocking his potentialities for growth.

The adolescent is intensely interested in his physical appearance. Farnham[7] says that "Mirrors act like magnets, holding the young entranced." He examines every inch of himself with more scrutiny than he did when he was first discovering that his body was a part of himself. Now he has a new body which is in a state of rapid development. Is it any wonder that he searches in the mirror to discover what he is really like? During preadolescence he creates an image in his mind of the type of adult he would like to be. Because our society glamorizes the Hollywood girl and characterizes the ideal man as being tall, broad-shouldered, strong and handsome, the adolescent dreams of being able to fulfill these requirements. In the process of discovering himself, many an adolescent becomes anxious because the self-image he sees in the mirror is unlike his fantasied ideal. He exaggerates the physical characteristics he identifies as "poor qualities," and becomes fearful lest his individual differences interfere with his capacity to be popular with the opposite sex. If he is markedly different from his friends, his sense of certainty becomes threatened.

Instead of parents berating their teen-ager's self-fascination, they need to give him insight which will help him to acquire a realistic appraisal of his appearance and to become assured that he is an attractive person. If the adolescent girl does not know how to make herself attractive, her mother needs to help her find ways to highlight her outstanding qualities. Criticizing the adolescent's self-preoccupation increases his uncertainty and intensifies his longing to be like others whom he admires more than himself. When he accepts himself and becomes proud of the self that he is, his preoccupation will cease. As a consequence of this inner change, his energy will be freed for pursuits which hold more potentialities for gratification. Until the physical changes of adolescence bring a newly formed body, the individual's self-image is that of a child. It takes repeated observation and many experiences in finding that his grown-up self is more attractive to himself, his parents, teachers, peers and adult friends to change his image to that which he really is.

The nurse has an important role to play in the life of the adolescent. The nurse who is with an adolescent at the time of a physical examination can assist him in understanding himself. If the nurse is sensitive to the fears which are characteristic in this phase of growth, she will create an atmosphere which makes it easy for the adolescent to reveal what is bringing him concern. If he knows that other adolescents are also troubled about their bodies, his anxiety will lessen because he recognizes that his feelings are not unique but universal and understandable. The adolescent often reflects his anxiety about his body with symptoms of ill health. The majority of adolescents need assurance that they are normal males or females. If assurance from the doctor or the nurse fails to relieve their anxiety, it is suggestive of emotional ill health.[8]

The school and the infirmary nurse have many opportunities to help adolescents. Most adolescents who frequent the nurse's office with vague symptoms of physical distress are manifesting the inner turmoils of adolescence. The school or the infirmary nurse who has insight into the adolescent's developmental needs will provide sympathetic understanding and will help him to obtain the help which he requires.

The nurse who cares for sick and physically handicapped adolescents needs empathy and the capacity to work with them in ways which increase their feelings of self-esteem. The adolescent wants to feel "whole," integrated and self-assured. A misshapen body threatens the adolescent's security at a time when he needs self-assurance the most. Discovering that one is *like* others is one of the adolescent's greatest needs. If an adolescent deviates from normality, he is without one of his greatest sources of security. If he has not had experiences which brought self-acceptance, he will need supportive care from a person who understands his feelings of inadequacy, can accept him as he is and has faith in his capacity to develop the personality qualities which will bring social acceptance and opportunities to contribute to society in ways which bring recognition, self-esteem and expression.

The sick adolescent is threatened by his illness and needs nursing care which alleviates his anxiety and gives him courage to face the problems with which he is confronted. A poised, secure nurse will strengthen his faith in himself and others and help him gain the courage he needs to face the reality of his illness or handicap. Illness is a blow to the adolescent's pride. Many adolescents experience feelings of depreciation. They need nurses who can help them regain their feeling of self-esteem and respect. If the nurse can relieve some of their anxiety, they will see her as a supportive person whom they can trust.

The adolescent feels respected when his need to understand his illness and treatment is recognized. His self-esteem is strengthened when his doctor and his nurse sit down and discuss his illness with him. He has the capacity to understand, and he resents it when hospital personnel keep him in ignorance, and it is understandable why he does. In this period he is greatly concerned about his body and its powers. The more he knows about his body and the care it requires, the more responsibility he will take in keeping it healthy. The adolescent rebels at authority. If his need for health supervision or treatment is presented in a way which helps him understand his need for it and leaves him free to use his own good judgment, he will take responsibility for his own health needs and be proud of his self-made decision.

The physical growth of puberty changes the individual's status and brings awareness of new responsibilities and a need to become ready to meet them. When the individual becomes an adolescent, new demands are made upon him. His parents and his teachers expect him to take more responsibility and have goals which bring concentration and diligence. They forget that he has not yet formulated his goals. First he must test out his powers, master his fears and come to terms with himself. In early adolescence his energy is not goal-directed outside of himself—he has too many personal problems to solve. He is keenly aware of his responsibilities and experiences pressures from within to accomplish and to attain emotional equilibrium.

The adolescent is not only absorbed in his own body and physical development; he is also engrossed in his own problems, his feelings and his relationships to the world of people about him. He is concerned about his status, his personality qualities, his intelligence and his potentialities for successful achievement. He goes through a period of wondering who he is and what he is to become. He is absorbed in the subject of the future. He wonders what it holds for him, and if he will be fitted to meet the responsibilities of adult life. He ponders about marriage, deliberates over the possibilities of getting a mate and having children and attempts to evaluate his personal worth. He reflects upon his capacity to become an independent, self-reliant creature and searches for a philosophy and an interest which will make life meaningful to him. His self-absorption reflects his uncertainty about himself and gives us clues concerning his needs.

Pondering over the above questions has its roots in the adolescent's uncertainty; it also brings anxiety. The teen-ager does not know what adolescence or adulthood holds for him. The unknown is frightening for every adolescent no matter how well prepared he is to meet it. Every day of his life he is confronted with new experiences which make demands upon him. He does not know his strengths or his limitations until he tests himself in each new experience. Life in adolescence is a succession of test experiences. Is it any wonder he is irritable, unstable, aggressive and oblivious to other people's needs?

The adolescent daydreams and seeks interested listeners to prepare himself to meet his problems. He craves solitude and freedom to daydream. He also wants the opportunity of talking over his problems with his parents, his teachers and his friends. He utilizes "bull sessions" with his peers to air his views and to get hints from them which will give him confidence in meeting his problems. *He needs opportunities to daydream.* Unless daydreaming is excessive and unassociated with constructive activity it can be considered purposeful, helping him to appraise himself and reality and to master his fears, and preventing him from having to act out impulses that he is unprepared emotionally to express.

The adolescent's feelings of inadequacy often become expressed in compensatory braggadocio and exaggerated competitiveness. He needs to make himself feel competent and superior. He is competitive, egotistical and arrogant because he is trying to master his fear of failure by proving to himself and the world that he *is* what he longs to be and what his parents and society expect him to be.

Because the adolescent is insecure and in the process of testing himself out, *he needs poised, secure parents, teachers and nurses who understand his anxiety and can provide the calm, consistent support which communicates security and faith in him as a person.* The adolescent must find answers to his questions. If his dependency upon his parents forces him to accept their solutions to his problems, he will feel weak and resentful; he will not be master of himself. Nor will he be in harmony with his conscience or his infantile impulses; he will not be integrated; he will be forever torn apart with inner turmoil and conflict.

The adolescent will find the answers to his own problems if his parents and his adult friends believe in him, give him freedom to think independently and find ways to increase his feelings of self-esteem. He values his parents' opinions and wants his society's approval more than he has ever wanted it before. After the adolescent has mastered his fear of dependence and discovered some of the joys of independent activity, he will seek the counsel of his parents if they are skillful in expressing their views in a way which leaves him free to make his own decisions.

It is normal for adolescents to seek the help of an older friend. They do it because they are threatened by their dependence upon their parents. The adolescent craves attention and interest in his person. If he cannot tolerate it from his parents, he will seek an older friend or teacher who has recently emancipated himself and appears to have all the answers.[2] He usually denies his dependency upon his parents by seeking a friend of his own generation—someone he says is "progressive and in tune with the present times." If his parents understand his fear of dependence, they will not be threatened by his temporary rejection of them. When an adolescent masters his fear, he will be able to turn to his parents without fear of being dominated by them or fear of yielding to his wish to remain a child.

Physical Growth Brings New Fears and the Need for Personality Reorganization. When pubertal changes come, the adolescent not only experiences new bodily sensations but also has an influx of energy which increases the potency of his sexual and aggressive drives.[10] The pubertal changes not only stimulate sexual daydreams, but also threaten the adolescent's ego, bringing anxiety and a need for defenses which will both bring impulse gratification and satisfy the demands of his conscience.

The adolescent's awakening sexuality is frightening; he is threatened by instinctual drives which are potent, unfamiliar and striving for expression.[24] The adolescent senses that these drives are dangerous. The adolescent whose development has progressed normally does not need any warnings; they only increase his fear to a degree which may become overwhelming. *Instead of warnings, he needs guidance which helps him to understand and to accept his sexuality and to sublimate his drives until he has reached adulthood.*

The adolescent's ego senses his danger; it functions to bring emotional equilibrium and balance the demands of his id, his conscience and society. The teen-ager is in conflict and consumed with anxiety. He is also frustrated because he is neither emotionally ready for direct sexual expression and complete independence nor yet able to channelize his drives into satisfying, constructive pursuits. Little wonder he is aggressive, erratic and inconsistent! He is unstable because he is not yet integrated; he has not resolved his conflicts in a way which harmonizes with all parts of his personality. The young adolescent does not understand himself, and cannot yet depend upon his own powers of control. In addition, he has had insufficient experience to master his drives in ways which bring consistent control, relief from anxiety and provide socially acceptable outlets for his powerful drives. Anne Frank[9] reflected her inner conflict when she wrote the following lines in her diary:

> I believe that it's spring within me, I feel that spring is awakening, I feel it in my whole body and soul. It is an effort to behave normally, I feel utterly confused, don't know what to read, what to write, what to do, I only know that I am longing. . . . !
>
> Thank goodness the others can't tell what my inward feelings are, . . . Above all, I must maintain my outward reserve, no one must know that war still reigns incessantly within. War between desire and common sense. The latter has won up until now; yet will the former prove to be the stronger of the two? Sometimes I fear it will and sometimes I long for it to be!*

The adolescent needs a strong ego to master his drives. If his ego is weak and he yields to his instincts, he will break down emotionally, becoming mentally ill or delinquent. If he becomes delinquent, he will be in conflict with the outside world and torn apart with a guilty conscience. If his ego succumbs to his conscience and mobilizes rigid defenses which give him no opportunity for instinctual pleasure, he will be saddled with the character structure of the school-age child. He will have a rigid character, be over-controlled and experience perpetual frustration which will bring hostility, tension and feelings of inadequacy. The ego which has become strong through constructive experiences prior to adolescence gives in to neither the id nor the conscience; it finds ways to provide instinctual pleasure without threatening his peace with either his conscience or the standards of his society. The strong, healthy ego balances instinctual demands and the demands of the conscience and keeps the balance satisfying.[23] When it does the individual has a balanced or integrated personality, is free from neurotic anxiety and has emotional freedom for productive activity.

Emotionally the adolescent is still a baffled, frightened individual who is struggling to find solutions which will bring him peace of mind. He is experiencing what Freud[11] calls *instinctual anxiety*. In preschool years he could give in to his infantile impulses to obtain gratification.[10] The individual's situation is not so simple in adolescence. If his ego yields to his instincts in adolescence, he has to face conflict with his conscience[10] and with society, which is equally painful. In early adolescence when his anxiety is at its

---

* From Anne Frank: *The Diary of a Young Girl*, copyright, 1952, by Otto H. Frank, reprinted by permission of Doubleday & Company, Inc.

height, his ego struggles to bring the harmony which it experienced in latency or the school-age period.[10] His ego redoubles its effort to master his instincts, and utilizes all the defenses it has used in earlier periods of personality development.[10] In writing of adolescence, Freud[10] describes the way the young adolescent's ego handles the increased potency of his instinctual drives. Freud says:

> In this struggle to preserve its own existence unchanged the ego is motivated equally by objective-anxiety [fear of those in the outer world*] and anxiety of conscience and employs indiscriminately all the methods of defence to which it has ever had recourse in infancy and during the latency-period. It represses, displaces, denies and reverses the instincts and turns them against the self; it produces phobias and hysterical symptoms and binds anxiety by means of obsessional thinking and behavior.

To establish heterosexuality the adolescent must free himself from his infantile conscience which forbids it.[20] His childish conscience gave him security; he was sure that he would not do anything which would bring the disapproval of his parents. In adolescence his impulses are stronger, and he discovers that it is difficult to check their expression even when he maintains the standards that he had prior to the onset of puberty.[20] If he lets down his inner standards to the slightest degree, his anxiety mounts and he redoubles his efforts to master himself.[11]

The young adolescent redoubles his efforts to master his drives with asceticism, religiosity and intellectualization.[3] If an adolescent is afraid lest his instinctual urges overpower him, he may renounce all desire for sexual pleasures. Asceticism can spread and deprive the adolescent of legitimate, wholesome, acceptable pleasure. He may refuse an adequate diet or social activities and concentrate on activities which are arduous and frustrating.[11] Usually the defense is only a temporary solution to his problem. When his fear of his instincts has lessened, and he feels power within himself to master his drives, he can become more lenient with himself and indulge in pleasures which he knows are safe and harmless for his growth. Temporarily, the young adolescent may also use religiosity and intellectualization[11] for the same purpose.

Until the adolescent finds constructive, satisfying solutions to his conflicts, he will be frustrated and react with aggressiveness toward those whom he feels are responsible for it—his parents. All adolescents react aggressively to frustration, and many of them react overtly rather than turning their aggression against themselves. The teen-ager's aggressiveness is understandable, but it takes tolerance,

---

* The words interpolated within brackets are the author's.

a sense of humor and patience to endure it. If his parents understand his frustration, give him opportunity to vent his feelings verbally and encourage and support his constructive interests, the adolescent will discover substitutes and find ways to sublimate his sexual and self-assertive strivings into activities which bring him pleasure.

It takes a great deal of time and help for the adolescent to re-organize his personality. In preadolescence his personality was disorganized. Then pubertal changes flooded his body with hor-mones and reawakened and strengthened his instinctual drives. Fortunately, the adolescent is creative and ready to express himself in art, music, athletics, literature and idealistic community projects. When he finds outlets for his creative drive and the need to express himself, he will feel less frustration and tension, and the conflict between him and his parents will become less acute.

NEED OF EMANCIPATION FROM ONE'S PARENTS FOR MATURITY

Emancipation from his parents becomes intensified in preadoles-cence and continues until the individual solves his conflict between independence and dependence or abandons the struggle and re-gresses to a phase of development which is less frightening. *To make a mature heterosexual adjustment, the individual must give up his parent of the opposite sex, free his conscience of the chains which prohibit sexual expression[20] and discover that independence is more satisfying than childish dependence, protection and support.*

NEED OF THE ADOLESCENT TO FREE HIMSELF FROM HIS LOVE OF HIS PARENT OF THE OPPOSITE SEX

When puberty comes, the adolescent's love for his parent of the opposite sex becomes revived. The repressions and conflicts of preschool years come to the surface, and he is confronted with the most difficult of all problems—withdrawing his affection from his parent so that he has love to invest in a mate. Anne Frank[9] wrote of her feelings toward her father, saying: "I'm not jealous of Margot, never have been. I don't envy her good looks or her beauty. It is only that I long for Daddy's real love: not only as his child, but for me—Anne myself."*

The adolescent feels frightened and endangered when he again feels intense love for his parent of the opposite sex. He was dis-appointed in preschool years and he cannot tolerate a repetition of that experience. Now he recognizes reality, and flights into fan-

---

* From Anne Frank: *The Diary of a Young Girl,* copyright, 1952, by Otto H. Frank, reprinted by permission of Doubleday & Company, Inc.

tasy do not bring him relief from anxiety as they did earlier. In preschool years he was inadequate sexually. Now he is sexually developed, and goal-directed impulses threatens his security.

To defend himself against the anxiety which comes when he feels love for his parent of the opposite sex, the adolescent *denies* his love and rebels against that which he unconsciously desires. Outwardly, he acts as if he hated his parent of the opposite sex but he is merely defending himself against his unconscious feelings of love. The boy, for example, criticizes his mother, refuses her affectionate overtures, and berates her sexual powers. This behavior is uncomfortable for the parent but essential if the adolescent is to retrieve the love he has invested in his parent. Unless he withdraws his love from his parent of the opposite sex, he will not have it available for a heterosexual mate outside his family.[21]

In adolescence, the individual struggles between his love for his parent and the wish to grow up, to find a mate and to establish a family of his own. This struggle entails tasks which are not easy to surmount. He does not dare to be like the parent of the same sex because he fears his rival's hostility and his own feelings toward his parent of the opposite sex. Yet to win a mate like his parent of the opposite sex, he must acquire the qualities of his rival parent.[19] His predicament brings confusion and vacillating behavior. One minute he copies his rival parent; the next minute he feels compelled to be different from his parent, and he searches for ways to accomplish his purpose.

To hide his confusion about himself, the adolescent projects his feelings of inadequacy onto his parents. He does not know why he is disturbed, confused and hostile. He feels ambivalent and anxious and does not understand from whence these feelings come. He cannot talk it over with his parents or his friends because the real causes of his misery are unconscious. He is secretive with his parents. He does not dare bare his soul to them lest they discover his real desires. What we see are his defenses against his unconscious feelings and fantasies. The adolescent does not understand himself but he cannot face this thought because it threatens his feelings of self-esteem. To hide his feelings of inadequacy about himself, he projects his feelings onto his parents and says it is *they* who do not understand him. Again Anne Frank's[9] writing exemplifies adolescent characteristics. She shows her ambivalence toward her mother and the commonly experienced feelings of being misunderstood.

I am always making resolutions not to notice Mummy's bad example. I want to see only the good side of her and to seek in myself what I cannot find in her. But it doesn't work; and the worst of it is that neither Daddy nor Mummy understands this gap in my life, and I blame them for it. I wonder if anyone can ever succeed in making their children absolutely content.*

To free himself, the adolescent must enact the drama of adolescence within his home[7] and reach maturity through his interpersonal relationships with his parents. He has grown up within his own family, been sensitive to the qualities existent in both his parents and absorbed their ideals, those attributes they love in one another and the characteristics which appear to be unacceptable to each other. His emotions are attached to his parents, so it is logical to assume that the "battleground of adolescence" must be in the place where his conflicts developed. It is a painful process for both the adolescent and his parents but it is one which must be lived through if emancipation, emotional freedom and security are to become a reality. Anne Frank's concern about parents' capacity to make their children completely contented is an interesting comment and may well reflect her conflict between independence and dependence. Undoubtedly, she sometimes longed to remain a protected, loved child. However, had her parents made her completely contented she would have been in deeper misery and hated them for keeping her a child.

Need of the Adolescent to Free Himself from the Wish to Remain a Child

The adolescent needs to fight gradually for his freedom as he becomes ready to handle it constructively. If he has to struggle to obtain his freedom, he will do it at his own pace as he becomes able to utilize it, and he will value it when he gets it. If he is given too much freedom, he may be overwhelmed with it and decide that staying a dependent child is safer.[7] In preadolescence the youngster asserted his independence and denied his need for dependent gratification. However, inadvertently he did receive dependent gratification. The girl received it from her female friends, and from her mother when she regressed and turned over to her the responsibility of keeping herself clean, tidy and orderly.[4] In adolescence, the teen-ager's assertion of independence is more marked, but it is threatening then because he realizes the responsibilities entailed in it. He cannot possibly admit that he wants complete freedom or that he is threatened by it, so he covers his insecurity by projecting it onto his parents. He cannot say, "Free-

---

* From Anne Frank: *The Diary of a Young Girl*, copyright, 1952, by Otto H. Frank, reprinted by permission of Doubleday & Company, Inc.

dom is scary. I don't know what to do with it yet," so he says, "My parents don't know that I am grown up and ready for freedom. They are scared to give it to me lest I not use it wisely." Josselyn[16] clarifies the adolescent's conflict between independence and dependence when she says:

The childhood fantasy of attaining adulthood, with all its powers and privileges, is about to be realized. The adolescent wishes not only to be an individual, but an independent and grown-up one. Accepting the advice or the direction of a parent is an acknowledgement of inadequacy. This is intolerable. The only way to be an adult is to act like one. Therefore decisions must be made, clothes must be purchased, hours must be controlled, independent of the parents who treat him "like a child." To agree with the parent—be it on the subject of friends, the color of Mary's hair, the political situation, or the proper time to end a party—is to acknowledge one's status as a child. To disagree is to manifest one's strength as an adult. Freedom from the parent and agreement with him are incompatible.*

The adolescent's conflictful feelings bring vacillating, contradictory behavior.[14] Extremes in behavior are characteristic during this final period of personality development. One minute he refuses all advice; the next minute he demands more help than he has sought since infancy.[19] Then when he gets it, he does not dare to use it for fear that he will feel like a child. The following example illustrates this natural trait.

Jim was 15 years of age when his dance club planned its first formal party. Each member of the club was to bring his own partner. Jim told his father about the party and said he was not going because he had to invite a girl. "If I ask a girl, she'll think I'm crazy about her and expect me to keep on dating her," he said, as his father tried to point out the values of the party. The more his father encouraged him, the stronger Jim's resistance became.

The subject of conversation changed when Jim's younger brother joined them. After fifteen minutes had elapsed, Jim said, "What would I say to Mary if I called her and asked her to the dance?" When Jim's father proceeded to help him with his problem, he flew into a rage and said, "Aw! Dad, that's not the way they do it nowadays! Never mind, I'll figure out a way to do it myself. Times have changed! Mary would think I was nuts if I said that to her."

The dynamics involved in vacillating behavior are understandable when one views the struggle the adolescent is having to free himself from dependence and to keep himself free of anxiety at the same time. His behavior is a cycle of self-assertion, fear and retreat. He asserts himself to hide his fear of dependence and to save his feelings of self-respect; he argues, berates his parents and calls them

---

* Reprinted by permission of the author and the Family Service Association of America.

old-fashioned, shows off and demands his rights to independence. When his aggressive behavior brings results and he gets a measure of independence, he feels the impact of responsibility and gets scared. His anxiety brings regression and he takes flight from independence with childish behavior; he gorges excessive quantities of food, submits with the blind obedience of the preschool child and makes excessive, unreasonable demands. But living with his childish self is equally disturbing to his peace of mind. And the cycle begins anew and repeats itself over and over again.

The adolescent's contradictory behavior and instability reflect his conflicting feelings and his inner turmoil. When he feels strong, he can devaluate his parents because at the moment he does not feel as if he needed them. When he is scared and longing for the security and comfort that he experienced earlier, he feels weak and childish; he idealizes his parents and feels protected with their strength. The moment he does, he feels his immaturity which is unbearable because he is struggling to achieve faith in himself. Anne Frank[9] says:

> Sometimes I believe that God wants to try me, both now and later on; I must become good through my own efforts, without examples and without good advice. Then later on I shall be all the stronger. Who besides me will ever read these letters? From whom but myself shall I get comfort? As I need comforting often, I frequently feel weak, and dissatisfied with myself; my shortcomings are too great. I know this, and every day I try to improve myself, again and again.*

Verbally, the adolescent violates the mores of his family and society but simultaneously lives within the confines of his incorporated parental standards. Josselyn[19] says his verbal violations are attacks upon his own conscience. He recognizes that his conscience must become modified before he can express himself sexually but for many years most adolescents can only permit their feelings to be expressed in words. Josselyn[19] describes some of the adolescent's contradictory characteristics in the following way:

> His verbalizations and his actual behavior are, from day to day, characteristically contradictory. He seems to be an idealist and yet his behavior does not always bear this out. At one time he too rigidly follows an idealized code of conduct, and then, as if by a sudden metamorphosis of character, he violates—or more often *talks* of violating —every acceptable code of behavior.
> His relationship with other people is confusing. One moment he hates, the next he loves. The object of this emotional response may be the same person or it may be a different person.
> He rejects his parents as if they were lepers in a community of healthy people. In almost the next breath he idealizes them, picturing

them as more saintly than the saints, more learned than the sages, more omnipotent than God.

It is plainly evident why adolescents need parents, teachers and nurses who understand them and also provide relationships which are steady and consistently supporting. When the adolescent's behavior is accepted as a natural phenomenon which is characteristic of growth and necessary before personality reorganization can take place, the adult remains poised and supports with his understanding. If the adult does not have insight into normal adolescent behavior, he grows anxious when he observes the adolescent's erratic, disorganized behavior. This scares the adolescent for it portrays the adult's weakness and lack of faith in him.

The adolescent needs to feel strength in his parents during the period his ego is strained with conflict. In adolescence he does not have strength within himself; he must absorb it from those who are guiding him. If it is given in the way which it was given in earlier years, he will rebel and become defiant. It must come from deep understanding of him as a person. There is no formula which can be applied indiscriminately. The adult needs intuitive capacity to sense the adolescent's needs of the moment. When experience has prepared the adolescent to utilize a degree of independence, he should be granted the privilege of using it. When he needs protection and dependency gratification it should be given in a way which maintains his self-esteem and helps him to accept it without being threatened. The example which follows illustrates the application of this principle.

Elicia was a 14-year-old, tempestuous, disorganized adolescent. She flew into rages whenever her mother would not grant her wishes. She demanded independence and got more than she could use. There were no limits in her home except those which Elicia set for herself. When Elicia flew into a rage her mother did likewise, and gradually Elicia's anxiety became acute because she did not have her mother's strength to rely upon. Elicia's behavior provoked her mother to anger, and her mother's anger intensified her anxiety and hostility. Elicia's instability increased. She could not apply herself to her daily tasks because she was consumed with anxiety. She had no security at home, and her mother's response to her aggression prevented her from getting the help that she needed to channelize her feelings into socially acceptable forms of behavior.

Elicia wanted limits which would help her control her impulsivity. Her provocative behavior was a method of seeking them but instead of kindly imposed standards, she got hostility and her own way. She wasn't ready for independence. She needed inner strength to channelize her powerful emotions. She was seeking understanding and help to control herself and she did not get it. As a result she felt deserted, depreciated and as if nobody cared anything about her. It deepened her hatred of her mother, which brought feelings of guilt and a need to be punished. When she was punished by her mother's hostility, it relieved her guilt and justified her feelings of hatred.

Through the help of a nurse, Elicia's mother sought psychiatric help. She came to understand herself and the reasons why she utilized Elicia's behavior to meet her own needs. Through this help she gained increased control of her own feelings and curtailed expressions of her own anger when Elicia flew into rages. When her mother remained calm, Elicia's anger quickly abated, and her mother was free to study the need Elicia was seeking to satisfy in her behavior. When Elicia needed limits she got them; when she showed a readiness for independent activity, her mother gave her the freedom that she needed for growth.

NEED OF THE ADOLESCENT TO GO THROUGH VARIOUS PHASES IN THE PROCESS OF EMANCIPATING HIMSELF

The adolescent goes through various phases of experimentation in the process of freeing himself from his parents. During the period he is emancipating himself from his parents, he feels lonely, deserted and many times unloved as well. Anne Frank[9] wrote of these feelings within herself. She says: " 'For in its innermost depths youth is lonelier than old age.' I read this saying in some book and I've always remembered it and found it to be true."* In her loneliness Anne found Peter. When Anne[9] felt that she was not progressing in her relationship with him she wrote:

I shall have to go on alone once more, without friendship and without Peter. Perhaps soon I'll be without hope, without comfort, or anything to look forward to again. Oh, if I could nestle my head against his shoulder and not feel so hopelessly alone and deserted!*

Temporarily, in his loneliness, the adolescent may need to make compromise solutions to his problems. When he discovers that they do not bring fulfillment, and he becomes more secure, he gets the courage to broaden his field of experience and to tackle the problems of interpersonal relationships with a mixed group of teenagers. After a period of dating with many friends, he tries going steady. Gradually, he narrows his field of interest and finally finds a mate with whom he would like to establish a home and rear a family.

Masturbation is one compromise solution which is commonly practiced in adolescence.[7] Because the adolescent has a sexual drive which cannot be expressed directly, he has to make compromises to relieve his tension and frustration until he has found better ways of obtaining satisfaction. In adolescence, masturbation has purpose even though it is accompanied by fantasies which are guilt-provok-

---

* From Anne Frank: *The Diary of a Young Girl*, copyright, 1952, by Otto H. Frank, reprinted by permission of Doubleday & Company, Inc.

ing. Temporarily, it solves his problem; it relieves his tension and prevents him from experimenting with sex before he is emotionally mature enough to enter into a truly creative sexual relationship. Farnham[7] says that masturbation serves a useful purpose. "The pathways are kept defined. The supremacy of the genital as the source of final pleasure is reaffirmed and maintained."[7]

Continued relationship with members of the same sex is another temporary compromise solution which the young adolescent may need to choose.[7] In Chapter 8 this phase of development was described. In adolescence the teen-ager finds further advantage in a group of friends who are of the same sex. He can talk about his anxieties pertaining to himself and to the opposite sex. Through group interaction, he discovers that other adolescents are experiencing similar problems and his conscience becomes modified with group standards.

The adolescent cannot give up parental codes of behavior without a substitute so he accepts and abides by those his group formulate. The codes of the group are usually strict, and, until he gains increased self-assurance, he is a slave to them not only because he is afraid of his own impulses but also because he will submit to almost anything to belong to his group and to win its approval. His need for belonging to the group is of paramount importance to him because he cannot endure the loneliness which comes if he does not have friends. He cannot return to his parents. The drive to obtain adult satisfaction is too strong.

The above phase of development is prolonged if the adolescent is fearful of the opposite sex or of his own reawakened sexuality. If the purpose of his relationships with members of his own sex is understood and if he is helped to master his fears, he will become ready for broader social experiences.

The adolescent who is fearful of members of the opposite sex or of himself needs help to master his fears and to develop social skills which make him attractive to others and confident of himself. Many times the adolescent needs more than the help of his group. If he is afraid of members of the opposite sex, he needs understanding of the psychology of the opposite sex and help to discover ways he can function to enhance his relationships with them. If he is afraid of his own sexual impulses, he needs guidance which helps him to understand them and to know how to handle situations which arouse his sexual desires. The young adolescent does not know how to manage himself with the opposite sex. He not only needs guidance which helps him decide how he wants to use his creative powers, he also needs experiences with members of the opposite sex to become acquainted with them, comfortable in his relationships and secure in his ability to think instead of reacting with thoughtless impulsivity.

Adolescence is a time for gaining understanding of members of the opposite sex. In early adolescence the boy is competitive and driven to test his powers of conquest. The girl wants to prove that she is attractive and desirable, and much of her behavior is motivated by a need for companionship and competitive strivings. If the adolescent cannot compete with his parent of the same sex and take his mate from him or her, he can compete with his friends. And he does. The adolescent's conversations are full of his conquests and successes. When a teen-ager has succeeded in "stealing" his friend's girl or boy friend, his feelings of rivalry become partially mastered. Later in adolescence, when he has proved his popularity, feelings of tenderness and love will supplant his feelings of rivalry and competitiveness. When he masters his rivalry, he can use his energy in appraising the qualities he would like in a mate. He will also be free to see that there are advantages in postponing marriage until he finds someone whom he loves and respects and with whom he would like to spend the rest of his life.

Prematurely given advice usually falls upon deaf ears. The adolescent is consumed with anxiety concerning his status with the opposite sex. He has to "play the field," work out his own problems and learn through experience. Again, parents will be wise if they refrain from dictating and giving advice. Helping the adolescent improve his powers of discrimination is an infinitely more constructive method of guidance. A few pointed questions which help the adolescent to think and to observe bring better results than criticism and constant needling. If his current love object is criticized, he may prolong the relationship to defy his parents. Many hasty marriages serve this purpose, and, because they are rooted in defiance rather than mutual respect and love, are doomed to failure.

In hospital wards there are adolescents who need experiences with members of the opposite sex to help them master their fears and to become comfortable in their relationships with them. In orthopedic wards, convalescent homes and residential hospital schools, there are adolescents who spend months, sometimes years, being physically rehabilitated. The teen-ager cannot make a heterosexual adjustment unless he has social opportunities with members of the opposite sex. The handicapped, hospitalized adolescent has fewer opportunities to seek friends of the opposite sex. He also has more fears in relation to his potentialities for acceptance. For these reasons, nurses need to plan ward social experiences which give their adolescent patients opportunity to become acquainted with one another. They should also be able to recognize the adolescent's need for privacy. Adolescents need supervision but deeply resent intrusion, domination and spying. Nurses as well as parents need to supervise adolescents' social experiences in a way which provides both protection and feelings of confidence and faith in their ability to have fun and pleasure with each other in socially accepted ways.

NEED FOR PREPARATION FOR ONE'S ADULT ROLE IN SOCIETY TO BRING SUCCESS

In adolescence the individual evaluates his interests, ideals, aspirations and strengths not only because he is anxious about himself but also because he recognizes his need to become prepared for his future role in society. Many individuals come to this phase of growth with clearly defined vocational or professional goals. There are many more adolescents who do not know what they want to be or what they want to do with their lives. Some adolescents have their life work mapped out for them by their parents. From early childhood they have sensed their parents' ambitions for them and take for granted that they must submit to their desires.

The adolescent needs to know himself if he is to find a career which will bring success, satisfaction and fulfillment. Parents and other professional workers must help the adolescent learn the opportunities existent within the various professions, study his interests, talents and special abilities and think through his potentialities for success in the different fields which are open to him.

A person must be fitted for his work to enjoy it and he must enjoy it to be creative, productive and truly successful. For this reason *the adolescent needs freedom to select his own career and opportunities to become prepared for it.* An adolescent who is coerced into a profession or business to meet his parents' needs is doomed to frustration. He will resent his parents' domination and hate the dependence which forced him into submission. The youngster who has had his childhood ambitions encouraged by interested parents will turn to them again for guidance when the time comes for him to choose his career. He will also seek the advice of his teachers, club counsellors and adult friends. In these experiences, the adolescent needs an interested listener who can encourage him to think through his problems independently. He can give the exploring teen-ager information to increase his understanding of the responsibilities and growth and economic opportunities in specific careers, but he needs to leave him free to make his own decision.

Many girls choose marriage and motherhood as their career and begin it as soon as they leave high school. Unfortunately, many of them have had little preparation for the most socially important of all professional careers. Some girls are well prepared for marriage and parenthood because they have an opportunity to learn to be good wives and mothers from able teachers in their own homes. But there are many young women who have been denied the most valuable education of their lives.

Those girls who have not had preparation for marriage and motherhood in their own homes need educational experiences with teachers who can help them gain increased understanding of themselves, for self-understanding is fundamental to understanding others. Many high school students get everything else but this—advanced algebra, ancient, medieval and contemporary history, English, physics, chemistry and a variety of languages. They learn to write themes, to typewrite and to take shorthand. Occasionally, they have the opportunity to learn to cook and to sew but often the requirements for graduation are so rigid that there is little opportunity for electives which would prepare them to be homemakers.

Few children in America are graduated from high school with increased understanding of themselves, human development or the factors which make for successful and happy family life. They have knowledge of plant and animal life but are woefully ignorant of human development. They know infinitely more about the life cycle of the ameba than they know about babies. Yet adolescence is the period when they are motivated to learn. The girl's wish for a baby is revived and she seeks ways so satisfy her longings. Courses in child care and family life meet the adolescent's need. The teacher who is interested in human beings and family life gives her feminine students more than knowledge; she gives them a motherly person with whom they can identify themselves.

Many college and nursing school graduates are equally ill-prepared for marriage and parenthood. They graduate knowing little about the anatomy and physiology of the personality but they can trace fetal circulation to perfection. Is it not equally important to help them understand themselves so that they may become ready to meet this fundamental need in others?

Gibran[13] expresses some of children's developmental needs in the following poem. This poem also expresses the wishes and the aspirations of every parent regardless of how ill-prepared he is for his role. Parents want to give to their children. They want them to have freedom to develop their individual creativeness. When they are hampered in giving because of inner conflict and frustrations, they experience a defeat that disheartens them. Parents need empathy; they do not consciously stifle their children's growth; they do so because of unconscious striving which they cannot control.

And a woman who held a babe against her bosom said, Speak to us of Children.
And he said:
Your children are not your children.
They are the sons and daughters of Life's longing for itself.
They come through you but not from you,
And though they are with you yet they belong not to you.

You may give them your love but not your thoughts,
For they have their own thoughts.
You may house their bodies but not their souls,
For their souls dwell in the house of tomorrow, which you cannot visit, not even in your dreams.
You may strive to be like them, but seek not to make them like you.

For life goes not backward nor tarries with yesterday.
You are the bows from which your children as living arrows are sent forth.
The archer sees the mark upon the path of the infinite, and He bends you with His might that His arrows may go swift and far.
Let your bending in the Archer's hand be for gladness;
For even as he loves the arrow that flies, so He loves also the bow that is stable.*

QUESTIONS TO GUIDE OBSERVATION

1. What physical changes come at puberty? How do physiologic changes affect the teen-ager's emotional development?

2. What are the developmental tasks of adolescence? How can guidance help the adolescent accomplish his developmental tasks?

3. How does an adult establish and maintain a constructive relationship with an adolescent?

4. How can emotional problems affect the adolescent's physical health?

5. How does development in all preceding periods of growth affect personality growth during adolescence?

6. How do family relationships affect an adolescent's personality development?

7. What personality characteristics would lead you to think that an adolescent was having problems and conflict in weaning himself from his parents?

---

* Reprinted from *The Prophet* by Kahlil Gibran by permission of the publisher, Alfred A. Knopf, Inc. Copyright 1923 by Kahlil Gibran; renewal copyright 1951 by Administrators, C. T. A. of Kahlil Gibran Estate, and Mary Gibran.

8. What principles of nursing care have you formulated from the study of normal adolescent behavior?

9. What may illness mean to an adolescent?

10. How can illness or a physical handicap affect personality development?

11. Observe adolescents in high school. How did they respond in the classroom? How did their behavior differ after class was dismissed? What characteristic adolescent behavior did you observe?

12. Observe adolescents in a clubhouse or a social hour in high school. What did they do? What did they talk about? How did they respond to you?

13. Observe one of your adolescent patients in a hospital ward. Describe him and his behavior. Describe his family situation from reading his history and listening to him tell about it. What does he do in the ward all day? Who are his friends? What kind of relationship does he have with them? Describe his relationship with you. How do you respond to him? What problems have you encountered in giving him nursing care? Why do you think they arose? How did you handle them?

14. Think back to your own adolescence. What problems did you encounter in the process of growing up? What help did you want during those years? How did you seek it? Did it meet your requirements? Do you find it easier to empathize with the adolescent than with a younger child?

15. How did you feel upon entering the school of nursing? Why did you enter the nursing profession? How did you feel as a student entering a new school? What did you want which you did not receive? How did you feel about the rules of the residence, the hospital and the nursing procedures? How do you feel after a morning with patients in the ward? What help do you feel you need in learning to work with them?

REFERENCES

1. Alexander, Franz: Emotional maturity, Mental Health Bull. 26:1, Nov.-Dec., 1948.
2. Babcock, Charlotte: Emotional needs of nursing students, Am. J. Nursing 49:166, 1949.
3. Blanchard, Phyllis: Adolescent experience in relation to personality and behavior, p. 691, in Personality and the Behavior Disorders, vol. 2, New York, Ronald, 1944.
4. Deutsch, Helene: The Psychology of Women, vol. 1, New York, Grune and Stratton, 1944.
5. Elliot, M. M.: The family today: its needs and opportunites, Social Casework 34:47, 1953.

6. English, O. S., and Pearson, G. H.: Common Neuroses of Children and Adults, New York, Norton, 1937.
7. Farnham, M. F.: The Adolescent, New York, Harpers, 1951.
8. ————: The teens discover themselves, Parent's Magazine 26:36, 1951.
9. Frank, Anne: The Diary of a Young Girl, New York, Doubleday, 1952.
10. Freud, Anna: The ego and the id at puberty, Chapter 11, p. 149, in The Ego and the Mechanisms of Defence, New York, Internat. Univ. Press, 1946.
11. ————: Instinctual anxiety during puberty, Chapter 12, p. 166, in The Ego and the Mechanisms of Defence, New York, Internat. Univ. Press, 1946.
12. Gallagher, J. R.: Adolescents have special health problems, The Child, 15:29, 1950.
13. Gibran, Kahlil: On children, p. 21, in The Prophet, New York, Knopf, 1923.
14. Gittleson, Maxwell: Personality development in adolescence, p. 72, in Personality Development and Its Implication for Nursing and Nursing Education, Springfield, Ill., Department of Public Health, 1949.
15. Havinghurst, R. J.: Developmental Tasks and Education, New York, Longmans, 1948.
16. Josselyn, Irene: Adolescence, Chapter 9, p. 93, in Psychosocial Development of Children, New York, Family Service Association of America, 1948.
17. ————: Treatment through supportive measures, Chapter 8, p. 76, in The Adolescent and His World, New York, Family Service Association of America, 1952.
18. ————: Physical aspects of adolescence, Chapter 1, p. 9, in The Adolescent and His World, New York, Family Service Association of America, 1952.
19. ————: Psychological problems of the adolescent: Part I, Social Casework 32:183, 1951.
20. ————: The fate of the conscience, Chapter 7, p. 67, in The Adolescent and His World, New York, Family Service Association of America, 1952.
21. Kirkpatrick, M. E.: The mental hygiene of adolescence in the Anglo-American culture, Mental Hygiene 36:394, 1952.
22. Lander, Joseph: The pubertal struggle against the instincts, Am. J. Orthopsych. 12:456, 1942.
23. Redl, Fritz, and Wineman, David: Children Who Hate, Glencoe, Ill., The Free Press, 1951.
24. Ross, Helen: Fears of children, (pamphlet), Chicago, Science Research Associates, Inc., 1951.
25. Saul, Leon: Emotional development and preventive psychiatry, Chapter 1, p. 3, in Emotional Maturity, Philadelphia, Lippincott, 1947.
26. Schultz, G. D.: Letters to Jane, Philadelphia, Lippincott, 1948.

Index